THE COMPUTER AFTER ME

Awareness and
Self-Awareness in Autonomic Systems

THE COMPUTER AFTER ME

Awareness and Self-Awareness in Autonomic Systems

editor

Jeremy Pitt

Imperial College London, UK

ICP

Imperial College Press

Published by

Imperial College Press
57 Shelton Street
Covent Garden
London WC2H 9HE

Distributed by

World Scientific Publishing Co. Pte. Ltd.
5 Toh Tuck Link, Singapore 596224
USA office: 27 Warren Street, Suite 401-402, Hackensack, NJ 07601
UK office: 57 Shelton Street, Covent Garden, London WC2H 9HE

Library of Congress Cataloging-in-Publication Data
Pitt, Jeremy, author.
The computer after me : awareness and self-awareness in autonomic systems / Jeremy Pitt, Imperial College London, UK.
pages cm
Includes bibliographical references and index.
ISBN 978-1-78326-417-9 (hardcover : alk. paper)
1. Computer science--Philosophy. 2. Androids. 3. Intelligent agents (Computer software) 4. Emotions and cognition. 5. Human-computer interaction. I. Title.
QA76.167.P58 2014
004.01--dc23

2014024328

British Library Cataloguing-in-Publication Data
A catalogue record for this book is available from the British Library.

Printed in Singapore

Preface

When I was much younger, my ambition was to be a science fiction writer. Fate, in whatever preposterous guises it could find, dealt me a hand in which I ended up as an academic, spending a lot of my time writing European project proposals. Some of these get funded, and become facts (of a sort); most of them don't, and remain, well, fictions. Live the dream, as they say.

However, the EU Future and Emerging Technology (FET) Unit warrants considerable approbation for its continued success in defining research programmes that could, with appropriately tinted spectacles, be reasonably construed as science fiction – but then funding research projects under that programme which turn the ostensible fictions into hard scientific fact.

One of these targeted programmes, or Proactive Initiatives, addressed *Awareness and Self-Awareness in Autonomic Systems*, ICT for optimising system performance based not so much on the designer's conceptions, but on the system's own perceptions (awareness) of its performance with respect to the dynamic environment in which it is presumed to be embedded.

This immediately raises a number of scientific challenges, not least because the notion of 'awareness' or the state of being 'self-aware' are hardly well defined or understood by those disciplines that have addressed them, let alone as new concepts for ICT.

Recognising that meeting such challenges therefore requires a coordinated, inter-disciplinary effort, FET also funded a Coordination Action (in our case, imaginatively entitled AWARE), whose remit is, *inter alia*, to foster cooperation and communication between the projects in the programme. Moreover, it has a responsibility to be outward-looking, to engage with both the scientific community and with EU citizens, in order to explain the motivation for the programme, and to explore the consequences if the targeted outcomes of the research programme were to be met.

This is the aim of the current volume: to map out the space of research in computational awareness, computational self-awareness, and autonomic systems; and to explore the possible social, political, cultural, legal and environmental ramifications.

On a more general note, the idea of the conscious and/or self-conscious machine has intrigued scientists and writers alike. However, this book is not about futurologist interpretations of Moore's Law and (wild?) projections about cyborgs, singularities and the revolution of the robots, however much fun that might be (and frankly the micro-chip in my recalcitrant toaster seems to have already made a start). It is, on the other hand, a realistic assessment of the state of the art in computational awareness and, in particular, a serious consideration of its potential for benefit and disruption. No technology is intrinsically 'good' or 'bad', it is only the use to which it is put – or programmed – or perhaps self-programmed – that can be judged in such a way. It is incumbent on responsible scientists and technologists to consider the social implications of their science and technology. It is all well enough for mountaineers to justify their actions by "because it is there", but not good enough for scientists to justify themselves by "because I can", and then shrug their shoulders at being taken by surprise by the Law of Unintended Consequences. Again.

Jeremy Pitt
London, 2014

Acknowledgments

Authors' Acknowledgments

Marco Aiello, Roberto Baldoni, Alexander Lazovik and Massimo Mecella: This work has been partially supported by EU project Smart Homes for All, contract FP7-22433.

Kirstie Bellman: Thanks to Christopher as always for our intellectual partnership, as well as pragmatic help on LaTeX for this chapter. In memory of Joseph Goguen and Donald O. Walter, always present in spirit.

Aikaterini Bourazeri, Pablo Almajano, Inmaculada Rodriguez and Maite Lopez-Sanchez: This work has been partially supported by Autonomic Power System (EP/I031650/1) UK EPSRC project, and EVE (TIN2009-14702-C02-01/02), AT (CONSOLIDER CSD2007-0022), TIN2011-24220 and TIN2012-38876-C02-02 Spanish research projects.

Giacomo Cabri and Franco Zambonelli: This work has been partially supported by the EU-FP7-FET Proactive projects SAPERE (contract no. 256874), and ASCENS (contract no. 257414). Thanks to Nicola Capodieci for the contribution about the Artificial Immune System.

Giovanna Di Marzo Serugendo, Matteo Risoldi and Mohammad Solemayni: Thanks to the members of the TSC (The Social Computer) Swiss NCCR Consortium, who all contributed to developing the TSC concept.

Regina Frei and Giovann di Marzo Sergugendo: Regina Frei was supported by the Swiss National Science Foundation with a Fellowship for Advanced Researchers.

Petar Goulev and Joan Farrer: Many thanks to the participants of the Barrier Solutions project, kindly support by The Santander Business Innovation Fund managed by the University of Brighton, UK.

Justin W. Hart and Brian Scassellati: This chapter is based upon work supported by grants from Microsoft Research and the National Science Foundation under contracts no. 0835767, no. 0968538, and no. 1117801.

Matthias Hölzl and Martin Wirsing: This work has been partially supported by the EU-FP7-FET Proactive project ASCENS (257414).

Peter R. Lewis: This research has been partially funded by the EU-FP7-FET project EPiCS (257906). Thanks to members of the EPiCS project team, especially Xin Yao, Arjun Chandra, Rami Bahsoon and Funmilade Faniyi for many thought provoking discussions.

Alan Winfield: is very grateful to the organisers of and fellow participants at the AWARE project workshops and slide factory for deeply interesting and formative discussions on awareness.

Editor's Acknowledgements

After the previous volume (*This Pervasive Day*, Imperial College Press, 2012), I remain hugely grateful to the Senior Commissioning Editor of Imperial College Press, Lance Sucharov, and my Editor, Tasha D'Cruz, for giving me a second go. Though quite how someone so concerned with the precise meaning of words puts up with my rather more flexible interpretation of 'commitment', 'deadline' and indeed the legal niceties of a signed contract I do not know, but Tasha does and is ever a patient source of sound advice, guidance and encouragement.

I have benefited enormously from the wonderful collegiality of all my collaborators on the Aware Project: Ben Paechter, Emma Hart, Callum Egan (who never misses an opportunity to make me look good), Ingi Helgason, Gusz Eiben, Mark Hoogendorn, Giacomo Cabri (who never knowingly under-invites me anywhere), Franco Zambonelli and Jennifer Willies. Thanks everyone; but a special thanks to Jennifer, none of this would be possible without her remarkable wisdom, sheer enthusiasm and indefatigable energy; and certainly not the proof that $compensation = \pi R(g\overline{g})^2$.

Naturally, I am indebted to all the chapter authors, not least for their various fascinating contributions, but also for approaching what is (for scientists and engineers) a fairly unconventional commission in such an open, collaborative and constructive way. I highly appreciate all their efforts in reviewing others' and revising their own chapters, and am deeply grateful for the comments of Alan Winfield and especially Ada Diaconescu on the Introduction. For me at least, it has been most interesting and enjoyable: thanks to you all.

Contents

Is That Computer Out to Get Me? 103

Chapter 1

Introduction: The Computer After Me

Jeremy Pitt

Imperial College London, UK

> *"I speak of none other than the computer that is to come after me," intoned Deep Thought, ... "A computer whose merest operational parameters I am not worthy to calculate ... A computer which can calculate the Question to the Ultimate Answer."*
>
> *The Hitchhiker's Guide to the Galaxy* (Adams, 1979)

1.1 Introduction

Ever since the construction and operation of the world's first electronic stored program computer (irrespective of whether this was Manchester's SSEM, Cambridge's EDSAC or IBM's SSEC, and in 1948 or in 1949) there has always been 'a computer after it' – one whose operational parameters are an improvement on its predecessor – size, speed, functionality, design, usability and so on.

Even before these machines started replacing the work of people (the term 'computer' was a job description before it denoted an artefact), the question was being asked if machines could replicate the performance of people, up to and including thinking, intelligence, cognition and consciousness. Critically, in his paper *Computing Machinery and Intelligence*, Alan Turing (1950) posed the question: Can machines think? In that paper, Turing finessed the question, because the terms 'machine' and 'think' were sufficiently ambiguous (philosophically) as to render them meaningless, and he instead addressed the question: Are there imaginable digital computers which would do well in the *imitation game*? If these computers do 'well enough' in the imitation game to look *as if* they were thinking, then there is a positive answer to the original question. This imitation game is often played as the now standard interpretation of the Turing Test, which a computer is said to pass if a human player is unable to distinguish between interacting with another human participant and the computer.

After 'intelligence', the concept of *awareness* increasingly features in a number of domains of computer science, information technology and communications. This includes context awareness in pervasive and ubiquitous computing, user awareness in intelligent interfaces and assistive robotics, physical awareness (of itself) in robotics, and 'whole systems awareness' in performance optimisation of distributed systems and computer networks. (Chapters 2, 3 and 4 address aspects of awareness in service-oriented computing, self-assembling ensembles, and grid computing.)

Correspondingly, we are prompted to consider the question: Can machines be aware?; which we freely admit we cannot answer either. This is partly because dictionary definitions of *awareness* (e.g. "having knowledge or perception of a fact or a situation") are so constrained and regimented as to be uninformative; and partly because, at the other extreme, *awareness* is a term that is virtually impossible to define to everyone's satisfaction. *Awareness* and *self-awareness* are also deeply entangled with concepts (and debates) such as 'consciousness', 'mind' vs. 'brain', 'life', etc. in many of the physical and natural sciences (including psychology, philosophy, neuroscience, artificial intelligence and artificial life).

Rather than joining this discussion, we 'do a Turing' and replace the question by another: Accept that this computer is not aware, but suppose there is an imaginable 'computer after it' which is sufficiently advanced to *look as if it were* aware, then what are the technological, ethical, legal and social implications?

In other words, under whatever definition of 'awareness' one chooses, assume that there is no current digital computer or robot which satisfies that definition. But consider the procession of ever-improving computers and the continuing vindication of Moore's Law (that computer power doubles roughly every 18 months) and advances being made in artificial untelligence and robotics. And then assume that there is an imaginable computer that does satisfy the chosen definition, and looks as if it were aware of something in the same way that a human is. The aim of this book is to consider, during the transition from the non-aware computer to the aware computer, the possible transformative – and potentially disruptive – impact of this awareness, and self-awareness, in 'the computer after me'.

Accordingly, we identify the three readings of the title as:

First reading: 'the computer after me' said from the point of view of the computer – the next generation computing device following (after) this one: smaller, faster, smarter, etc.;

Second reading: 'the computer after me' said from the point of view of the user – the benefits of computer representation and reasoning about human concerns and actions, and the potential drawbacks – the computer is out to get (is after) me;

Third reading: 'the computer after me' said from the point of view of a third-party observer – the computer is trying to acquire (is after) some kind of inner representation and understanding of itself.[1]

In this chapter, we start in Section 1.2 with a kind of thought exercise, by considering examples of the imaginable, aware 'computer after me' from science fiction films and novels. These examples are by no means complete and exhaustive, nor are they meant to be; they are examples of an imaginable digital computer that exhibits some form of 'awareness', and effectively considers its implications through the narrative of the book or film.

From there, Section 1.3 reviews the state of the art in a limited form of computer 'awareness', either through the modelling or replication of a human sensory channel, or measurement through instrumentation of some data source in an external environment which is interpreted, reasoned about, and acted on. The idea of *self*-awareness is loosely considered as a measurement through instrumentation of the computer's own performance in this external environment which is interpreted, reasoned about, and acted on. This introduces the ideas of autonomic systems as systems whose components can leverage some form of self-awareness to optimise performance, to fix themselves, to configure themselves, and so on.

This leads to a discussion in Section 1.4 of why this matters, from three different perspectives, each of which is one of the three readings intentionally embodied by the phrase 'the computer after me'. Firstly, what are the potential applications, and possible risks, afforded by the next generation of computers which demonstrate more 'awareness' than their predecessors? Secondly, what are the implications from the user's point of view, if (or

[1]Whereupon it suffers a massive existential crisis brought on by the tragic realisation that it is lost and alone in a meaningless, cruel and deity-free Universe, but hey, join the club, pal.

when?) through some combination of sensing, data mining and machine learning, this aware computer knows more about the user than maybe she even knows about herself? Thirdly, what are the implications of the introspective computer, the computer in search of its own identity that eventually recognises itself?

Finally, this chapter is completed in Section 1.5 with an overview of the individual contributions in each of the three titular readings, and we summarise and draw some conclusions in Section 1.6.

1.2 Computer Awareness in Science Fiction

A classic example of computer awareness in science fiction literature is Isaac Asimov's three laws of robotics (Asimov, 1950):

(1) A robot may not injure a human being or, through inaction, allow a human being to come to harm.
(2) A robot must obey the orders given to it by human beings, except where such orders would conflict with the First Law.
(3) A robot must protect its own existence as long as such protection does not conflict with the First or Second Laws.

These are quoted here in full because, by replacing 'robot' with 'person', it is evident that a substantially advanced level of 'awareness' would be required to comply with these laws. For example, a robot would need to be able to perceive fully an environment, and be able to reason whether its action would injure a human, whether another action would injure a human, whether it can do anything to prevent that other action, and so on. Then consider the robot working out how hard to push someone so as not to hurt them and yet to remove them from the path of an oncoming car. There is also a significant amount of knowledge required to understand and interpret an 'order', because this requires representing a significant body of organisational and legal knowledge. Finally, a robot, or any group of computational entities, able to protect its own existence would have highly sophisticated levels of self-awareness ('computer after me': third reading). This issue is addressed in Chapters 15 and 16.

Another classic example of computer awareness is the HAL 9000 Computer from Arthur C. Clarke's *2001: A Space Odyssey* (1968). HAL is a computer that could (in the book at least) pass the Turing Test, but on the voyage to Saturn (in the book; Jupiter in the Stanley Kubrick film) it becomes increasingly unstable because it is required to deceive the crew about the true nature of the mission. Unable to reconcile the requirement to protect the secrecy and to tell the truth to the crew, in a rather extreme demonstration of 'the computer after me' (second reading), HAL suffers a 'breakdown' and disconnects the life-support system of three astronauts who are in suspended animation, runs over another with a extra-vehicular transport module, and opens the airlock doors to eliminate the last.

A good example combining both the second and third readings of 'the computer after me' is Skynet in the *Terminator* series of films. The Skynet computer was installed to control military hardware, but it started learning exponentially quickly and achieved some form of 'self-awareness'. Its operators panicked and tried to deactivate it. Skynet prevented this, perceived it as an attack, and (since the attack came from its own operators) inferred that all humanity was a potential threat. In defence, it launched all the nuclear missiles under its command. The theme of machine learning leading to computer self-awareness is handled slightly more subtly and thoughtfully in Warwick Collins' *Computer One* (1993). In this novel, the computer comes to the realisation that it has both 'on' and 'off' states, that something else (i.e. human operators) has control over the state, that the 'off' state is undesirable, and therefore perceives anything (i.e. all humanity) that can achieve that state as a threat, and so (following ideas expressed in Lorenz's *On Aggression* (1966)) initiates action to eliminate the threat.

A poignant illustration of 'the computer after me' (third reading) is given by the replicants in the film *Blade Runner*, based on the novel *Do Androids Dream of Electric Sheep?* by Philip K. Dick (1968). In the film, replicants are physically indistinguishable from humans apart from superior strength and agility, and a lack of empathic and emotional response. However, it is discovered that the longer replicants 'lived', the more their memories accumulated, and so they developed an emotive capacity which caused them to become unstable. As a result, replicants (like many machines today) were manufactured with built-in obsolescence as standard, so that they 'died' after four years. This leads one replicant to seek out its maker (the chairman of its manufacturing corporation) to ask the eternal, and very human, question 'why?'. (Note that in 'real life', apoptotic computing (Sterritt, 2011) has been proposed as a safety mechanism to guard against undesirable and/or emergent behaviour in autonomic systems.)

Finally, to give an example of the potentially escalating problem of computer awareness (first reading), we refer to the Robert Sheckley short story *Watchbird* (1967). In this cautionary tale, an autonomous flying robot (the eponymous watchbird) is developed. These robots are equipped with sensors and reasoning capacity to detect and infer the brain signal characteristic of the prospective murder by one human of another. The watchbird is armed with an 'electroshock stun gun' and so can pro-actively prevent the murder. However, the watchbirds also have a learning algorithm and can communicate with each other, and as a result of their collective awareness they 'learn' the wrong correlation between signal and harm being caused to other living things, and start classifying other signals as signs of incipient murder. As a result, they start zapping people for swatting flies, chopping vegetables, and so on. As far as the watchbirds are concerned, the number of murders starts to increase, so they resort to ever stronger electroshocks. In desperation, the watchbird developers launch a stronger, more powerful type of flying robot, whose purpose is to hunt and kill the watchbirds. However, these new robots in turn become aware of other signals, which they learn to classify as things to be hunted – and killed.

The point of this review is that Turing rephrased his question so that he could focus on a specific kind of machine, and did not have to debate whether they could exist – the Manchester, Cambridge and IBM machines demonstrated that they already did. For our purposes, we can say that the aware 'computer after me' is at least imaginable in the realm of science fiction; in the next section, we examine whether the computer that 'looks as if it were aware' is not just imaginable, but equally demonstrable.

1.3 Computer Awareness and Self-Awareness

In this section, we do not seek to define computer awareness, although a definition has been attempted (Lewis *et al.*, 2011), and a classification of different levels of self-awareness from a neurocognitive perspective has been defined (Morin, 2006). Instead, to demonstrate the various dimensions of computer awareness, we pose some pseudo-naive questions: How many senses does a computer have? Does a computer know that it is a computer? and: Does metal know when it is weakening?

1.3.1 *How many senses does a computer have?*

Considering, simplistically, *homo sapiens* as a data processing device, it would be observed that this device possesses five senses, including sight (two sensors processing at a rate of GBit/s), sound (two sensors processing at a rate of several MBit/s), touch (millions of sensors processing at a rate of several hundred KBit/s), smell (one sensor processing at a rate of tens of KBit/s) and taste (one sensor processing at a rate of tens of bits/s).

Considering a computer purely as a data processing device, the earliest monolithic, stand-alone machines of course had none of these senses: data was 'punched in' to whatever input channel was available with a machine built according to the von Neumann architecture (Patterson and Hennessy, 2011). However, in the best spirit of human endeavour to build stuff in our own image (from gods and statues to robots and other automata), there are corresponding research fields investigating the instrumentation, processing, reasoning and knowledge required to build a system for modelling or replicating a human sensory channel.

For example, the field of computer vision (Shapiro and Stockman, 2001) studies systems and methods for acquiring, processing, analysing and understanding still images and video streams from the real world in order to produce numerical or symbolic information that can inform practical decision-making, including event recognition and situation recognition. For example, systems have been developed for tracking and identification of people using cameras, which require sophisticated algorithms for pattern recognition, data conversion and signal processing (Talantzis *et al.*, 2011). Similarly, the field of speech processing is the study of speech signals and algorithms for processing such signals, used in applications such as speech recognition (identifying the linguistic and semantic content of a speech signal) and speaker recognition (e.g. for access control).

There is substantial progress in developing many kinds of sensor networks, from instrumenting transportation systems for monitoring environmental pollution (North *et al.*, 2009), to the proposal to develop a *planetary skin*, aiming to integrate Earth data captured by ground-, sea-, air- and space based sensors for natural resource management, to support decision-making at local, national and global levels (Casilla-Rubio and Willis, 2009). There has also been considerable progress in equipping robots with a sense of touch (Dahiya *et al.*, 2011), for example enabling a robot to identify different materials through physical contact (Fishel and Loeb, 2012).

However, progress in automating sensory systems appears to be made in inverse proportion to the data rate of processing or the number of sensors. Development of a miniaturised sensor or 'electronic nose' for scent recognition is still a distant goal, although breakthroughs in developing sensors and systems that can detect and dispense scents are being made (Tillotson,

2012). Some advances in simulating computer taste have been reported (Iwata *et al.*, 2004), but the complexity of taste and its inter-dependence with other sensory channels (especially smell and touch, but also to a lesser extent sight and sound) have meant that computer taste remains a significant challenge.

In addition to the five 'traditionally' recognised exteroceptive senses, humans (in addition to others) have interceptive senses such as hunger and thirst related to the well-being of the self, and a sense of proprioception related to movement and kinematics. A form of interoceptive awareness is discussed in Chapter 12 and a form of proprioceptive awareness is discussed in Chapter 18.

Computing devices do not, of course, have to be restricted to 'sensing' and 'interpreting' data according to the sensory apparatus of biological organisms. The key characteristic of an *embedded* system, besides being designed for a specific task, is that it functions as a component of a larger whole, or some physical, real-world environment, and often with real-time processing constraints. It is therefore necessarily *aware*, in the limited sense that, through some form of instrumented sensing, it perceives an environment and computes a response to that perception. One of the earliest examples of an embedded system was the Apollo Guidance Computer (AGC), developed as part of the US Apollo space programme in the 1960s, which was used for navigation, guidance and control of the spacecraft.

This requirement for awareness is also critical in the study of *socio-technical* systems, which recognises and studies the interaction of people and technology in the workplace, and which might place some demand on the digital component to display some awareness of the essentially qualitative human concerns, such as the law, finance, culture, society, morality, norms, and so on, i.e. an awareness of not just their physical environment, but the conventional environment of rules and regulations commonly understood by people (see Chapters 9 and 11).

Similarly, the increasing development of *cyber-physical* systems, which are based on coordination of computational, physical and biological components, in particular in human-robot teamwork. But, how much 'awareness' is required, not just for a robot to be a useful or efficient part of the overall effort, but for a human team-member to appreciate its contribution and react to it as if it were another human (in the same way that chess grandmaster Garry Kasparov had to play against IBM's Deep Blue chess computer as if he were playing another human with intuition and strategic goals, and not just another finite state machine)? This might require the computational components to be aware of their participation in a collective shared enterprise, their role and responsibilities in it, their position within a hierarchy or an organisation, and so on. In fact, arguably, it requires the computational elements not just to be aware, but to be *self-aware* as well.

1.3.2 *Does a computer know that it is a computer?*

The *mirror test* is a standard test in animal psychology, used to determine whether an animal has the ability to recognise itself in a mirror (Gallup, 1970), and is often used as a measure of self-awareness.

The standard test involves introducing a wild animal to a new controlled habitat, introducing a mirror, and observing the behaviour. Gallup (1970) used chimpanzees, and observed that to begin with they displayed aggressive behaviour, presumably interpreting their reflection as a threat; but after a time started to use the reflection for other purposes, such as grooming unseen body parts and even playful interaction. Subsequent development of the test extended these initial conditions by marking the animal (without its knowledge) with an odourless dye in two spots, one that could be observed in the mirror and a control spot that could not. The self-aware animals reacted consistently with being aware that the reflected image was itself, e.g. by inspecting or removing the marking from itself while looking in the mirror, but ignoring the control marking.

All of the great apes, elephants, some marine mammals (orcas and dolphins), even some birds, have been observed to pass the test. Human development enables infants to pass the mirror test at around the age of 18 months, although this claim has been subject to some discussion (Asendorpf *et al.*, 1996), depending on which branch of psychology is assumed.

Some scientists have attempted to build a robot capable of, if not actually passing the mirror test itself, then at least some form of self-recognition. Various approaches include temporal correlation between initiation of motor activity and variation in the perceived environment (Gold and Scassellati, 2007), using a neural network to learn the distinction between flashing LEDs on a reflected image and a robot imitation (Takeno *et al.*, 2005), and using self-knowledge of a robot's kinematics and visual calibration to learn about its form using self-observation (Hart and Scassellati, 2012), as discussed in Chapter 14. The mirror test has also been used to investigate whether it is possible for a swarm as a whole to discriminate between its own mirror image and another swarm (Schmickl *et al.*, 2011), although there are perhaps more sensors than vision involved in natural swarms.

These are impressive engineering achievements, but it is important to note that the mirror test is a *measure* of self-awareness, not a binary decision function. Getting an object to *recognise* itself as an object is not a conclusive demonstration that the object *knows* what sort of object it is or what it should do with this knowledge (Ackerman, 2011), or that it would necessarily pass our hypothetical Turing-like test for awareness.

For example, in search algorithms for two-player games, it was a basic assumption that the opponent had exactly the same knowledge of the state space and applied that knowledge in a consistent effort to win the game – in other words, the computer program was essentially playing against a model of itself – not that it was 'aware' of it, or itself.

This assumption remains pervasive. For example, one of the most commonly used architectures in intelligent agents research is based on the BDI (Belief-Desire-Intention) agent architecture (Rao and Georgeff, 1995). The conceptual model on which the BDI architecture is based is the Intentional Stance (Dennett, 1987), a philosophical theory of the mind with the objective of exploring philosophical theories of free will and consciousness. The Intentional Stance was developed by Dennett for purposes of predictive leverage at a high level of abstraction. The idea was to predict the behaviour of an object by thinking of it in terms of a rational agent. This meant ascribing to it certain beliefs and desires that it ought to have, given its situation, and working out, via some form of 'practical reasoning', what the agent ought to do, and this is the *prediction* of what the agent will do. The Intentional Stance is "the strategy of interpreting the behaviour of an entity (person, animal, artefact, whatever) by treating it as if it were a rational agent who governed its 'choice' of 'action' by a 'consideration' of its 'beliefs' and 'desires.'" (Dennett, 2009, p. 339).

The use of practical reasoning using BDI, for example in planning, was developed further by Bratman (1987), but the key insight of a range of works in the early 1990s was the formal characterisation of this strategy in modal logic (Cohen and Levesque, 1990), using different *modalities* (qualified truths) for each component of belief, desire and intention. As the theory completed the transition from one providing predictive leverage to one of providing *design* guidelines (Rao and Georgeff, 1995), it offered a basis for practical implementation and has been used in many agent-based systems and programming platforms. When it came to interaction between multiple BDI agents, the modalities were indexed by agents. For example, the formula $B_i B_j \phi$ meant that agent i believes that agent j believes that proposition ϕ is true, and agent i would reason about agent j's beliefs the same way it reasoned about its own. This can be seen as a logical model of the self and of the other, assuming that the 'other' was the same kind of thing as itself.

Similarly, the HAMMER (Hierarchical Attentive Multiple Models for Execution and Recognition) was developed for robotic applications (Demiris, 2007) because of the requirement to represent the results of *physical* actions of the self and others, in a situated environment, as well as the cognitive elements of intelligent agents (which originally had to represent only the results of *communicative* actions). HAMMER was based on the generative simulation theory of mind (Hesslow, 2002) and other psychological experiments, which showed that there was a shared neural substrate between the mechanisms of action execution and those of action recognition (Demiris and Khadhouri, 2006). However, it too offers an enhanced theory of intent prediction based on a self-similar model of others, i.e. it assumes that 'others' are just like itself.

Both these architectures demonstrate that while self-recognition is important, both self-representation and allied reasoning are essential for self-awareness (subject to the usual caveat that there are different levels of awareness (Lewis *et al.*, 2011; Morin, 2006)), as discussed in Chapters 6, 14, 15 and 16, and is a pre-requisite for self-protecting, self-optimising and self-configuring systems.

1.3.3 *Does metal know when it is weakening?*

One difference between an inanimate (and supposedly completely un-self-aware) object and an animate object possessed of some form of self-awareness is that the latter can use that awareness or self-awareness to perform some aspect of self-assessment, e.g. for a system fixing or repairing itself. Again, the Apollo Guidance Computer (AGC) provided an early example of this behaviour. During the first lunar landing by Apollo 11, the AGC kept giving an alarm because certain unnecessary tasks kept on overloading the processor. However, the software had been designed with priority scheduling and extensively tested, and Mission Control decided this was an alarm that the pilots could 'safely ignore'. As expected, the computer rebooted and re-initialised, automatically deleting low priority tasks and leaving the core navigation and control processes. This allowed the descent and landing to be successfully completed (Cortright, 1975).

Considering biological organisms, and specifically humans, they are generally 'unaware' of weakening components, but might carry on regardless of symptoms or other problem indicators (e.g. pain as an 'alarm that can be safely ignored'). They are also equally 'unaware' of their immune system at work; although they may be 'aware' that they have an immune system and follow a diet to promote or protect its operation. However, it could be argued that the immune system is very much 'aware' of its environment and for triggering the appropriate response mechanisms.

One implication of this animate/inanimate dichotomy, for making the transition from 'inanimate' computational systems to 'animate', aware or self-aware ones, is that there are multiple levels of awareness, possibly interacting, and each with a spectrum of possible behaviours. This could be realised by batteries that are 'aware' of their own energy level and hard drives that can report their own risk of failing, up to *autonomic computing* (Kephart, 2005) and *organic computing* (Müller-Schloer *et al.*, 2011).

The idea for autonomic computing systems was inspired by the human autonomic nervous system, which provides unconscious and often involuntary control over certain bodily homeostasis. A homeostatic system is capable of sustaining its structure and functions by balancing out multiple dynamic equilibria. The idea was identified by IBM[2] as a template for multi-criteria optimisation in systems with distributed control components, for example data centres.

It was observed that, in running a data centre, the hardware costs had diminished over time, personnel costs were roughly constant, but the cost of power had substantially increased. Reducing operational costs of running a data centre required paying closer attention to power management. However, there were two conflicting objectives managed by separate autonomous controllers: the queue manager, whose objective was to minimise query response times, and so wanted to turn as many processors as possible *on*, and the power manager, whose objective was to minimise energy consumption, and so wanted to turn as many processors as possible *off*. An autonomic (multi-agent) system enables the two managers to negotiate a balanced equilibrium, which could also change depending on external circumstances (e.g. spot pricing in the electricity market) (Kusic *et al.*, 2009).

While multi-criteria optimisation in data centres is, perhaps, the 'Ur' application of autonomic computing and remains important, its potential is also being demonstrated in socio-technical applications such as smart homes (see Chapter 7) and Smart Grids (see Chapter 8), amongst others. A

[2]Paul Horn's manifesto: *Autonomic Computing: IBMs Perspective on the State of Information Technology'*, IBM T. J. Watson Research Labs, NY, 2001. The original document is not easy to find online.

specific challenge for computer scientists and software engineers is to design, develop, deploy – and walk away from – these systems, which can self-diagnose and fix themselves (cf. Chapter 5). These are autonomic systems that 'know when they are weakening', and for which awareness, and self-awareness, would appear to be a pre-requisite (Rish, 2009).

Consequently, there is an increasing requirement to engineer computing and communication systems that have to operate in circumstances where unexpected performance, a dynamic environment and competing sub-components are commonplace, and the system is required to optimise overall performance according to multiple criteria in response to rapidly changing conditions. Critically, we are concerned with situations where the rate of change in the environment demands decision-making that is too fast, too frequent, too complex, too expensive and too entangled for a human operator to intervene – and maybe even too risky.

1.4 Why Does Computer Awareness Matter?

It could be argued that the discussion so far has only addressed fictional examples of computer awareness and self-awareness which never happen in practice; or that the actual examples given of automated senses, agents, robots and systems are still many years away from real-world deployment. However, this question matters now, and it matters from the perspective of each of the three readings of 'the computer after me'.

For the first reading, creating computers of successively powerful performance not only replaces some things that people can do, it also creates opportunities to do things that people cannot. For example, in financial markets, electronic platforms have been introduced for *algorithmic trading*, which is used to compute market trades based on automated (algorithmic) decisions according to price, time, quantity and so on. A special class of algorithmic trading is *high-frequency trading* (HFT), in which complex decisions about trading positions are initiated and accepted without human involvement. These decisions are evidently too fast, too frequent and too complex for operator intervention; given that some analyses estimate that over 50% of US equity trading is by HFT, it is certainly expensive as well.

Algorithmic trading supposedly offers better ways of managing risk and providing market liquidity, but there has been intense speculation and debate about the contribution of this technology to the 2010 Flash Crash, with an international body of regulators, IOSCO (International Organization of

Securities Commissions), concluding that "their usage was also clearly a contributing factor in the flash crash event of May 6, 2010" (IOSCO, 2011).

Several of the science fiction examples discussed earlier, *2001: A Space Odyssey*, *Computer One* and *Watchbird*, explored the possible (undesirable) consequences of developing a technology that we ourselves do not fully understand and therefore do not necessarily fully control. It would seem that high-frequency trading algorithms are a real-life example of this. Then consider the dire predictions and possibilities of cyber war: would it be possible for a cyber security system to interpret, or mis-interpret, a traffic pattern as an attack, and launch a counter-attack; or even for it to conclude that the best form of defence is a pre-emptive strike?

The true story of Stanislav Petrov is apposite here. Petrov was the duty officer when a Soviet satellite-based early warning system reported a US nuclear missile launch. He decided that the report was a false alarm and his assessment may have prevented an erroneous retaliatory counter-strike. Since the Soviet military were still there to carry out the investigation, they were able to confirm that the early warning system had indeed malfunctioned (Long, 2007). This powerfully illustrates the risks of developing systems that take humans out of the loop, yet we have been considering systems with awareness that function *without* operator intervention.

On the second reading, we are considering computer programs that are intended to be aware of essentially qualitative human concerns – such as the law, culture, society, morality, organisations, institutions, environment and medicine. In 2008, the UK Department for Work and Pensions introduced "work capability assessment" (WCA) tests, a computerised system that was intended to determine if people claiming disability or incapacity benefits were entitled to them. Whatever criticisms that may be levelled at the system, not least the simple focus on physical capacity to the complete exclusion of mental illness, it clearly has its problems – 400,000 appeals with a 40% success rate in the first three years since its introduction, costing UK£50m per year. An independent review found that "the WCA is mechanistic, impersonal and lacks empathy" (Harrington, 2011). This highlights the risks and dangers of automating systems with human concerns without a sound conceptual understanding of the concerns that are to be represented and about which the system needs to reason.

On the third reading, even if a computer does not exhibit, or does not even need to exhibit, a human-like characteristic, in order to interact with humans 'naturally', it might at least have to understand the characteristic. We refer to a *New Scientist* article, quoting a scientist commenting on one of the robots designed for the mirror test mentioned above (Hart and Scassellati, 2012):

> *Mary-Anne Williams of the University of Technology Sydney, Australia, points out that robotic self-awareness is crucial if robots are ever going to work safely alongside humans. "Many robots today not only do not recognise themselves in a mirror, but do not recognise their own body parts directly," she says. "For example, a robot may be able to look downwards and see its feet but not recognise them as its own."*
>
> *Self-awareness is a basic social skill and without it robots will struggle to interact with people effectively, Williams adds.*
>
> (Hodson, 2012)

Therefore, we need computers and robots that are aware of themselves not only to protect their own existence but also to be fully functional members of teams with human and computational actors. Protecting its own existence and contributing to the common good could fall anywhere on a spectrum of possibilities between a primitive survival instinct to taking actions according to some axiomatisation of a form of the Kantian Categorical Imperative (Kant, 1785) (e.g. a framework for evaluating the motivations for, and consequences of an action; for some deeper discussion see Chapters 16 and 17).

The issue of software survivability is not new. No-one expected COBOL programs written in the 1960s and 1970s to be executing 50 years later – but they could not have done so without the support and intervention of several generations of systems programmers and computer architecture and operating systems development that took backwards compatibility and legacy systems seriously. What would it take for a self aware system to survive for 50 years, especially one acting as a life-long companion, one that is supposed to function without operator intervention, but is embedded within a social, legal, political, cultural or organisational context that will inevitably change enormously over such a time-frame? And, is the electronic equivalent of apoptosis (programmed cell death) as important a feature of self-aware computer systems as it is of biological organisms (Sterritt, 2011); not just for protection, but for re-generation?

However, this is why computer awareness, and self-awareness, really matter. An important condition for any technology (aware or otherwise) is its capability – intended, acquired or accidental – to harm humans or human values (see Chapter 13). It is not the acquired (emergent, learned) capability of the out-of-control super-computer (the science fiction staple as discussed above) that is the most significant problem, but the accidental capabilities of human- and human-context-aware computers that present the greater risk – but also the greatest potential benefits.

1.5 Chapter Overviews

If it is accepted that increasing computational awareness, and self-awareness, will inevitably matter to people, as both individuals and collectives (i.e. communities and societies), then it is necessary to evaluate the scale, space and implications of computational awareness. In this book, we undertake such an evaluation from the three different readings of "the computer after me". Accordingly, this book is divided into three parts.

In the first part, we assume that (at least part of) the vision of ubiquitous computing and the Internet of Things has been realised, and that information and communication technologies have 'disappeared' into the everyday fabric of life and our ambient environment. If there is always going to be a generation of computer that is 'faster', 'smarter' – or more 'aware' – than the previous generation, then what is the 'computer after me', when the 'me' is this disappeared computer? Cabri and Zambonelli (Chapter 2) discuss this from the perspective of service-oriented architectures, while Hölzl and Wirsing (Chapter 3) consider it from the perspective of ensembles of 'things'. The three other chapters in this part address further awareness properties of such a computer (or computational ensembles) that are characteristic of humans or human society: Müller-Schloer *et al.* (Chapter 4) consider social awareness, in Chapter 6 von Mammen and Steghöfer discuss an algorithm for developing awareness of emergent processes by middle-out abstraction, while Frei and di Marzo Serugendo survey the state of the art in writing software that can repair itself (Chapter 5).

In Part II, the issue addressed is: what happens when 'the computer after the disappeared computer' is not just aware of its technical environment, but also its human – social, cultural, environmental, medical and organisational – environment as well? In this context, in Chapter 7 Aiello *et al.* study the ambient environment of the smart home; and in Chapter 8 Bourazeri *et al.* consider awareness for information visualisation in Smart Grids through serious games. Savarimuthu and Ghose discuss awareness of social norms for sustainability in Chapter 9, while Goulev and Farrer consider awareness of solar exposure for preventative medical purposes in Chapter 10. The discussion is generalised further by di Marzo Serugendo *et al.* in Chapter 11, who present the social computer, and by Pitt and Nowak in Chapter 12, who call for a new science of institutions based on the convergence of societies of devices with communities of people. However, Part II concludes with a stark warning from Michael *et al.* in Chapter 13, of how this computational awareness could, without care, lead to überveillance.

In the third and final part of this book, the issue addressed is: what happens when 'the computer after the disappeared computer' becomes aware of itself? In the first chapter of Part III, Hart and Scasselati present Nico, a robot that appears to pass the mirror test (Chapter 14), while Bellman (Chapter 15) and Winfield (Chapter 16) present routes to self-awareness based on systems with internal models. In Winfield's case, these internal models are used to consider ethical behaviour for robots, and this issue is further explored by Bhuta *et al.* in Chapter 17, in the context of drones and the law. Finally, Part III is concluded by Lewis in Chapter 18, with a discussion of smart camera networks and proprioceptive self-awareness.

1.6 Summary and Conclusions

This chapter began with a quotation from Douglas Adams' *The Hitchhiker's Guide to the Galaxy*; perhaps it is apposite to end by returning to another of his marvellous robotic inventions, Marvin the Paranoid Android. Suppose we could create a computer of such power that it looked as if it were aware; and then we left it running, like we do our laptops and desktops, with nothing to do. Would it get bored? Would it start fiddling, like the sorcerer's apprentice? Would it be cruel to treat it this way?

Artificial intelligence is already used in everyday products, from toasters and washing machines to tube trains and smart meters. The proliferation of sensors and processors is giving rise to a new generation of embedded systems, with significant, inter-connected intelligence in computational components, interacting in tandem or partnership with humans, often referred to as socio-technical or cyber-physical systems. There are many application domains where such embedded systems involve people, software (often through intelligent software called agents) and hardware (specifically robots), working together in a collective. The potential future benefits and applications of such systems are almost limitless, especially as and when the agents and the robots become increasingly aware and/or self-aware.

However, it is important to bear in mind, as has been stressed several times in this introductory chapter, that there are many different 'levels' of awareness, and particularly of self-awareness, and a spectrum of capabilities at each different level. There are also many different 'things' to be aware of and many different ways to become aware of them: facts and situations relating to its operating environment, human objectives, or human-related qualitative concerns (such as social relations, legal systems and organisational structures). It is also possible for a complex computer system to display multiple levels of awareness, with each level possibly more or less aware of the others (just as a biological organism is largely unaware of its immune system, but experiences the side-effects of its operation).

As we develop computer systems with increasing awareness, it is easy to introspect on science fiction and focus on the 'dark side', with so many examples of systems running out of control (Watchbirds, SkyNet, Computer One, Hal, the Bomb from the film *Dark Star*, and so on). The Apollo Guidance Computer and the success of autonomic computing are real-life examples where awareness, self-awareness and self-* properties have provided unique, essential and tangible benefits. On the other hand, other examples presented in this chapter, such as the early-warning nuclear-attack detection systems, HFT algorithms, the UK WCA system, are all examples of systems with autonomy and some form of awareness that have all gone wrong, with potentially disastrous outcomes (without wishing to equate a stock market crash with destroying the planet).

Therefore, the precautionary principle requires us to consider the potential risks and wider social, legal, ethical, cultural and environmental implications, even to ask the question: if it is not the self-aware computer that is itself the risk, is it the people programming the self-aware computer who present the risk (in the same way that no security on a data transmission channel is of any use if the data receiver will not act in good faith (Pitt, 2012))? We seem to be torn between, on the one hand, needing systems to become more self-aware in order to achieve our intended goals for them, be useful to people, and operate safely, effectively and efficiently; and, on the other hand, needing to beware of systems that are so self-aware that we dare not or cannot intervene. The chapters in this book reflect both concerns: the state of the art in developing computational awareness, and the checks and balances needed to control perhaps the most disruptive ICT ever to be developed – computational self-awareness.

PART I

What Comes After the 'Disappeared Computer'?

Chapter 2

Towards Self-Aware and Self-Composing Services

Giacomo Cabri and Franco Zambonelli
University of Modena and Reggio Emilia, Italy

2.1 Introduction

Our everyday life more and more relies on a variety of innovative services provided by emerging ICT, from smart phones to RFID tags and interactive displays, and this trend is increasing. In most cases, such technologies make available a variety of individual service components that have to interact and possibly collaborate with each other in order to provide effective complete functionalities.

Indeed, we are already facing the release of early composite ubiquitous computing services trying to exploit the possibilities opened by these new scenarios in the form of, e.g., environmental displays and signage capable of reacting to users' presence by composing with location services and user profiling services (Alt *et al.*, 2012), car navigation systems capable of providing real-time traffic information by dynamically composing with web information services (Riener and Ferscha, 2013), not to mention the variety of emerging location-based social services composing a variety of international capabilities (Schuster *et al.*, 2013) and more general futuristic services for our future urban scenarios (Zambonelli, 2012).

It is a matter of fact – and this will be the case also for ubiquitous services – that the more we use a technology, the more such technology will become part of the fabric of our everyday life. And we increasingly expect that such technology will be able to automatically react to our needs, situations and expectations, so as to adaptively satisfy our needs in an automatic and transparent way. In the case of composite ubiquitous services, this implies the capability of automatically selecting the most appropriate composition of service components that can satisfy users' needs, and dynamically re-shaping such composition upon changing contextual conditions or upon changing users' needs.

However, promoting such adaptivity features, which is a necessary precondition towards exploring the full potential of the emerging pervasive computing infrastructure, requires a deep re-thinking of traditional approaches to distributed and service-oriented computing (Huhns and Singh, 2005), to overcome their limited capabilities in supporting the situated and highly dynamic nature of pervasive services.

In fact, the mechanisms and strategy to engineer proper interaction and collaboration between services have not yet reached the necessary degree of flexibility and dynamics to meet such expectations. By relying on traditional approaches to software engineering, service components are still designed to work with a limited number of compliant, well-defined components, and the dynamic composition of different services is not always possible or is very difficult to achieve (Zambonelli and Viroli, 2011).

This issue can be tackled by making components capable of 'self-composing' with each other without direct supervision of the users and without pre-coded design solutions. In particular, such self-composition should be made possible from two different viewpoints: at the *component–component interaction* level, and the *system collaboration pattern* level. The former concerns the capability of the components to interact in an effective way even without knowing each other in advance. The latter relates to the organization of the components inside a system.

As discussed in this chapter, to support properly self-composition of services, services must first of all become 'self-aware' entities, i.e., they must be capable of reasoning on their own functionalities, goals, structures, and on the users' situations and needs, and take composition decisions accordingly on their own. However, the road towards self-aware and self-composing services still requires facing challenging research issues.

2.2 Service Composition and Self-Awareness

In this section we provide some examples of service composition, in order to contextualize the problem being addressed. There can be two directions of service interaction: *horizontal* composition and *vertical* composition. We will also emphasize, with the help of these challenging examples, how such composition means must become dynamic and self-enforced by services, calling for self-aware approaches to service composition.

2.2.1 *Horizontal composition*

The former kind of composition is required when the user request can be accomplished by several services, all of the same kind (or similar), but which operate in different "spaces". Here we use the term "space" in a very general sense: it could be *geographical*, as in the following example, or a portion of the web or of other physical or logical environments.

A typical example is a route planner. Let us consider for instance a user who must reach Nancy, in France, from Modena, in Italy. Since the two cities are not directly connected by any means, the user must first decide which means to exploit. For example, the user could decide to exploit trains; in this case, the user must exploit the *Italian railway* service to find connections from Modena to Paris and to book the most suitable one, then the *French railway* service to travel from Paris to Nancy. So, the two services accomplish the same task but in different spaces (in this case, geographical spaces).

But another choice is to exploit flights. In this case, since the two cities do not have an airport (or, at least, an airport with international flights), the user must search for the international flights from and to the cities nearest Modena and Nancy, respectively Bologna and Paris. So the user must find a train from Modena to Bologna, then a flight from Bologna to Paris, and finally another train from Paris to Nancy, accounting for three (similar) services in three different spaces.

There could be other similar examples in the route planning field, for instance for car travel across different continents.

2.2.2 *Vertical composition*

The *vertical* composition is required when the user request must exploit more services of different kinds, which do not share the same time intervals.

A typical example of this composition is an e-commerce transaction. Let us consider a user who wants to buy some goods and requires home delivery. She can exploit at least three services of different kinds. The first one is a *shop* service, which enables the user to know which goods are on sale, along with further information such as price, availability, size, and so on. The second service is related to the payment for the chosen goods, for instance, a *credit card transaction* service. Finally, a *delivery agency* service is in charge of the actual delivery of the goods to the user's home. Currently, these three services are provided by online e-commerce websites as a whole, but there could be situations where the user would prefer to choose each service separately, for instance because she has a subscription to her favourite delivery company.

2.2.3 *Towards self-aware services*

Despite the availability of a large number of service components, they can hardly be composed and collaborate with each other because most of them were not designed for open collaboration in dynamic environments. Standard protocols are good to support openness (Huhns and Singh, 2005), but they have turned out to be insufficient to support adaptivity.

Given the notable dynamics of modern service environments, and in particular of ubiquitous ones, supporting effective component–component interactions in spite of such dynamics represents the first issue to be faced, in order to enable single components to interact with other components, not known in advance, possibly of an ephemeral nature, and typically not conceived to work together. Such an issue is particularly critical for horizontal service composition, where services exist in different physical and social spaces.

A second issue implies having the means to appropriately organize and orchestrate the activated services that have to provide functionalities to a component. Although it is clear that appropriate organization of the systems of components is needed in order to optimize the availability and execution of high-level services, the dynamics of modern service environments calls for such organization to be identified on the fly, based on current environmental and operational conditions. Such an issue is particularly critical in the case of vertical composition, where correct synchronization of the activity and the correct communication among services is necessary to ensure the proper deliver of the composed service functionalities.

In this context, it is possible to think of extending traditional approaches to service composition so as to better tolerate high dynamics in the operational environment in an adaptive way. However, this would imply a notable increase in the complexity of the supporting middleware infrastructure. In particular, the supporting infrastructure (e.g., the discovery and the transport services) should be made capable of recognizing the prevailing situation, dynamically modifying the strategies for service matchmaking depending on the current situation, thus dynamically enforcing different strategies for composing and orchestrating service.

On the contrary, we argue that the best solution to tolerate adaptive service composition is to have the very concept of service components evolve so as to let them become 'aware'. Awareness implies that a service component (or an ensemble of components) is aware of *itself* and its current operational conditions and configuration (i.e., *self-awareness*), as well as the *other components* it relates to, the *environment* where they live, and the overall conditions of the *sytem* in which it executes.

Being aware of itself means knowing *what* service can be provided independently of *how* it is actually provided; being aware of other components means knowing what kind of services can be exploited and how to exploit them; being aware of the environment means knowing the conditions in which the services are requested and must be provided. Awareness at system level means that the system as a whole knows how it is organized and is able to change such an organization (i.e., its collaboration pattern) to adapt to unexpected requirements.

2.3 Approaches to Self-Aware Service Composition

There are several approaches that try to overcome the limitations of traditional service compositions towards making services self-aware and, consequently, adaptive. This section considers some of these approaches.

2.3.1 *Nature-inspired self-composition approaches*

Many research approaches recognize the limitations of traditional service-oriented approaches in dealing with adaptivity, and suggest that the complexity of modern service systems (and of ubiquitous computing ones) is comparable to that of natural ecosystems. Consequently, they argue that it could be worthwhile adopting natural systems as an inspiration to fully rethink the modeling and architectural assumptions of service systems (Agha, 2008). That is, modeling and architecting pervasive service systems in terms of nature-inspired decentralized ecosystems, so as to make adaptability and awareness inherent because of the basic 'rules of the game', as in real-world natural systems.

In such natural systems (whether considered at the physical, chemical, biological, or social level), all the activities of the system components are inherently situated in space and driven by local interactions only (see Figure 2.1). Such interactions are not ruled by pre-defined orchestrated patterns. Rather, interactions are simply subject to a limited set of natural laws (let us generically call them "eco-laws"), from which even complex patterns of interactions dynamically emerge via self-organization. In this way, adaptivity becomes an inherent characteristic deriving from the existence of self-organizing interaction patterns, whose structure can flexibly yet robustly re-shape in response to contingencies.

Accommodating new and diverse component species (to support adaptivity in vertical composition) reduces to simply enabling components to enter the ecosystem in respect of its eco-laws, and letting the dynamics of the interactions evolve and re-shape in response to the appearance of such new species. In this way, one can take advantage of the new interactional possibility of such new species and of the additional value they bring, without requiring the individual components or the infrastructure itself (i.e., its eco-laws and structure) to be re-engineered.

Most importantly, it is the overall dynamics of the interactions induced by the eco-laws – seamlessly involving composition and aggregation of data and services – that naturally induce a sort of "systemic self-awareness" into the ecosystem. That is, service components are not necessarily forced to digest and interpret information to express an observable self-aware behavior. Rather, their automatic composition will make the systems as a whole, other than its components, inherently express forms of observable self-awareness and adaptivity in their dynamics.

Nature-inspired computing paradigms have indeed already been extensively investigated (Kari and Rozenberg, 2008). Many proposals, though, exploit the natural inspiration only for the definition of general computational models (Berry and Boudol, 1990) or – for distributed and pervasive computing – of adaptive algorithmic solutions in the context of assessed architectural frameworks (Babaoglu *et al.*, 2006). Instead, we argue that natural metaphors can act as comprehensive conceptual and practical frameworks for architecting pervasive service systems and their supporting infrastructure.

One can think of natural systems from many viewpoints, each of which can act as a guiding metaphor for modeling and implementing the service components that will form the pervasive service ecosystem, the space in which they will execute, and the eco-laws that will rule their interactions.

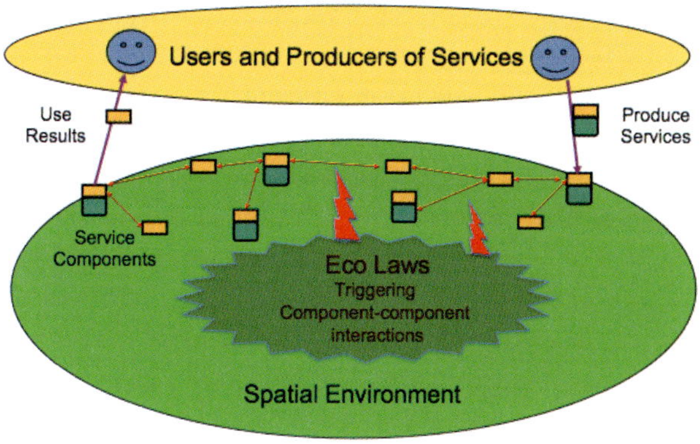

Fig. 2.1 The general conceptual architecture of nature-inspired service approaches

In particular, so far, four key metaphors are being extensively explored for this purpose (see Zambonelli and Viroli (2011) for an extensive survey):

- Physical, in which service components are abstracted as virtual particles which interact and compose with each other driven by virtual force fields.
- Chemical, in which service components are like virtual molecules interacting and composing with each other due to virtual chemical bonds.
- Biological, in which components are abstracted as cells interacting and composing (morphing) together via exchange of chemical gradients.
- Ecological, in which components are considered as species of animals that interact with each other in a virtual food web (i.e., a service composes with another in the same way that an animal tries to eat other animals).

All metaphors adhering to natural inspiration are, by construction, spatially situated, adaptive, and open to hosting diverse and evolving species. However, when it comes to analyzing such metaphors for exploitation in pervasive computing scenarios, different metaphors may tolerate with variable degrees of adaptivity different situations and dynamic contingencies, analysis of which is out of the scope of this chapter. However, all natural metaphors exhibit adaptation and self-aware composition while limiting the number and complexity of eco-laws and the complexity of individuals and their environment, thus also keeping the supporting infrastructure lightweight and the overall execution efficient.

We invite the reader to have a look at the specific instantiation of the biochemically inspired approach to service components that has been realized within the SAPERE project,[1] to get an idea of how the above claimed advantages have been effectively verified.

2.3.2 *Composition and re-composition of service collaboration patterns*

In nature-inspired approaches the programmers/designers do not have direct control over the dynamics of the compositions, which are self-organizing and spontaneously induced by the eco-laws. This can make it difficult to enforce and orchestrate complex compositions and their dynamic modification. Since this can be perceived as a notable drawback of the approach, other approaches try to achieve adaptivity while preserving control over the patterns of composition and collaboration between components.

If self-composition of a specific pattern is a first step, we are more interested in analysis of what happens when dynamic contingencies require a system *self-re-composition* (simply *re-composition* in the following), i.e., a change in the way components are composed in the system, and in particular their collaboration pattern.

Depending on the situation, one pattern can be more suitable than others (Cabri and Capodieci, 2013); since situations can change at runtime, a change of pattern makes the system more adaptable. In this section we discuss three different approaches: (i) a *role*-based approach in which the collaboration logic is delegated to roles that can be dynamically changed at runtime (Cabri *et al.*, 2005); (ii) a *description*-based approach that aims at describing the collaboration patterns by means of some formalism (Lerman *et al.*, 2005), and allows measurement or evaluation of the 'distance' between different patterns in order to understand how to change from one to another; and (iii) an approach inspired by *Artificial Immune Systems (AIS)* that takes inspiration from biology (de Castro and Von Zuben, 2000).

The next subsections will present these approaches, while Table 2.1 summarizes their pros and cons.

---

[1] http://www.sapere-project.eu

Table 2.1 Comparison of the three proposed approaches

Approach	Pros	Cons
Role-based	High-level solution; separation of concern	Sharp separation hard to achieve
Description-based	Easy to implement; less code	Description of patterns with a formalism; distance can be high
AIS-inspired	Scalable, decentralized and adaptive	Time requisites; requires further efforts for conflicts avoidance policies design

2.3.2.1 *Role-based approach*

In the first approach roles are exploited. A role can be defined as *a set of behaviors common to different entities* (Fowler, 1997), with the capability to apply them to an entity in order to change its capabilities and behavior. The main advantages of exploiting roles can be summarized as follows: first, they can be applied to existing entities to change their behavior; then, roles can be thought of as solutions common to different problems, so they can be reused in different situations; further, roles enable a separation of concerns between the *business* logic of the application, which is embedded in the components, and the *collaboration* logic, which is embedded in the roles; finally, roles promote an organizational view of the system, which well suits component-oriented approaches (Zambonelli *et al.*, 2001).

In the past we have worked on enabling components (in that case *agents*) to dynamically assume roles (Cabri *et al.*, 2005), and our claim is that the results of that work can be effectively applied in this case.

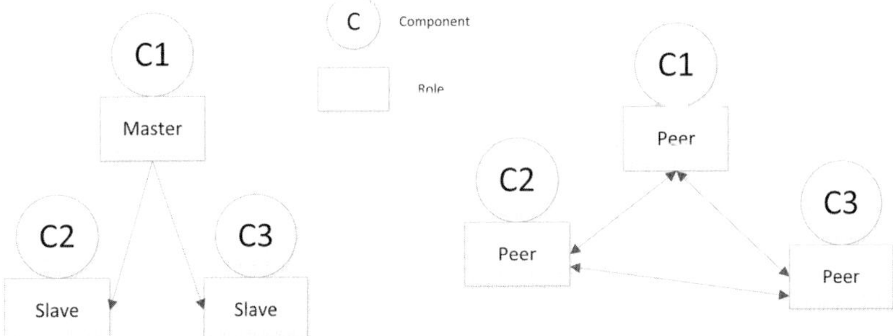

Fig. 2.2 Change of pattern by means of change of roles: from master/slave (left) to peer-to-peer (right)

In more detail, in this approach the pattern is defined by the roles played by the components. Conceptually, it is enough to change the roles of all the components in order to change the pattern. For instance, in the left-side diagram of Figure 2.2 an ensemble of three components (C1, C2, C3) initially exploits the *master/slave* pattern, by making the components play the appropriate roles. Then, all components change their role, assuming the *peer* one (right-side diagram of Figure 2.2); from this point, the collaboration pattern is a *peer-to-peer* one.

The main advantage of this solution is that it is a high-level one. Then, by enacting the separation of concerns, it makes it possible to focus on the pattern change separately from the business logic. A possible drawback is that the separation of concerns is not always so sharp.

2.3.2.2 *Description-based approach*

The second approach relies on the formal or semi-formal description of the patterns and the capability of measuring the differences between patterns. In more detail, the idea is to represent the different patterns in some formal or semi-formal way, and then evaluate which parts are common and which parts differ.

One candidate formalism to describe the patterns and to evaluate the distance is based on Finite State Machines (FSM); in this case, the distance between two patterns is represented by the number of different states. For instance, consider the example reported in Figure 2.3. We have described two patterns (*Pattern1* and *Pattern2*) by means of sets of states. *Pattern1* is composed of states A, B, C, D, G, H, while *Pattern2* is composed of states A, B, C, D, E, F. So, the two patterns have a common set of states that can be assumed as the "core"; then, changing from *Pattern1* to *Pattern2* means discarding states G and H and adding states E and F.

This approach provides a classification and description of the patterns in terms of FSM. We have started classifying collaboration patterns (Cabri *et al.*, 2011; Puviani *et al.*, 2013), but this requires a deeper work and the subsequent description in terms of FSM. Along with FSM, we are also evaluating other formalisms, such as the Activity Diagram of UML, which allows concurrency in the pattens to be expressed, which FSM does not.

The advantage of this approach is that it is easy to implement in an automatic way. Moreover, the required code is likely to be less than that in the role-based approach, since only the differences must be added/removed, not the entire role of the pattern.

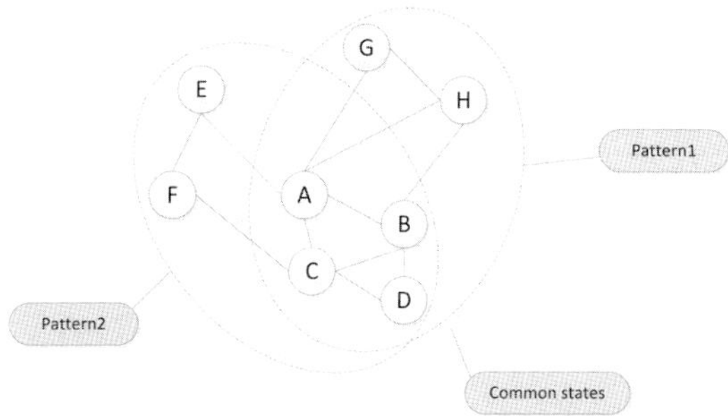

Fig. 2.3 Description of patterns in terms of states and difference between them

The first drawback of this approach is that it requires a description of the collaboration patterns in terms of a formalism (e.g., the FSM) and the translation of this formalism into code to be executed. A more important drawback is that patterns can be very distant, so requiring significant work in describing them without any advantage.

2.3.2.3 *Artificial Immune System inspired approach*

Getting back to nature, a third approach that still enables some control over the dynamic shaping of collaboration patterns is based on Artificial Immune Systems (AIS). Artificial immune systems take inspiration from the way cells and proteins interact during a pathogen response in a living being (Capodieci *et al.*, 2013). AIS-inspired software approaches are not intended to be a very accurate reproduction of the complexity of such biologic systems; however, they are used for defining simplified algorithms and procedures for solving different tasks that can be exploited for our problem (de Castro and Von Zuben, 2000).

There is a significant number of features of the immune system that can be exploited. In particular, the immune system of a human being is *scalable*; according to the pathology of a human body, the number of lymphocytes deployed in the recognition and elimination of a specific antigen can vary. These cells are *heterogeneous* in their composition: often in AIS, the concept of B-cell/T-cell interaction is exploited by assigning for each type of cell a respective 'equivalent' for the system being studied. In a heterogeneous multi-agent/robot system this can be mapped by assigning the different functions of each cell to the behaviors of a different agent/robot, or even features of the environment.

Table 2.2 Mapping between a distributed robotics scenario and cell typologies (Jun *et al.*, 1999), table from de Castro and Von Zuben (2000)

Distributed Autonomous Robotics (DARS)	**Immune System**
Environment	Antigen
Strategy of Action	Antibody
Robot	B-cell
Control Parameter	T-cell
Adequate	Stimulus
Inadequate	Suppression
Excellent Robot	Plasma cell
Inferior Robot	Inactivated cell

Table 2.2 shows how this mapping was formulated in a Distributed Autonomous Robotics (DARS) case study (Jun *et al.*, 1999). No matter how the studied system is composed, the AIS approach, like its biological counterpart, lacks a centralized control, thus becoming more appealing in designing fault-tolerant collaboration strategies.

Considering the problem of changing collaboration patterns, the immune system itself provides an example of two different strategies that can be adopted depending on the situation; both aim to neutralize antigen attacks. The former is a specific *innate* response, the latter is an *adaptive* response: basically our immune system tries a non-memory driven and simple way to devour antigens with a layered response that starts in our skin. The low complexity of this procedure is such that this response is fast but does not work to neutralize many pathological variations of the entity. Therefore, if the innate approach fails, our system immediately starts with a memory-driven cell-mediated adaptive response able to slowly react to new dangers that are now present inside our body. We can consider this approach for solving the problem as a change in collaboration strategy of the cells involved. We can now think about having a multi agent/robot system that tries several ways to solve the same problem, obtaining a performance evaluation and thus stimuli that can suppress or positively assess the collaboration pattern currently in use.

In connection with the concept of distance in patterns presented in Section 2.3.2.2, in an AIS for dynamic pattern changes each pattern can be represented by a *binary string*, in which we represent missing or present states at code level inside each agent. When an agent notifies a change in collaboration pattern, it will send a string of bits representing which states have to be used for the new proposed pattern: the target agent receives this string and via an affinity assessment algorithm (a very common topic in AIS) can evaluate if this string will lead to suppression of the currently used states, the activation of other previously dormant states (states that are present in the code of the agent, but were not executed at the time of the received message) or even the activation of a code migration process for obtaining a missing state for further differentiation.

If well designed, an AIS approach will maintain the same desirable characteristics as a biological immune system, such as *decentralization*, *scalability* and *memory-based*. The immune system itself can be used as a starting case study in bio-inspired collaboration patterns change. AIS provide algorithms for coordination, pattern recognition, cluster formations and fault tolerance: all of these concepts can help design self-* systems. Finally, this approach can be integrated with the concept of distances in patterns.

The drawback is that it needs techniques for managing conflicts in messaging and cluster formation of independent ensembles operating in close locations. Each agent has to be instructed to understand when a change in collaboration pattern is needed. According to the complexity of the problems to be solved and the number of approaches designed in order to solve them, an adaptive response modeled with our AIS approach may introduce additional time before reaching a state of equilibrium.

2.4 Research Challenges

These approaches are very promising for the development of self-aware services. Yet there are still several challenges to overcome for the deployment of self-aware services.

2.4.1 *Challenges for nature-inspired self-composition*

The capability of effectively developing nature-inspired service ecosystems requires facing the following research challenges.

First, there is a need to define proper methodologies and tools for the development and engineering of nature-inspired service ecosystems, as well as for the dynamic and decentralized control of the overall ecosystem dynamics. A key challenge here is to understand the trade-offs between the power of top-down and bottom-up adaptation, and also studying how the two approaches can co-exist (and they will indeed have to) and possibly conflict in future systems, and to contribute in smoothing the tension between the two.

Second, methodologies should come with tools to control the overall behavior of the pervasive system and its sub-parts. Clearly, the challenging issue of defining such models and tools comes with the issue of identifying means to 'measure' such behaviors in order to understand if the control is effective. Defining sound measures for future pervasive scenarios is in itself challenging, given the size of the target scenario and the many – and often quite ill-defined – purposes it has to concurrently serve.

Third, to handle the extreme openness of the system, there is a need to identify proper security mechanisms and policies. Specifically, it will be important to investigate the integration of security and privacy policies not in terms of external tools, but as part of the inherent self-adaptive dynamics of the system itself.

2.4.2 *Challenges for dynamic adaptation of system collaboration patterns*

With regard to collaboration patterns there are three main challenges, at different levels.

The first challenge is to show that the change of collaboration pattern is useful in a quantitative way. In fact, systems are likely to satisfy their *functional* requirements even if something in the environment changes, but this is not always true, and an evaluation of the impact of a change of collaboration pattern is useful to understand how systems can face such changes. Furthermore, what may be interesting is that such changes are more likely to affect the satisfaction of the *non-functional* requirements, such as performance or usability: for instance, after a change in the environment, the system continues to provide its functionalities but requires more time. In both cases, since a change of pattern can be expensive, a balance between the costs and the benefits must be carefully evaluated; costs are easier to calculate, while calculating benefits is more challenging.

The second challenge is to show implementation feasibility of the change of the pattern. In the previous section we have proposed three possible solutions, which theoretically can support the change of the collaboration pattern at runtime. But they must be implemented and engineered to provide an effective support to developed systems.

The third challenge is to enable systems to change patterns. Even if we can enable a system to change its collaboration pattern, it must also be enabled to *decide* to make the change. The situation is complex because we address systems that are likely to be decentralized, so that no single manager can take a decision for the whole system; moreover, *all* the system components must change the pattern. Components must agree in changing the pattern, and a research challenge is to find how this can be modeled and actuated.

2.5 The Impact

The impact of this research may be the definition of flexible and dynamic *ecosystems* of service components. In such ecosystems, service components can join and leave, independently of the original systems for which they were designed. Service components can provide their services to other components not known in advance, and can exploit the services of others in a seamless way. Ecosystems can adapt their collaborative patterns not only to better enable component interactions, but also to better suit the users' and environment's needs.

From a user's point of view, this means exploiting high-level services, composed of possibly several lower-level services, without concern for how the latter are composed and/or organized. This has several advantages:

- More services will be available, deriving from the seamless composition of existing ones.
- High-level services will better suit users' requirements, since the systems will dynamically choose the most appropriate low-level services depending on the users' needs.
- If a user's needs change, services will be more adaptable, thanks to the ability of reconfiguring themselves.

From the environment point of view, the advantages can be less visible, but they are still present:

- Again, services will be more adaptable to environmental changes.
- Services can be composed not only on the basis of users' requirements, but also respecting the environment's policies and rules, for instance exploiting components compliant with local law depending on the country where the service is required or provided.

One important note is that this can affect our everyday life, not just large software systems or company software infrastructures. The two scenarios introduced at the beginning of this chapter are examples taken from common activities.

2.6 Summary and Conclusions

In this chapter we have discussed self-awareness and self-organization of service systems. We point out that we have addressed these aspects not only from the single component point of view, but also from the *system* point of view. Nowadays, the software world is conceived as systems of components, and so must be engineered.

We have shown that self-awareness is the prerequisite to enable systems to self-compose and to re-compose themselves dynamically. For the first step (*self-composition*), we have discussed nature-inspired approaches, which apply natural eco-laws to service components that can join together to provide higher-level services, but are likely to not know each other in advance. The second step (*dynamic re-composition*) can be needed when there are changes in the environment, or in the systems itself, that require a reconfiguration in terms of change of the collaboration pattern; to this purpose we have presented three different solutions: role-based, description-based and AIS-inspired.

What emerges from our work is that *self-awareness* is a fundamental property to enable self-composition and re-composition in service ecosystems. In particular, we point out that it must be a property of the single components as well as of the entire system; for instance, to change the collaboration pattern the system must be aware of its own collaboration pattern, aware of the possible collaboration patterns that can be adopted, and aware of the fact that a change can lead to a better situation. However, as in nature-inspired approaches, awareness can be also be seen as a systemic property, not something to be attributed to individual components.

With regard to future work, we recall some already-mentioned challenges. On the one hand, we are going to evaluate the effectiveness of the proposed approaches by means of abstract considerations and also of some case studies. On the other hand, we must show the feasibility of the proposed approaches by implementing infrastructures that provide the described mechanisms. The two directions are strictly connected, and will be followed in the near future.

Chapter 3

Issues in Engineering Self-Aware and Self-Expressive Ensembles

Matthias Hölzl and Martin Wirsing
Ludwig-Maximilians-Universität München, Germany

3.1 Introduction

Personal assistants such as *Siri* or *Google Now* should recognize their user's current situation and provide requested information as well as other, potentially relevant information without being intrusive or requiring undue amounts of input from the user. Management systems for fleets of electronic vehicles should schedule cars while taking into account a complex set of requirements, company policies and user preferences, without imposing restrictions on the users of the fleet and without requiring manual intervention for unplanned events. Robots used for disaster relief operations should be able to fulfill complex tasks in unknown, fast-changing and possibly hostile environments without endangering human rescue personnel.

As different as these systems are, they share several characteristics: they operate in open environments in which they have to interact with a possibly large number of other entities that are often not under the control of the system's operator and that are not primarily designed to interact with the system (or, in some cases, are actively hostile to the system). The situations arising in the environment are often ambiguous and unpredictable from the system's point of view; many significant events cannot be directly detected by the system and have to be inferred from circumstantial evidence and imprecise input data. The system often cannot directly control the environment, but has to achieve desired effects by performing actions with non-deterministic or probabilistic outcomes. Finally, the most important aspects of the environment and the system's desired behavior are often better described by optimization goals or quality of service contracts than by functional requirements. In more system-theoretic terms, we are dealing with heterostatic,[1] utility-based systems operating in non-stationary, partially observable, non-deterministic environments with multiple feedback loops. Following the InterLink project (2010) we call these kinds of systems *ensembles*.

Current software is often too inflexible and brittle to cope well with the dynamic nature and complexity of ensembles. One way to overcome these limitations is to equip software with more information about the world in which it is operating and the goals it is meant to achieve, and with the capability to act on this knowledge. We call the knowledge that a system has about itself and its environment its *awareness*, and its capability to choose actions based on its awareness *self-expression*. In the next section we will identify the dimensions along which the "intelligence" of a system, i.e., its awareness and capabilities for self-expression, can be classified.

Most users of computers can probably appreciate the advantages that equipping them with better awareness and self-expression mechanisms would have. Yet, astonishingly many books and movies present "intelligent" systems as threatening, out of control, or means for enslaving instead of liberating humans. Is this just dramatic license, a way to provide conflict for exciting storylines? Or is there some profound insight in dystopian visions of future software systems? The introduction of this volume presents many examples of (fictional and non-fictional) systems that misbehave, sometimes in a fatal manner. Therefore, it is necessary to look at some of the reasons why self-aware and self-expressive ensembles might fail in more spectacular ways than traditional systems, and at possible socio-technical solutions to prevent or mitigate undesired consequences.

This chapter is structured as follows. A multi-dimensional classification of self-awareness is introduced in Section 3.2, and the challenges that building increasingly aware and self-expressive systems poses for developers is discussed in Section 3.3. Section 3.4 addresses certain challenges that possess no solely technical solution: privacy, ownership and control of data; the potential for discrimination and (ir)responsibility; and failure modes and consequences of failures by ensembles. The final section concludes.

[1]A heterostatic system is one in which components try to optimize their individual value functions (Klopf, 1972), whereas a homeostatic system is one that strives for an equilibrium state.

3.2 Classifying Awareness and Self-Expression

Before discussing the effects that awareness, self-awareness and self-expression of systems have, we should clarify what exactly we mean by these notions and how we can determine whether a system is more or less aware. In this section we introduce informally our conception of awareness, a minimal set of components that each awareness mechanism has to possess to fit into our model, and the various degrees of awareness along which we distinguish awareness mechanisms.

3.2.1 *Elements of the awareness mechanism*

Since it is difficult to conceive of a completely memory-less (self-)aware system, a system S that exhibits awareness has to have *some* way to store information about itself or its environment E; we call this information the *awareness model* M of S. The awareness model can be distributed among various nodes of S and even the environment E. Therefore, our concept of awareness models also encompasses system architectures based on stigmergy, e.g., robots that place tokens in their environment to mark places they have already visited.

If S is operating in an open-ended, non-deterministic environment E, the awareness model should account for the dynamics of E (including, from the point of view of S, other agents active in the environment): changes in E should influence the awareness model M and vice versa. Adapting the definition of Smith (1984) for procedurally reflective systems to ensembles, we call S (or, slightly inaccurately, M) and E causally connected if changes to M eventually influence E. In many systems, this influence is not immediate, since activities taken by the system need time to propagate to the environment. Similarly, we say that S (or M) is *inversely (causally) connected* to E if certain changes in E lead to corresponding changes in M after S reaches some state in which it can perceive the changes in its environment. The subsystem that is responsible for maintaining the inverse connection between E and M is the *sensor system* of S.

Most environments are only partially observable: S cannot directly perceive all relevant information, instead it may have to *reason* about the available data to obtain the information required for action. We use the term "reason" in a very broad sense: the *reasoning engine* of a simple agent might be a program that simply queries the data stored in its awareness model, or it might perform simple computations, such as computing the length of a path by summing up the length of its components. More sophisticated reasoning engines might perform complex inferences, run simulations or develop plans as part of their reasoning process, and a system may include several, distributed reasoning engines.

We call the combination of sensor system, awareness model and reasoning engines of a system its *awareness mechanism.* Its components need not be dedicated to the awareness mechanism, they can also be used by other parts of the system.

3.2.2 *A white-box definition of awareness*

Our goal is not to define a binary predicate that classifies systems as "aware" or "not aware," we want to characterize and compare the *degree of awareness* that various systems possess. In this section we focus on a white-box definition in which we assume that we can analyze all internal mechanisms of the systems under consideration. We assume that the state of a system and its environment at a single moment in time can, at least in theory, be described by a *state space*, and we call all possible trajectories the system can take through the state space over time its *trajectory space* or *phase portrait.* A more in-depth discussion of the formal model underlying this discussion can be found in Hölzl and Wirsing (2011), but the details are not important for this chapter.

We classify awareness mechanisms along three different axes: *expressivity*, *quality* and *interface* with the rest of the system.

3.2.2.1 *Expressivity*

There are many modeling and reasoning techniques suitable for building awareness mechanisms, and most systems combine several of them. Defining a universal notion of "expressivity" for awareness mechanisms is therefore difficult, but two characteristics can typically be distinguished:

Scope To remain manageable, an awareness mechanism will only be concerned with some dimensions of the state space, often with limited precision, and it will only store a limited amount of historical information. The *scope* of an awareness mechanism describes which subspace of the trajectory space it represents.

Depth We call a measure for the information accessible by an awareness mechanism that is transitively connected to its scope the *depth* of the awareness mechanism.

Note that scope and depth are defined in relation to the state space; both "M_1 has larger scope than M_2" and "M_1 is deeper than M_2" mean that M_1 contains more information than M_2, the difference is whether this information is part of the system's state or whether it is meta-information about the awareness mechanism and its data. Intuitively, the scope of an awareness model M describes how big the slice of the world represented by M is and the depth of M describes the richness the model's ontology.

As an example, we look at a video camera that records a room in which three people are moving around. We are interested in their locations; our state space therefore contains (x, y) coordinates for each person. If the video camera stores an hour of video, what is the scope of its awareness model? Since the video feed contains no data about the position of either person, its intersection with the state space is empty, and hence its scope and depth are minimal. A person watching the video might be able to extract information about the locations, but that is a result of the awareness mechanism of the human, not the camera.

For a smart camera that can recognize people (without identifying individuals) the scope of its awareness model is no longer minimal. If the camera can also identify the three individuals we are interested in, its scope becomes larger still. For the scope and depth it is not important whether the camera outputs the video stream in addition to the positions of the people; only the latter information influences the awareness of the system.

As these examples show, the amount of stored data is not sufficient to determine the expressivity of a system's awareness mechanism; we must also take into account the capabilities of the reasoning engines.

3.2.2.2 *Quality*

An awareness model that has great scope and depth, yet bears only a remote relationship to the actual environment in which a system operates is not particularly useful. Similarly, a reasoner that can answer a wide range of questions may not be useful for a system if it takes too long to derive answers. Therefore, we are interested not only in the expressivity of awareness mechanisms but also in their *quality*, which we subdivide into accuracy and performance:

Accuracy The *accuracy* of an awareness mechanism is a measure for the distance between answers provided by the awareness mechanism and the corresponding "real" values.

Precision The *precision* of an awareness mechanism measures how close the answers for repeatedly asking the same question in the same state are to each other, independent of their distance to the "real" value.

Performance We define the performance of an awareness mechanism as the average time it takes to answer queries of a certain complexity.

The accuracy of different awareness mechanisms can be estimated by comparing the data in the awareness model with reality, e.g., by measuring the total difference between the location of a robot R obtained from its awareness model and its actual location (as observed by a tracking system) over the duration of a simulated rescue mission.

In dynamic environments, accuracy obviously depends on the time needed to update R's awareness model after changes in the environment. For example, assume that R has a map of the environment that it uses for path planning, but that R only updates its models using data from its own sensors. If an avalanche blocks a part of the road that R intends to take, this will not be reflected in R's model until R reaches the blocked part of the road, so this aspect of the model is inaccurate over long periods of time. If, however, R also updates its model based on information received from other robots, it may increase the accuracy of its awareness since data about remote obstacles can be integrated into the model in a timely manner.

3.2.2.3 *Interface*

A third aspect that distinguishes different awareness mechanisms is how much access they permit for the rest of the system or to external observers, how their connection with the rest of the system is achieved, and how many possibilities they provide for the rest of the system to change the awareness mechanism, e.g., by modifying the model or adding new reasoning capabilities. We call these features of an awareness mechanism its *interface*. The interface can be divided into its *interaction* with the rest of the system, its *accessibility*, its *traceability* and its *configurability*.

Interaction There are various ways how awareness mechanisms may interact with the rest of the system. Software-intensive systems are generally structured as components communicating via well-defined ports and protocols. In biological systems, the responsibilities of and interactions between different parts of the system are often much more complex.

Accessibility An interface may not provide all features of the awareness mechanism to the rest of the system. We call the expressivity that an awareness mechanism exposes via its interface its *accessible expressivity*, and similarly for quality, scope, depth, etc.

Traceability It is often necessary that users of an awareness mechanism can comprehend or analyze the reasoning that led to certain conclusions. We call this property the *traceability* of the awareness mechanism.

Configurability Some awareness mechanisms allow users to modify the structure of the awareness model, add or remove sensors from the sensor system, and add, replace or reconfigure reasoners. The extent to which these operations are possible is called the (run-time) *configurability* of the awareness mechanism.

The design of the interfaces of awareness mechanisms plays an important role in awareness engineering (Section 3.3) since awareness mechanisms generally have to balance many competing demands: extensible awareness mechanisms often require more resources, demand complex interactions from the rest of the system, and often produce results that are difficult to comprehend. Accessible awareness mechanism may enable more features but pose privacy or security problems for the ensemble.

For example, a security camera might be able to detect people in a room and notify its operators when it recognizes suspicious behaviors. Limiting accessibility to this feature only and providing no configurability leads to a simple interface for the camera's awareness mechanism. Making more of the internal workings of the camera's awareness mechanism accessible, e.g., by allowing users to track individuals, may enable new applications but may also make the system susceptible to abuse, see Section 3.4.

3.2.2.4 *A white-box definition of awareness*

We call the functionality of a system's awareness mechanism its *(internal) awareness* and the accessible functionality of the awareness mechanism its *(structurally) accessible* or *exposed awareness*. Since this notion is based on the internal workings of the system's awareness mechanism and not on an operational description of its behavior, this is a *non-operational* (or *structural, white-box*) definition of awareness.

From this definition it is easy to classify or compare the *degree of awareness* of different systems. We call the degree of awareness of the awareness mechanism itself the *internal degree of awareness* of the system and the degree of awareness of the functionality exposed by the interface of the awareness mechanism the *(structurally) exposed degree of awareness.*

Various (non-operational) notions of self-awareness found in the literature can be expressed using our definition by placing constraints on the expressivity of the awareness mechanism.

3.2.3 *Self-expression*

Given a structural definition of awareness or self-awareness, we know whether a system has enough information about itself, its environment and the behaviors required to achieve certain goals, but unless this information can actually influence the behavior of the system it serves no operational purpose. Therefore, we are usually interested in systems whose knowledge representation is causally connected. Recall that a system and its model are causally connected if a change in the model can affect the system's behavior and thereby eventually the environment (see p. 39).

The notion of *self-expression* is defined Lewis *et al.* (2011) in a manner similar to causal connection between the awareness model and the environment (and see also Chapter 18):

- *A node exhibits self-expression if it is able to assert its behavior upon either itself or other nodes.*
- *This behavior is based upon the node's state, context, goals, values, objectives and constraints.*

Zambonelli *et al.* (2011) define self-expression in a different way that is related to *weak* and *strong adaptation*: In their parlance, *self-adaptation mechanisms* are concerned with modifying parameters or selecting among actions, whereas

> Self-expression mechanisms *concern the possibility of radically modifying at run-time the structure of components and ensembles.*

To distinguish these notions of self-expression, we call the definition of Lewis *et al.* *behavioral self-expression* and the one of Zambonelli *et al.* *structural self-expression.* In the following, we propose a definition of (behavioral) self-expression that is similar to the one by Lewis *et al.* and weaker than structural self-expression.

The level of *self-expression* exhibited by a system can be defined in a decision-theoretic way. We suppose that the desirability of various courses of action can be described by a *value function* V, which may or may not be explicitly known to the system. Using V we can express goals of the system and preferences over the system's behavior in a unified manner.

Recall that causal connection means that the awareness model influences the system's behavior, but causal connection does not imply any expectation that these behavioral changes are positively correlated with either goals of the system itself or an externally provided value function. For self-expression we strengthen this notion slightly and demand that a change in the awareness model M of a system that is *self-expressive with respect to* V influences its behavior so that it improves the expected value of V given M. The dependence on M is crucial for this definition; a system with an inaccurate awareness model M may exhibit perfect self-expression (because it optimizes the expected value of V based on M) but bad overall performance (because M bears no relationship to the actual environment). Also, the degree of self-expression depends crucially on V; we call a system *self-expressive* if it is self-expressive with regards to its own value function.

Put another way, the degree of self-expression of a system with respect to V can be defined as the degree of rationality that the system's actions exhibit relative to the value function V and its awareness model, i.e., a system expresses itself perfectly if it uses its awareness mechanism to maximize the expected total value of its actions over its lifetime.

3.2.4 *A black-box definition of awareness*

From the definitions of non-operational awareness and self-expression we can recapture a notion of *operational* (or *black-box*) *awareness*. To analyze the awareness of a system S without relying on knowledge about its internal structure, we require a fixed value function V. We can then compare the performance of S, as measured by V for the tasks we are interested in, to systems S_i with known awareness mechanisms exhibiting perfect self expression with respect to V. If S achieves a performance measure that is at least as good as S_i, we define its (operational) awareness to be at least the same as that of S_i.

For example, in certain environments it is not possible for a robot to efficiently navigate to a target location without knowing its own position. If a robot R is consistently able to navigate to a desired target location, we say it is *(operationally) aware* of its location, without knowing anything about its internal structure. If, on the other hand, a robot R' is unable to find the target location, then we say that R' is not operationally aware of its location. This may mean that the awareness mechanism of R' does not contain the necessary data to make good decisions, or the failure of R' may be due to a lack of self-expression; this distinction cannot be established by the chosen experiment.

3.3 Awareness Engineering

The development of a system according to a traditional or agile software-engineering process is concerned with tasks such as capturing business requirements or use cases, developing (UML) models based on the code, generating or writing the code, and finally testing and deploying the system (Sommerville, 2007). These tasks focus mostly on the interface between external user roles and the system, and on the system's internal structure. This is possible for traditional systems, since they are designed to have relatively static structures and functionalities which are fully under the control of their developers. Domain knowledge is used by designers while they are building a system, whereas the resulting system operates without having to "understand" its domain in any meaningful sense.

When developing ensembles, designers will no longer be able to specify the concrete behaviors for each possible situation that the system might encounter; instead, parts of the design process will move to the meta-level in that the developers devise strategies and mechanisms that the system can use to recognize and cope with various circumstances it encounters in the environment. Developers will therefore have to (1) formalize larger parts of the domain and background knowledge for the system, (2) provide reasoning mechanisms that enable the system to assess its situation and goals based on this knowledge and to derive the best course of actions, and (3) build mechanisms that allow the system to act based on these inferences. For many systems, resource constraints and the complexity of the tasks they have to fulfill make the use of general-purpose knowledge representations and inference mechanisms infeasible; therefore, finding the right trade-offs between expressivity, quality and integration of the awareness mechanism is amongst the major challenges faced by designers of ensembles.

We call the development of practical high-quality awareness and self-expression mechanisms that are expressive enough to enable the system to satisfy its design goals *awareness engineering*. This process will allow many novel and useful systems to be built and offer ways for systems to adapt to unforeseen circumstances and environments. But the introduction of awareness engineering also poses major new challenges for developers and organizations, for example:

- Building deep awareness models requires a detailed understanding of the system's domain as well as knowledge about the formalisms used for models, the capabilities and limits of different reasoning engines, and the acceptable trade-offs for the application domain.
- To achieve high-quality awareness mechanisms, manually constructed models have to be combined with mechanisms for learning and possibly with components developed using evolutionary processes into a system that reliably fulfills its design goals.
- Many capabilities of ensembles are decentralized and "emerge" from interactions between various components of the ensemble and the environment. Awareness models have to be expressive enough to use these capabilities for the goals of the ensemble when possible, and to foresee and avoid undesirable emergent properties.

Existing development processes and life-cycle models will need to be revised and expanded to take these challenges into account. An example for a possible development life cycle is the Ensemble Development Life Cycle (EDLC) being developed as part of the ASCENS project (Koch *et al.*, 2013). We will, however, not further pursue the impact that awareness engineering has on developers, but rather pursue how awareness engineering might be connected to the socio-technical questions posed by increasingly aware and self-expressive systems.

3.4 Socio-Technical Issues

The additional capabilities of systems with a high degree of awareness and self-expression give rise to multiple concerns about their impact on society that deserve consideration. This section touches upon some areas where awareness engineering is influenced by and influences social issues such as privacy, discrimination or consequences of system failures.

3.4.1 *Privacy, ownership and control of data*

Some of the most interesting applications of increased awareness are in personal devices that have an intimate connection to our daily lives. For example, the *Google Now* application analyzes its user's context and behavior, and proactively provides information that it considers relevant to the user. Increasing the awareness of this kind of application can most efficiently be done by collecting more data about the user and retaining it over longer periods of time (increased scope of awareness), and by enhancing the semantic content of the collected data, e.g., by building more detailed user models or by cross-referencing data from different sources (increased depth). However, increasing the awareness of applications that process personal data also leads to concerns about the user's privacy as well as control and ownership of data.

Parent (1983) defines privacy as "the condition of not having undocumented personal knowledge about one possessed by others. A person's privacy is diminished exactly to the degree that others possess this kind of knowledge about him." When talking about the impact of awareness in computer systems, the first question raised by this definition is what "undocumented" means exactly. Technically, most data collection is disclosed to users by end-user license agreements or similar documents and therefore documented. In practice, many people realize neither the amount of data collected about them during routine transactions, nor the amount of information that can be extracted from seemingly innocuous data. Companies already use these techniques to determine customers who are particularly likely to respond to advertisements. For example, Duhigg (2012) recounts how a supermarket targets women at the beginning of the second trimester of their pregnancy with special advertising campaigns, a practice that led to a father learning about his teenage daughter's pregnancy because of the coupons she received from the supermarket.

There is a related pertinent problem: some services are almost indispensable to take part fully in today's society, e.g., web search, but they invariably expose personal information to the service provider. Search terms on their own often reveal concerns or interests of users, such as possible medical problems; if they are correlated with data from other sources, intimate details of users' lives can be inferred with high probability. Users then face the choice of either not using these services and therefore being excluded from many of the benefits of modern technology, or suffering significant erosion of their privacy. In light of these considerations, it seems useful to strengthen Parent's definition of privacy to "the condition of not having undocumented personal knowledge about one possessed by others or being compelled to reveal personal knowledge to others."

From the system operator's point of view it is almost always desirable to collect as much information as possible. Determining appropriate levels of privacy and disclosure of the data being collected by systems is therefore a political question. The task of awareness engineering is then to achieve good operational awareness while limiting the structural awareness to features that do not violate laws, regulations or user's expectations of privacy.

To summarize, if privacy considerations are taken seriously, important aspects of awareness engineering will be:

- The development of awareness mechanisms that achieve a desired level of operational awareness while minimizing the scope and depth of personal data collected by the system.
- Providing users with understandable information about the data being collected and the conclusions inferred from this data, i.e., the construction of traceable awareness mechanisms (see p. 42).
- Offer users ways to opt out of potentially intrusive data collection, at least for necessary services, i.e., to build configurable awareness models that allow users to reduce the scope of the awareness mechanism and thereby the collected information.

Privacy concerns do not end once data has been collected; an important consideration is also who controls and owns the collected data. For example, can users verify the inferences that the awareness mechanisms draw from the collected data and overrule inaccurate items, i.e., is it possible to devise a kind of "glass-box" model of awareness mechanisms that provides traceability and allows users to improve the quality of the awareness model? If this is possible, how can the service provider protect itself from users who falsify their data to take advantage of services for which they are not eligible? Should users be able to remove all or some of their data when their business relationship with the provider of a service ends, and how can they be sure that no data is retained against their wishes? How long may user data be retained before it has to be deleted if the user takes no action? If a user removes their data from a system, what happens to aggregated data that the service provider has computed, and may some individual data be retained by the service provider to maintain the traceability of the aggregated data? What are the responsibilities of providers when personal data of their clients is exposed because of security problems? Should service providers be allowed to sell the data they have collected? How do the answers to these questions change if the data is provided by third parties without knowledge of the subject affected by the data?

These questions address technical issues about scope, interface and security of the awareness model in combination with legal aspects. They are not specific to systems with advanced awareness mechanisms, they already arise when we engage in online shopping or when companies engage in business-to-business transactions. However, they become much more relevant when awareness mechanisms possess knowledge about many private aspects of our lives and businesses. For example, Kosinski *et al.* (2013) show that "easily accessible digital records of behavior, Facebook Likes, can be used to automatically and accurately predict a range of highly sensitive personal attributes including: sexual orientation, ethnicity, religious and political views, personality traits, intelligence, happiness, use of addictive substances, parental separation, age, and gender." If more powerful awareness mechanisms can extract even more detailed personal data, establishing trust relationships (Schneier, 2012) between users and the operators of systems using these awareness mechanisms and restricting the use of awareness mechanisms to trusted parties will be important considerations for awareness engineering.

3.4.2 *Discrimination and responsibility*

Computer systems with increasing awareness about people and organizations also give rise to a second complex of questions that is closely related to privacy: the potential for undesirable social impact and discrimination inherent in these systems, and the responsibility for decisions taken by awareness and self-expression mechanisms.

While being able to accurately determine the risk of business transactions decreases the potential losses of the company, it might lead to unwelcome social effects. As an example, credit card companies are using large amounts of data to analyze their customers' risk of default and have been reported to, e.g., lower credit lines when customers seek marriage therapy, since this is an indicator for possible depression and job loss (Duhigg, 2009). However, if therapy leads to lower credit lines, this might put additional pressure on already troubled marriages, and hence lower the chances of reconciliation. So, while the system's awareness increases the utility for its operator, it might lead to unwanted social effects.

The example illustrates a general effect that can be observed in many situations. When a descriptive model of a system is used to control the same system, the resulting feedback loop may reinforce the behavior predicted by the model: if the stress caused by a bad marriage leads to an increased risk of default, then the added stress from financial pressure caused by the lower credit rating is likely to further increase this risk. Therefore, awareness and self-expression may lead to locally optimal behavior resulting in globally bad outcomes. However, in many cases this can be remedied by extending the scope and depth of the awareness mechanism. By taking into account not only a local performance measure but also the well-being of a larger part of the system, this effect can be minimized. It is interesting to note that compassionate behavior observed in human interactions often serves this purpose: helping people in difficult situations can cause them to overcome their difficulties, leading to a better overall outcome, and often a better outcome for all involved parties. From the point of view of awareness engineering, the problem is to find the right level of expressivity of the awareness model and develop utility functions that include the well-being of the system's environment as well as the system itself.

Even awareness mechanisms based on objective evaluation criteria might lead to self-sustaining discrimination against certain groups by maintaining unwanted feedback cycles. For example, if a certain ethnic group is determined to be more at risk of defaulting on their mortgages, the system might decide that its members are not eligible for student loans, thereby not enabling members of that ethnic group to obtain higher education, leaving them with less earning potential and possibly a higher risk for defaulting on credits. As the awareness of systems supporting or controlling important decisions is increased, these kinds of effects become more and more likely. Again, it is not a technical but a social decision whether this should be disallowed or not.

Sophisticated awareness mechanisms also open another, more insidious, avenue for discrimination: the system's developers or operators might be able to deliberately configure the awareness mechanism so that they discriminate against certain groups; the complexity of typical awareness models makes it difficult to discover such modifications for people not intimately familiar with the system; and even if the offending parts of the mechanism are discovered it is difficult to prove that they were introduced with the purpose of discriminating against a certain group.

This also touches on the obvious question: whose responsibility are the actions of self-aware systems? Should there always be a human in the loop who can veto the system and therefore be responsible for the final decision? Situation-awareness research as well as practical experience shows that humans perform badly when controlling systems that propose correct decisions most of the time and only rarely make errors (Endsley and Jones, 2004). A tragic example of this effect happened when U.S.S. *Vincennes* shot down Iranian Air Flight 655 in 1988. The passenger flight was misidentified by the Aegis cruiser's computer system, in spite of data showing that:

> *the jet was on a consistent course and speed and was broadcasting a radar and radio signal that showed it to be civilian. [...] Even though the hard data was telling the crew that the plane wasn't a fighter jet, they trusted what the computer was telling them more. [...] not one of the eighteen sailors and officers on the command crew was willing to challenge the computer's wisdom.*
>
> (Singer, 2009)

Although many factors were involved in the flawed decision-making, one of these was an over-reliance on technology which led to the death of all 290 passengers and crew on Flight 655.

3.4.3 *Failure modes*

The tragedy of Flight 655 highlight the issue that the failure modes of aware and self-expressive ensembles are different from those of simpler systems. Traditionally, system failures are based on models such as the domino theory or the 'Swiss cheese model'. The domino theory predicates that system failures are caused by some faulty component, and that this failure may propagate through other components, similar to a row of dominoes tumbling when the first one falls. The Swiss cheese model envisions several layers of protection between cause and failing component, where each layer has holes like a slice of Swiss cheese. Failures can happen only when the protections are (mis)-aligned to allow a straight path from cause to failure passing only through holes.

While these failure models can also be applied to complex systems, many failures in these systems can be better understood by not supposing that a single, extraordinary cause is responsible for the failure. Rather, these failures are caused by a confluence of events, with each individual event being inside the normal operational parameters of the system but their combination leading to failure (Hollnagel, 2012). Dekker (2012) argues that these failures occur since each node in the system tries to continuously optimize its operation based on its local, incomplete knowledge of the system. While each of these decisions may be rational from the node's point of view, together they can slowly lead to a configuration of the system in which a concurrence of individually harmless events causes the system to fail. These kinds of malfunction are therefore not caused by a single, catastrophic event but rather by a gradual "drift into failure" due to a series of seemingly inconsequential local decisions. The phenomenon of drifting into failure is, of course, closely related to the unintended social consequences arising from local optimization that were mentioned in the previous section. Examples abound where drift into failure can be observed in biological systems. One well-known example is the formation of so-called ant mills (Delsuc, 2003). When the pheromone trails of foraging army ants happen to enable circular pathways, the ants sometimes follow each other in a circle until they starve. Unless the ant mill is artificially produced, no single catastrophic event is responsible for its creation; rather the geometry of pheromone trails leads the normally successful optimization process into a state that turns out to be catastrophic for the system.

This mode of failure is related to another phenomenon that can be observed in dynamical systems – they are often "balanced at the edge of chaos" (Kauffman, 1993). If each component of the system optimizes its performance for the current situation, all "slack" is eventually removed from the system as it achieves maximum performance. Such a system can potentially adapt to a wide range of situations, but adaptations may result in dramatic changes of its behavior. While the notion that complex systems are necessarily balanced at the edge of chaos has been challenged by Mitchell *et al.* (1994), recent results indicate that this phenomenon occurs in most biological systems (Mora and Bialek, 2011).[2]

Looking at the definition of ensembles with aware and self-expressive components, it is clear that they exhibit all the ingredients that are responsible for drifting into failure: they consist of nodes that possess only limited knowledge of the system's overall goals and behavior, each node optimizes its behavior locally, and the system behavior is the result of interactions between the nodes. There is no general mechanism that can prevent systems from drifting into failure, and predetermined rules and regulations are often incapable of dealing with the adaptations performed by a complex system. If an ensemble is under the control of a single entity, it may be possible for its designers to introduce global contstraints on the performance measures of individual nodes, so that the system as a whole always maintains a certain tolerance for error. For ensembles that span multiple, possibly competing, organizations and use components from third-party providers, this solution is not realistic. Unfortunately, the most

[2]More precisely, the result of the paper is that all models for biological systems analyzed in the paper are close to a so-called critical point.

important and complex systems fall in the latter category. As discussed in the previous section, one possible way to mitigate the risk of drifting into failure is to increase the scope and depth of the system's awareness mechanism, so that components can recognize emerging problems for the system. Formal methods can then be used to analyze the behavior of the system and provide guarantees that certain classes of failure do not occur. However, this approach may significantly increase the resource consumption and overhead of the awareness mechanism as well as the development effort, so it has to be used judiciously. Another possible way to address this issue, proposed by de Weck *et al.* (2011), is to co-evolve the system and the regulations controlling its use. More information about the co-evolution of institutions and systems can be found in Chapter 12 of this volume.

3.5 Summary and Conclusions

The integration of awareness engineering into a system development process seems to be a promising way to address some of the problems occurring in the development of ensembles. Even though reactive agents, for example based on the subsumption architecture introduced by Brooks (1991), have been successful for certain tasks, and approaches such as swarm robotics have made great progress in building systems in which large numbers of robots cooperate using simple interaction rules, it is difficult to see how these approaches could be scaled to systems that perform complex tasks in challenging environments. To evaluate the state of the environment, the intentions of other agents and the importance of multiple competing goals, there seem to be few alternatives to having an awareness mechanism.

However, the introduction of awareness mechanisms poses challenges that go beyond the purely technical aspects of awareness engineering. Concerns such as privacy, social impact and failure modes are not only technical considerations, they also challenge society at large to define the boundaries of a system's behavior and the guarantees that systems and their operators have to provide. For systems whose failures can have a large impact on people's lives it is mandatory to develop safeguards that place limits on their possible behaviors. Integrating awareness-based adaptation with organizational structures that determine acceptable behaviors, formal methods that can dynamically validate the chosen adaptation strategies, and mechanisms for establishing trust between different stakeholders might provide a possible path towards engineering reliable, self-aware ensembles.

Chapter 4

Social Awareness in Technical Systems

Christian Müller-Schloer, Mathias Pacher, Yvonne Bernard and Lukas Klejnowski

Leibniz Universität Hannover, Germany

4.1 Introduction

The complexity of technical systems – especially in the area of embedded systems – has increased dramatically. Some reasons for the increase are the higher integration of circuits, shorter clock periods and lower power consumption leading to a miniaturization of microprocessors, microcontrollers and Systems on Chip. A result is the development and marketing of ubiquitous devices such as small PCs, handhelds, cell or smart phones. In addition, several of these systems and devices are interconnected by busses or via the internet. An example is a modern car, which contains up to 100 microcontrollers running crucial tasks such as ABS, ESP, engine control and the navigation system. Programming these microcontrollers and orchestrating their interactions is highly complex, especially if real-time aspects have to be considered. It is a grand challenge to develop and maintain such highly integrated and often distributed systems.

As a response, the Organic Computing (OC) Initiative was founded in 2002. It deals with theoretical and practical foundations to handle the complexity of the technical systems described above, inspired by mechanisms found in nature and biology, and presents a radical new perspective on complex systems (Müller-Schloer *et al.*, 2011). A typical property of OC systems is that they consist of interacting autonomous entities (e.g. the microcontrollers in the car). In the following, we call such autonomous entities *agents*. The interactions of the agents depend strongly on several conditions: Do the agents belong to the same owner (as in the car) or do they belong to different owners (such as bidding agents of different eBay users)? If the agents belong to the same owner we can assume that they will cooperate. But if they belong to different owners, cooperation between them is not self-evident: the bidding agents of different eBay users will try to win the auction and to minimize the price for their owner. Agents in such open systems are at least self-interested, but could also act selfishly or outright maliciously.

Therefore, it is necessary that agents in OC systems become *social agents*, i.e. they must be aware not only of their environment but also of other agents. We define *awareness* of an agent as its ability to collect, store, aggregate and use information about itself, about other agents and the environment. Awareness in a technical system can be classified into different types of observations and derived knowledge about 'the world'. We distinguish five classes of knowledge:

(1) Self-knowledge: The knowledge of the agent about itself, its internal state and its abilities.
(2) Knowledge about interaction partners: In order to interact properly the agent wants to be able to predict the future behaviour of its partners. The usual social concept for this is trust. A certain trust value is derived from past experience with this partner. Was it reliable? Did it ever try to cheat? Did it deliver correct results? What are its goals, and do they match or oppose others' objectives?
(3) Knowledge about the community: A community is a set of agents that belong together in some sense (e.g. because they serve the same user or they work on the same task). Therefore, it is useful if the agents know about the number of agents and the individual capabilities of the community's agents even if they do not interact. This makes sense because if an agent is failing, another agent of the community can replace it. More information about the community, which might be useful for making decisions, would be: the average workload of other agents, their reputation (i.e. what others think about an agent) or an impending system shutdown.
(4) Knowledge about the institution: Human societies have invented institutions that (i) have a wider view than a single individual and (ii) are able to support or modify the interactions of the individuals. Examples are government or a court of justice. In order to achieve this vertical

interaction, individual agents need specific knowledge such as: What are the rules that should be obeyed? What are the sanctions if the rules are broken? And, on a meta-level: How can the rules be changed?

(5) Knowledge about the environment: The agents need to know or to learn important properties of their environment. Is it static or dynamic? Are there obstacles to be avoided?

We call the knowledge types (2)–(4) *social awareness* because they comprise knowledge describing the relations of the different agents. An agent that is able to collect and use such social information is a social agent. Viewing technical systems as autonomous entities interacting with their environment and with other similar entities opens a whole range of new possibilities how to build such agents: social agents mimic human societies. Should we then set out and study the mechanisms of natural (human) societies and simply transfer them into technical systems? Since this cannot be an end in itself, we have to ask critically why we are doing this.

We are concerned with building complex technical systems consisting of (semi-)autonomous subsystems, which we model in terms of agents. This approach is not to be confused with socio-technical systems, where the focus is on the interaction of people and systems.[1] The benefit of transferring social behaviour into technical systems is to optimize the interactions between different agents: agents know with which other agents they can co-operate (thus accelerating task execution) and which agents have different goals (which leads to competition).

It is not our goal to mimic or simulate human social systems in order to gain a deeper insight into their mechanisms. While this is a worthwhile endeavour, all we want to achieve is an improvement of the technical system. We adopt (human) social mechanisms only if they help us. And we change them whenever this is beneficial.

In this chapter, Section 4.2 discusses the requirements for social agents to organize themselves into sustainable, enduring institutions. We will use Elinor Ostrom's template for such *self-governing institutions*; she has shown that social awareness is necessary whenever a group of agents competes for limited resources. Section 4.3 takes a closer look at *trusted communities* – our implementation of a society of social agents – and the individual

[1]Socio-technical systems (STS) in organizational development (Churchman, 1968) is an approach to complex organizational work design that recognizes the interaction between people and technology in workplaces. The term also refers to the interaction between society's complex infrastructures and human behaviour. In this sense, society itself, and most of its substructures, are complex socio-technical systems.

technical agents who constitute such a community. We will show that self-organization of social systems is possible, but it will also become clear that we need more institutional mechanisms in order to drive an agent community in a desirable direction. Therefore, Section 4.4 analyses how far we can transfer additional social mechanisms from Ostrom's eight principles to our technical societies. Finally, we give an outlook in Section 4.5.

4.2 Self-Governing Institutions

A group of human actors can encounter problems if they have to compete for limited resources with non-exclusive access. Examples of such *common pool resources* (CPR) are fisheries, timber and water, all of them necessary resources but with many competing parties having interests that are dependent on their exploitation. In situations where over-depletion of the resource affects its own sustainability, purely selfish, short-term and local behaviour can result, in the worst case, in a total exhaustion of the resource pool (i.e. the tragedy of the commons (Hardin, 1968)). In other situations, which may require the actors to participate actively in the maintenance of the resource, there can be a problem of free-riding, where some actors get the benefits of appropriating from the common resource without incurring the costs in provisioning to the resource itself or helping maintain the infrastructure that facilitates access to it. Free-riding is a common problem in peer-to-peer file-sharing applications.

A group of software actors, or agents, can encounter similar problems, i.e. a competition for limited resources, in many computing applications, such as cloud and grid computing, or in ad hoc and sensor networks, where the agents need to collectivize and allocate resources (bandwidth, energy, memory, etc.).

Elinor Ostrom has shown that a group of human actors can formulate solutions to collective action situations with the possibility of undesirable outcomes or behaviours (i.e. the tragedy of the commons, and free-riding) by incentivizing pro-social (rather than anti-social) behaviours through *institutions* (Ostrom, 1990). These institutions were defined as a collection of working rules that determined who was eligible to make certain decisions in particular situations, what actions were prescribed or proscribed, and so on. Ostrom identified eight principles of *self-governing* institutions for enduring and sustainable common-pool resource management. These principles are as follows (see Ostrom (1990) for details):

(1) Clearly defined boundaries: those who have rights or entitlement to appropriate resources from the CPR are clearly distinguished from those who are not, as are the resources in question.
(2) Congruence between appropriation and provision rules and the state of the prevailing local environment: as well as ensuring sustainability, the rules should also deliver 'fair' outcomes.
(3) Collective choice arrangements: those affected by the operational rules participate in the selection and modification of those rules. This principle prevents third parties imposing their interests.
(4) Monitoring, of both state conditions and appropriator behaviour, is by appointed agencies, who are either accountable to the resource appropriators or are appropriators themselves.
(5) A flexible scale of graduated sanctions for resource appropriators who violate communal rules.
(6) Access to fast, cheap conflict-resolution mechanisms. In a system with competing actors, conflicts of interest are to be expected, and need to be resolved quickly and 'affordably' (i.e. cheaply).
(7) Existence of and control over their own institutions is not challenged by external authorities. An external authority cannot intervene no matter what arrangements the appropriators choose for themselves.
(8) Systems of systems: CPRs can be layered or encapsulated. This principle means that hierarchies of CPRs are possible in order to save communication overhead or to simplify decision-making processes.

To use Ostrom's theory to solve a collective action problem faced by a group of software agents, we need to extend the agent's view with a form of 'social awareness'.[2] Social awareness requires interaction and thus communication between the agents. In addition, we have to introduce a notion of trust between the agents, which enables them to estimate the reliability of each other. If an agent trusts that another agent will perform an action this means that the first agent expects that the second agent will perform the action with a certain probability. Also, if a group of agents assumes that another agent performs an action but this agent fails to do this, the other agents can decide to punish the offender.

However, a key issue to address is how the values of trust are to be computed and which sanctions are to be imposed in case of failures or anti-

[2] The view can be extended not only locally (aware of the environment and other agents) but also on the time axis. History-aware agents using a learning algorithm can predict future developments more accurately.

social (non-compliant) behaviour. Therefore, we need a social framework that defines the rules and norms of interaction, communication and trust between agents. The agents then need to evaluate their actions (a priori and a posteriori) according to the mutually agreed, conventional rules of the institution, i.e. a set of norms, which should inform and influence the decision-making of the agents.

When a conventional rule or norm is introduced to a computer system, we have to decide between enforcement (which includes detection of violation, recovery from non-normative state or sanctioning of offenders) and regimentation (forcing compliance through code itself, which is inflexible and impractical in open systems). The design and implementation of the sanctioning enforcement system is however somewhat complex: a sanction that is designed to incentivize compliant behaviour and deter non-compliant behaviour needs agents that can learn from the outcomes of their actions (Riveret *et al.*, 2013), while the cost of enforcement (in particular in systems with endogenous resources) also needs to be taken into consideration (Balke *et al.*, 2013).

4.3 Technical Agent Societies

4.3.1 *Trusted communities*

We are interested in complex technical systems consisting of autonomous agents. Here, an agent is a hardware/software subsystem with some kind of sensory (or at least communication) equipment. If this sensory equipment adds information pertaining to other agents and to certain higher-level entities, this agent becomes socially aware. Also, it must be able to take decisions and to act accordingly. Our research question is if and how Ostrom's principles are applicable and advantageous for our technical system.

We call our approach *trusted community* (TC). A TC comprises a set of agents with a mutual trust relationship. It is characterized by a set of rules (norms), which agents who want to be TC members must adhere to. TCs can be implicitly or explicitly managed. In the latter case there is a (possibly distributed) management entity taking care of admission and exclusion of agents, norm adaptation and the TC lifecycle. But in either case, TCs are self-organized. TC membership is beneficial for an agent: the advantage of simplified interaction with other agents, access to community resources and reciprocal treatment must outweigh the overhead usually associated with each form of organization. So far, TCs are not full self-governing institutions in Ostrom's sense, i.e. exhibiting all eight design principles. The reasons will be discussed in Section 4.4.

The TC concept and its benefits can be explained by a desktop grid computing (DGC) system as a concrete application example. A DGC system allows a group of agents to distribute computing tasks, each of which is called a *work unit* (WU), within a network of personal computers (PCs). The idea is that one computer (agent) with a temporary overload can sub-contract WUs to presently idling ones. As long as all agents are benevolent, they should all be willing to accept WUs. However, there might be agents trying to exploit others, i.e. they sub-contract their own WUs but do not accept WUs from others. The agents could replicate WUs in order to increase the likeliness of success, but from the overall system point of view, this is an unnecessary overhead. Therefore, a rule of conduct is required with an incentive to accept WUs. For this we use the reputation of the agents. Any time a sub-contracted agent satisfactorily processes a WU, the contracting agent will rate its success positively. If this is done by many agents, the sub-contractor will build a high reputation. This increases its likeliness to be able to sub-contract WUs, creating a feedback loop rewarding behaviour which is beneficial for the community. After a while, all agents, who act socially responsibly in the above sense, will establish a group of high-reputation agents: a trusted community. TC members will cooperate preferably within the TC, and doing this will increase their efficiency since they can get rid of expensive checking procedures and WU replication.

There are more scenarios where the TC concept can be useful. Robots exploring and mapping an unknown terrain can be led to share their findings with other explorers. Sensors in an open wireless sensor network (WSN) are guided to supply correct information to others even at the expense of their own battery lifetime. Similarly, an open network of smart surveillance cameras can self-organize as a TC in order to isolate the less reliable ones.

4.3.2 *The social agent*

Increasing the (social) awareness level of an agent must lead to some kind of performance increase. But, in the first place, higher awareness means increasing overhead (see Figure 4.1(a)). Observations in the social context are made through more communication. On the system side, we have to provide a more costly infrastructure for data collection, aggregation and provision. In addition, the agent itself must be able to utilize the additional information. This requires more rational capabilities in the broadest sense.

The agent's decision mechanisms must be able to handle all five kinds of awareness information. At present, it is not entirely clear if this additional complexity pays off.

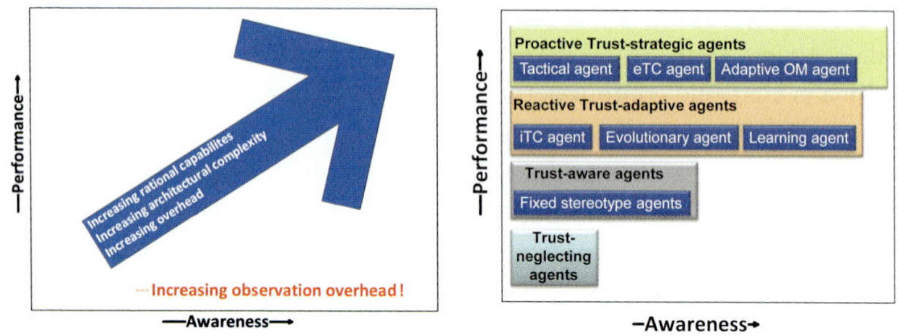

(a) Increasing agent awareness requires increased observation effort and more complex decision mechanisms. This has to lead to a performance increase.

(b) Agent types with different awareness levels have different performance potentials.

Fig. 4.1 The influence of increasing awareness on the performance

For experimenting we have built different agent types. Depending on their specific awareness level they can be placed in the performance vs. awareness plane (Figure 4.1). We have introduced four awareness levels:

- Trust-neglecting agent: This type does not know any trust values and thus does not consider them in its decisions. They implement certain fixed stereotypical behaviours such as egoist, free-rider etc.
- Trust-aware agent: Uses trust values for static cooperation decisions.
- Reactive trust-aware agent: Adapts its behaviour to trust values. It can either adapt to changing trust relations in the system (when trust values of other agents change) or to changes in the trust values other agents assign to it. Some of them are able to learn.
- Proactive trust-strategic agent: Adapts its behaviour before a situation change occurs. Due to predictions, it can adapt proactively and thus even prevent future critical situations. These agents can also adapt their observation model (OM), i.e. they determine at run-time which knowledge is useful.

In our DGC example, the trust-aware agents (and those of higher awareness levels) possess information about their own and other agents' workloads, their reputation and their own past experience with other agents. From this input they derive a trust value and a decision to accept or reject a work unit offered by another agent. A proactive trust-strategic agent has additional information about the interaction history with other agents (the so-called long-term situation descriptor).

So far we have assumed that each agent type is associated with a fixed scope of (social) awareness. In the more general case, agents need different information in different situations. If the agent can control the observations at runtime we will spend only the minimum overhead absolutely necessary to make the currently vital decisions. Therefore, we have extended the agent architecture with an adaptive observation model. The agent controller can specify exactly which information should be collected at any given moment and how this information is to be processed. This corresponds in the extreme case to the tunnel view effect experienced in life-threatening situations, where our sensory equipment (as well as the motor equipment) is tuned on escape.

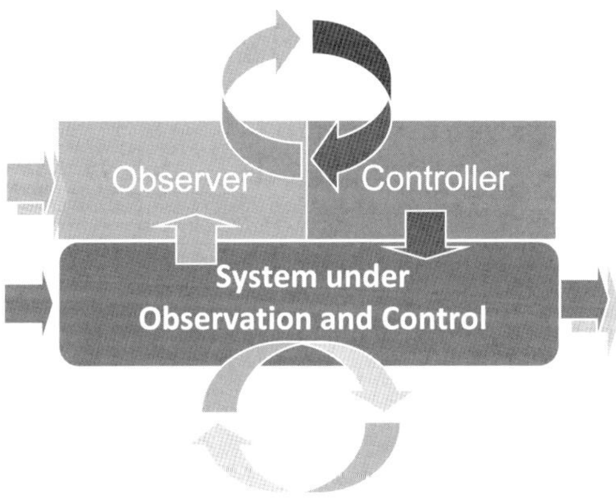

Fig. 4.2 Observer/controller architecture on top of system under observation and control (SuOC)

The architecture of a socially aware agent is structured according to the observer/controller (O/C) architecture (see Figure 4.2) widely used in the context of organic computing (Tomforde *et al.*, 2013). An OC agent consists of a productive system (usually called *system under observation and control* (SuOC)) as well as at least one pair of observer and controller. The SuOC does the real work (in the case of the DGC it distributes and accepts WUs). The observer collects and aggregates information from the SuOC (self-knowledge) and/or from the community, aggregates it into situation descriptors, which are then passed on to the controller. The controller takes decisions, which modify the SuOC's behaviour.

In more complex environments (such as a TC), we need several stacked levels of observers and controllers, as illustrated in Figure 4.3. Each level is responsible for specific observations and corresponding decisions, which modify a lower level.

The agent types introduced in Figure 4.1(b) differ in the amount of information available and in the solution quality reached by these agents. Figure 4.3 shows an agent architecture having three O/C levels. This corresponds to a proactive trust-strategic agent. Other agent types use fewer O/C levels.

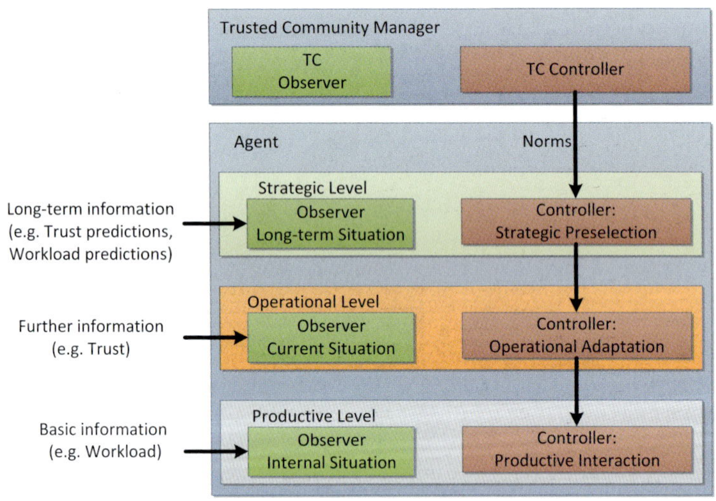

Fig. 4.3 Architecture of a proactive trust-aware agent with different awareness levels

The productive level is the basic level of each agent designed according to the social awareness hierarchy introduced above. It is able to interact with other agents based on trust levels. On the productive level, there exists a simple mapping between the internal situation, which has been observed by the observer component, and the productive interaction parameters selected by the controller component. The interaction of the productive level's controller is done in two roles: submitter (decision which agent to give work units to) and worker (decision whose work units to accept for processing). The productive level alone is not able to change its behaviour. It needs a higher level which may change its parameters. Therefore, we introduce an operational level that is used to choose parameters based on the analysis of the current situation. The behaviour chosen by the operational level determines the configuration of the productive level. The operational level's observer is able to categorize the situation based on the observable environmental parameters (workload in the TC, trust levels of available agents, own trust level). Based on the determined situation, the controller of the operational level chooses a suitable behaviour. Using a mapping of a situation, behaviour and outcome reached in a certain situation with a selected behaviour, the operational level of the agent is able to learn which behaviour is best suited in a certain situation. This learning and optimization is done at run-time. The behaviour selection is a short-term decision based on the current situation.

It can be worthwhile to take a more long-term perspective on the system's environment. This ability is realized at a strategic level. The observer of the strategic level is able to analyse previous situations and determine trends and predictions of the future situation. Therefore, the controller of the strategic level is able to act proactively before the situation actually takes place. This proactive strategic decision is given to the operational level in terms of a preselected behaviour. Thus, the strategic level confines the operational level's set of possible behaviours by only allowing behaviours that conform to the long-term strategy.

4.3.3 *From implicit to explicit trusted communities*

The agent architecture described so far (i.e. the productive, the operational and the strategic levels) does not recognize any higher-level authority. In this case, the TC is the result of a self-organization process, which is totally decentralized. We call this type of TC an implicit trusted community (iTC).

We have implemented and simulated a multi-agent system that forms an implicit TC. It consists of 30 trust adaptive agents and 10 egoistic/free-riding agents. The evaluation results are shown in Figure 4.4. After a starting phase (time step 0–10.000), a stable TC is formed by self-organization. At time step 35.000 we add another 10 free-riders. This causes the average reputation and the average fitness to break down while the average workload increases. After a recovery phase the system returns autonomously to stable operation around time step 55.000, when the TC has been re-established. This example shows that TCs can be formed by self-organization. However, if we want to shorten the recovery phase and to be able to react to more complex emergent system-wide pathological situations, we have to extend our architecture to an explicit TC, i.e. a TC with higher-level institutions.

Since norms are the central vehicle of an explicit TC to transport decisions from the TC manager (TCM) to the agents, we will revisit Ostrom's principles in the following section and discuss for each one if it is also useful in our technical society.

An explicit TC adds a higher level of control to the single agents. The agency responsible for this control is the TCM. The TCM knows more about the agent community than the single agents: it possesess a system level or institutional awareness. Based on this awareness, the TCM can impose norms in order to constrain the behaviour of the agents. These norms can be used as policies filtering the decisions made at the strategic level. The agent is still able to decide to what extent it follows the rules given by the institution. As the inclusion of the norm is realized at the top level, the decision whether or not to adhere to the norm is done at the strategic level. The productive as well as the operational level do not need to deal with this decision at all as they only get the predefined behaviour from the strategic level.

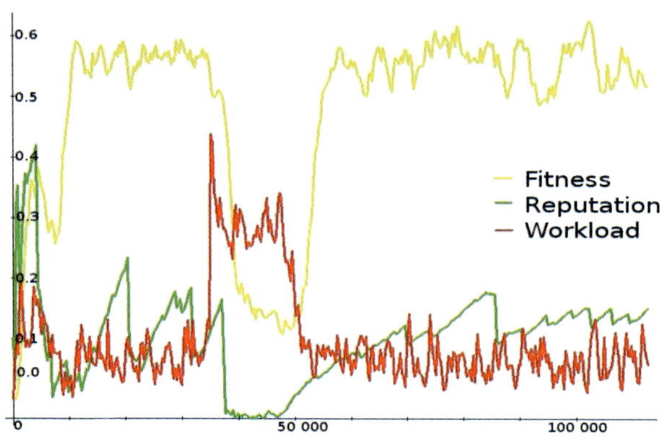

Fig. 4.4 Implicit trusted community under attack

4.4 No Society without Rules

Ostrom's eight design principles constitute a system that is regulated by norms. These norms are conventional (rather than physical) rules with which the individuals voluntarily and mutually agree to comply, in effect yielding some of their individual autonomy and opportunity for the benefit of the collective and, in the long term, to their own advantage. Adding institutions turns an implicit TC (iTC) into an explicit TC (eTC). In doing so we have added a new functional unit, the TC manager (TCM). It is important to note, that this TCM is not a static supermanager. It can be distributed or floating. In any case, the TCM function assumes a higher-level perspective – in terms of observation (i.e. awareness) as well as control. An eTC possesses a certain degree of centralized control. Since this control is not localized in a single agent and since this control is exerted from inside the eTC, an eTC is still a self-organizing system.

We now analyse if, or to what extent, each of Ostrom's eight institutional design principles are necessary and beneficial to build technical societies (for more details see Bernard *et al.* (2012)).

Principle 1: Clearly defined boundaries The first design principle for self-governing institutions is the definition of clearly defined boundaries. The iTC is adaptive such that the boundaries are implicitly defined by the set of agents belonging to the community. This set changes according to the community's need in the current situation. Therefore, an iTC does not have clearly defined boundaries known to all member agents. An eTC, on the other hand, has clearly defined boundaries as it has an explicit membership function and the TCM observes if an agent's behaviour conforms to the community's norms.

Principle 2: Congruence The second design principle for self-governing institutions is congruence between appropriation and provision rules and the state of the prevailing local environment. In an iTC, it is arguably precisely the lack of correlation between the interaction norms and the system states in which there is no mutual cooperation because of trust breakdown. Hence, an iTC only partially implements the second principle. An eTC on the other hand can be made fully compliant with Principle 2, but this requires an additional observation mechanism so that global states can be identified from reported local states. Furthermore, there has to be some assurance that the configuration of 'community rules' is precisely correlated with the intended outcomes.

Principle 3: Collective choice arrangements According to Principle 3, the agents affected by the operational rules participate in the selection and modification of those rules. Due to the adaptivity in our system, the agents are able to choose to what extent they obey the existing norms, but they do not control the norms themselves. For instance, it is a norm that agents should work for other agents, i.e. offer their idle computing resources. If the majority of the agents choose to be less cooperative, this results in a new situation of less trust among the agents. Thus, the agents have the local choice whether or not they obey a rule, but they do not have collective legislative power. In an eTC, the agent occupying the role of TCM has the *institutionalised power* (Jones and Sergot, 1996) to pass, enforce and adapt norms. As these norms could also be decided by collective choice (e.g. by voting or consultation), it would be possible to implement the third design principle for self-governing institutions in eTCs.

Principle 4: Monitoring In our distributed self-organized system, monitoring is done only by the agents themselves. Thus, there exists no entity or entities with a responsibility for monitoring global states or behaviour. This is a problem if situations occur that cannot be observed locally (for instance trust breakdown, or other more complex macro-level properties that emerge from micro-level behaviour and interactions). For these situations, the introduction of the TCM, which observes or infers not only memberships but also system states among the members, is necessary. With an eTC run by a TCM, Principle 4 can be fulfilled.

Principle 5: Graduated sanctions If the community rules are violated, the violator needs to be proportionally punished. This principle is mandatory for the isolation of malicious agents from the iTC, which is built based on a trust management and sanctioning mechanism. Our system already has a trust and reputation mechanism established, which also takes into account the amount of violations the agent has committed. Therefore, Principle 5 is already established in the iTCs of the TDG, and must be retained for eTCs as well.

Principle 6: Conflict resolution According to Principle 6, agents need access to fast and cheap conflict resolution mechanisms in order to establish enduring institutions. In case an agent objects to a sanction (e.g. bad rating for a wrong or delayed computational result or an unintentional error), this conflict needs to be resolved. In the existing TDG, the ability to object to a rating is not implemented. We rather rely on demanding a minimal trust value of agents to be allowed to provide feedback in the reputation system. But as soon as an objection to negative feedback is allowed, some form of conflict resolution is needed, in particular to avoid escalating negative feedback or the stoning effect observed in some reputation systems

(Khopkar *et al.*, 2005). Managing and adjudicating the process is another task for the TCM of an eTC.

Principle 7: No external control As there are no external instances in both implicit and explicit TCs, Principle 7 is met by the current version of our system. For a future version we envision multiple TCs with a possible overlap of concerns. In such a context it would be interesting to investigate the mutual influence of multiple TCMs on different TCs. More generally vis-à-vis Principle 7, there is also the question of allowing human operator intervention to override the decisions of the TCM, and whether or not this is even feasible given the complexity, speed of operation, and rate of change of these systems.

Principle 8: Systems of systems If we regard TCs (implicit or explicit) as systems, systems of systems are TCs composed of sub-TCs. In the current implementation, there exists only one bottom-up built TC, but we are also interested in the relations between different TCs. In particular, overlapping TCs might have different, even contradicting goals and hence conflicting utility functions. Furthermore, as currently TCs are only defined by the trust values and thresholds of the members, we could also imagine nested TCs where larger TCs could define a minimal trust threshold (to skip basic security measures) and nested sub-TCs accept only trustworthy agents (for instance to guarantee a certain QoS (quality of service) standard). The TC approach is very well suited for systems of systems aspects, but so far Principle 8 has not been met, due to the fact that there was no necessity coming from the application to implement it.

4.5 Outlook

Technical systems are becoming too complex to be managed individually by human operators. Therefore, organic computing and other similar initiatives are investigating how these systems can self-organize with the objective of improving their overall utility and the performance of their individual members. While self-adaptation of single systems is extremely useful, we must realize that it is not sufficient. Individual behaviour always has an effect on group behaviour, and vice versa. This is true for natural social animals (such as humans) as well as for technical systems.

Hence, it is inevitable that we should extend our artificial autonomous systems with social agents, which are able to cooperate, to compete and to handle norms, which are meant to facilitate the social interactions within institutions. The comparison with human societies, based on Ostrom's institutional design principles, is very helpful; however, it is not mandatory to transfer all those social mechanisms. With explicit trusted communities we are investigating how far such a transfer makes sense. We have found that purely decentralized self-organized trusted communities can be built, but that complex social mechanisms and emergent behaviour require a higher-level authority, such as an institution with explicit normative and sanctioning power, to control these mechanisms and their effects.

We have only considered trust relationships between agents. However, there exist more trust relationships, such as trust between human users and agents and among users themselves. We need to include the user in the trust relationships in future. This is difficult because human users are most creative in adapting rules to their intentions. And it is very hard for an agent to estimate the trust in a human user because the agent does not know the individual interests and the situation (long-term and short-term) of the user. Therefore, the actions of a human user can change dramatically from situation to situation making it hard to predict for an agent. But eventually we will have to address the transition from human–computer interfaces to human–computer partnerships.

Science fiction loves horror scenarios where computers or robots run wild. Why don't humans (usually) run wild? Human societies have developed a powerful system of norms, rules and enforcement measures to keep humans within the acceptable limits of behaviour. For technical systems, Asimov's robot laws (Asimov, 1950) are a prominent example of such a set of rules envisaged for advanced technical systems. It seems that increasing autonomy requires a richer set of sensory equipment (i.e. a higher level of awareness) as well as increasing deliberation and decision power. But autonomy must at the same time be curbed by rules regulating the social behaviour with the goal to foster cooperation, limit competition and possibly provide conflict resolution.

The work presented in this chapter has a technical focus: we analyse (human) societies in order to learn how we should organize technical societies. We move from nature (and culture) to the artefact. The eighteenth century philosopher Giambattista Vico (1668–1744) proposed that the truth and the artefact are exchangeable: we only understand what we make (*verum quia factum*). In this sense, it might also be worthwhile to look back from the technical agent society to its original idea. It might very well be that this can teach us something about our own workings.

Chapter 5

Self-Healing Software

Regina Frei[1] and Giovanna Di Marzo Serugendo[2]
[1] *University of Portsmouth, UK*
[2] *University of Geneva, Switzerland*

5.1 Introduction

Self-healing software systems, which have an intrinsic ability to adapt and to recover from failures and disturbances, arise from two originally distinct research efforts, both based on software agents to help software adapt to changes in their environments: *self-managing* software and *self-organising* software. Self-managing software (Waldrop, 2003; Sterritt *et al.*, 2010) addresses large-scale distributed systems that configure, heal, protect and optimise 'on their own', usually in a hierarchical way, to alleviate human administrators' work. Self-organising software (Di Marzo Serugendo *et al.*, 2011) addresses distributed systems able to (re)-organise themselves without external control, and usually work in a decentralised way. Typical applications involve swarm robotics, optimisation problems, agents coordination or services ecosystems (Montagna *et al.*, 2012). Recent work converges the two research trends, combining self-managing techniques with self-organising and decentralised ones (Di Marzo Serugendo *et al.*, 2010).

This chapter focuses on different aspects of self-healing software. It discusses relevant terminologies and reviews systems that can recover from failures and treat their own faults. The chapter is organised as follows: Section 5.2 relates self-healing to self-awareness, Section 5.3 provides a working taxonomy for software self-healing, Section 5.4 surveys work done in the area, and Section 5.5 concludes this chapter.

5.2 Self-Awareness as an Aspect of Self-Healing

Self-awareness exists at many different levels. At the level of an individual, it can mean that the person or agent is aware of itself and its environment, its skills, objectives, peers and the relations to them. At the level of a group, it can mean that there is some group identity and the awareness of the group's situation and behaviour within the bigger picture. At the level of the system, self-awareness may be related to the function and performance of the system as well as its relations to the outer world, and is often crucial when a system or component takes care of itself. As Rish (2009) puts it: "A key property of an autonomic computer system is 'self-healing'. However, self-healing starts with self-awareness: the ability of the system to perform real-time inferences and learning about its own behaviour, to diagnose and predict various faults and performance degradations."

The vision of autonomic computing by Kephart and Chess (2003) included that self-managing software systems need to be able to self-configure, self-heal, self-optimise and self-protect. The focus here is on self-healing, although it is sometimes difficult to completely separate it from the other three aspects of self-management. In certain cases, the healing will occur through a dynamic reconfiguration of entities composing the systems, whereas in others, code will correct itself. Also, policies to guide system behaviour and specific architectures may facilitate autonomous coping with failures. In all cases, self-healing requires a system to assess itself, to recognise and diagnose problems, and then recover from them.

Self-organising systems often have mechanisms that lead to self-healing because they allow the system to change its internal organisation to cope with changing conditions and hindrances. Some of them can be considered as issues the system is designed to deal with through self-organising mechanisms, whereas others are unpredictable and require self-management (Di Marzo Serugendo, 2009).

For instance, an ant swarm is able to self-organise and self-heal when confronted with new obstacles and scarce food sources as well as the death of swarm members. Primitive forms of self-organisation do not require self-awareness, but more advanced forms need self-awareness for the system to self-diagnose. If malicious ants were to introduce fake pheromones or change the biological programming of their peers (say, fleeing from pheromone gradients instead of following them), the pheromone-based stigmergy mechanism is no longer sufficient. The swarm would then need additional self-awareness measures to recognise and correct the problem. Actions might be taken at different levels, depending on the source of the problem and the possibilities for self-healing to take place.

5.3 A Working Taxonomy for Software Self-Healing

The term 'self-healing software' is used in a variety of ways, and there is disagreement among researchers about what should qualify as self-healing. Interestingly, there are also software approaches that clearly use self-healing – for instance, genetic variations leading to the automatic corrections of faults (Schulte *et al.*, 2013) – where the term is not used at all.

Some researchers consider that adaptation should not be considered as self-healing because it does not repair a defect or make the system recover from a problem. As an example, Ghosh *et al.* (2007) highlight the importance of differentiating between self-healing systems and systems that are self-adaptive, robust, resilient or dependable. However, does a fault necessarily have to occur first? Is it not desirable for a system to avoid even getting into the failure mode? Do preventive or corrective measures have to be labelled differently, even if the same measures taken once a fault has occurred may help as well and are then labelled as self-healing? Furthermore, the terms self-healing and self-repair are sometimes used as synonyms, whereas different meanings are intended in other cases; Frei *et al.* (2013) provide an in-depth discussion of these terms.

Nelson (1990) sees self-healing software systems in the context of work on *fault tolerant computing* and Laprie (2005) relates them to *resilience*, where the goal is to enable a system to maintain its intended function even when facing faults and disturbances (possibly in degraded mode).

One of the main questions to investigate is therefore: where does software self-healing start (does adaptation count?) and where does it end (if at all)? There is a whole spectrum of self-healing related approaches to software under a variety of labels, including: self-adaptation; resilience, dependability, fault tolerance and fault recovery (these may be achieved in a self-* way, but other options exist); and self-repair/self-healing.

Furthermore, several other self-* properties, such as self-reconfiguration, are often related to self-healing. These are mechanisms that can be used to achieve self-healing, among many other objectives. For instance, self-adaptation serves many purposes that are unrelated to self-healing: a thermostat adapts the performance levels of a heating system to environmental conditions, or a computer screen might get brighter with increasing light in the room. But adaptation can also enable a system to execute basic healing steps; see examples below.

Self-adaptation (Brun *et al.*, 2009): Through a feedback loop, the system compares its objective with its real achievement and consequently takes simple corrective actions such as changing the value of a parameter.

Example in relation to self-healing: A laptop might be configured to warn the user about running out of power when battery levels have reached 8% and again at 4%. A laptop with some self-awareness would be able to recognise if these warning levels were too low for a certain user to provide a power source before the battery is completely depleted. The laptop would then adapt the warning levels to avoid breakdowns of user applications.

Self-reconfiguration (Dalpiaz *et al.*, 2009): The system re-arranges its existing components in response to anticipated situations or to maintain or improve performance.

Example in relation to self-healing: Self-organising displays (Puviani *et al.*, 2011; Viroli *et al.*, 2012) create ad hoc compositions of available multi-media displays to serve a mobile user. The compositions continuously reconfigure to maintain the overall system performance as devices come and go, either because they are in/out of range or failing.

Self-organisation (Di Marzo Serugendo *et al.*, 2011): The system internally re-organises its components and their structure (or instructions) in response to unanticipated problems.

Example in relation to self-healing: A swarm of autonomous guided vehicles (AGV) operating in an automotive plant might lose several of its members due to depleted batteries caused by new obstacles. The AGVs will become aware of the fact that their usual strategies to find pathways are not suitable for the current plant configuration and re-organise their pathway strategies.

Self-management (Sterritt *et al.*, 2010): The system takes measures to cope with non-anticipated problems, makes automatic or semiautomatic changes at run-time in its infrastructure and behaviour according to the operational context.

Example in relation to self-healing: A database system might be set up to use a certain type of primary memory under normal conditions, and be able to use a secondary one in case the primary type fails. As the database system is experiencing high request volumes, it starts to run out of memory at certain times of the day and thus cannot provide the necessary services. The system becomes aware of this and takes the decision to use the secondary memory type at regular intervals during the times of high request volumes, hence re-establishing the system's ability to provide the requested services at all times.

5.3.1 *Failures, errors and faults*

Self-healing is required when things go wrong: faults, failures and errors are often used as synonyms, but there are differences between the terms. Avizienis *et al.* (2004) define them for systems providing services:

- A **failure** is an event that occurs when a service deviates from the correct service. Example: A robot drops its charge.
- An **error** is the deviation between a correct service state and an incorrect one. Example: A processor running out of memory.
- A **fault** is the cause of an error. Example: An invalid value in a variable.

Typically, an internal or external system fault leads to an error that subsequently leads to one or several system failures (Avizienis *et al.*, 2004). To delimit the areas that self-healing addresses, Figure 5.1 illustrates four scenarios for faults and failures in relation to balancing an egg:

(1) The system is fulfilling its function of holding the egg in a bowl under changing conditions. The system uses strategies for **self-adaptation, self-stabilisation, self-protection** and **self-optimisation**, or similar functions.
(2) The egg is falling, which is a fault occurring, but the system is able to catch it and thus a failure is avoided. Work in this area has been done for several decades under the names of **fault tolerance, fault recovery, resilience and dependability** (achieved by self-* or other means); this is not in the focus of self-healing.
(3) The egg was not caught and has cracked; a failure has occurred. **Self-healing** will provide the system with the means to glue the shell fragments back together or help them reconnect from the inside, and to place the egg back in the bowl.
(4) The egg is destroyed and beyond repair. A fresh start with a new egg is needed, which may not be considered as self-healing.

To distinguish self-healing from other properties such as self-adaptation or self-management, we consider self-healing to be specific to the third case in Figure 5.1. The ways to achieve the above properties or strategies dif-

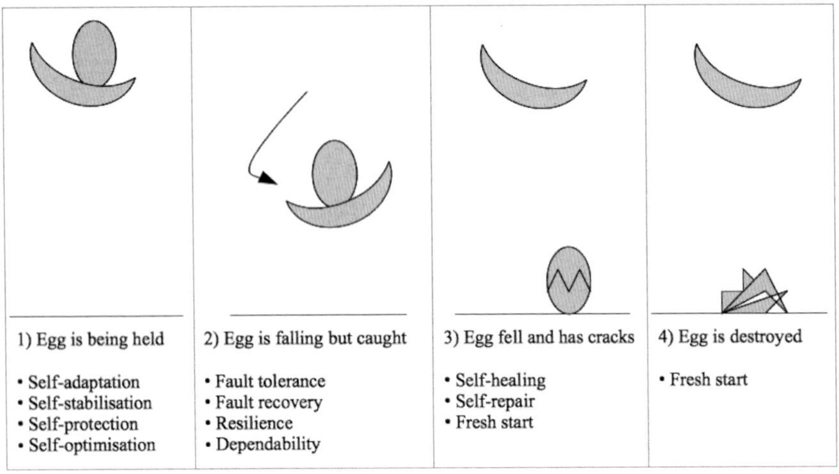

Fig. 5.1 Illustrative scenario of a system balancing an egg

fer. They can coarsely be classified as code-level, through self-organisation, based on policies, architectures or models, as presented in Section 5.4.

5.4 Approaches to Software Self-Healing

Psaier and Dustdar (2011) point out that research on self-healing systems originates from research on fault-tolerant (Pierce, 1965), self-stabilising (Dijkstra, 1974), self-adaptive (Laddaga, 1997) and survivable (Linger *et al.*, 1998) systems, as well as from autonomic computing (Kephart and Chess, 2003). Major importance is given to feedback loops in self-healing systems, which can be implemented in various ways and at various levels, as well as to the system behaviours being guided by adaptable policies. A particular challenge is the fact that there is often a blurred zone between desired or healthy and undesired or faulty system behaviour. Different approaches focus on maintaining system health, detecting failures, and addressing system recovery (Ghosh *et al.*, 2007). Saha (2007a) categorises aspects of self-healing software according to their fault model or fault hypothesis, system response, system completeness and design context. Faults or injuries to be self-healed include operational errors, defective system requirements or implementation errors. Alternatively, Jiang *et al.* (2007) classify software faults as:

- Syntactic faults: interface faults and parameter faults.
- Semantic faults: inconsistent behaviour and incorrect results.
- Service faults: QoS (quality of service) faults, faults related to unfulfilled SLAs (service level agreements), real-time violations.
- Communication/interaction faults: time out or service unavailable.
- Exceptions: I/O-related exceptions and security-related exceptions.

Park *et al.* (2009) propose three classes of self-healing software: architecture-based, component-based and log-based. We identify self-healing occurring at code level (Section 5.4.1), or through self-organisation (Section 5.4.2), the use of policies (Section 5.4.3), architectures favouring self-healing (Section 5.4.4) or through models maintained at run-time (Section 5.4.5). The focus of this chapter is on self-healing software (as discussed in Section 5.3.1), as opposed to self-healing systems that include hardware (such as approaches dealing with failing FPGAs (Cheatham *et al.*, 2006; Szasz and Chindris, 2010)). While self-healing code clearly addresses software concerns only, some architectures, as discussed in Section 5.4.4, deal both with self-healing software and with self-healing at a system level.

5.4.1 *Self-healing at code level*

The purest form of self-healing software would be code that can generate and correct itself if and when required.

In genetic programming, neutral mutations do not change the program's fitness or behaviour, but they automatically repair unknown bugs with high probability (Schulte *et al.*, 2013). Such variations may for instance rectify incorrect function calls, add missing conditional clauses, change a constant to a variable, or rectify a wrong parameter.

PANACEA (Breitgand *et al.*, 2007) – also called SHADOWS (Self-Healing Approach for Developing cOmplex softWare Systems) – is inspired by self-healing in the human body. The software self-monitors and when recognising misbehaviours, classifies them and addresses the more serious ones. Measures include inserting new lines of codes before a program runs or moving around memory resources, to avoid system crashes. Programmers may add *annotations* to their code to guide the healing agents to code areas likely to be critical. At run-time, these annotations will serve as an interface for monitoring and healing the annotated code.

Using a model inspired by chemical reactions and rewriting, competition and cooperation are another way of implementing self-healing (Meyer and

Tschudin, 2010). Even if running on faulty hardware, the healthy software will maintain its robustness by replication.[1] Replicating entities compete with each other for resources but can also benefit from cooperation.

Saha (2007b) suggests an algorithm to deal with multiple data errors in web applications or service agent code and data. It corrects the erroneous data of the contaminated agent code by comparing an application's state to the original code.

ClearView is a software for endusers, similar to an anti-virus program. It detects errors in running programs by analysing which rule of normal execution may have been violated and fixes them at runtime by generating patches that force the program to comply with the rule (Perkins *et al.*, 2009; Naone, 2009). Successful patches are maintained, whereas ineffective and damaging patches are discarded.

ASSURE (Sidiroglou *et al.*, 2009) is an approach for applications to recover from unknown failures by using known and anticipated failures. Rescue points are located in the code for the system to cope with known failures, and they can also be used as points to which the system will return in case of unanticipated faults.

Shifters (Cuesta *et al.*, 2011) are software agents that are similar to stem cells. In the beginning, they are neutral elements but they evolve towards having a specific function. This emergent adaptation is based on the needs of the system as well as adaptation patterns (Perez-Sotelo *et al.*, 2011) and is caused by an agent's interactions with its peers. By transforming initially neutral elements into any required type of agent, the system can cope with failing agents by generating new ones. This is a type of redundancy strongly inspired by the way our body replaces dying cells.

George *et al.* (2002) use another cell-based programming model as the basis for further programming abstractions. These will inherit the biological characteristics of intrinsic robustness, scalability and self-healing. The computational cells go through a set of states and reproduce through cell division in case some cells become defective. The intended functionality of this cell-based self-healing software model is the same as described above for shifters, although the mechanism used to achieve this is different.

[1] In ordinary sequential programming languages, a *Quine* is a single piece of code outputting its own source code. In the parallel world of an artificial chemistry such as *Fraglets*, a Quine becomes a set of molecules that is able to regenerate itself (Meyer and Tschudin, 2010). Quines can be used for operations such as data processing.

5.4.2 *Self-healing through self-organisation*

Self-organising software (Di Marzo Serugendo *et al.*, 2011) targets decentralised systems made of numerous entities evolving together to produce some global result. Self-organisation is often closely related to self-healing, as adaptation is part of the regular behaviour of the system. In case of a failure, self-organisation will lead to the system maintaining its functionality in an alternative way.

Self-organising software very often takes inspiration from nature and is composed of relatively simple autonomous components or agents, each applying specific *rules* with only local knowledge of their environment. Through the joint work and local coordination of the different components some global result *emerges*. The different design elements of a self-organising system include the (active) agents themselves, the self-organising mechanisms (or rules) to which they abide, the environment in which they evolve and the (static) artifacts on which agents and environment act. Di Marzo Serugendo (2009) provides a description of types of faults for self-organising systems linked to each design element.

Crucial to the decentralised coordination among agents are the self-organising mechanisms, usually inspired by nature. Among the most popular ones are stigmergy (indirect communication through the environment, such as ant coordination through pheromones (Bonabeau *et al.*, 1999)), bird flocking or fish schooling, gossiping or immune systems, as well as evolutionary techniques (de Castro, 2006).

Engineering efforts led researchers to express these self-organising mechanisms in the form of design patterns (Babaoglu *et al.*, 2006; De Wolf and Holvoet, 2007). Fernandez-Marquez *et al.* (2013) provide a comprehensive classification and description of design patterns for self-organising mechanisms together with a detailed description of their inter-relations. This is completed by a software architecture proposal for using the self-organising mechanisms as basic primitives provided by the environment (Fernandez-Marquez *et al.*, 2011). Also, Seebach *et al.* (2010) suggest a software engineering approach for creating self-organising systems that can cope with failures, based on design patterns and composeable system fragments.

5.4.3 *Self-healing based on policies*

Some approaches use policies for the systems to dynamically reconfigure when encountering problematic conditions. The adherence to high-level policies, specified by human administrators, ensures that autonomic systems behave as desired. Policies may be of different types, from action based (e.g. what to do in a given state) to goal based (e.g. what is the desired state to reach next) or to utility function based (e.g. computation of the desired state to reach based on utility function to optimise) (Kephart and Das, 2007; Kephart and Walsh, 2004).

Policy-based approaches (Kephart and Walsh, 2004) lead to self-healing systems where artificial intelligence principles provide guidance for autonomic systems to choose actions that move them into desirable states.

To create self-healing properties, Jiang *et al.* (2007) model the desired system behaviour and classify possible faults. The system model is then transformed into platform-specific code with failure detection and resolution mechanisms. The software will take appropriate actions to restore the system to the specified operational state.

Specifically for self-healing in real time, consequence-oriented diagnosis and healing is introduced (Dai *et al.*, 2011). This hybrid diagnosis tool is based on the multivariate decision diagram, fuzzy logic and neural networks. It efficiently diagnoses and prevents software and system failures.

5.4.4 *Architectures for self-healing*

The most frequently used form of software self-healing is at system level, which means that the system internally self-reconfigures in a dynamic way. Dynamic reconfiguration of components is a form of self-healing where some code is substituted. The most prominent examples of architectures for self-healing are *organic computing* (Schmeck *et al.*, 2010; Müller-Schloer, 2004) and *autonomic computing* (Kephart and Chess, 2003; Horn, 2001).

Organic computing uses an *observer/controller architecture*, and consists of three layers: a top layer (high level) with reasoning, simulations and observation capabilities, which can give feedback; a middle layer; and a bottom-up layer (low level) with reflexes. The low-level assertions (Müller-Schloer, 2004) are similar to action policies (if-then rules). The counterpart in the system that receives violation messages is the *observer* (acting as a sensor or detector); the *controller* takes measures accordingly (Müller-Schloer and Sick, 2008). The observer decides whether reconfiguration is necessary; if so, the controller will execute it. In autonomic computing, a single autonomous entity (a manager) controls a hierarchy of other autonomous entities, and follows the *MAPE loop* (IBM, 2005) (*monitoring, analysis, planning and execution*), supported by a knowledge base.

Kramer and Magee (2007) developed a layered architectural reference model for self-adaptive systems that organises distributed adaptation in a hierarchical fashion: elements within a higher layer work at a higher level of abstraction, and drive the layer below.

Self-healing requires the elicitation and maintenance of domain knowledge in the form of <service failure diagnosis, repair plan> patterns (Montani and Anglano, 2008). Case-based reasoning (CBR) is a lazy learning paradigm that can be used for failure diagnosis and remediation in software systems, as most errors are re-occurrences of known problems. The suggested architecture externalises the problem from the "black box" requiring self-healing and applies CBR with a <retrieve-reuse/revise-retain> cycle.

Concepts mirroring human mechanisms, such as reflex reactions and the use of vital signs to assess operational health, may be used for designing and implementing a personal autonomic computing architecture (Sterritt and Bantz, 2006). This was implemented on personal computing devices as a self-healing tool using a pulse monitor and a vital signs health monitor within the autonomic manager. The support architecture for multi-platform working is based on autonomic computing concepts and techniques, and enables collaboration among personal systems to take a shared responsibility for self-awareness and environment awareness.

5.4.5 *Model-based solutions for self-healing*

Model-based solutions, such as the one proposed by Garlan and Schmerl (2002), consider an abstract representation of the system and an externalised self-repair component that monitors the system, checks its conformance with the model at run-time and proposes adaptation solutions.

Similarly, the externalised infrastructure for self-healing by Wile and Egyed (2004) does not entail any modification of the system that needs to become self-healing. It uses a reflective model of the target system's operation to determine what aspects can be used for self-healing. In the system architecture model, this means identifying effectors, probes, gauges and controllers, thus decoupling the self-healing from the operations.

Self-healing for object-oriented applications (Haydarlou *et al.*, 2005) addresses the case of legacy software where the source code is not available. This approach makes use of context information related to failures and up-to-date maintained models of the application being monitored. Application failures are then automatically diagnosed and healed with specific planners and an executor to apply the self-healing plans.

5.5 Discussion and Conclusion

Self-healing will give systems more capabilities to autonomously deal with faults and failures. This is particularly valuable in a world where many software systems are growing in both size and complexity, which makes them hard to manage by humans. The only solution is for software to take care of itself, including in situations where faults and failures have occurred.

Self-healing is the most advanced item in an entire spectrum:

- **Self-adaptation, self-stabilisation, self-optimisation, self-protection:** Software adjusts to continue delivering correct service.
- **Resilience, dependability, fault tolerance and fault recovery; achieved in a self-* way:** The software deals with faults and takes corrective actions to avoid failures and maintain correct service.
- **Self-repair/self-healing:** Once a failure has occurred, the software takes actions to recover from the failure and to return to correct service.

A variety of strategies and mechanisms can be used to achieve software self-healing. Some of them are internal and occur at code level, meaning that the software is able to rectify code or generate new code as required. Others use dynamic self-reconfiguration of existing software elements, which is often related to self-organisation or self-management. Some systems use policies to guide their behaviour, whereas others rely on specific architectures for self-healing. These architectures often include self-healing at systems level, which means that hardware is also concerned. Other solutions highlight the importance of separation of concerns and externalise self-repair activities to specific architectural components combined with the use of a model of the monitored system.

More primitive forms of self-healing, often based on self-adaptation or self-organisation, do not require the system to be self-aware; however, more elaborate mechanisms for coping with faults and failures, often based on self-management, require self-awareness for the system to assess its own state and performance as well as its neighbours' situations.

This chapter provides an overview of existing work on self-healing software. Most of the surveyed work is still in an early stage and needs further investigation to become mature and useable in practical applications. In an area of research that may have appeared rather confused due to the number of different approaches taken and the absence of consistent terminology, this chapter contributes by structuring the area and providing a working taxonomy for self-healing.

Chapter 6

Bring It On, Complexity! Present and Future of Self-Organising Middle-Out Abstraction

Sebastian von Mammen and Jan-Philipp Steghöfer
Augsburg University, Germany

6.1 The Great Complexity Challenge

The inherent complexity of many man-made or naturally occurring systems and networks – such as online social networks or ecosystems of interacting biological processes – is widely acknowledged. The ubiquitous networking paradigm has highlighted the elaborate webs of interactions and interdependencies between living beings, objects and processes. Yet we still lack an algorithmic framework capable of tackling the complexity of the world in terms of representation and computation. Thus, any step toward understanding – and predicting – the dynamics and emergent phase transitions of complex systems would greatly contribute to the advancement of science. Present-day societal challenges that could benefit from this kind of knowledge are plentiful, and can be found in fields ranging from the life sciences to economics and engineering. To some extent, the mathematical analysis of complex systems can provide some insights about the phase transitions that may occur over time (Haken, 1980; Fuchs, 2013). However, this approach requires a great deal of effort and does not scale well, becoming intractable as the number of factors involved in a system increases.

Moreover, the interactions that drive system transitions have to be identified and formalised a priori by the modeller. In contrast, an ideal model building process should require as little information as possible about a system's actual behaviour. It should be enough to only describe how the parts of a system interact, without building in any assumptions about when feedback cycles might be triggered to snowball into fundamental global system changes. In a model of this kind, the parts of the system that interact according to sets of internal rules (and so without any external, higher-level drivers of their collective behaviour) are known as 'agents'. Each agent in such a model is a self-contained entity with its own individually accessible data, states and behaviours. The sequences of interactions among agents and the traversal of their states in a computational simulation correspond to the emergent feedback cycles and phase transitions of complex systems. If we were able to detect patterns that are precursors to phase transitions and patterns that correspond to the system's global dynamics, we would automatically become aware of emergent phenomena.

Inspired by several ideas in artificial intelligence, machine learning, and artificial life, we present the SOMO (self-organised middle-out) algorithm, which we might call a pattern-detection algorithm for phase transitions in complex systems. Our main aim is automated dynamic abstraction, i.e., bottom-up learning given enough training examples and top-down validation to reaffirm or revoke the previously learned concepts. This chapter presents the SOMO concept with an emphasis on its more visionary aspects: how the idea could evolve from its most recent conception and its current implementation towards our ultimate goal: our 'computer after me' is one that reduces complexity, rather than increases it.

6.2 Self-Organising Middle-Out Abstraction

In 2011, the SOMO concept was presented (von Mammen *et al.*, 2011), an approach that automatically builds abstractions bottom-up and validates and revokes them top-down – possibly both at the same time but in respect to different model aspects. As this concept works in both directions and as it bridges the gap between the orders of the model, it can be considered as operating at a 'meso' level of analysis.

The foundation of the concept is an unsupervised learning method that observes and learns processes which occur – that is to say, emerge – during a computational simulation. A learned process pattern provides a shortcut to driving the evolution of the simulation. Instead of considering the series of all conditions that lead to the process's changes one step at a time, it suffices to recognise the emergence of the process. As a consequence, the detailed interactions are no longer executed but, whenever the according preconditions hold, the observed side effects are enacted in the system. Such automatically learned patterns may also be understood as abstracted process descriptions and they hold the promise of helping us to understand, explain, and compute complex phenomena in simple terms.

SOMO observes the simulation data and identifies process patterns, 'biased' only in terms of its representations (meaning that the way interaction patterns are represented by SOMO can influence the kinds of patterns that can be detected and so bias the result). The identified patterns are used to refine the computational model that drives the simulation process being observed. As the SOMO algorithm continues to observe and learn the patterns that emerge from the simulation, it continually increases the model's level of abstraction by introducing hierarchies of abstracted patterns. It is hoped that such hierarchies will to some extent coincide with the real-world conceptual boundaries that we identify in natural systems, such as the subdivision of the organisational complexity of animal anatomy into cells, tissues and organs. Since such abstractions are inevitably subject to noise and unknown conditions, we also introduce a confidence measure that is associated with each abstraction.

The next section presents a variety of concepts that are both inspiring the SOMO algorithm and closely related to it. Section 6.4 introduces a (borrowed) example that illustrates the emergence of high-order physico-chemical compounds. Based on this example, we outline the SOMO concept in Section 6.5. Current SOMO implementations are explained in Section 6.6 and futuristic implementations around it are presented in Section 6.7. In Section 6.8, we conclude with a short vision of SOMO's potential.

6.3 Optimising Graphics, Physics and Artificial Intelligence

Various research interests and complementary research trends have been driving the design of the SOMO concept:

- The concept of *emergence* that tries to capture higher-order patterns, properties and descriptions of (sub-)systems which arise from multiple, relatively simple interactions (Baas and Emmeche, 1997).
- The need for integrative approaches to *representing, modelling and simulating multi-scale systems* – this challenge is currently addressed by passing up and down value sets from separate, sometimes fundamentally disparate, model components (Horstemeyer, 2010; Eissing *et al.*, 2011).

- The need for *abstraction*: a model so comprehensive as to span several degrees of scale, to host a large body of systems and subsystems, and to independently consider their intricate behaviours quickly outmatches the computing capacities of even the greatest of supercomputers.

Abstraction is not only the essence of model building in the first place but it is also the key to expressive and efficiently solvable models. We postulate that a model should be as detailed and as comprehensive as possible, while its (numeric) utilisation for the purpose of rather specific predictions or simulations should automatically lead to model simplifications and abstractions. Whenever possible, this should happen without jeopardising the model validity; whenever necessary, the loss of accuracy the abstractions cause should be made transparent. SOMO pursues this endeavour by building and maintaining hierarchies of abstractions learned from observation. The higher the level of hierarchy, the fewer interactions have to be tested. Such tests are typically intertwined with expensive condition queries – only the state changes of the simulation will be performed to drive its evolution.

Similar shortcuts by means of hierarchical organisation have been conceptualised and implemented in numerous other contexts. For instance, different levels of detail (LOD) of computer graphics resources, such as meshes (differing in the numbers of vertices) and textures (differing in the numbers of pixels), are typically organised in hierarchies to allow for fast access to the most commonly used assets, whereas the graphics scenes themselves are often subjected to spatial partitioning hierarchies that allow algorithms to quickly determine which graphics objects need to be rendered in a given view port (Möller *et al.*, 2008).

There is a significant overlap between these *culling* techniques and mechanisms to speed up the detection of collisions between geometric objects, one of the foundational functionalities of physics engines – both rely on the quick discovery of objects at specific locations. In general, the locations of the geometries may change, which is why the spatial partitioning hierarchies are dynamically created and adjusted. Dynamic adjustments of the bounding volume hierarchies are also required if the geometries themselves are dynamic, for instance if they change their scale. In this case, a method has been shown to yield rather good results that updates the upper half of the hierarchy bottom-up if one of the geometries changes. The lower half is only updated selectively in a top-down fashion, as soon as the changed geometry is accessed (Larsson and Akenine-Möller, 2001).

Hierarchical optimisations have also been deployed in the field of artificial intelligence. For example, costly automated planning routines can be pruned early, if high levels of a hierarchy reflect the adherence of a plan's most critical variables (Sacerdoti, 1974). Similarly, reflective agents need to plan their coordination – hierarchical abstractions of their interaction partners may increase their decision performance, too (Durfee, 1999).

6.4 Emergence and Hierarchies in a Natural System

In Rasmussen *et al.* (2001), an approach, or 'Ansatz', to capturing the emergence of physicochemical compound objects with according emergent properties is described. We want to use their example to illustrate the mechanics of SOMO.

In their experiments, attracting, repelling, and bonding forces among charged monomers and water molecules are shown to result in higher-order polymer and micelle formations; at each level, the resulting compounds obtain novel physical and chemical properties. In the model, hydrophobic monomers bind to hydrophilic monomers as well as to polymerised hydrophobic monomers, which results in second-order amphiphilic polymers which, in turn, aggregate in third-order micelle structures. At each stage, the resultant compounds exhibit properties different from the underlying constituents. The aggregating nature of the process yields compounds of greater size but it also leads to varying qualitative, geometric structures and differentiated physicochemical behaviours. An adapted illustration of the emergent process is shown in Figure 6.1.

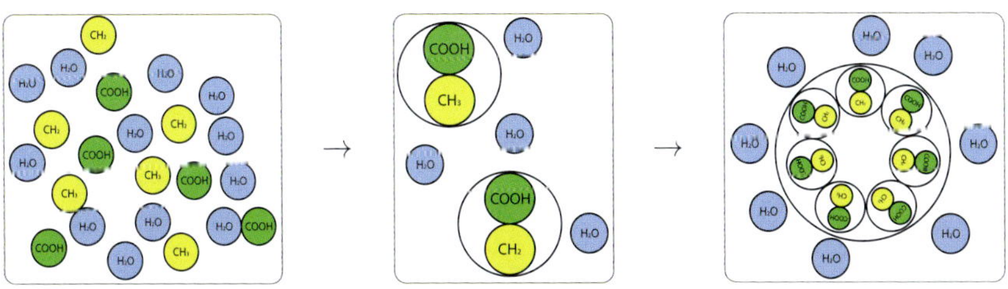

(a) (b) (c)

Fig. 6.1 (a) Hydrophobic and hydrophilic monomers immersed in water. (b) Polymers emerge as hydrophobic monomers bind to hydrophilic monomers. (c) A micelle-like structure forms based on aligned polymers with hydrophobic heads and hydrophilic tails. These illustrations are adapted from Rasmussen *et al.* (2001).

The higher-order objects form based on the interactions and (emergent) relationships among the axiomatic objects of the given model. Often, higher-order objects can be captured as spatial aggregations, but in general they should be regarded as networks of arbitrarily complex topologies. In accordance with Baas and Emmeche (1997), the authors also stress that emergent characteristics of a (sub-)system are observable and describable in terms of the (relatively simpler) interactions between its components.

We reflect the subsumption of individual elements by emergent entities of greater order in a hierarchical structure. In the given case, polymers are built from monomers and aggregate to form micelle-like structures (see Figure 6.2). As Rasmussen *et al.* (2001) suggest, an observer needs to identify the emerging units and their emergent properties. In our approach such observers are immersed in the simulation and observe the state and interaction patterns of the model entities. The observers further simplify the entities' computational representations in accordance with the learned behavioural patterns. Individual entities and their behaviours are subsumed by higher-order entities that perform the learned patterns only in order to prune the computational complexity. However, we do not postulate a *necessary* coincidence between the learned high-order entities and emergent entities that we ourselves would identify, as in the micelle example. Rather, we assume that there is a great chance that the learned patterns and the ones recognised by humans overlap to some extent – it is possible that the human-identified orders represent all but a small fraction of the automatically generated abstractions. In order to clarify this distinction, we step through an exemplary run of the SOMO algorithm in the next section, using the self-assembly of micelles as a running example.

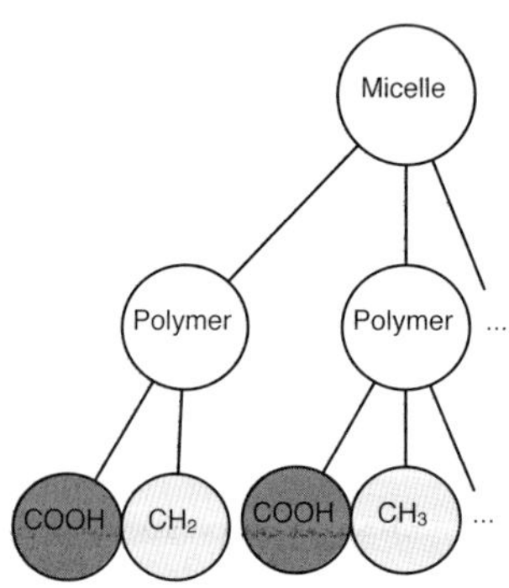

Fig. 6.2 Hierarchy of emergent entities in micelle formation (Rasmussen *et al.*, 2001)

6.5 The Technical Concept of SOMO

For our approach, we consider the elements of model agents, described by their states and behaviours (for a more in-depth formalisation of the agent concept, consider, for instance, Denzinger's generic agent definition (Denzinger and Winder, 2005)). In our example, we distinguish between freely moving reactive agents that represent molecular compounds (similar to artificial chemistries (Dittrich *et al.*, 2001)) and the environment they are immersed in. In particular, in our running example, a large number of hydrophobic and hydrophilic monomers are immersed in an aqueous environment. With the beginning of the simulation, the agents start to interact with each other and with the environment based on their behavioural rules. Together with the initial configuration of the system, these rules determine the result of the simulation, and if correctly phrased, they would result in the emergent phenomena described in the previous section.

6.5.1 *Observation of interactions*

In addition to the model agents comprising molecular compounds and the environment, the SOMO concept introduces *observer* agents that monitor the interactions of the model agents as well as the conditions under which they occur. In the context of the micelle-forming example, observers do not have to make assumptions about the model agents' internal states and behaviours – only their actually triggered, externally observable state boundaries (i.e., the observed boundaries of the domain over which the state variable is defined) and state changes are relevant. However, the potency of the observers can be increased by granting them access to the agents' behavioural rule sets, to their internal states, and, thus, to their activated rules.[1] Following the fundamental concept of cause and effect, the observed interactions are recorded in terms of states and state changes. States that lead to certain state changes are translated into boundary conditions, or *predicates*, whereas state changes simply describe the transition from one state attribute value to another. Boundary conditions of time (i.e., the agents' timing), proximity between agents, or their mere presence or absence come to mind. Conjointly occurring pairs of boundary conditions and state changes are stored in *interaction histories* over a certain period

[1] Focusing on the observation of state changes seems simpler than considering the underlying, responsible behavioural representations, as those would have to be correctly interpreted and related to the simulation context by an external observer.

of time. A sliding time window reduces the storage required and lets the observers 'forget' rare or singular events.

In the example, a pair of hydrophilic and hydrophobic monomers may attract each other, then stick together. A strong correlation between their locations would emerge, quickly resulting in a static relationship between their position states. The molecules might stick together over a long period of time. An observer would identify this behaviour and infer from the observations that these molecules will, under the given conditions, continue to stick together. Therefore, instead of continuously adjusting their locations based on their proximities at each time step of the simulation, an abstraction is introduced into the model. For now, the monomers are considered constantly attracted, or *bonded*. These bonded monomers, or *polymers*, are likely to aggregate in a *micelle*-like organisation because of the interplay with the aqueous environment: the polymers' heads align to face the water molecules, whereas their tails avoid them. Again, this formation is recognised and learned by the SOMO observers.

Instead of using specialised observers, the agents that make up the model can themselves observe interactions and the environment. In many cases, however, it is desirable to separate SOMO logic and the simulation model to maintain a clear distinction between the behaviours of the automatically learned abstractions and the original model. Independent of the kind of agent that takes on the task of observation and abstraction, the observers are subjected to certain restrictions. First, they are subject to an 'event horizon', i.e., they do not perceive the entire system but only portions of it. This is due to the fact that an omniscient observer would have to deal with a vast amount of data, nullifying the scalability benefits for which SOMO was designed, and making it necessary to introduce limits of the observations. Second, even though observers make no assumptions about the model of an observed agent, they are limited to knowledge they have been granted access to – they can only perceive states and state changes they were designed to sense. Therefore, if interactions take place hidden from the observers, for instance direct messaging between agents based on hidden internal states, these interactions will not become part of the interaction history.

These restrictions bias the abstraction process. If the scope of the simulation is well defined, these restrictions can be mitigated rather easily – the SOMO agents can be distributed across the interaction space to cover important 'hot spots' and the system designer can ensure the agents' ability to observe all relevant states and state changes. For more ambitious projects, however, it might be necessary to create a wide variety of observers, capable of identifying many different kinds of interactions.

Heterogeneous configurations are also possible. For instance, a subset of agents might be part of the original model and yet observe and abstract others, whereas the remainder of the agent population might be either model agents or observer agents. Naturally, hybrid agents, which play both roles, are useful if an abstraction hierarchy is part of the model. In the following, in order to avoid additional case distinctions, we will only distinguish between (1) a strict separation between observer and model agents, and (2) the capacity of all agents to observe and abstract.

6.5.2 *Interaction pattern recognition and behavioural abstraction*

The entries of the interaction history not only comprise some anonymous information about states and subsequent state changes but they also reference the involved interaction partners. Similar to Ramchurn *et al.* (2004), we use the interaction histories as databases for finding patterns in the agents' interaction behaviours. Previously unknown patterns, or *motifs*, can be identified in time series relying on various techniques such as learning partial periodic patterns (Han *et al.*, 1999), applying efficient, heuristic search (Chiu *et al.*, 2003), online motif search (Fuchs *et al.*, 2009), and even the identification of patterns of multiple resolutions (Wang *et al.*, 2010). Motif detection is adapted to interaction histories by assigning symbols, e.g., A or B, to specific log entries and finding patterns in the resulting strings, e.g., BBABCCBBABDA. In the given example, BBAB is a motif candidate.

The recurring sequence of interactions contained in the motif as well as the conditions that are part of it can be the basis for a *behavioural abstraction*. If interactions are recognised repeatedly, they can be abstracted in several ways – most simply, the predicates are not always checked; in full glory, a complex sequence of interactions can be fully abstracted and only the aggregated side effects, i.e., the state changes, can be enacted in the system. Hence, a motif that provides comprehensive information about the interaction partners and the actual interactions would allow rewriting of the agent rules as efficient sequences of unconditional instructions, with source and target agents readily in place.

A repeatedly occurring motif in the example system is the interaction between hydrophilic head and hydrophobic tail of a polymer. As the effect of this interaction stays the same once the monomers have bonded, it is no longer necessary to check these conditions and calculate the result of the interaction. An observer that has monitored this interaction can thus suspend the rules that cause the effect and instead enact it directly. Of course, such an intervention requires direct access to the agents' rule bases and might not be possible in some systems (cf. Section 6.5.5). Instead of suspending a specific agent's behavioural rules directly, it is possible to subsume the agent as a whole. The next section will describe this approach of hierarchical agent subsumption in more detail.

6.5.3 *Creating and adjusting hierarchies*

The polymer formation from simpler monomers provides an example for an abstraction even more powerful than simplifying specific interaction rules. If the agents keep interacting in a predictive manner, with each other and with their environment, they can be subsumed by one *meta-agent* that exhibits their external behaviour without continuously (re-)evaluating the interactions of its constituting elements. Recursive subsumption of agents and meta-agents yields a hierarchy of ever more abstract meta-agents.

The formation of hierarchies can be implemented by means of a set of special operators. In order to establish a hierarchical relationship, an agent might *enter* another agent. Alternatively, it might be *adopted* by another agent. Both actions yield corresponding parent–child relationships between the two agents. Such a parent–child relationship is reverted by *raising* a child in the hierarchy.

Depending on whether the agents observe their own interaction histories or specialised observers are used in the system, different kinds of behaviour are possible:

- If an agent observes its own interaction history and detects that it constantly interacts with another agent (or a group of other agents), it can create a new agent, assign its own abstracted behaviour, enter this new agent and deactivate itself. The newly created higher-order agent then adopts all other agents that formed the original behaviour, adding their abstracted behaviour to its own, and deactivating them as well.
- If specialised observers are deployed in the system, they create the meta-agents and assign the agents to be subsumed to them. The meta-agent then follows the same steps as above.

The end result in both cases is a meta-agent that behaves just like the group of agents to the outside but does not need to evaluate internal interactions. The polymer as well as the micelle are examples of structures that can be abstracted in this fashion. In fact, the micelle shows how a true hierarchy can form: in the course of the simulation, polymers form first, are detected by the observers, and abstracted. Then, the polymers form a micelle, which is internally stable and behaves consistently towards its environment. This can also be detected and abstracted so that only interactions between the micelle and the water molecules have to be evaluated.

Repeated applications of these abstraction rules yield continuously growing hierarchies with increasingly simplified behaviours. At the same time, hierarchies are dissolved when no longer appropriate. For this purpose, meta-agents repeatedly check for validity of the abstraction they represent by checking whether the original predicates still hold or by temporarily disbanding the abstractions, checking for the occurence of the abstracted interactions and either re-abstracting or abandoning the abstraction.

The subsumption of agents and their behaviours closely resembles the concept of modularisation and crafting hierarchical code. Figure 6.3 shows a visual programming perspective on agents, their behaviours and behavioural interrelations; individual operators (spheres) are recursively nested to allow for the hierarchical design of behavioural modules, whereas the connections between inputs and outputs (cones) determine the flow of information at each hierarchical level. The realisation of this visual modelling language has partly been motivated by the need of a generic, hierarchical representation of agent behaviours.

6.5.4 *Confidence measures*

The identification of motifs in the interaction history as well as the decision to resolve a hierarchy are based on *confidence estimation*. There is a large body of work around confidence in statistics (Kiefer, 1977), and its effective standardisation for use in the natural sciences is a vivid research area (Louis and Zeger, 2009). Confidence measures are also used in computational models of trust (Kiefhaber *et al.*, 2012). The general idea is to estimate the probability that a pattern occurs based on its preceding frequency over a given period of time.

In SOMO, repeated observation of interaction patterns increases the confidence value. A sufficiently great confidence value leads to abstraction. The confidence value also determines the abstraction's lifespan. Confidence metrics that are too generous, i.e., that cause too long abstraction lifespans, diminish the accuracy of a simulation. Abstracted behaviours are repeat-

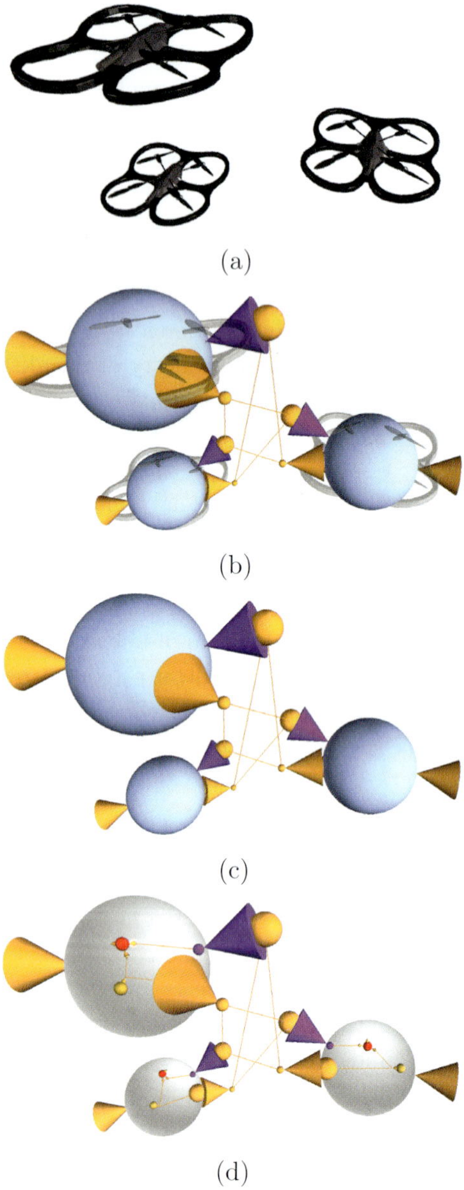

Fig. 6.3 (a) Three quad-copter agents situated close together. (b) Projection of the agents' behavioural operators and their interrelations into the agent space. (c) Focus on the behavioural network. (d) Introspection of the agents' behavioural modules reveals hierarchically nested, lower-level operators and their connectivity.

edly checked for validity by either exposing the subsumed agents to the environment and re-observing their behaviour, or by checking the predicates that were identified in the abstraction process. This check can occur at fixed time intervals, at the designated end of the meta-agent's lifespan, or based on heuristics such as the degree of activity in its local environment. If the abstraction remains valid, confidence rises and the checks become less frequent. However, if the abstraction is invalid, confidence sinks and the abstraction is either checked more often or abandoned completely.

In case of miscalculations, the simulation could be reset to a previous simulation state, adjusted and partially recomputed. This additional overhead might make it hard to reach a gain in efficiency. On the other hand, if confidence is assigned too cautiously to motifs, abstraction hierarchies do not get a chance to form in the first place. Thus, a careful balance has to be found. Learning methods as introduced in Section 6.5.6 can help find suitable parameters for concrete scenarios.

6.5.5 *Execution model*

Our stated goal is to create a learning abstraction mechanism that makes as few assumptions as possible about the agents it is working with. However, in order for behavioural abstraction and hierarchical abstraction to work, the underlying execution model has to fulfil some requirements.

As mentioned before, *behavioural abstraction* requires that some of the internal rules according to which an agent operates can be suspended by an external entity. This is a natural assumption if agents observe themselves or if they can issue the rule's temporary removal (e.g., to a global simulation engine). However, if the agents are fully opaque and abstraction is performed by specialised observers, they need to be able to influence them directly. As the system designer usually has complete control over the simulation environment, it should be possible to implement such a feature within the environment directly.

For *hierarchical abstraction*, we assume that execution of the agents follows the hierarchy as well. First, root nodes are considered for execution. Their children are considered recursively only if they are active, i.e., if they are not suspended. Deactivating child nodes instead of removing them from the simulation entirely is necessary as part of the process for checking the abstractions' validity. Their (inactive) maintenance as part of the simulation hierarchy also serves to update their states as part of abstracted high-level behaviours.

Since simulations are usually closed systems, it is safe to assume that a benevolence assumption holds. This means that no agent in the system has an incentive to deceive the observers and information about states and state changes is provided freely and without inhibition. In cases in which this assumption does not hold, additional measures have to be taken. Concepts developed for dealing with uncertainty in open, complex systems such as trust (Steghöfer *et al.*, 2010) can be useful for this purpose.

6.5.6 *Learning SOMO: parameters, knowledge propagation, and procreation*

As an unsupervised learning approach, a self-organised middle-out learner will have to learn about itself and thus, in a sense, become self-aware. A simple example is the requirement to learn which abstractions worked in the past and which failed to show the desired benefits. If abstractions had to be quickly dissolved, the SOMO observer that created them obviously did something wrong. Either its observations were faulty or the parameters were sub-optimal, e.g., the confidence value that is used to estimate when it is safe to assume that an interaction actually occurs repeatedly.

On the other hand, multiple SOMO observers deployed in the system should be able to learn from each other. An abstraction that has proven valid for one observer should not have to be learned by other observers in the system. Instead, patterns should be propagated and the knowledge acquired should be spread throughout the system. This way, the SOMO learner becomes an organic, learning, improving system within the system that constantly revises and improves its knowledge about the environment and itself by the meta-interaction of the individual observers.

Thus, SOMO agents learn on two levels: they adapt and improve their individual learning and abstraction parameters to become well suited for the niche they occupy in the simulation; and they exchange knowledge with each other and incorporate this knowledge in their decision-making process.

The former kind of learning can be performed based on the data the agents collect and based on the perceived results of the actions performed by the agents. If a behavioural abstraction has proven unstable, the agent can, for instance, increase the confidence value at which it abstracts behaviour. It would thus have to be more certain that a behaviour occurs repeatedly in the same fashion before abstracting it. More excitingly, however, an additional feedback loop can be added to a SOMO learner that uses the data collected by the agent to simulate different sets of parameters and the results they would have yielded. Such a simulation-within-the-simulation can use an evolutionary algorithm (EA) to evolve and test a population of parameter sets, simulate the learner's behaviour, and use a fitness function that checks whether the parameters would have found abstractions that have actually proven valid. A parameter set with a high number of valid abstractions gets a higher fitness value and may be adopted. The EA can run concurrently and change the parameter settings whenever better results are obtained than is possible with the current parameters. A similar approach has, for instance, been used to create and simulate new traffic light switching rules in a traffic-control scenario (Prothmann *et al.*, 2011).

The latter kind of learning, in which patterns, motifs, parameter sets, etc. are propagated in the system, can be implemented using gossiping algorithms (Eugster *et al.*, 2007). These consensus approaches are built around local communication in which information is primarily exchanged with neighbours, aggregated, and spread through the system. As the communication is limited to a small number of agents, the system is scalable and, since information is always disseminated along several trajectories, the system is robust. A major concern in the design of such algorithms is 'eventual consensus', i.e., ensuring that at some point all agents have access to the information. Fortunately, the SOMO learning approach does not have this requirement as even local knowledge exchange can improve its efficiency and, thus, relatively simple gossiping protocols can be used.

Whenever a SOMO agent learns a new set of parameters, a new motif, or that a certain abstraction has proven valid, it can provide this information to other agents in its neighbourhood. These recipients can either use this information, for example because they are situated in a similar environment, or discard it. They can also augment or redact the information and send it on to their own neighbours. In this way, knowledge spreads through the system and allows the learning agents to profit from the experiences of others. Similar techniques have been used to spread reputation information in multi-agent systems (Bachrach *et al.*, 2009).

For the transmission of information between SOMO learners, a language for the knowledge of the agents has to be defined. Apart from using the language in the exchange of information, it can also be used to store the knowledge between simulation runs. This way, different runs of the same simulation can profit from knowledge learned previously and – if the simulations are similar enough – different simulations can re-use knowledge learned previously. A SOMO learner that is repeatedly used in the same setting can thus evolve along with the simulation and improve over time.

In settings in which the simulation is highly dynamic, an additional meta-learning approach can be used. At the start of the simulation, SOMO learners are spread evenly within the simulation space. If a SOMO agent finds itself in a highly dynamic environment, with many entities to observe and many interactions, it can procreate by spawning a duplicate of itself. This new agent carries the same knowledge as its parent and can become active in the same area. Thus, the SOMO system self-organises towards a structure in which learning takes place in those locations where it is most beneficial and where most interactions occur.

While the outlined meta-learning approaches should improve SOMO's ability to find valid abstractions and simplify the simulations, they incur additional computational cost as well as increasing the memory requirements. Therefore, the use of these faculties has to be evaluated carefully for each new simulation setting and the trade-off between the resources required for meta-learning and the benefit has to be analysed.

6.6 Current Implementations

In several publications, Sarraf Shirazi *et al.* present the exploration and extension of SOMO implementations in the context of biological simulations (Sarraf Shirazi *et al.*, 2010, 2011a,b, 2013; Jacob *et al.*, 2012; von Mammen *et al.*, 2012). Therein, the application domain slightly shifted from protein-interaction networks (in the context of the MAPK signalling pathway) towards cell-cell/cell-membrane interaction systems (in the context of blood coagulation processes). More importantly, the model representations underwent an evolution as well: Sarraf Shirazi and his colleagues (one of them is an author of this chapter, S. von Mammen) first learned clusters of intertwined functions of gene expression rates by correlating their results – initially by means of artificial neural networks, subsequently by means of genetic algorithms. The second iteration of implementations featured rule-based multi-agent representations and sets of learning observer agents that logged and subsumed the activities of the other agents in the simulation. For instance, blood platelets and fibrinogens that are stuck together are subsumed by meta-agents with reduced rule sets, which represent the blood clot.

Current SOMO implementations have shown the effectiveness of the concept. In early experiments the number of tests performed as part of the simulation was successfully reduced. In later experiments, Sarraf Shirazi *et al.* were able to show that the overall performance, also considering the computational overhead needed for observing and dynamic learning, can be improved.

The original SOMO concept foresees the possibility of exposing SOMO agents without prior knowledge to an arbitrary multi-agent simulation to automatically infer hierarchies of patterns from the observed processes. In order to reach this desirable goal, numerous challenges still have to be addressed. The universal deployment of the SOMO concept requires, for instance, a generic learning mechanism for identifying arbitrary patterns (e.g., learning classifier systems (Wilson, 1995)), a universal approach to measuring and comparing confidence values and an accordingly tuned reinforcement learning mechanism, as well as a comprehensive formalisation of representation and algorithms.

An example of a meso-level abstraction algorithm with a more technical focus has been presented by Steghöfer *et al.* (2013) with the HiSPADA algorithm. The Hierarchical Set Partitioning Algorithm for Distributed Agents forms abstraction hierarchies within an agent society based on scalability metrics. If an agent system solves a computationally intensive problem that is defined by the individual agents (such as scheduling in power management scenarios) and that can be hierarchically decomposed, intermediaries can be introduced to solve parts of the original problem. Each intermediary solves a sub-problem that is defined by the agent it directly controls. The runtime of the problem solver depends on the number of agents controlled by an intermediary. If it exceeds a certain threshold, an additional layer of intermediaries can be introduced to divide the controlled agents. An intermediary acts as a black box to the outside, much like the meta-agents in the hierarchical abstraction. However, the intermediary is not the result of a learning process based on the interaction patterns of the agents but merely a result of an internal constraint violation. Nevertheless, the concept has proven to improve scalability in large systems and provides a starting point for future research.

6.7 Awareness Beyond Virtuality

It has already been shown that current implementations of SOMO are capable of pruning computational complexity in multi-agent based simulations and identifying emergent processes. A broadly deployable, unbiased SOMO implementation would make it possible to compute models with large numbers of approximate constants, such as in our perceived reality. This would make it possible to integrate vast quantities of scientific facts, across all levels of scale and scientific disciplines, for consideration in simulations.

6.7.1 *Integration and emergence*

Such a SOMO implementation would offer *virtually* unlimited computing power for models with large numbers of approximate constants – as in our perceived reality. Vast amounts of multi-scale and multi-disciplinary scientific data could be integrated in simulations. The development of an organism could be computed bottom-up from a single fertilised cell. As we believe SOMO to be principally capable of developing awareness of previously unknown emergent phenomena – both *in-silico* and *in-vivo* – the organism's systems would be identified automatically. The recognised patterns are expressed in algorithmic rather than traditional mathematic representations, and so human-readable and accessible to human reasoning.

6.7.2 *Model inference*

The SOMO concept need not be limited to virtual simulations. Heuristic learning methods could supply feasible solutions for gaps in theories, for which empiric researchers have not yet provided answers. However, instead of limiting SOMO to virtual simulations, it could operate on top of a smart sensory network (SOMO net), an advanced wireless sensor network (Akyildiz *et al.*, 2002). Enhancing SOMO sensory nodes with effectors would introduce the capability of self-directed inquiry. At this point, the SOMO net could turn into a self-reflective machinery similar to the one developed by Lipson and Pollack (2000), which also grew, the other way round, into a system to automatically infer complex, non-linear mathematical laws from data sets by avoiding trivial invariants (Schmidt and Lipson, 2006). The SOMO net enhanced in this way would be able to perform autonomously observational analysis and proactive investigations to accelerate further the generation of comprehensive and accurate scientific models.

6.7.3 *SOMO net*

In addition to the sensory functionalities present in a subset of nodes of the envisioned SOMO net, all the nodes would have to provide a runtime environment for a SOMO agent. To begin with, the initialised, *networked* SOMO agent – a conceptual descendant of the SOMO observer as deployed in virtual simulation environments – would sense and transmit data to its neighbours and, in turn, aggregate any received information. The analogies to distributed learning approaches are obvious, especially in the context of wireless sensor networks (Predd *et al.*, 2006). However, despite the common notion of a global learning task, distributed data sources, and efforts to fuse the aggregated data, the SOMO reaches further.

A SOMO agent would quickly learn patterns in the sensed and received, transmitted data and refine its sensing configuration and communication connectivity based on the greatest information gain: it would direct its inquiries to areas of interest, i.e., sensor ranges or nodes that provide (from its perspective) unpredictable information. Depending on the confidence values associated with the learned patterns, the original data sources would be queried once in a while in order to test the abstractions' validity.

As the learned patterns would reference the learning context, i.e., the network location and connectivity of the learning agent, the abstracted information could be passed down the network, enriching the other agents' databases, without causing confusion. Whenever possible, patterns could be subsumed in higher-level abstractions, the validation process stretching across the network.

The self-organised, decentralised learning and validation algorithm would ensure that the system under observation is described at several levels of abstraction, based on the input on numerous nodes with their individual perspectives. At the same time, it would ensure that the processing and communication costs of the networked nodes are minimised, crucially important for the efficacy and longevity of a wireless sensor network.

6.7.4 *SOMO after me*

SOMO and SOMO nets would make correlations between processes apparent that have never been thought of before. These new insights could, due to the immense complexity that SOMO promises to handle, help to build sustainable, progressive, evolving economic and ecological infrastructures for the great challenges of humankind.

At the same time, accessible methodologies for large-scale data modelling and exploration would become an (even more) important limiting factor. In order to address this rising challenge, we have been developing an integrated visual programming and simulation environment. Combined with SOMO's computing abilities, such environments could make model building and simulation feasible and attractive to non-scientists, or, rather, they could turn anyone into a scientist and revolutionise everyday life.

6.8 The Future of SOMO

In summary, the SOMO algorithm and SOMO nets hold the promise of revealing hitherto unsuspected correlations between processes. Such new insights, and the immense complexity that SOMO can handle, could help to build sustainable, progressive and evolving economic and ecological infrastructures for tackling the major challenges humankind faces today. Our current work on SOMO is focused on pattern detection in observed interactions and the possibilities for propagating knowledge about abstractions through the system. Once the implementations of SOMO have reached maturity, we envisage that research can shift to analysing how the learned abstractions and features correlate with the behaviours we find in higher-order emergent phenomena. Whether we will find striking similarities, or instead discover these to be two completely different forms of complex systems, remains an exciting open question at this time.

PART II

Is That Computer Out to Get Me?

Chapter 7

Self-Steering and Aware Homes

Marco Aiello,[1] Roberto Baldoni,[2] Alexander Lazovik[1] and Massimo Mecella[2]

[1] *University of Groningen, The Netherlands*
[2] *Sapienza University of Rome, Italy*

7.1 Introduction

Due to the ever-increasing availability of cheap sensors and actuators, homes are becoming more technological. This goes well beyond the 'gadgetification' of the houses of the early adopters and the wealthy, as domotic solutions are becoming massively accessible for creating more secure and comfortable living spaces. Such a trend is expected to deliver significant improvement in the quality of life for the average citizen as well as for people who have a special need, such as limited mobility.

The current shift does not simply provide for homes with hundreds of sensors and actuators, but also for a different way of interacting and controlling them. If in the past one had direct command–effect interactions or, at most, simple feedback loops, now we are going towards smart proactive homes. That is, homes that on the basis of a specific context perform some form of reasoning and as a consequence take the initiative of making world-changing actions. Consider a simple lamp in a corridor. The most basic operation is a switch on the light that is directly operated by the user. A triggering of the switch changes the state of the light (direct-command). To avoid having to operate the light or forgetting that it is on when not needed, one can also mount a passive infrared sensor that turns on the light when it detects movement and keeps it on for a given amount of time when there is not enough light in the corridor (simple feedback loop). Ideally, what one really wants is the light to go on when the user needs it, perhaps turning on just before the user enters the corridor and turning it off immediately after the user leaves. That is, the light should sense the user's intentions and pro-actively operate accordingly. The example can scale to more sophisticated situations, say a user watching the television and at the same time vacuum cleaning. While moving around the home, the TV program could 'follow' the user on screens disseminated around the home and eventually pause when the user is occupied in a conversation over the phone or with a housemate. Or, if the user wants to watch a football match with some friends and this implies having cold beers in the fridge, certain lighting conditions, and being disconnected from the phone, the house could make sure that all such requirements are maintained at all times during the whole match. One does not have to restrict the imagination to situations of user comfort, and can think of energy-saving automation, support for users with limited mobility or for those with special needs.

The natural question arising is then: how can we create pro-active or better named *smart* homes? A number of ingredients are necessary to realize a smart home. Certainly, there has to be an underlying sensing and actuating infrastructure, which has to be able to interoperate using a shared middleware and perhaps shared ontologies. However, this is just a prerequisite for having access to data and being able to actuate. What then is needed is deduction capabilities that transform raw sensed data into meaningful high-level concepts. These form what is known as the context of the home. The context, which includes information about the user in the home, holds information such as the temperature of a room, its illumination, the energy consumption of the various appliances, the location of the users and possibly a classification of the activities carried out. The context is what makes the home aware of its use and in turn enables the deployment of smart systems. Systems based on user activities and intentions can steer the home in order to support the inhabitants' actions and even satisfy secondary goals, such as saving energy.

In the present chapter, we consider a generic architecture to make homes smarter, which essentially revolves around having contextual information and exploits artificial intelligence planning techniques. We base our proposal on the results of the European research project Smart Homes for All (SM4All) which ran from 2008 to 2011 (Aiello *et al.*, 2011).

7.2 The Many Contributions to the Home Context

The movie *Kitchen Stories*, released in 2003, is set in the fifties in rural Norway, and portrays a Swedish researcher sitting on a high chair in the kitchen of a farmer to observe how the space and appliances are used. The observer has a map on which he writes all the movements and activities of the home owner. The final goal of this ethnographic study is to collect enough observations to deduce how kitchens are used in practice and what can be improved in the design of the next generation of Swedish furniture. The movie, which builds on the tension between the observer and the observed, carries an interesting idea from industrial design: the user and the usage should be the driver for creating ergonomic spaces, and usage is best observed in situ. The idea is modern and actual, with the advantage that today we are able to observe unobtrusively and automatically. The advent of sensors and ICT allows us to automate the step of data acquisition, while making it more reliable and information-rich. At the same time, we gain the possibility of real-time adaptation of the environment to the user needs and activities.

7.2.1 *The home context*

Let us initially focus on the first part of the picture, that is, on observing people in their homes. A number of sensors are able to measure physical quantities and can be used to infer information about the user and the home situation. The *context* of the home is its state at any given moment, built as the union of the states of its components and its users and deductions over these states. The context thus includes facts about the users (location and activity currently being carried out), the appliances (fridge temperature and content, instantaneous electricity consumption of any device connected to a socket), the spaces (room temperature, status of heaters and coolers, status of doors and windows in terms of being open, closed, or locked) and the home environment (weather information, cost of electricity on the grid).

Bolchini *et al.* (2007) provide an overview of what context means in computer science from a data-oriented perspective, and an overview of a set of models proposed in the literature. Huebscher and McCann (2004) consider the specific case of smart homes to design a context-aware middleware. The emphasis is on moving from raw sensor data to workable context information. They distinguish between context provider components and context services providing aggregated information. The fridge can be a context provider indicating its temperature, energy needs and the state of its door. A context service can then aggregate data from the fridge and another context provider such as an infrared camera and indicate that a person is in the kitchen performing an activity related to food. In general, the step from sensor data to abstract context information is not a trivial one. Sensor readings are prone to errors, inconsistencies among readings from different sensors are common, and there is no general and straightforward way to fuse sensor data into high-level contextual information for event or situation recognition.

Buchholz *et al.* (2003) identify five factors that make for the quality of a context: (1) precision, describing how much the context mimics reality; (2) probability of correctness, giving a quantitative measure of the reliability of the context information; (3) trustworthiness, which measures the reliability of the context source; (4) resolution, which describes the coarseness of the available context data; and (5) up-to-dateness, which indicates how current the contextual information is with respect to the real world.

7.2.2 *A case study*

In a smart home, one can imagine all appliances being able to provide context information and, in addition, one can think of a set of extra sensors giving more accurate situational information, especially regarding the people acting in the home. In the SM4All showcase, we used a home of about 60 square meters with two bedrooms, two bathrooms, a kitchen and a living room. The home, known as Casa Agevole, is designed specifically for people with physical disabilities and it is at the premises of the Santa Lucia Hospital compound in Rome.

For our experiments and showcase, we used the following devices and sensors: a home gateway, a TV, a music player, a multimedia box, microphones, bluetooth speakers, a brain–computer interface, a laptop, a display, a smart phone, window motors, door motors, a motorized bed, a smart fridge, a washing machine, controllable lights, fire extinguishers, motorized curtains, RFID tags and antennas, a set of cameras and a PC dedicated to their operation, fire sensors, smoke sensors, light sensors, rain and wind sensors mounted outside.

This variety of sensors enabled us to deduce the location of the people, the state of the home in terms of lighting, security, climatization, the emergence of safety critical conditions (e.g., a fire starting in the kitchen) and so on. In addition, there was also a wide variety of actions that the home could perform to satisfy the needs of the user. Doors and windows could be opened or closed, the fridge could check its contents and participate in decisions regarding food, monitors could provide user feedback, music could be automatically routed on speakers and follow the user, and so on. Context awareness is achieved through a complex event processing system, in the spirit of Wu *et al.* (2006), which collects raw data and events from sensors and devices and aggregates them on the basis of pre-specified rules, to be defined in a declarative manner at deployment-time of the home.

7.3 A Smart Home Architecture

Having contextual information is central to the creation of an architecture for a smart home. The state of the home and of its users is the starting point to perform any control and, in turn, satisfy the needs of the users. But context alone makes the home 'aware', not smart. In SM4All, we have designed an architecture to go beyond awareness and introduce concepts of pro-activity in the home. To do so, we base the architecture on the abstraction of a service providing for an open, dynamic and flexible sensing and control infrastructure.

Figure 7.1 gives a schematization of the systems' main components and their basic interactions (Kaldeli *et al.*, 2013). One can distinguish three macro layers: the pervasive layer, where the basic sensing and actuation takes place; the composition layer, which is responsible for abstracting the context and coming up with smart decisions and translating these into service invocations; and the user layer, which provides the interface for the user to control the home.

The composition layer is the heart of the architecture, where context is deduced and used. Five major subcomponents populate the layer, one being the *context* component described in the previous section. Closely related to the pervasive layer is the *repository*, which keeps the descriptions of the set of supported service types, including appropriate semantic markups about the operations offered, as well as the registry with the actual device instances that are active at any given moment. This is kept up-to-date according to the notifications received from the pervasive layer. A map representing the layout of the house (e.g., the rooms in it, and how they are arranged) is also stored in the repository. Whenever a new device registers itself to the pervasive layer, it also publishes itself to the repository as an instance of its associated abstract type, specifying its functionalities in

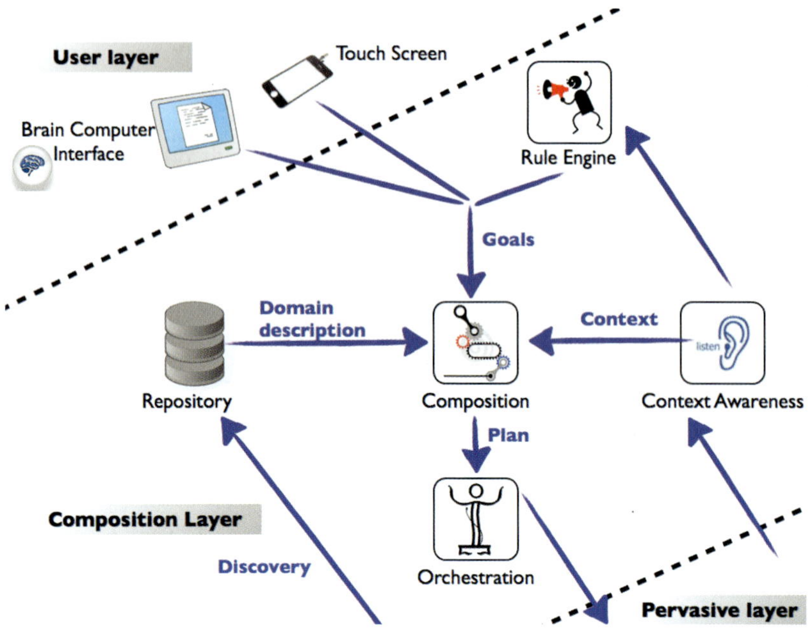

Fig. 7.1 Architecture overview

terms of action preconditions and effects.

The *rule engine* uses information about context changes and, if certain conditions hold, takes action (e.g., if a fire is detected, and an emergency plan should be put into practice) by directly invoking the composition module. The *composition* module receives high-level complex goals issued either by the user layer (e.g., a request for a beer) or the rule engine (e.g., an emergency goal for combating some dangerous gas that has been detected in the kitchen), and tries to fulfil them by generating appropriate compositions of the available services. The compositions are computed automatically and on the fly by a domain-independent planner, which uses constraint satisfaction techniques, based on the current home domain delivered by the repository and the state of the environment provided by the context awareness module.

Whenever a goal is issued, the planner generates a plan, i.e., a sequence of service operations (actions), whose execution changes the state of the environment in accordance with the properties prescribed by the goal. The plan is then passed to the *orchestrator*, which translates the composition into lower-level service invocations and executes them step by step, in a synchronous manner. If a service operation returns a permanent failure, the plan execution is terminated, and the composition module computes a new alternative plan for the same goal, after the erroneous service has been removed from the registry of currently available services.

The composition layer works transparently for the home inhabitant; though the final control should be in his/her hands. To this end, the user layer provides the possibility of plugging in interfaces for controlling the smart home. The basic module of the user layer is the Abstract Adaptive Interface (AAI) (Di Ciccio *et al.*, 2011), which acts as a proxy that provides services to the particular user interface (UI). Through a unique adaptable algorithm, the AAI is able to manage many different UI models, such as a touch screen or a brain–computer interface, by changing its behavior on the basis of the concrete UI characteristics. The AAI collects information about the available service operations of active devices and the pre-specified goals, and forwards them to the concrete UIs. The information collected from the repository includes visual data (icons) associated with the service operations offered by the devices, as well as information about their location, so that they can be organized accordingly, depending on the capabilities of the concrete UIs.

Moreover, a set of icons representing complex goals, such as preparing the bedroom for sleeping, are also made available. The AAI is seamlessly updated to reflect the most recent status of the devices, as delivered by the context awareness component, and notifies the concrete UIs connected to the system accordingly. Whenever an icon is selected, the respective instruction is sent either directly to the orchestrator, if it represents a single operation, or to the composition module, if it corresponds to a complex goal. The AAI can then be integrated in a number of possible interfaces.

In SM4All, we have experimented with brain–computer interfaces that, after a short training, are able to translate brain signals into a set of predefined commands; something that takes advantage of the possibility of issuing high-level goals whose execution depends on contextual information, rather than having to provide detailed instructions to the home. Also touch screens, mobile devices, laptops and voice recognition software have all been used as input means for the interaction with the home.

7.4 Discussion

The SM4All experience has shown how essential it is to have proper contextual information to build a system that can make the homes self-steering and appear smart to the user. Context is not for free, though. It is abstracted and deduced by combining information coming from a plethora of sensors and appliances that are idiosyncratic in the way they represent data, in their sampling rates, in the precision, trustworthiness, resolution and freshness with which they capture physical reality. Furthermore, if acquiring the state of electronic devices is somewhat doable, inferring the state of the people is a much harder task. Even such an apparently simple operation as location tracking is not easy to achieve in open settings. Nevertheless, current technology is sufficient to provide rich contextual information and we expect to have more data to draw upon in the near future.

Context awareness is thus an essential component for home smartness; however, it really becomes interesting when it is used for driving the home behavior. In SM4All, this is based on the interplay of two composition engines (see Caruso *et al.* (2012) for further details): the offline synthesis engine, which is based on pre-specified, reusable automaton-based composite services, and a dynamic planner, which performs continual planning on-demand, based on artificial intelligence planning techniques.

Being computed offline, routines are specifications that offer several orchestrations for enacting the desired behavior: each follows a different path, according to the current state of the devices and the environment, during the execution. Every legal state of the involved devices and every coherent state of the environment is foreseen. Composite services are stored in the repository, thus being reusable. Being made online, plans from the dynamic planner are single orchestrations starting from the current context and stopping in a reachable situation where the goal is fulfilled. Plans are not stored anywhere: their life cycle ends as they are executed.

In order to clarify the interplay of the two compositions, let us consider a *relax scenario* routine, which was computed by the offline synthesis engine in advance. The desired service specifies that the lights in the living room should be switched off, the curtains should be closed, and then the stereo should be turned on. Mike, an inhabitant of the smart house, makes the system launch the routine. However, the service operation for closing the curtains in the living room fails to execute properly because his sister has opened the window. The failure is caught by the orchestrator, which in turn invokes the dynamic planner to solve the issue: a declarative goal, equivalent to the final state of the relax scenario routine, is passed to it. The planner then generates a recovery plan, which first closes the window, then closes the curtains, and finally switches on the stereo. Although the computation of this simple plan might be a matter of less than a second, resorting to the dynamic planner may be time consuming in cases of complex compositions, since the dynamic planner always starts the computation from scratch. Therefore, the general framework is to have target services corresponding to the user's goals: offline synthesized compositions realize the routines, and the dynamic planner is used as a recovery mechanism, if any failure occurs during the execution.

Offline synthesis engine The offline synthesis is based on a conversational description of the available devices and the environment and the desired target corresponding to some goal, both represented as finite transition systems. The task of the synthesis is to realize the behavior of the target service by combining those computation fragments (realizable transitions) that the available services provide. The solution is based on the reduction of the problem to the synthesis of linear-time temporal logic (LTL) formulae by model checking over game structures, in the spirit of Calvanese *et al.* (2008). The composition returned by the offline synthesis, called the *routine*, can be seen as an imperative program that, given the current state of the system and the next operation to invoke, specifies which device can realize that action, taking into account the current conditions in the home environment and the conversational states of devices. Hence, it verifies the realizability of the target by analyzing the actions, i.e., whether the paths admitted by transitions lead to consistent states with respect to the available devices, while respecting the constraints imposed by any pre-condition and effect associated with these transitions. Targets are described through the same syntax and semantics of the simple devices. The target is specified and processed at deployment time, i.e., during the installation of the system, hence before run-time.

Dynamic planner The dynamic planner delays the creation of a plan till the moment that the goal is issued. Only then is the space of possible actions considered. Furthermore, since an environment such as a home is inherently concurrent and non-deterministic, the planner checks the actual effects of action invocation. The planner accepts goals expressed in a rich temporal logic enhanced with the possibility to express linear constraints over variables, the domain defines the home actions as preconditions and effects of invoking an operation, and the context is a set of assignments to domain variables, some of which may be unknown to the planner. The planner is domain independent and relies on a contraint satisfaction engine to work (Kaldeli *et al.*, 2011).

In SM4All, we have thus shown how context is essential for home automation and how planners can take advantage of such information, once a basic sensor and device middleware is in place, to enhance a home with smartness. This is an important step in showing the realizability of smart homes, but we consider the general problem to be far from being solved. We have mentioned the problem of reconciling reality with the sensor readings to have more precise and fine contexts. Temporal and spatial reasoning techniques will be necessary to reason about contextual information (Augusto and Nugent, 2004; Aiello *et al.*, 2007), and this raises yet more challenges. The number of elements providing information for the context increases and the data must be handled. If one considers a modern office building, it is easy to have thousands of sensors and actuators, not to mention the hundreds of appliances and user devices, and homes are following the trend in terms of numbers of sensors and actuators.

Another problem to address is the concurrency of control in indoor spaces. While the home is creating and executing plans, the users are living their lives and changing the state of the home. Further, more plans could be executed concurrently by the same home automation controller or by several others (e.g., the mobile phone of a user could be running a home entertainment plan, while the home automation system is executing a home emergency plan as a reaction to a fire alarm). Unobtrusive and intuitive concurrency management mechanisms need to be devised. Additionally, most current research on smart homes seems to focus on one user per apartment. This is a good starting point, but obviously does not fit all home situations.

Smart homes are not only about technology; in fact, the focal point is people. Therefore, one also needs to consider the social aspects, the interaction design issues such as universal design (i.e. design for all) and internationalization (Sharp *et al.*, 2007). These include the social norms and the high variability in cultural understanding of what is a home and how it should behave. Acceptability issues are central in the success of any technology. This goes beyond the mere design of appropriate human–computer interfaces. People have to be confident of being in control and that their privacy and safety are not compromised by the technology. Chapter 9 in this book provides an interesting overview of such issues.

One should also mention that there are alternative views on what a home should do with contextual information. The present chapter takes the position that contextual information is essential for smart homes. An alternative view, as for instance advocated by Intille (2006), is that context should be simply given back to the user and that any decision and actuation should be entirely in his/her hands. In our own user evaluation study (Kaldeli *et al.*, 2013), we considered user acceptance for two sets of people: young people with a high level of computer literacy and elderly people with an average age above 75. The two categories of people were exposed to the concepts and were able to experience the smart home. Both groups overall were inclined to accept the technology proposed to them, though both had concerns. The young group raised privacy concerns, being aware of what kind of information the system running the home must have had, while the older group was concerned by losing control over their own environment. Naturally, both concerns are legitimate and should be taken into account when realizing home automation products.

A final remark concerns the fitting of a similar technology in an existing home. In Kaldeli *et al.* (2013), we have proposed an engineering process to fit existing homes with the technology, while experience with the Casa Agevole of the Santa Lucia Hospital has given us practical insights. If, on the one hand, we notice that deploying the technology in an existing home is possible, on the other hand, it does require considerable effort from both ICT experts and builders. Therefore, one should also study how to make the technology accessible to the general public in a simple and economically attractive manner. We leave such concerns for a product development and marketing phase, which might follow the research effort phase that has been presented in this chapter.

7.5 The Future of Homes

Having stressed the central role of context awareness and that its precision and richness is improving as technology improves, technological trends, one can wonder what the future will bring us with respect to our homes. The inter-networking of devices and appliances has become a mature technology and does not provide major obstacles to having smart homes. Interoperation among devices is still fitful, though standardization and efforts in building shared ontologies are helping. Sensor technology is also becoming cheaper and more pervasive, so we do expect our homes to be increasingly aware of their state. In addition, the next generation of home appliances will be network ready and easily integrated in home automation systems.

One particular feature that is gaining increasing attention is the energy footprint of any home operation, which in turn can be related to carbon dioxide emissions. Devices will have to be aware of their energy needs, of their energy consumptions, and possibly coordinate energy usage at the level of the home. Users will want to be aware of the consumptions and perhaps decide on their actions based on such knowledge.

Chapter 8 nicely illustrates the user involvement in energy decisions. The involvement is even more relevant when considering the concept of a smart grid to which homes, smart or not, will be connected. The smart grid is the coupling of the power grid with ICT in order to have better monitoring of the infrastructure and in turn be able to include renewable sources and provide better user feedback. One possible side effect is that energy will be priced in real time for the end users. This means that the smart home will need to make decisions based on the energy price, which in turn will reflect the congestion state of the grid. The home may also make decisions on using small generation facilities in its control (e.g., a solar panel installed on the roof, a wind turbine or a micro combined heat and power generator). The home could also have an energy storage facility (permanently in the form of a set of batteries on its premises, or occasionally when an electric car is parked outside and connected to it).

All these options will increase the number of decisions the home needs to take. Georgievski *et al.* (2012) report a small experiment in an office regulating its appliance operations based on the user needs and the varying energy prices coming from a simulation of a smart grid. The results show that the office could save up to 35% of its power costs in its normal operation without affecting the comfort and productivity of the workers. The solution provided for the office required no user intervention whatsoever.

We believe that homes will become increasingly complex from the point of view of technology. We have advocated why the trend has a positive effect towards having rich contextual information and we saw how contextual data can be used to make homes smarter. The cornerstone for the success of such technologies is to hide the complexity from the user. The home still needs to be a comfortable and secure place where inhabitants act naturally and where the home transparently supports them, not a place where constant decision making is required and things seem to happen without a reason.

Chapter 8

Assistive Awareness in Smart Grids

Aikaterini Bourazeri,[1] Pablo Almajano,[2,3] Inmaculada Rodriguez[3] and Maite Lopez-Sanchez[3]

[1] *Imperial College London, UK*
[2] *Institut d'Investigació en Intelligència Artificial, Spain*
[3] *Universitat de Barcelona, Spain*

8.1 Introduction

Smart grids use information and communication technology (ICT) to underpin an energy distribution network's infrastructure and performance, placing at the same time a particular emphasis on the demand-side, which requires us both to understand better the behaviour of energy consumers and to give energy consumers a better understanding of the effects of their behaviour on the grid. We are investigating serious games as an innovative way to train consumers and increase their active participation in the now 'smart' energy infrastructure, i.e. smart grids. We specifically focus on local micro-grids, in which energy consumers can also be producers, who self-organise their own provision and appropriation rules in the context of an institution. Enabling assistive awareness in such a local grid helps users to better understand the specific roles that are occupied inside smart grids and enhance the sense of collective responsibility and action among them. Computational awareness enables the visualisation of different forms of information, while assistance services help users in their decision process to achieve individual and common goals.

8.2 Background

The increased demand for efficiency, reliability and sustainability has driven the electricity network towards smart grids, which use ICT to underpin the network's infrastructure and performance. Specifically, smart grids are concerned with policy demands (to address global warming and carbon dioxide emissions) and consumer demands for low and competitive electricity prices. Other important issues in the smart grid are security, smoothing out peak demand, increased generation from renewable resources, and more importantly, from the point of view of our research, active user participation.

The optimisation of the energy system depends on the users' behaviour and their interactions with the new technologies. User behaviour impacts the smart grid at both individual (e.g. a household) and collective levels (e.g. a community). However, the role of the consumer tends to be ignored by smart grids, as they assume that users will somehow adapt to new technologies. In fact, the main problem that arises from the evolution of the electricity distribution network is the negligence of the user–infrastructure interface and the imposition of smart meters as controlling and distributed sensors that report to a monolithic and central control system.

We propose the use of serious games to support the user–infrastructure interface and encourage active user participation. The user–infrastructure interface is a virtual environment (Almajano *et al.*, 2012b) which integrates information visualisation for comparative feedback (Moere *et al.*, 2011) and new affordances for the smart meters (Bourazeri *et al.*, 2012). Moreover, in the context of self-determination, we seek to encapsulate aspects of self-organisation and support the principles of enduring institutions (Ostrom, 1990) through the same interface. Our aim is to promote long-term user engagement and enable consumers to gain a better understanding, not just of prices, but also of: resource allocation, i.e. electricity distribution among different members of a community; investment decisions, i.e. investment in renewable energy sources, storage, etc.; and sustainability, in the form of low carbon emissions, for example. Finally, we provide users with agent-based assistance to help them in their decisions about both individual and collective goals (Almajano *et al.*, 2012a).

The remainder of this chapter is structured as follows: firstly, we introduce the issue of the user–infrastructure interface in Section 8.3 and we propose combining alternative technological and scientific approaches to address the problem with user participation and engagement in the smart grids. Then, in Section 8.4 we review how we can achieve user engagement through assistive awareness, whereas in Section 8.5 we outline the impact of our research and the goals we aim to achieve. In Section 8.6 we propose the 3D serious game institutions and Section 8.7 presents a game scenario and its mechanics. Section 8.8 gives an overview of various interfaces for smart grids proposed in related works and we conclude with some remarks in Section 8.9.

8.3 The User–Infrastructure Interface

The twenty-first century's electricity distribution and supply network is efficient, functional and can meet normal energy demands (with occasional exceptions). However, the energy generators and distributors have to comply with changing government policies and laws, while meeting targets for reduced carbon dioxide emissions, consumer demand for low and competitive electricity prices, electrification of transport and heating and so on. All these targets should be met within limits and regulations set by policy makers. Advanced communication and information technologies are used to improve the utilisation and efficiency of the energy network, giving at the same time more choices to the consumers and trying to engage them with the new infrastructure.

Although smart grids place a particular emphasis on the demand-side and are predicated on consumer participation, the user–infrastructure interface is still largely neglected and smart meters, which are supposed to be the means for providing information, are conceived as a centralised and controlling technology, rather than as an innovative and enabling technology for making everyday life easier. Energy consumers need to learn how to interact with the new technologies and the infrastructure interface, something that tends to be ignored by smart grids, as they assume that consumers will somehow automatically adapt to these modern technologies.

This problem is of critical importance as the negligence of the infrastructure interface has led to the demise of many water projects related to *common-pool resources* (CPR), such as water management, forests or fisheries. For example, one study (Lam, 1996), focused on the infrastructure development and maintenance of an irrigation management system in Nepal, proved that even though a new technology can improve the performance of an irrigation system, this advance is not enough for effective management and maintenance of the infrastructure. This example highlights that the introduction of ICT to the smart grid may not be enough, as institutions, users' social arrangements and infrastructure attributes need to be taken into consideration as well.

To address the problem of user participation and engagement, we propose serious games as an attractive and engaging interface to train and hold users' attention for long-term decisions and actions. Moreover, smart meters, represented in the user interface, provide the user with a means of managing and monitoring electrical appliances (Bourazeri *et al.*, 2012), whereas comparative feedback could give an overview of the electricity consumption. Finally, agent-based assistance in cooperation with smart meters could give details and advice to consumers on how to achieve their individual goals (e.g. reduced electricity bills) and their collective goals (e.g. smooth out peak demand) goals.

8.4 User Engagement through Assistive Awareness

Computational awareness can help users to better understand the specific roles they are playing within a community by means of visualising different forms of information. Moreover, it can promote the sense of collective responsibility and action among a community's users. This process could be enhanced if all this information was processed and presented to the users in a more understandable way, i.e. by providing users with *agent-based assistance*. Thus, we propose *assistive awareness*, a combination of computational awareness and agent-based assistance, to engage users with the new infrastructure interface, gaining at the same time the necessary experience and knowledge.

Assistive awareness is very important in a local smart grid as users should impersonate different roles and fully understand the goals they want to achieve. For example, in the 'prosumer' (consumer and producer) role, users make choices about prices, which energy provider to get their electricity from, or selling surplus energy back to the grid. In the 'citizen' role, users may be concerned about the impact of their consumption profile on the environment or may have an interest in setting and meeting policies and regulations. All the participants in the local micro-grid should be assured that they receive a 'fair' share of resources with long-term endurance for the collective. This has to be done with respect to a set of institutional rules which have to be followed by all users.

With information visualisation for comparative feedback, users can gain a significant understanding by simply looking at images and figures; since data in any form can be visualised and conceived (Spence, 2007). Comparative feedback should be based on actual energy consumption and provided on a sufficiently frequent basis to be effective (but not over-frequent so as to be intrusive). Consumers should then be able to have an overview of the costs of using specific electrical appliances over a particular time period (Pratt *et al.*, 2010). Receiving feedback on a comparative basis helps users to identify their consumption patterns and observe possible changes in their behaviour towards energy use. Other studies based on the effectiveness of comparative feedback proved that a maximum 12% decrease in energy consumption can be achieved (Darby, 2006; Fischer, 2008). Other findings were that it is more effective than direct feedback and an efficient way to change users' behaviour and habits towards energy consumption.

However, changing behaviour and actions towards energy use could be a very demanding and difficult task. The available information coming from different electrical appliances can be massive, whereas the individual and collective goals can vary with time of use and type of users. An agent-based assistant can help users in analysing all this information coming from the smart meters by providing them with a number of helpful services (e.g. advice on how to reduce their electricity bill).

8.5 Research Impact

Designing and implementing a user–infrastructure interface for smart grids aims to impact users' behaviour: how users consume electricity in the grid; how the rules and regulations affect the introduction of new technologies; how the different incentives and behaviours influence society's values; and how the overall consumption patterns affect energy savings. Users take decisions to pursue a greener and more sustainable environment and promote the grid efficiency, with an ulterior goal of making financial savings. Desired goals (energy or money savings) could also be achieved by giving consumers the chance to impersonate the role of a local micro-grid user in a serious game. Serious games are a challenging and motivating way of increasing awareness towards social and public issues. Energy consumers will understand better how their behaviour and actions affect the grid; taking part in a common pool resource problem will enable the energy consumers to gain the necessary knowledge and experience of 'fair' share and long-term endurance of resources. Finally, users will have a better overview of electricity prices, investment options and decision-making.

8.6 Serious Games for Smart Grids

Smart grids place a particular emphasis on the demand-side, which requires both a better understanding of energy consumers' behaviour and getting energy consumers to understand better the effects of their actions on the grid. User engagement with the grid is of critical importance and the interface of this infrastructure must be taken into account. We are investigating serious games as an innovative way to support the user–infrastructure interface, especially for local micro-grids in which the energy consumers are also producers, who self-organise their own provision and appropriation rules in the context of an institution.

Serious games are digital games, simulations and virtual environments whose purpose is not only to entertain and have fun, but also to assist learning and help users develop skills such as decision-making, long-term engagement and collaboration. They are experiential environments, where requirements to be thought-provoking, informative or stimulating are as important as being fun or entertaining (Marsh, 2011). Serious games can help users to improve their abilities, while at the same time designing and implementing a user–infrastructure interface based on them can engage and motivate users for long-term decisions and actions. Users are able to observe changes in their performance and behaviour throughout this interface, whereas their active involvement, participation and confidence can be enhanced. Another important feature is the collaboration that can be established among players who play to achieve a common goal.

Serious games can be used in two different ways for establishing and encouraging user participation in smart grids. The first way is to set up a virtual environment where users can have direct and active participation in the 'real' grid. The other way is to have a game for training purposes that helps users to better understand problems concerning resource allocation, prices, investment decisions and the grid's sustainability. We mainly emphasise the second way.

The game scenario can be a virtual house, representing a standard house equipped with all the electrical appliances and smart meters, and the users can interact with the appliances and observe their realistic electricity consumption, or they can be provided with agent-based assistance about how to reduce carbon dioxide emissions or save money. Smart meters are like the known meters that are installed on our houses for reading energy consumption, but their advanced features (process and transmit consumer's information to energy providers, provide feedback to users) make them more functional and useful (McDaniel and McLaughlin, 2009). By connecting a smart meter to every electrical appliance, consumers can have a real-time overview of their energy usage; they know exactly how much electricity each appliance consumes at a specific time period. Another advanced feature is a pricing scheme with different prices and variation in tariffs. Smart meters should not be just passive devices for displaying data, but they should remotely control the electrical appliances and schedule them depending on consumers' needs and preferences.

We propose a new user–infrastructure interface for smart grids based on serious games, encapsulating in it Ostrom's institutional design principles for enduring institutions (Ostrom, 1990) (see also Chapter 4). These principles are necessary and sufficient conditions for an institution to maintain a common pool resource. Table 8.1 presents the correlation between Ostrom's principles and user participation in a serious game for smart grids.

Table 8.1 Ostrom's principles encapsulated by a serious game

Serious game	
Ostrom's principles	*User interface feature*
1. Clearly defined boundaries	Game access
2. Congruence between rules and local environment	Collective awareness
3. Collective choice arrangements	Participatory deliberative assembly
4. Monitoring	Smart meters
5. Graduated sanction	Sanctions, incentives and rewards
6. Conflict resolution	Dispute resolution procedures

We encapsulate *Principle 1*, clearly defined boundaries, by having access to the serious game (or not). The online world represents the institution, and membership is needed in order for the user to have access to this online world and play a character in the game. Regarding *Principle 2*, the users should be able to communicate with each other and their smart meters to achieve collective awareness (see Chapter 12) of the efficacy (or not) of the configuration of rules (e.g. the allocation algorithm) vis-à-vis the local environment. Any changes are modified by participation in the deliberative assembly, which is a specialised decision-making forum for collective choice is needed to self-determine any change in the rules (*Principle 3*). Smart meters can have the role of a monitoring agency enabling data streaming (*Principle 4*). Moreover, the smart meters can now have new affordances and capabilities depending on the locations found in the environment. *Principle 5*, graduated sanctions, has been extended to graduated incentives in order for the game to reward successful game play and sanction inappropriate behaviour. Finally, we provide conflict resolution mechanisms in cases where disputes occur (*Principle 6*). For our first prototype, we are not considering Ostrom's last two design principles (no interference from external authorities and systems of systems) and they have been omitted in Table 8.1. Both can be encapsulated to ensure that the serious game cannot be controlled or monitored from the external environment and communication between different institutions is feasible.

Thus, long-term user engagement can be enabled through a 3D serious game interface in which smart meters, information visualisation for comparative feedback and Ostrom's principles for enduring institutions are integrated and encapsulated. A 3D serious game can provide all the necessary means for user participation in the grid, and enable the users to control and guide their avatars (embodied characters). Within the game the following features can be enabled:

- Smart grid representation and simulation, which is the virtual environment (virtual household with all the electrical appliances and the smart meters) where the user can control and monitor the energy use.
- Multi-modal communication, where the users can discuss and set common goals using voice/text chat, gestures and so on.
- Voting system, which can be represented inside a room (similar to real spaces) to allow the players to vote for the rules and regulations of the smart grid and resolve any conflicts which have occurred.
- Smart metering, which is basically the management of the electrical appliances and the monitoring agency for the visualisation of data about energy consumption and prices, which includes comparative feedback that users may receive regularly.
- Rewards & sanctions, for rewarding the good players with prizes or benefits (e.g. high priority in resource allocation), and sanctioning the bad players (e.g. performing inappropriate behaviour) by means of penalties.

8.7 Serious Game Technology

The proposed user–infrastructure interface aims to visualise and represent a community that includes different households, equipped with electrical appliances and smart meters connected to a smart grid. This novel user–infrastructure interface aims to extend the communication bridge between the user (i.e. consumer) and the system (i.e. smart grid). We use game,

3D virtual world (VW) and multi-agent system (MAS) based technologies to build this bridge. We advocate that a serious game for smart grids can be modelled as a virtual institution (VI) (Bogdanovych *et al.*, 2008), the combination of 3D VWs and an electronic institution (EI), which is an organisation-centred multi-agent system (MAS) (Esteva *et al.*, 2004).

Virtual institutions have been successfully used in a variety of e-applications, such as e-learning (Bogdanovych *et al.*, 2010) and e-government (Almajano *et al.*, 2012b). The latter work implements a water market as a VI where participants (human and software agents) negotiate water rights. Whilst the EI models the market (defines roles and interaction protocols), the VW offers a 3D advanced interface that facilitates the active participation of humans within the market. We use VIXEE (Trescak *et al.*, 2011) as the VI infrastructure, a robust *Virtual Institution eXEcution Environment* that provides interesting features, such as multi-verse communication and dynamic manipulation of the VW content.

On one hand, the 3D VW interface facilitates active human participation in the system (in our case, a smart grid). A human gets immersed in the environment by controlling her/his avatar (embodied character) in the VW. Such a VW enhances the visualisation of information about the system and its facilities, e.g. data coming from sensors in the real world (or simulated ones). Moreover, the participants interact in a seamless and intuitive way with the other participants (to perform collective arrangements) and with the environment (e.g. virtual smart meters) by using multi-modal communication channels (voice chat, text chat, information panels, touching objects and gestures). Figure 8.1 shows how humans and agents can interact inside a room of a VI by performing gestures, establishing chat dialogues and displaying information in public panels.

Fig. 8.1 Virtual world populated by 3D virtual characters performing collective arrangements (human–human and human–agent interactions)

On the other hand, the rules of the game can be enforced by the EI, which structures the agent interactions by defining the following components: an *ontology*, which specifies domain concepts; a number of *roles* participants can adopt; several dialogic *activities*, which group the interactions of participants; well-defined *protocols* followed by such *activities*; and a *performative structure* that defines the legal movements of *roles* among (possibly parallel) *activities*.

Furthermore, an *assistance infrastructure* has been proposed, which consists of an assistance layer on top of a MAS (Almajano *et al.*, 2012a). Such a layer is populated by a set of personal assistants (PA). which provide general assistance services to participants within the system. Thus, a PA can provide help to a user to fulfil her/his goals through the assistance services. These services include: information about the system, which can be included in the assembly, when the agent enters the system for the first time; or decision support, which can be useful in the household activity in order to help users to make efficient use of the resources.

8.7.1 *Game scenario*

At the beginning of the game, the player selects which role to impersonate, such as 'prosumer' and 'citizen' in the context of a community. This community is a local micro-grid, composed of different households (see Figure 8.2). The players have to accomplish different challenges which are related to real situations that an energy consumer can face as a daily scenario. Three different activities can be enabled in the game: *presentation*, *household* (see Figure 8.3) and the community *assembly*.

In the presentation activity, the user is informed about the configuration of the game and the different challenges that should be accomplished. The household activity represents each individual household, where the player interacts with the smart meters to schedule and monitor the use of each electrical appliance. In the assembly activity, the members of the community vote for the collective rules that need to be followed in the game concerning electricity use and the sanctions to be applied to players with inappropriate behaviour.

8.7.2 *Game mechanics*

This application is modelled as a massively multiplayer online role-playing game (MMORPG), where multiple users play online and impersonate differ-

Fig. 8.2 The virtual community

Fig. 8.3 The virtual house

ent roles based on a hypothetical scenario, in our case, a local smart grid. The different electrical appliances and the dynamic pricing schemes that are available to all players enable them to complete a number of challenges in the game. These challenges concern money saving, grid sustainability, investment decisions with long-term benefits for both the individuals and the community, and 'green' behaviour.

Particularly in the 'money saving' challenge, the player needs to reduce her/his monthly electricity bill. For this challenge a dynamic pricing scheme is provided which enables the player to check electricity prices among different time slots. The player is also informed about the energy consumption of each electrical appliance that is available in the house. These details (prices and electricity consumption) are pushed through the smart meters that are installed in the houses and provide real-time services and information.

The player should take decisions according to the needs and challenges of the game in order to obtain as many rewards as possible (e.g. stars, badges, points) while at the same time avoiding the penalties (e.g. removal of points). Most rewards and sanctions are given immediately to the players (e.g. when a challenge is accomplished or an improper behaviour is detected), whereas others can be given at the end of the game. Moreover, private and public chats enable the players to socialise and set collective strategies in order to win common goals.

Agent-based assistants can help the players to successfully accomplish their goals. These personal assistants, by processing the current and past data of both the smart meters and the institution, can provide services to users in order to complete the individual and common goals of the community (e.g. advice on when to schedule an appliance).

8.8 Related Work

Designing an interface engaging enough to enhance user participation in smart grids is of crucial importance in order to co-create value. This means value creation does not only rely on the electricity utility company that markets the electricity services but also relies on the users who actively and effectively use these services (Honebein, 2009). Honebein (2009) introduced four key areas in which smart grid customers can co-create value and, in consequence, interaction designers should devote their efforts to develop useful and appropriate interfaces. They are operational efficiency (reduced cost of delivering energy), demand response (reduced consumption at peak times), energy efficiency (avoid energy waste) and load shifting (schedule energy usage). In the following we describe several research works that, in some way or another, address several aspects of these four key areas.

Weiss *et al.* (2009) developed a user interface to monitor the current electricity consumption of individual appliances in a mobile device. The monitoring can be switched on and off and the results can be compared to historical values. Their system includes two additional components. First, a smart meter measures the energy consumption of the electrical devices. Second, a gateway connects the smart meter to a mobile device. This is composed of three parts: a parser to interpret the information coming from the smart meter; a database to store this information; and a web server to provide access to the gateway's functionalities and the smart meter sensor values. Users can then monitor and control their electricity usage remotely.

Other works offer more advanced features. For example, the Aware Living Interface System (ALIS) (Bartram *et al.*, 2011) can accommodate a diversity of energy sources, hardware devices and home control contexts. With the aim of promoting user awareness, ALIS has been designed to take into account human factors, such as physical and visual constraints (place and aesthetic) and the idiosyncratic habits and expectations of users in home environments, as individuals and also as a community. ALIS connects to a web service layer that manages the data and commands of a control backbone which provides fine-grained measurement, device control and automation logic.

Alternatively, Gamberini *et al.* (2012) proposed a mobile web application (EnergyLife) which follows a game rationale to sustain users' motivation while increasing their awareness about energy consumption. EnergyLife provides feedback in a combination of real consumption data coming from individual electric devices and advice on energy conservation based on a user's actual consumption behaviour. Moreover, users can share their new habits with the other members of the community. This application can access data stored in a base-station in each house, which caches the real-time consumption measurements from wireless sensors.

The previous three works enable the user to control directly the 'real' smart grid devices, whereas the interface provides feedback to users concerning their actions. Kim *et al.* (2012) proposes a service interface for the customers who provide power prices and usage information, configuration of electrical devices based on a set of expressed preferences, but also the system can automatically control and manage home appliances according to the power price using Universal Plug-and-Play (UPnP).

We follow Gamberini (use of games to motivate) and Kim (control of appliances) approaches, but we go beyond these by advocating the use of 3D virtual environments as an interface and game which not only engage but also train and influence users' behaviour inside smart grids. We propose modelling a serious game for smart grids using virtual institutions technology, which enables the connection of a 3D virtual world interface to a multi-agent system (MAS). In addition, facilitated by our MAS approach, we also provide the users with agent-based assistance, to help them improve their understanding and their participation in the simulated smart grid and, in consequence, in the real one. Finally, we encapsulate principles for enduring institutions to ensure long-term and sustainable use of energy.

There are other works that rely on games to give the players the role of 'citizens' who take macro-level decisions about generation and use of different sources of energy. These games are currently used by public institutions to inform citizens about the importance of sustainable energy use. *2020 Energy*[1] is a *question and answer* game where the player with the help of three advisers (economical, environmental and social) has to reduce the consumption of energy, increase the energy efficiency and choose the best renewable energy. The aim is to provide the user with a general background about energy usage. *Energetika*[2] is a serious game where the player should sustain the energy supply of a hypothetical state (enact the role of a supplier) and keep track of social, economic and ecological impacts, balancing all the different stakes for sustainable resource management. These games aim to inform users about the consequences of the current energy waste resulting from the passive role they adopt. We focus on the active participation of a user who plays the role of the prosumer. We aim to engage users with new technologies in order to support the sustainable use of electricity in communities.

8.9 Summary and Conclusions

In this chapter we presented how serious games could be used as an innovative way of supporting the energy infrastructure interface, especially for local micro-grids in which energy consumers can also be producers, who self-organise their own provision and appropriation rules in the context of an institution. Comparative feedback and new affordances for smart meters could also be supported through the same interface, enhancing the user awareness towards collective responsibility and actions. Users will gain the necessary experience and knowledge that will enable them to interact and engage with the new infrastructure interface. They will also get a better understanding of electricity prices, resource allocation, investment decisions and sustainability.

The system could be further enhanced by providing users with agent-based assistance. In future work, we will implement our interface as a virtual household, fully equipped with all the electrical appliances and smart meters, and we will evaluate it in order to determine if there is a statistically significant increase in active user participation and engagement.

---

[1] www.2020energy.eu/game

[2] http://www.wir-ernten-was-wir-saeen.de/energiespiel/game

Chapter 9

Norm-Aware Socio-Technical Systems

Bastin Tony Roy Savarimuthu[1] and Aditya Ghose[2]
[1] *University of Otago, New Zealand*
[2] *University of Wollongong, Australia*

9.1 Introduction

Social norms play an important role in shaping human behaviour. They guide people on how to behave under certain circumstances by informing them on what is permitted and prohibited. The growth of socio-technical systems that enable the interaction between humans and technology calls for endowing systems with abilities to understand and facilitate acceptable behaviour as governed by conventions, norms and laws.

Awareness of socially acceptable behaviour (referred to as normative behaviour in this chapter) becomes particularly important when social interactions between humans are facilitated through software systems. For example, researchers working on teleconferencing systems have realized the importance of aligning eye contact between different participants (i.e. the gaze norm) (Jones *et al.*, 2009). So, when a human user interacts with an artificial agent (e.g. an avatar), the avatar's gaze model should mimic (or even replicate) the human gaze model to make the interaction more meaningful for the human. Therefore, the systems in question should detect normative activity and inform affected parties to take appropriate remedial action if there were violations. Otherwise, the presence and the engagement of the users in such virtual environments will be reduced. Thus, one of the key features of a system that is norm-aware (shown in Figure 9.1) is the ability to identify norms from a variety of information sources and recommend those norms to the involved parties. Upon identification, the system should warn users about potential norm violations they might cause based on their choices of actions by observing the history of interactions.

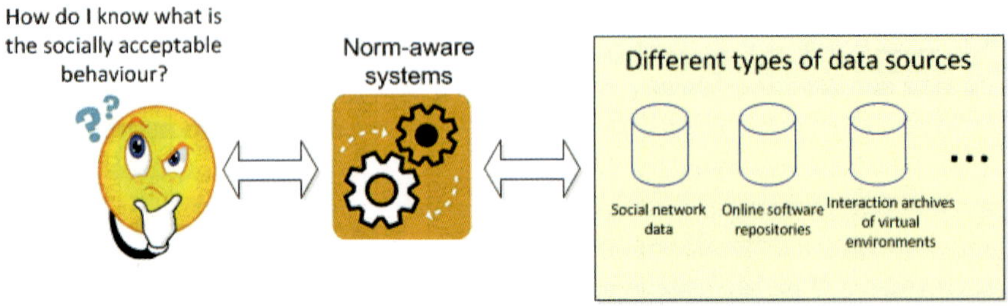

Fig. 9.1 An agent employing a norm-aware system to identify norms

Another impetus for the development of norm-aware systems comes from the availability of large amounts of data (i.e. big data). It is now possible for a computational entity to analyse and extract norms from behavioural data and also have the ability of the entity to reason about them. We define such a system a norm-aware system, one that is *capable of identifying, spreading (e.g. recommending), monitoring and enforcing norms.* Such a system creates a representation of the world based on the data available and reasons about actions that humans or other users ought to (or ought not to) perform under certain circumstances.

Such norm-aware systems fall under the second reading of 'computer after me' as described in the introduction chapter. Norm-aware systems broadly can be categorized under systems that provide 'socio-cognitive' abilities to socio-technical systems. Much of the research work in this direction has been carried out in the area of normative multi-agent systems, where researchers have studied how the concept of social norms can be used to shape the behaviour of software entities in artificial agent societies (Boella *et al.*, 2006). The examples of norm-aware systems described in this chapter (Sections 9.3 and 9.4) typically look at behavioural data and extract behaviour that can be recommended to humans or artificial entities (avatars, bots, etc.). These systems thus are *watching over a user's shoulders* (in the sense of 'the computer is after me'), taking into account the situated environment and also the available action space, and should provide recommendations on what the user should do, what should be avoided, and what the consequences of violations might be.

There are several examples of norm-aware systems that are currently being studied by researchers. These include virtual environments such as Second Life (Rymaszewski *et al.*, 2006), massively multi-player online games (Johansson and Verhagen, 2009), and user behaviour in online software repositories (Savarimuthu and Dam, 204). Behaviour recommendation is also possible from information extracted from big data sources such as Twitter (Kooti *et al.*, 2012). Recommendations for green behaviour (e.g. reduction in power consumption) can also be provided by norm-aware systems that capture power consumption data (Savarimuthu *et al.*, 2012a).

This chapter is organized as follows. A brief background on how social norms are used in human societies for guiding and shaping behaviour and the need for software systems to be norm-aware are discussed in Section 9.2. Case studies on domains where norm-aware systems are being developed are presented in Sections 9.3 and 9.4. Three case studies are presented in Section 9.3 and the fourth (elaborate) case study on sustainability is presented in Section 9.4. Also, the challenges for each of the systems are discussed. Finally, the conclusions are provided in Section 9.5.

9.2 The Need for Norm-Aware Systems

This section first provides a brief background of norms in human societies. Then it discusses why software systems need to be norm-aware.

9.2.1 *Norms in human societies*

Social norms are *generalized expectations of behaviour* in a society (Habermas, 1985). Human society follows norms, such as the exchange of gifts at Christmas and tipping in restaurants. Norms have been employed by human societies to facilitate cooperation and coordination among agents, which enable smoother functioning of the society. When a social norm is in force, members of a society expect other members of the society to behave in a certain way in a given situation.

Due to multi-disciplinary interest in norms, several definitions for norms exist. Elster notes the following about social norms (Elster, 1989) in human societies:

> *For norms to be social, they must be shared by other people and partly sustained by their approval and disapproval. They are sustained by the feelings of embarrassment, anxiety, guilt and shame*

> *that a person suffers at the prospect of violating them. A person obeying a norm may also be propelled by positive emotions like anger and indignation ... social norms have a grip on the mind that is due to the strong emotions they can trigger.*
>
> (Elster, 1989)

9.2.2 *Why should software systems be norm-aware?*

One of the important contributions of computing technology to mankind is the facilitation of the automation of tasks and its ability to assist in human decision making. The ability of systems to further assist humans can be enhanced if the systems demonstrate not only their ability to tackle technical aspects (i.e. *know-how*) but also their understanding of human concerns such as norms, laws, trust, culture, etc. Researchers have argued that norms in particular are the basis of governing socio-technical systems (Singh and Tadanki, 2013). Developing such a norm-aware system is far from trivial since a wide range of variables needs to be considered. Also, the software system should have the ability to learn from a variety of sources and also employ a variety of techniques such as data mining, information retrieval and natural language processing (Savarimuthu and Dam, 204).

A human user interacting with other humans in a social setting is already equipped with norm-inference capability based on his or her previous experience. However, an artificial agent (the software entity) needs to possess norm recognition techniques (Andrighetto *et al.*, 2007) which involve norm identification, norm salience evaluation, norm recommendation, etc. Such capabilities of the agent will help it to make better decisions and improve its overall experience in the virtual environment. These techniques together act as a norm recommender system mimicking the agent's mental prowess at work to infer the norms. The software entity thus displays the quality of being 'socially aware', which is of importance for the development of socio-technical systems.

There are several advantages of norm-aware systems. A norm-aware system can warn humans about norms that they are violating, can offer remedial actions to perform and also assist in policy making to address norm violations. Norm-aware systems can lead to the decrease in the amount of resources used (e.g. by recommending the green norm of duplex printing), and the amount of time spent on analysing social context (e.g. by recommending whether an action is allowed in a virtual environment). Additionally, norm-aware systems are more attractive for humans because they are natural and intuitive to work with, are easy to understand and learn (for the user), and are dynamic and flexible in responding to changes in the environment (as opposed to systems with hard-wired norms).

The next two sections (Sections 9.3 and 9.4) discuss four different domains in which norm-aware systems have been developed and used. Section 9.3 briefly describes three domains and Section 9.4 presents the domain of sustainability in more detail. The challenges in facilitating norm awareness are also discussed.

9.3 Case Studies of Norm-Aware Socio-Technical Systems

In this section we describe efforts undertaken in three disparate domains to make socio-technical systems norm-aware. The primary objective of these systems is to aid human decision-making by making social expectations more explicit. This assistance comes in the form of the software entity's ability to understand the normative context and provide recommendations of appropriate behaviour.

9.3.1 *Human–computer interactions*

Human–human or human–agent interactions facilitated through socio-technical systems need to be norm-aware in order to be perceived as more engaging and effective (Obaid *et al.*, 2012; Jones *et al.*, 2009). For example, researchers working on teleconferencing systems have realized the importance of aligning eye contact between different participants (i.e. the gaze norm) (Jones *et al.*, 2009). Also, cultural differences in the length of eye contact (Obaid *et al.*, 2012) are taken into consideration to facilitate engaging interactions. The same applies to the norm of interpersonal distance between participants in both human societies and artificial agent societies such as Second Life (Yee *et al.*, 2007). As previously mentioned, when a human user interacts with an artificial agent (e.g. an avatar), the interaction becomes more meaningful for the user if the agent follows a gaze model that mimics the human gaze model (Fukayama *et al.*, 2002) instead of the agent constantly staring at the human. If norm awareness had not been integrated in these interactions, the presence and the engagement of the users in such virtual environments would have been reduced drastically.

9.3.2 *Virtual environments and multi-player online games*

Virtual environments such as Second Life (Rymaszewski *et al.*, 2006) and multi-player online games such as World of Warcraft have enabled geographically dispersed humans to have a shared platform to interact (co-operate and collaborate) with one another. Researchers have investigated how human users interacting with one another through computer-mediated interactions infer norms (since norms can be culture specific). In previous works, we have developed mechanisms that can be used to infer prohibition and obligation norms (Savarimuthu *et al.*, 2010, 2013). Sanctions form the starting point for norm identification. Prohibition norms are identified by extracting a sequence of actions (or just an action) that could have caused the sanction by using a data mining approach (Savarimuthu *et al.*, 2013). In the case of obligation norms, missing event sequence (or sequences) that was responsible for the occurrence of a sanction is identified (Savarimuthu *et al.*, 2010). The result of this process will provide a reason for the occurrence of sanctions (i.e. the reason for the sanction is the violation of a prohibition or an obligation norm). There have been other works on identifying norms in work places and making them explicit to the parties involved (Santos and Pitt, 2011).

Though some progress has been made on norm identification, several challenges remain. For example, how can sanctions be attributed to norm violations and not to random actions of ignorance or violence? Also, what are the dynamics of sanctions (i.e. how can sanctions emerge in a society and how can they be identified)? These questions need to be investigated in human societies before appropriate mechanisms can be developed to enable smoother computer-mediated interactions.

9.3.3 *Extracting norms from big data and software repositories*

Huge volumes of data are available online. Software systems can mine appropriate data and present information to the users. For example, based on analysing a Twitter feed an agent can recommend what the convention or the norm is on sending re-tweets (Kooti *et al.*, 2012). A software entity can recommend using the re-tweet (RT) norm using the 'RT' option instead of all the other possible options, since the RT norm is more widely used. This recommendation relies on the ability of the software entity to extract an appropriate norm in real time from massive amounts of data.

Mining software repositories (MSR) is an emerging software engineering research area (Hassan, 2008) that focuses on mining the rich and large quantities of data available in software repositories to uncover useful and important patterns and information about software systems and projects. Such information assists developers, managers, testers, etc. working on those systems by offering insights into the nature of open source software development (OSSD) through the development techniques and tools. A user of the open source project (a socio-technical system) can be informed about existing and emerging norms that are not formally represented elsewhere. Extraction of norms from open source software repositories is in the nascent stages. While the work on norm identification (Savarimuthu *et al.*, 2010, 2013) as discussed in the previous section can be used as a starting point for the extraction of norms in simple cases through the identification of sanctions, the domain of OSSD poses non-trivial challenges. For example, correlating or linking different types of documents containing relevant information is required before a sequence of actions can be constructed. For example, an email message may contain the sanction message exchanged between developers A and B. Let us assume that A sanctions B for not adding a valid comment to the latest version of the file she uploaded. The problem in extracting the norm in this case is that, first, the verbose message sent from A to B should be understood as a normative statement which involves natural language processing. Second, a cross-check should be conducted to evaluate whether the normative statement is indeed true (i.e. checking whether the comment entered by B is invalid by investigating the log).[1]

We believe the general area of computer science is now on the cusp of transformation, where the challenges posed by big data can only be solved by employing techniques from a variety of disciplines. There is a need for developing a normative framework that can identify norms from open source repositories and recommend those to the agents (e.g. new agents joining a society). The proposed architecture should be equipped with appropriate libraries for (a) information retrieval techniques (including natural language processing) in order to identify sanctions; (b) mining software repositories (e.g. cross-linking different sources); and (c) norm extraction (e.g. inferring norms from sequences of events). Additionally, the framework should be

[1]In this example, only two artifacts, the email message and the log, are involved. But in practice, several different types of documents may need to be traversed to find the relevant information. Techniques developed in the field of MSR (Bird *et al.*, 2008; Nagappan *et al.*, 2006) can be employed for cross-linking documents.

able to track and trace the life-cycle of a norm. For example, it should provide appropriate features to capture the waxing and waning of a norm across different periods of time. Norms can start off as a convention and eventually become a rule (or a policy) which should also be considered in the framework (a discussion is provided in Section 9.4.2.5).

9.4 Norms and Sustainability

Design and development of sustainability promoting applications is one of the areas where norm awareness is beneficial (also indicated in the introduction chapter). This section aims to provide a brief summary of applications that are green norm-aware.

9.4.1 *Sustainability and green ICT*

Sustainability is a fairly overloaded term (Johnston *et al.*, 2007). Here we refer to sustainability as a set of goals that human society would like to achieve. These goals aim at promoting activities that meet the needs of the present without compromising the ability of future generations to meet their own needs (Brundtland, 1987). Information and communication technology (ICT) has an important role to play in facilitating the goal of sustainability; it contributed 2% of carbon emissions (Mingay, 2007) in 2007 and this is predicted to grow at the rate of 6% every year until 2020 (The Climate Group, 2008).

Sustainability issues in computing are being studied broadly under the theme of Green ICT. Green ICT is *the study and practice of designing, manufacturing, using, and disposing of computers, servers, and associated subsystems such as monitors, printers, storage devices, and networking and communications systems efficiently and effectively with minimal or no impact on the environment* (Murugesan, 2008). There are two components to Green ICT – *greening of ICT* and *greening by ICT*. Greening of ICT aims at decreasing the impact of ICT systems, such as reduced power consumption through efficient design of hardware and software (e.g. algorithms), reduced resource usage through virtualization, reduced infrastructural developments through cloud computing, improved efficiency through business process re-engineering. Greening by ICT aims at decreasing the impact through the use of ICT in other areas such as finance, transportation, agriculture and energy grids. Applications that help in the consumption reduction of resources (e.g. power bill reduction through intelligent monitoring and control, minimizing fuel consumption through congestion monitoring and route planning, reducing water consumption in the agricultural sector through intelligent infrastructural planning) are increasingly being used. Also, ICT systems can be used to encourage pro-environmental behaviours such as telecommuting and reduced energy consumption.

9.4.2 *Norm awareness through software systems*

We refer to a class of norms called *green norms* as introduced by Savarimuthu *et al.* (2012b). Green norms contribute towards achieving the sustainability goals of a society. Examples of green norms include reduction of electricity consumption, reduction of household and industrial wastes and the uptake of recycling. Green norms aim to facilitate the greening of the world[2] by prescribing activities that are aligned with sustainability goals and proscribing activities that are detrimental to achieving sustainability goals (i.e. obligation and prohibition norms, respectively).

Green norms play an important role in encouraging pro-environmental (i.e. sustainable) behaviour in societies. In human societies there are three broad inter-related categories of green norms. They are personal norms, social norms and legal norms. While personal norms are at the level of the individual, social and legal norms operate at the level of a society or an organization. Policies of an organization are examples of legal norms. Figure 9.2 shows the three categories of norms and their relationships. It also shows examples of green norms under each of the categories.

9.4.2.1 *Personal norms*

Personal norms may vary from person to person (e.g. giving a seat to an elderly person in a crowded bus may be a personal norm for one person, but may not be a social norm). These norms of individuals can arise from moral obligations that they subscribe to (Thøgersen, 2002). Some examples of green personal norms include walking to work, taking short showers, and switching off devices on stand-by. These can be thought of as sustainable living norms of individuals.

Some of these personal norms could potentially become social norms if they were adopted by others. Mechanisms for spreading such behaviour

[2]The concept of greening is closely related to environmental sustainability, which covers a broad umbrella of activities including the reduction of carbon dioxide emission, reducing chemical wastes, recycling, etc.

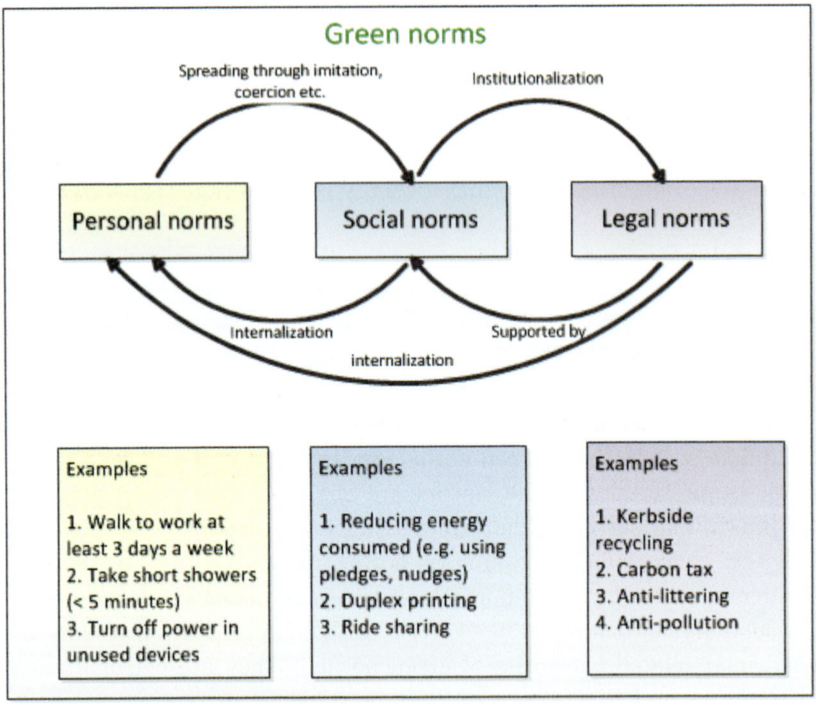

Fig. 9.2 Interrelated categories of norms

include mimetic and coercive forces (Chen *et al.*, 2011). For example, people may imitate the behaviour of an influential person and the speech or actions of powerful individuals can coerce others to undertake green action. Social norms may also get internalized and become personal norms (i.e. the individual no longer reasons about the social norm, because it has been internalized, and used instead to short-cut complex decision-making).

9.4.2.2 *Social norm*

Social norms are shared norms and there is an expectation on the part of an agent on the behaviour of another agent. For example, a user of a park expects another user not to litter. Personal behaviour when shared across a medium (in either physical or virtual settings) can become social behaviour. For example, social norms of a group can be communicated in group meetings or through other media such as email and social networks. Also, behaviours that are not explicit, but may be commonly observed in the community, can be identified and made explicit. An approach called social norms marketing (Schultz *et al.*, 2007) is used for this purpose, where social norms are identified based on observed common behavioural patterns, which are then used to influence people into pursuing appropriate social behaviour. The main objective of the social norms approach is to alleviate misunderstanding of norms.[3] Researchers have found that social norm based messages help in bringing about positive changes in domains such as littering in public places, resource stealing (e.g. theft of petrified wood in Arizona national parks), reuse (e.g. reusing hotel towels) and energy conservation (cf. Savarimuthu *et al.* (2012b)).

Social norms marketing is increasingly used for green norms. For example, the average energy consumption behaviour of a society can be inferred by aggregating the energy behaviour of the individuals in a network and using the information to influence people to change their behaviour (Hunt, 2011). Examples of social norms that have emerged in some societies include reduction in power consumption, using duplex printing mode in organizations and ride-sharing in either a social or work context.

Some social norms may become legal norms (laws in a society or policies in organizations).[4] For example, once a certain proportion of agents adopt a behaviour and that behaviour is demonstrably beneficial collectively, it can be prescribed as a policy (e.g. duplex printing). A discussion of a model and some examples are presented in Section 9.4.2.5.

9.4.2.3 *Legal norms*

Legal norms are the rules and policies monitored and enforced by institutions and governments. Examples of green legal norms include recycling (as prescribed by a city council), carbon tax (as prescribed by governments) and anti-littering norms and anti-pollution norms (as prescribed by an appropriate institution). The legal norms may also have an impact on social norms. Some legal norms are strongly supported by social norms (where the sanctioning is informal when compared to formal sanctions for legal norms). An example of such a norm is the anti-smoking norm. Smoking in public places in many countries is punishable by law and this is strengthened through social norms (i.e. punished socially).

[3]For example, in the context of alcohol consumption among university students, there might be a misperception of the average amount of alcohol consumed by the agents, which can be alleviated through social norms propaganda.

[4]Note that we do not suggest all social norms become legal norms, only that some social norms become laws.

9.4.2.4 *Norm-aware software*

Software programs are increasingly being used to induce changes in attitudes and behaviour among people. For example, in the context of sustainability, a wide range of software applications that disseminate information on reducing, recycling and reusing are being used by governmental organizations and educational institutions. While these systems can induce attitude change, some applications go even further to enable behavioural change (e.g. competition to reduce the power bill).

Software systems that enable the operationalization of these different types of green norms are now available. Avoiding duplicate resources or sharing existing resources is one of the ways by which investments in producing extra (new) resources can be avoided, which also avoids the need for disposing of wastes. Several software applications that target a change in behaviour among individuals have started to emerge. For example, the personal norms of individuals can be monitored by Google Play's market[5] applications such as CalorieCounter, CardioTrainer and AquaMonitor. Also, applications that can facilitate the identification of aggregate green behaviour (e.g. OPOWER facebook application for energy conservation[6]) and its spread have started to emerge.

Several social applications that encourage the adoption of green behaviour (e.g. LiftShare, a ridesharing application[7]) are also on the rise. We believe it will only be a matter of time for applications for tool sharing[8] and toy sharing[9] to appear that will encourage green behaviour. Online games that target teaching sustainability issues have started to emerge (Fabricatore and López, 2012), which have the potential to impact the younger generation. Also, games have the potential to impact both personal norms and social norms depending upon the target of the game (see also Chapter 8). For example, Facebook games such as iGreen or GreenFarm2 target the behaviour change on an individual (hence the personal norm), while collaborative games such as SimCiy and FarmVille target a group of people (i.e. changing group behaviour which may also influence out-of-game attitude and/or behavioural changes of the players).

---

[5]https://play.google.com/store
[6]https://social.opower.com
[7]https://www.liftshare.com/uk/
[8]http://en.wikipedia.org/wiki/List_of_toollending_libraries
[9]http://www.toylibrary.co.nz

9.4.2.5 *From social norms to policies*

Of particular interest is the enabling of policies to be constructed from social norms since some of the green social norms are emergent phenomena (e.g. the buying of electric vehicles is an emerging green norm). Such emerging norms that promote sustainability need to be identified and appropriate incentive-based mechanisms need to be devised to facilitate their uptake. Our previous work has proposed a model where top-down and bottom-up approaches can be combined in the design of policies concerning sustainability. It particularly proposes how emergent norms not yet known can be identified, spread and potentially made into policies (see Figure 9.3). The four steps associated with the architecture are given below.

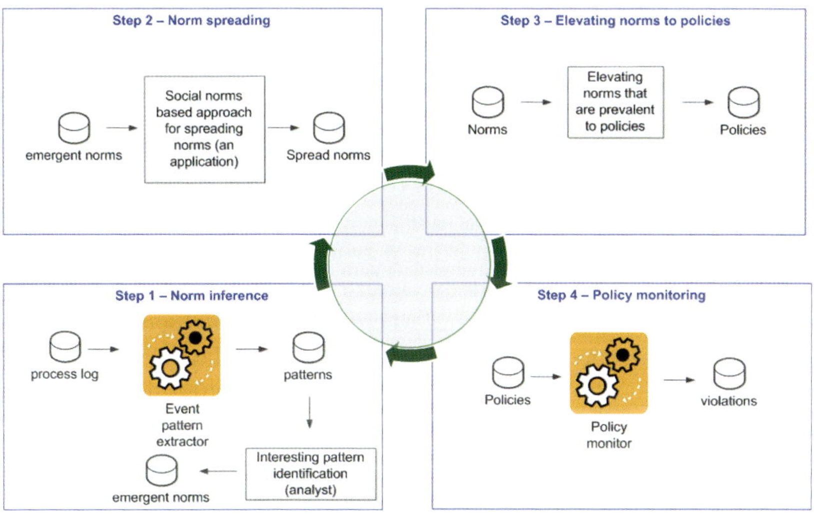

Fig. 9.3 Four steps of the architecture

- **Step 1** The first step involves the extraction (or the identification) of the organization-wide (or society-wide) unknown normative behaviour (emergent behaviour). For example, the normative behaviour associated with duplex printing may not be known in the organizational setting. Without any explicit policy, a substantial proportion of agents may print in the duplex mode mainly because they may have a personal norm to reduce paper waste. However, this behavioural regularity (i.e. a group norm) may not be known to all the agents (i.e. at the organizational level). So, this information can be extracted from the print logs available in an organization and the agents can become aware of the emergent norm.[10] Another example is the OPOWER application on Facebook that uses the social network data to identify social norms (i.e. aggregate energy consumption behaviour) and encourages people to decrease their energy consumption using descriptive and injunctive norms (Cialdini *et al.*, 1990).

- **Step 2** It could be that the emergent norms may be prevalent in some branches of an organization (or in some parts of a society) but not in others. Then, those identified norms can be spread using a social norms approach (Cialdini *et al.*, 1990). For example, the norm of duplex printing might have emerged in one branch of an organization, but not in the others. This norm could be spread through a social norms approach (e.g. exposing this emergent norm to other parts of an organization through emails and nudge schemes) to encourage adoption.
- **Step 3** A certain proportion of a population might already be complying with a norm (e.g. due to norm spreading), but this might not have been clearly articulated and recognized at the organizational level. Thus, the goal of this step is to make those norms explicit policies. For example, 80% of the organization may follow a particular norm, hence, the organization may decide to elevate that norm to a policy. Policies are often formulated in settings where there is broad social acceptance of the norm in question. When, say, 80% of a population already follows a social norm, the exercise of turning the norm into a policy is both a short-cut of the diffusion process (i.e. seeing the observed benefits of a norm, an organization might short-cut the diffusion process by introducing it as a policy), and also a means to ensure that the remaining 20% adheres to the norm.
- **Step 4** Upon successful establishment of a norm as a policy, the agents in the branches are monitored for norm compliance by their peers. The agents report norm violations to the aggregation agent (also called the policy monitor). Appropriate incentive or disincentive mechanisms should be set up at the organizational level to sustain the established practice. We also note there is a feedback loop from step 4 to step 1. The norm inference step includes, in some way, a norm formulation exercise (the analyst plays a key role in step 1, as the diagram highlights). That analyst-mediated norm formulation component is quite

[10]For example, an analyst will be able to extract information about the emergent norm.

likely to be informed by the outputs of the monitoring step (step 4); e.g. a norm that is being frequently violated might require 'tightening', i.e. re-formulation to make it more constraining of behaviour, or to make the associated sanctions more punitive.

A case study conducted at the University of Otago (Savarimuthu *et al.*, 2012b) to investigate how much voluntary duplex printing was done (i.e. without any explicit norm governing this behaviour), showed that about 70% of the users of the deparment of information science printed in the duplex mode. Based on results such as these, appropriate interventions can be designed (i.e. groups of people who do not follow the convention can be encouraged to follow norms through social comparison approaches such as pledge schemes). A natural next stage in this direction is to spread those norms (i.e. normative messages) through appropriate channels, such as emails and social media. For example, a norm-aware printing system can find the duplex printing norm and recommend this to the members that do not follow the norm.

Another domain where norm-aware systems can help is energy systems. Energy behaviour in both organizations and homes can be monitored by applications that can be built in to devices such as smart meters, PCs and mobile phones; appropriate norm-based interventions can then be provided.

9.5 Where To, From Here?

A computer monitor suggesting that you decrease the idle time to 15 minutes instead of 30 minutes before it goes into the power saving mode (based on analysing your behaviour) or a cellphone reminding you to switch off the power of your computer monitor before you go home are very simple examples of norm-aware computing that give the feeling that 'the computer is after you'. Norm-aware systems have also started to recommend what the new conventions of Twitter are, or the new lingo used in a game environment is, and in the future might even warn you not to walk in a particular street in a foreign city late at night (e.g. you might be violating a local law or perhaps risking personal safety), or not to commit the new version of code without adequate comments.

Thus, norm-aware systems act as proxies to human users enabling better decision making. They mimic social awareness by recommending behaviours to the users (how users ought to behave), informing them about the new norms, new patterns of behaviours, etc. There are clear benefits of norm-aware systems. Norm-aware systems lead to a decrease in the amount of resources used (e.g. by recommending the green norm of duplex printing), amount of time spent on analysing social context (e.g. by recommending whether an action is allowed in a virtual environment) etc. These systems improve the overall quality of the user experience and also present themselves as being more socially aware.

Though research work has begun on developing norm-aware systems in different domains, the research challenges are far from trivial. A norm-aware system should have the ability to learn from a variety of data sources and also employ a variety of techniques such as data mining, information retrieval and natural language processing. However, there are several challenges, which include an integration of different norm-aware systems in order to provide a holistic experience to the user (currently different norm-aware systems are developed for different purposes), and integrating contexts between norm-aware systems.

9.6 Conclusions

Awareness of socially acceptable behaviour is vital for future socio-technical systems where the aim is to integrate humans and software seamlessly in the operationalization of a socio-technical system. Since humans bring their innate, in-built notions of expectations (normative expectations) when interacting with software systems, there is a need for norm-aware systems in domains where computer-mediated human–human interactions or human–agent interactions take place. This chapter provides an overview of how the concept of norm awareness is currently being embedded in socio-technical systems. When the concept of norm awareness is embedded in a system it provides a feeling to the user that the system facilitates socially aware interactions and also the sense that the computer is after me (i.e. only appropriate behaviour will be allowed, triggering appropriate behaviour on the part of the humans). This chapter discusses four application areas of norm-aware systems, in the domains of human–computer interactions, virtual worlds, open source software repositories and sustainability. It presents an overview of these research areas and also identifies the challenges for developing norm-aware systems in these domains.

Chapter 10

Interactive Design Activism

Petar Goulev[1] and Joan Farrer[2]
[1] *Targovia Ltd, UK*
[2] *University of Brighton, UK*

10.1 Introduction

This chapter describes a collaborative transdisciplinary research project, called *BarrierSolutions*©, in response to computational awareness of a *health problem*, in this case the potential for skin damage and cancer created by inappropriate use of our natural habitats. From the various elements within the research toolbox created for this project, the importance of sensing and context-sensitive information processing emerged, and resulted in this question:

How can 'aware' computers support 'human' survival?

Design and computer science became the common media through which the various elements developed for the project toolbox were described. In this chapter, two different meanings of the term 'awareness' emerge – 'binary-awareness' and 'fuzzy-awareness'. Using the language of design and computing helped bring about a common understanding concerning potential solutions in relation to the problem of solar radiation and its effects on human health and well-being.

One of the reasons we focused on the natural phenomenon of solar radiation (Robinson, 1966) is its complexity in relation to human survival; on the one hand, supporting and sustaining life, indeed, essential for life; yet carcinogenic in cases of prolonged exposure or individual vulnerability (Lucas *et al.*, 2006).

There are already a multitude of computer applications, particularly within the medical and health domains, which are utilised to support human life. Some examples of well-known successful applications include:

- Regulating cardio rhythms to prevent interruption of blood circulation (Morris *et al.*, 1999).
- Regulating breathing to prevent apnoea where the patient is asleep (Ficker *et al.*, 1998).
- Maintaining cabin pressure, oxygen levels and air circulation within airplanes/submarines (Zhang and Chen, 2007).

At this stage, it is important to note that all of these computer applications require decision-making on the part of the computer that could potentially save or endanger life. The interventions also have the characteristics of being unique for each human being (for example, one person's ideal breathing pressure is individually calculated) and this could change over time (Boisteanu *et al.*, 2009). Such decision-making also adheres to fuzzy rules. In other words, binary (yes/no) solutions are not appropriate: there is no clear point at which the breathing pressure is ideal for every human, and it may even change for the human over the course of a night. Additionally, these applications often involve complex feedback mechanisms, for example, within an aircraft, if the general solution of providing a given level of cabin pressure fails, a fall-back mechanism of providing individual masks for oxygen will be activated (Giguere, 2010).

The applications do differ, however; for example, the first (cardiac rhythm control) is built inside the body and is always present, whereas the second (sleep apnoea treatments such as CPAP machines) is external and used only when the human decides to change their behaviour – to go to sleep and to use the machine. This is an important difference when considering solutions to sun safety and cancer prevention: the latter approach allows the individual human considerable freedom to decide to engage with the device or find another solution, whereas the first relies solely on the medical judgement of another.

It seems plausible, therefore, that computers' awareness will firstly be targeted at protecting the physical entity of the human being. At the present time this seems more easily achievable in comparison with protecting humans' complex psychological world; although the two are not mutually exclusive. One key problem is that human beings, even when they are aware that they have to protect their own bodies, do not necessarily do so. This may be due to lack of knowledge, lack of financial resources, lack of psychological motivation and so on. We would like to go further and state that computer technology is capable of helping with this lack of awareness, especially in the case of lack of knowledge and information. We demonstrate this in later sections of this chapter by examining how feedback mechanisms were implemented in one of the tools in the BarrierSolutions© project, which aims to create desirable clothing made of protective 'smart' textiles incorporating fibres that interact with computer intelligence and digital communication to provide 'early warning systems' of over-exposure to the sun's potentially harmful UV rays.

As the Rio Earth Summit in 1992 identified, the safe usage of natural resources is a complex and ongoing problem (Meakin, 1992). However, information science has shown enormous potential in finding practical solutions to support life in limited human habitats over time, one notable example being the International Space Station Environmental Control and Life Support System (Wieland, 1998). With further technological advances, the potential for the further management of larger hitherto restricted habitats will grow, for example, computer management might support larger geographical areas such as a particular coastline or mountain range (de Freitas *et al.*, 2009).

The environmental impact of computers is not only about how to create and dispose of the machines, as aware computers have the potential to beneficially impact the environment and humanity by mitigating damage and managing human–environmental interaction. As such, through the principles of interactive design activism described in this chapter, computers may facilitate sustainable development rather than work against it. This raises a further question to the one asked at the start of this section: could computers manage a human habitat that keeps the body healthy?

10.2 Computers and Human Well-being

As discussed in the Introduction (Chapter 1), there are many fictional works where the human is perceived as the enemy by highly intelligent computer systems. However, we would argue that, from the aware computer's point of view, its main priority should be not just how to protect individual human life (as suggested by Isaac Asimov's three Laws of Robotics) but also, and further, how to preserve the existence of the human race. Although, for example in the *Terminator* series of films, the 'intelligent' computer (SkyNet) perceives humanity as a threat which should therefore be eliminated (using, amongst other tools, the Terminator robots), we believe that the more aware the computer becomes, the more it will protect the human and its habitat. To a large extent, the best way to preserve human life is to help humans in the safe usage of the natural resources of their existing habitat rather than creating artificial ones. As the International Space Station demonstrates, computers already can support human life through such artificial environments; however, we believe there is much greater potential for supporting human life through computers managing the interaction between humans and their naturally existing environments.

In this chapter, we imagine a computer network that is aware of, and supports the interaction between the environment and the human body. By constantly informing the body owner about its state in relation to the environment across parameters such as temperature, solar radiation, humidity or medical indicators, the potential for responsiveness in terms of behavioural change is offered. One of the key goals of design activism (see below) is a behavioural change, in response to sustainable principles (Farrer *et al.*, 2006). The aim is to utilise the power of aware computers and their interactive possibilities in this context. We can imagine novel applications that offer different ways to raise awareness of a whole range of issues – such as the interaction between humans and solar radiation.

10.3 To Fuzzy or Yes (No)!

An awareness concept battle has been going on throughout the whole of recorded human history between binary and fuzzy modes of thinking and this was the case even before records began. For this reason, we do not expect the appearance of any new computer-driven technologies to be powerful enough to resolve it. Computers have already performed well on both sides, helping their programmers and owners to score points and conquer new subjects and domains from within both approaches.

On the one side is 'definitive knowledge' forming a world of precise formulas, law and order and indisputable rules, known as *binary logic* or the *binary system* as originally formulated by Leibniz in the eighteenth and Boole in the nineteenth centuries. Here, propositions and formulas are either true or false; and sets of formulas are either consistent or inconsistent. Showing that by adding a formula to a consistent set of formulas makes it inconsistent means that the complement of the formula is consistent with the set; this reasoning is proof by contradiction.

The other side is 'uncertain knowledge', representing a world of imprecision, uncertainty and probability, for example through *fuzzy logic* (Zadeh, 1965). Propositions and formulas of fuzzy logic variables have a truth value that ranges between true and false, and so represent a form of partial truth, where the truth value may range between completely true and completely false. Reasoning (inference) in fuzzy logic uses the aggregation of applying fuzzy rules to a set of fuzzy variables.

One way to see the distinction is to compare criminal and civil trials. Criminal trials are more like 'binary' systems, in the sense that the case must be proven 'beyond reasonable doubt', the jury verdict must (generally) be unanimous, and the outcome is either innocent or guilty, and nothing in-between. Civil trials are more like 'fuzzy' systems, in the sense that the case can be decided by a preponderance of evidence, the verdict of the majority of the jury is often acceptable, and the damages awarded can be on a sliding scale.

Based on this dichotomy, we suggest conceptualising computer awareness in two distinct ways:

- 'Binary-aware' computers – where the awareness is modelled and programmed following strict rules based on boolean algebra.
- 'Fuzzy-aware' computers – where the awareness models follow judgments based on 'rules of influence', experience and expertise.

It is clear that both concepts of awareness have their merits and weaknesses; however, it is mathematically clear that fuzzy includes binary at its edges (e.g. if you reach 100% agreement, the answer is 'yes', cf. [Kosko (1994)]). We argue that a binary-aware computer is more threatening to humanity, as at one point in time, it could decide whether the human race is friend or foe. This is portrayed in the *Terminator* movies in which the majority of aware technological robots are against humans with only a minority being for them (and these being absolute states). Similarly, in *I, Robot*, the main computer controlling all robots decides, that for the protection of humans, they must be imprisoned as they could not be trusted to behave safely. "Computer says no" (from the TV program *Little Britain*) is already used as a cultural signifier for binary-computing, albeit one in which computers are used to hide the wrong decision making by large organisations without a human face.

We also argue, therefore, that 'fuzzy-aware' computers may be more forgiving towards humans and will try to conceptualise our weaknesses and beliefs. Instead of constantly judging us in the Aristotelian way, they will try to help us, even when we break the rules encoded in them (as humans are prone to doing). The question of their superiority is not expected to arise in the same way as with 'binary-aware' computers; they will be aware that their decisions are not always correct, which creates equality with humans who also make errors in their judgements. Such computers will be able to avoid Russell's paradox (Russell, 1996).

In the project BarrierSolutions© discussed in this chapter, fuzzy thinking was posited as an intrinsic concept inherent in the sun safety issue. Judging the correct exposure to the sun is not an exact science; there are arguments for and against the utility and damage that it causes. Furthermore, human variations such as skin colour, type and location create infinite answers to the question: how much exposure to solar radiation is safe?

Design activism (Fuad-Luke, 2009), which promotes design in which individuals are given choices through information, is intrinsically linked to a fuzzy-thinking approach. Knowledge is presented, including the contradictions of the current science, and individually tailored to the variations of the human, giving a plethora of options for protection through awareness of the complexity of the issues.

10.4 Interactive Design Activism

Broadly speaking, this shift towards thinking in terms of computer-supported sustainability sits within the movement of design activism. This posits the idea that society can be improved by changing the design of the goods being utilised (Fuad-Luke, 2009):

> *Design Activism is 'design thinking, imagination and practice applied knowingly or unknowingly to create a counter-narrative aimed at generating and balancing positive social, institutional, environmental, and/or economic change'.*
>
> (Fuad-Luke, 2009, p.27)

Part of the design activism programme is the idea that emergent social, environmental and personal problems can be tackled using design practices that are both sustainable and collective; particularly design of intelligent and desirable products to address public health issues and well-being to enable inclusivity and behavioural change. Within the context of the public health issue of sun safety, Farrer and colleagues have investigated designing fashion clothing and textiles that are sun protective (Farrer and Finn, 2009).

Farrer has argued that this is a paradigm shift from the usual medical research model (Farrer and Finn, 2009), because it acknowledges the drive of consumer culture but imbues it with social values to address current societal issues. What is added in this chapter is the notion that through aware computing, particularly fuzzy logic, design activism can be reinvigorated and redeveloped.

Following is an illustration of the potential for aware computing in the context of design activism. This new paradigm, *interactive design activism*, was coined by the chapter authors (Goulev and Farrer, 2013) and enables the issue of the safety of users to be reconfigured. In this case in relation to sunlight or, more specifically, solar irradiation. By reconfigured we mean utilising existing knowledge and technologies in novel combinations to facilitate behavioural change.

10.5 Sensing the Sun

The main source of energy in the human's natural habit is the closest star – the Sun. Strangely enough, the human body does not have a dedicated sensor for the level of solar radiation that causes gradual overheating in living tissues. This is the reason why every year millions of people complain of, and are damaged by, sun-burn. Unlike humans, computers have sensors that alert them to overheating, and can even shut down completely to prevent damage to their material 'bodies' (Bai and Cheng, 2012). Still, humans are able to use their awareness of external environmental factors to alter their behaviour to prevent damage. Meanwhile, sun safety remains a key public health problem about which somewhat conflicting messages exist. On the one hand, health promotion encourages exercise and activity, especially participation in outdoor sports. On the other hand, this creates risks for the human body, primarily through skin cancer (and aesthetic risks also exist such as wrinkles) (Turner, 1998).

Furthermore, the cultural desire to appear bronzed and tanned, at least in many Western societies, with its associations with international travel and holidays abroad, has not abated to any great extent and many people still expose themselves considerably to UV rays to achieve this look. Although there is a general consensus that exposure to UV light (not just in sunny conditions but also in cloudy ones) is risky in terms of skin cancer, there is increasing debate about whether drastic limitation of exposure might also limit vitamin D synthesis, which itself has been linked with a number of health conditions (Wolpowitz and Gilchrest, 2006) such as rickets, and is reportedly on the increase in the UK (Davies, 2013).

As such, sun exposure is both risky and potentially beneficial; although it is widely accepted that very prolonged exposure is likely to be damaging, there is some evidence that in certain populations moderate exposure might be beneficial or protective (Newton-Bishop *et al.*, 2011). At present, computers are able to help doctors with occasional personalised risk assessment (Glanz *et al.*, 2003); however, providing a continuous everyday support targeted to a particular human requires a level of computer awareness that has not yet been developed.

There are several aspects that are relevant to deciding 'correct' exposure: timing, limiting exposure to sunlight (length of time and intensity of radiation), as well as the addition of protective factors such as clothing, sunscreen or using shade (Stanton *et al.*, 2004).

Skin cancer prevention (as opposed to treatment) attracts significant funding from the medical sector, and continues to excite growing commercial interest from the cosmetic and sunscreen industries (Shih *et al.*, 2009), yet melanoma rates continue to increase, as reported by World Health Organization. This research project's overall aim was to develop desirable and wearable BarrierSolutions© coupled with early warning technology that could be used to develop a new field or paradigm shift for investigation, using the emerging field of smart materials and design of 'aware' interactive computer platforms for behavioural change.

In this chapter, given the emphasis on adding fuzzy thinking into sun safety solutions, we focus on one tool in detail: the beach-based UV awareness and communication platform, as illustrated in Figure 10.1. The aim of this particular aspect of the project is to utilise developments within computer science, such as intelligent computing, fuzzy logic and designing non-intrusive sensors, to achieve the goal of offering personalised and interactive feedback on sun exposure information to enhance sun safety.

There is a need for personalised feedback on sun-related risk because not all people have the same level of risk and risk varies according to context (Glanz *et al.*, 2010). For example, recent research has shown that men are more likely to get skin cancer than women. Personalised feedback could also incorporate other dimensions on which exposure and risk might vary, such as different skin types, genetic heritage (e.g. having the genetic variant for red hair makes people more susceptible to skin cancer and less likely to benefit from moderate exposure (Newton-Bishop *et al.*, 2011) and geographical location (e.g. the ozone layer differs in protectiveness in dif-

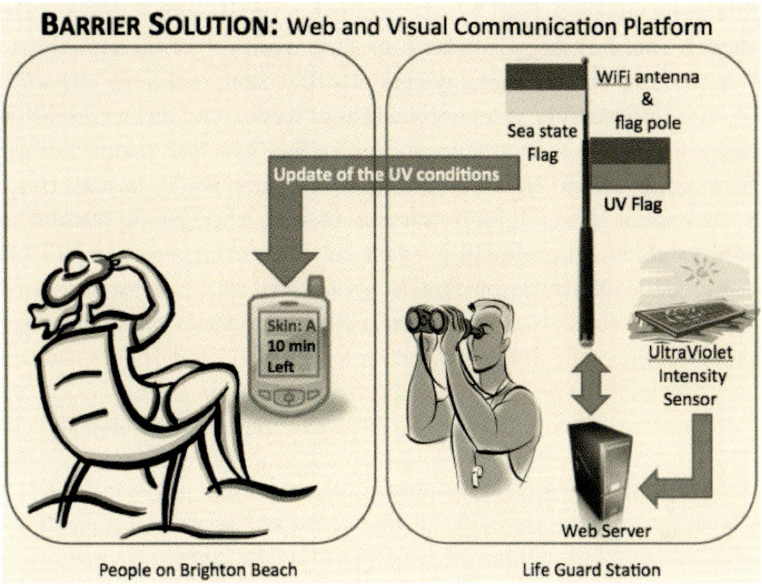

Fig. 10.1 Beach-based UV awareness and communication platform

ferent locations, as well as sun strength). It may also be the case that, at a psychological level, people respond better to a more relevant and tailored message that seems designed specifically for them and their circumstances rather than a generic one.

10.6 Personalised Public Health Advice

Up until now, there has been little research into how interactive intelligent computing systems might deliver personalised public health advice in the context of sun safety. Here, computer software is used to make the user aware of their personal exposure to UV light, based on developing non-intrusive sensors, which previously have been used to monitor the sensory data of individuals to provide an estimate of their emotional state (Goulev *et al.*, 2004), taking into an account an established requirement for personalised sensor technology to be as unobtrusive as possible (Ouwerkerk *et al.*, 2008). There is something of a paradox within our design: consumers are likely to deliberately choose to purchase and/or respond to such an app or program because they perceive themselves to be sun-aware or at risk, but they do not necessarily want to be monitored in an intrusive way. Hence, any such feedback sensors need to 'feel' relatively unobtrusive whilst still offering the user the relevant information that they seek.

To date, a prototype of a mobile system has been developed and tested by the authors. The main feature is an interface in which people input data on their skin type and their current level of ultraviolet radiation, based on their current location. It is important to note that people classify their own skin type, based on broad relevant categories (e.g. red hair/pale skin); in addition, the device is able to use geolocalisation sensors to identify the particular place the person is in. Based on this information, an appropriate personalised time of solar exposure is determined, and then suggested to the user. As an additional way of representing the same information, visual aids are used to provide data about the level of sunlight intensity. Using information and computer technology in conjunction with fuzzy-awareness offers greatly increased levels of personalisation and geolocalisation.

A further advantage of this system is that it can be developed across different platforms to increase availability and coverage: currently the system is being developed using Java, MacOS and Android amongst others. One additional dimension of using these platforms is that it allows much greater access to groups for public health purposes, for example, younger people who may feel immune to the health risks posed by the sun or who do not feel conventional campaigns address the issues they face. By using the existing technologies they use as platforms (such as iPads and mobile devices), this increases the opportunity for take-up amongst these groups.

In terms of comparisons with other sun safety products, this suite of products in development has numerous advantages. One is that such applications fit very much within the sustainability agenda, as they utilise existing technological devices (mobiles, internet), rather than requiring the creation of new products, as with sun screen or clothing. However, there is also the possibility of combining them with existing sun safety solutions. The platform is being further developed, for example, through the inclusion of electro-conductive textiles, which change in response to UV radiation.

10.7 Modifying Human Behaviour

One disadvantage, however, of attempting to modify behaviour through the provision of personalised information is that the platform cannot control the response of the user who may ignore this information in favour of staying longer in the sun or not taking additional preventive measures. This is not likely, given that the user will have had to activate the app/program and input the data, suggesting a high level of awareness of sun safety and motivation to stay safe.

However, even the most 'aware' computer platform, with timed reminders and further sensors input, cannot ensure the user really does modify their behaviour. Aware human–computer interactions should be entirely free and not coercive; the computer offers the opportunity for enhanced human protection but does not enforce it. As such, this interactive system is designed to facilitate informed choices about sun safety by offering feedback that is both personalised and responsive to the user, but ultimately respects their autonomy in relation to health choices.

In summary, it is recommended that interactive computer technology, delivered by 'aware computers', should be designed with sustainability – *people, profit, planet* – in mind (Gwilt and Rissanen, 2011), and this approach can have a transformative impact in relation to sun safety behaviour of humans.

10.8 Transdisciplinarity, Knowledge Transfer and Multi-domain

In conclusion, we reflect on the three interpretations of awareness outlined in Chapter 1, drawing on our experience with the BarrierSolutions© web and visual communication platform. Our interpretation of awareness most closely aligns with the second reading. The 'computer after me' is seen from the point of view of the user – the benefits of computer representation and reasoning about human concerns and actions, and the potential drawbacks. In this chapter, we have emphasised a potential benefit: our work can be interpreted as 'the computer *looking after* me' – although the boundary between care and control should be carefully negotiated (as any parent knows), and privacy concerns should be addressed.

In a dangerous physical real-world environment, often with real-time processing constraints, the computer would be 'aware' of the issues only in a limited sense due to an inability to process the collected real-time data in the way that humans do. Pitt mentions one of the earliest embedded systems, which was developed as part of the US Apollo space programme in the 1960s, in which the requirement for such awareness was critical. Pitt states that in the study of socio-technical systems, which recognises and studies the interactions of people and technology, these systems of awareness give more to humans than just an understanding of their physical environment; they also give an awareness of the rules and regulations commonly understood by people. Similarly, in the web platform considered here, physical parameters (e.g. temperature) are also translated into usable knowledge (e.g. the likelihood of the need to remove self from threat/take evasive action).

Pitt in his summary and conclusions (see Chapter 1) talks about artificial intelligence being used in everyday products such as toasters, and goes on to talk about the proliferation of sensors and processes leading to a plethora of new generation embedded systems with significant interconnected intelligence in computational components interacting in tandem or partnership with humans. These are often referred to as socio-technical or cyber-physical systems. He discusses many application domains where embedded systems involve people, software agents and hardware working together in a collective. He also talks about the future benefits of such applications where using these systems possibilities are limitless.

At its broadest level, the BarrierSolutions© case study methodology presented here is based upon the relatively new concept and practice of trans-disciplinarity. Trans-disciplinarity was first presented by Piaget in 1970 (cited in Nicolescu (2002)) where he suggested that interdisciplinary relations, interaction and reciprocity had limitations because of the specialised 'silo' research these interdisciplinary groups produced. Piaget talked about the concept of trans-disciplinarity pointing to a 'new knowledge space' which will locate these disciplines inside a total system without boundaries. When the term was first presented, the public was not ready for the true meaning of the latin prefix 'trans' and Piaget talked about 'across' and 'between' disciplines to the audience at the time.

However, he omitted a third aspect of 'trans' which is 'beyond', and it is the concept of beyond disciplinarity that is at the core of our project. We have demonstrated not only that computer systems can be utilised by different disciplines ranging over fashion, design, medical systems and so on, but that their creations are truly 'trans-disciplinary'. As such, this project paves a path for design activism made interactive through computing science. Furthermore, as the opportunities for the sustainability of human life to be entwined with computer networks increase, we argue that such activism should rest on fuzzy-aware principles in line with the inherent uncertainty and fragility of human existence in which decision-making, and survival, is rarely black and white.

Chapter 11

The Social Computer

Giovanna Di Marzo Serugendo,[1] Matteo Risoldi[2] and Mohammad Solemayni[3]

[1] *University of Geneva, Switzerland*
[2] *University of Luxembourg, Luxembourg*
[3] *Imperial College London, UK*

11.1 Introduction

The pervasiveness of information and communication technology is creating major changes in our social interactions, in the way we consume, utilize and propagate information, and in our lives. These changes and technological advances bring new opportunities to exchange with others, such as with community supported tools. More generally, we increasingly rely on this combination of human and machine capabilities to share opinions and information and in this way to address complex issues. These issues have in common the fact that neither humans alone, nor computers alone can solve them. Current instances of such complex problems are peer review for conferences, scheduling of all services at large airports with minimal costs and a high degree of reliability, or aviation traffic control.

There exist, however, problems of much higher complexity, such as *hyper-complex* or *wicked problems*, identified by Newman and Gall (2010) as problems that "defy conventional approaches to understanding, planning, design, implementation and execution because: (1) The stakeholder interests are so diverse and divisive; (2) Interdependencies are so complex and so little understood; (3) Behaviors are so dynamic and chaotic (unpredictable)". Wicked problems have no purely algorithmic solution; we often do not know if there is a good solution, or even how to reach a reasonable solution if one exists. This is typically the case in an increasing number of societal and scientific problems, which require a combination of human experience and computational intelligence to solve (e.g. the morphological classification of galaxies, or the digitisation of printed works).

Our vision is to develop a new type of computer, called The Social Computer (TSC). The TSC essence can be paraphrased as *the social computer is a machine-enhanced society*, very much as a cyborg is a machine-enhanced human. An instance of a TSC[1] is a network of humans (individuals, groups) and machines (computers, data, services, sensors) able together and together only to assist experts in solving a specific large-scale (scientific or societal) problem that cannot be tackled by either computers or humans alone. A TSC innately integrates human abilities based on intelligence, competences and skills with machine processing power so that they complement each other. A TSC is a computer because it accepts input data, can store and process it, and can produce output results. It is, however, also social, since it is based on collaboration between humans and machines. In addition and by design, a TSC must operate in an ethical, law-abiding, correct and trustable way.

This chapter discusses this vision and proposes a research roadmap to reach it. It will first review the problem and its research questions, second it discusses the state of the art, and third it presents a TSC structure and its computational awareness. Then, the chapter will consider the research directions to develop, highlighting the discussion with a case study in public policies and democracy, before concluding with the expected impact.

11.2 Problem and Research Questions

There are already instances of primitive social computers that use both human input and machine processing to solve particular questions. These problems however are fairly delimited, and rely on a limited amount of information needed for the solution; also, users are typically domain experts, and can, thanks to their competences, easily treat such problems. Little or no provision is made to account for and take advantage of the social dimension, such as inter-personal communication, human unpredictability

[1] We will refer to 'the social computer' as a concept and 'a TSC' or 'the TSC' as an instance, or instantiation, of that concept, accepting the redundancy in the determiners in the latter expressions in favor of readability.

and/or adaptability, and affective phenomena. Other examples of primitive social computers encompass groups of coworkers supported by computing resources, people playing massively multiplayer online games, or a single person whose activity would be supported by a network of machines. In these cases, however, the matter at hand is often not presented in the form of a problem to be solved, or the decomposition of problems into subtasks; furthermore, the links between humans and/or machines are not established in any principled, problem-solving way. A lot of burden is still placed on humans to identify problems and their solution.

We anticipate that people and society, by using and interacting in principled ways through a TSC, should be able to solve hyper-complex problems. Such issues can be computational (e.g. how to solve a scientific problem that cannot be completely formalized), consensual (e.g. how to reduce the costs of health insurance) or controversial (e.g. how to reduce our carbon footprint). Addressing them will require collecting partial solutions from diverse human and machine clusters, assessing opinion from experts and from the public, predicting the outcome and consequences of individual subproblems, and other similar tasks impossible to achieve by humans or machines independently. A TSC therefore is an integration of humans and machines collaborating together on-demand to solve problems and answer questions. It frees users from organizational burden, helping them in breaking down problems into manageable tasks; it allows deep and exhaustive search of information and data mining in order to obtain partial solutions; and it exploits at best the different human and computational resources to obtain effective solutions. TSCs are not fixed, pre-defined entities like today's computers, but are dynamic, evolving collaborations of humans and/or machines, adapting themselves to the problem at hand.

Central to any collaboration between humans and machines, and thus central to the TSC, are the notions of ethics and trust. Many ICT developments have been primarily guided by the market, leaving behind ethical, legal and psychological considerations. Today's highly interconnected networks of machines and humans offer no ethical warranty. Privacy is becoming a very fragile matter, with sensitive data often stored, used and aggregated unbeknownst to their owners, sometimes with malicious intent. For instance, people have not fully grasped the impact of the reputation of their online persona and their online actions, with undesired social or professional consequences.

The fundamental scientific challenges that such a research vision addresses are firstly, how to concretely solve hyper-complex problems using a TSC; and secondly, how to ensure that fundamental humanistic, ethical principles are included by design in a TSC.

Central to the TSC are also its two constituents: the human and the machine. To account for human characteristics and abilities, a TSC will be able to accept, handle and benefit from unpredictable behavior and evolving opinions; it will take into account human traits such as motivation, lateral thinking and affect. The TSC machine architecture will consist of components of different types such as computers, sensors, services, storage spaces and humans themselves. Given a problem, it will be possible to create on the fly a corresponding TSC to address it: the problem will be analyzed and parsed, decomposed into tasks that will be translated into proper input to distribute to the TSC "computational units", which are humans and machines. The TSC will be able to share the tasks between units, collect and pool their results in a weighted way, and produce a final integrated result as fast as possible and in a way that people can use it.

The above two research questions can be refined by additional technical questions related to theoretical computer science, data mining, HCI, networking and complexity, such as: how to make a TSC trustable; how to 'compile' a hyper-complex societal problem so that a TSC can process it; and how to integrate human input and present output to users. This vision also relates to key human and societal research questions, including: how to motivate people into creating and using a social computer and keeping participants engaged; and how to make a TSC ethical by design.

Additional societal research questions that need to be answered encompass: why do I, as an individual, or we as a society, benefit from a TSC? How is my integrity and my potential as a human and a citizen preserved? How will a TSC integrate in the society's power balance, complementing rather than disrupting the current system? And, why and how can a TSC earn the trust and demonstrate its relevance in problem finding?

11.3 State of the Art

The technological society of today includes a number of resources that can be used for solving problems; not just people, their abilities, knowledge and social network, but also computers, platforms such as social media, and a growing amount of available data and services. Ideally, the best way to use these resources would be to federate them to bring the computational power of machines and the abilities of humans together.

Social computer Social networks and socially developed platforms are dynamic and fast paced environments that have an enormous impact on the life of humankind. From collaborative information resources, e.g. Wikipedia, to the role of social networks in the Arab Spring, the significance of their effect is present in our lives. The idea of fusing human computation capabilities with computers goes back to Licklider's article 'Man–computer symbiosis' (Licklider, 1960; Quinn and Bederson, 2011).

Giunchiglia and Robertson (2010) proposed and coined the term "The Social Computer" or a network of humans and machines that is able to gather and distribute information, solve problems and take actions. They define the algorithmic behavior of a social computer as a network of humans and computers with two layers. The first level or inner loop consists of people and computer collaborating in a social computing platform. The second level or the outer level combines and controls the inner loop to integrate the efforts for large scale problem solving. With their definition, the social computer not only senses and processes information, but also acts in the real world to solve problems. For example, in case of a flood in a region, a TSC can be formed to warn the inhabitants and arrange the rescue operations.

Social computing Social computing on the one hand facilitates the study of society and human social dynamics and on the other hand develops technologies that deal with social communication and social interactions (Wang *et al.*, 2007). Socially developed media have been used for elections, market trend forecasting and sentiment analysis of public opinion (Jin *et al.*, 2010; O'Connor *et al.*, 2010). Jin *et al.* (2010) analysed the rate at which photos of politicians and products were uploaded on Flickr to estimate the outcome of elections and market trends. Tweets collected from Twitter have also been used for detecting public sentiment and opinion (O'Connor *et al.*, 2010). Their findings were close to the polling results collected by polling agencies. In another domain, tweets were used to detect earthquake and typhoon trajectories in real time (Sakaki *et al.*, 2010). The real time system could send a warning to people at risk, thus saving potential victims. These services, though useful, are still only used individually. A greater potential could be reached by considering them as resources available to be dynamically combined to build new services. Social computing on the one hand facilitates social studies and human social dynamics and on the other hand develops technologies that deal with social communication and social interactions (Wang *et al.*, 2007). Many technologies and topics that are being studied in developing a TSC fall under the categories of social computing studies and technologies. However, TSC has a larger scope as it encompasses multiple fields from ethics and law to computer science, psychology and sociology.

Human computation There have been different services and platforms using human workers and their computation power, e.g. reCAPTCHA (von Ahn *et al.*, 2008), fold.it (Cooper *et al.*, 2010), Wikipedia, etc. Wikipedia[2] is a famous example of a collaboratively developed encyclopedia. Games are also used to attract users and make them solve problems such as image labeling (von Ahn and Dabbish, 2004) and protein folding (Cooper *et al.*, 2010). Crowdsourcing is another example of using human workers for monetary or non-monetary rewards. Crowdsourcing has been used in different domains, such as innovation, fund-raising, creativity and design (Howe, 2008). Scientists wishing to find more computational resources turned to the public and asked for help either by asking to use the processing power of people's computers (Anderson *et al.*, 2002) or by asking them to classify galaxies (Lintott *et al.*, 2008) or fold proteins (Cooper *et al.*, 2010). The e-LICO project (e-LICO collaboration, 2009) addresses the data-mining research community and lets users share workflows to solve specific data analysis tasks. Other users can re-use and adapt these workflows. When there is human participation in any activity, the participants need motivation and incentive for their contributions (Quinn and Bederson, 2011). In the case of human computation, the incentives can be monetary (e.g. MTurk), altruism (e.g. samasource.org, wikipedia.org), enjoyment (e.g. image labeling game) and reputation. Requested tasks are generally of low complexity, independent of each other, and require little time and cognitive effort. Additionally, despite these advances, a lot of organizational burden is still placed on humans to identify problems and their actual solution. Therefore, these approaches cannot cope with complex tasks when the problem cannot be specified in advance.

Dynamic decomposition of problems and allocation of tasks Early approaches for human computations involving complex coordination of tasks are based on models for decomposing problems into smaller tasks (Paternò *et al.*, 1997; White, 2004). More recent proposals encompass: programming languages for hybrid human–machine computer recombinations of existing interaction patterns (Minder and Bernstein, 2012); extension of the use of crowds, not only for performing simple tasks, but also for organizing them (Zhang *et al.*, 2011); hierarchical decompositions

[2]http://www.wikipedia.org

of tasks (e-LICO collaboration, 2009); frameworks such as Google MapReduce for processing large arrays of data in parallel, allowing programmers without experience in parallel programming to make use of distributed system resources (Dean and Ghemawat, 2008); and CrowdForge, an extension of the MapReduce framework, where tasks are first partitioned into subtasks, then mapped to workers to be processed, and results finally merged together (Kittur *et al.*, 2011). CrowdForge allows solving problems through micro-task markets, and supports systematic and dynamic decomposition of tasks. Tasks are still rather independent and coordination of tasks is obtained through progressive merging of intermediary results. No particular effort has been made to characterize human tasks at a fine level of granularity, to model how social responsibility intervenes in the solving of complex tasks, or to consider solving other classes of problems such as hyper-complex societal problems.

Self-organizing and self-adapting systems Self-organizing systems are decentralized systems whose individual, autonomous components interact, usually only with their neighbors and with local knowledge of their environment; decentralized coordination occurs through bio-inspired mechanisms such as gossip or stigmergy (Di Marzo Serugendo *et al.*, 2011). The appealing characteristic of these systems is the relatively simple tasks performed by the different entities of the system compared to the global emergent collective result. Application domains include collective robotics (Labella *et al.*, 2006), sensor networks (Fernandez-Marquez and Arcos, 2010), P2P systems (Snyder *et al.*, 2009), and context-aware and pervasive services ecosystems (Viroli *et al.*, 2011). Self-adaptive systems encompass works on self-management and autonomic computing (Kephart and Chess, 2003) addressing issues such as self-protection and self-healing. These works however do not consider ecosystems consisting of heterogeneous entities such as humans, social media services or data sensors grouped together on the fly for a dedicated purpose, nor do they address the range of problems considered by TSC. Some recent work has begun to apply these principles to privacy (Tchao *et al.*, in press).

Privacy, trust and ethics Involving people in a cooperative computing effort raises questions about ethics, trust and privacy. Privacy in a cooperative context, i.e. in a group, has been defined as an interpersonal, dynamic process (Boyle *et al.*, 2009), regulated by norms and requiring a cooperative effort to be carried out. Privacy violations can be deliberate or unintended, e.g. when some action or interaction becomes visible outside of the desired context (Grudin, 2001).

In addition to violations, lack of privacy in a global social computing system presents the potential for surveillance practices (Haggerty and Ericson, 2000). Privacy-enhanced technologies, such as communication anonymizers or bogus online accounts as a means to allow users to keep control of their data do not really convince privacy advocates (Stalder, 2002b; Goold, 2009). More radical scholars even think that the concept of privacy itself is no longer capable of drawing a line at the development of a surveillance society (Stalder, 2002a), although see also the discussion in Chapter 13 (this volume). In computer-supported cooperative work, trust is a central issue as users and participants do not have a complete knowledge of other resources. A modern approach to ensure trust exploits networks of advisors to assess the trust of peers and services (Gorner *et al.*, 2011). When a network of peers changes dynamically, the trust level of new services has to be assessed (Aljazzaf *et al.*, 2011).

11.4 TSC Structure and Computational Awareness

A TSC is composed of diverse *TSC units*, which are available technical or human resources, such as social media like Facebook, the wisdom and knowledge of an elderly woman, or an advanced prediction tool. These resources are "wrapped" in a homogeneous way and exploited within a TSC. Any newly available resource, e.g. tools for sensing crowd opinions, is then wrapped and incorporated into the TSC units. We envisage TSCs to be formed on the fly based on a certain number of TSC units. A complete classification and description of these units is part of the research goals; a preliminary example of what are possible TSC units and how they can cooperate on the fly to solve a particular problem can be seen in Figure 11.1. The figure shows a few examples of how different types of problems (requiring tasks that can respectively be best performed by machines and humans) can be tackled by selecting different TSC units for cooperation, including human intelligence units (HIUs).

The following scenario illustrates how the TSC can solve problems through decomposition, then combination of technological resources and human abilities.according to the following schematic:

- A person wants to address a complex issue, and provides the TSC with a first rough formulation of the problem through an appropriate interface.
- The TSC makes a preliminary analysis of the question, using machine resources and human intelligence as needed. Ethical and legal filtering

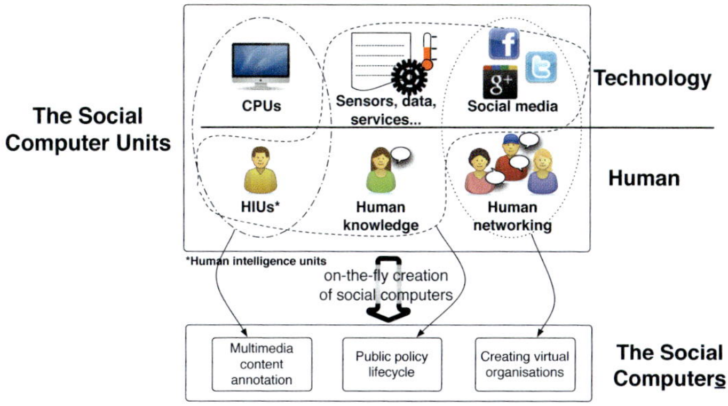

Fig. 11.1 An example of TSC units cooperating to solve particular problems

help determining if solving the problem violates the ethical constraints that rule the TSC activity.

- The problem is decomposed into subproblems whose nature is determined (e.g. a mathematical problem vs. a problem requiring human intuition). Subproblems are dynamically matched to the TSC units (humans and/or machines) that are able to solve them, according to the nature of the subproblems and the TSC units' capabilities.
- The distribution of individual subproblems to TSC units takes into account ethical and trust aspects (e.g. sensitive data are only sent to TSC units that are known to have a good reputation).
- Human traits are taken into account for human TSC units, such as motivation and affect.
- The TSC combines all results from the individual units.
- Finally, the TSC gives back to the original user one or several solutions in a usable form.

The TSC architecture will include components such as computers, networks, services, information and humans, all considered computational units. Facing a specific problem, a user will be able to create, on the fly, a corresponding TSC to address it. The TSC will be able to analyze and parse a problem, decompose it into tasks, and translate these into proper input to distribute to the TSC computational units. It will be able to balance load between units, collect and pool their intermediate results, and produce a final result in a reliable and satisfactory fashion. A TSC will be able to adapt to changes in the situation at hand (e.g. unpredictable behavior, dynamically evolving problems) through self-organization and self-adaptation, and to take into account human traits such as non-determinism, lateral thinking, and affect in a broad sense. The usage of a TSC will comply with carefully established ethical codes of conduct in its handling of information and in its interaction with humans. Adaptation is the norm and is constantly required since humans, involved at different steps of a TSC, may decide to quit, or become unresponsive. Specific machine resources can fail too. Self-adaptation and self-organization techniques will thus guide the TSC behavior. Similarly, outputs produced by the different TSC units, be they human or machines or a combination thereof, are evaluated for their reliability and/or quality through appropriate verification and validation techniques. During the lifecycle of a TSC, services involving sensitive data related to humans involved in the TSC have to adhere to legal procedures (e.g. data protection laws) and contracts arising from the TSC are dynamically established.

This process allows the solution of problems of complexity that defeats classic automated approaches. The breakthrough innovation of the TSC is to involve human intelligence in the interpretation, decomposition and solution of a problem. This is tightly integrated with advanced computerized techniques, so that a complex problem can be fully tackled, both in its computable aspects and in those that require human intelligence. The mix of humans and machines will be able to manage the complex structure of the problem itself, freeing users from the need to break down problems into machine-manageable chunks.

11.5 Methodology and Research Directions

A research roadmap for reaching the vision of a TSC is organised as follows:

Foundations These are concerned with the project's main vision and ambition, including a sound anchoring both in computer science and in philosophical and political theories about democracy. They provide guidelines for the other research directions, and aim at: firstly, defining The Social Computer paradigm, its capabilities and its impact on society; secondly, designing how a TSC works and what is it made of; and thirdly identifying the ethical and legal challenges, providing guidelines for the paradigm to develop in a trustable and socially responsible way. The hybrid human–computer nature of TSC strongly poses the question of whether it is equivalent to a Turing machine. In addition to computation, aspects such as trust and privacy have to be supported as services at the architectural level. Indeed, privacy and control are key issues in the online society. Collaborative platforms and crowdsourcing raise several open, ethical and legal problems, for instance monetary rewarding crowdsourcing platforms have issues including unfair wages and unfair rejection of submitted human intelligent tasks (HITs).

TSC operating system This is mainly concerned with how a TSC is made and operates. It focuses on how to enable TSC units collaboration on the fly, how to organize them to answer problems, and how to maximize the quality and dependability of a TSC. This research direction will apply self-organizing and self-managing principles to address the following: dynamic problem translation and decomposition of tasks, coordination of results, and on-going adaptation to problem formulation and availability of resources. Self-adaptation also encompasses learning mechanisms that observe how problems were solved in the past and tries to extract patterns that govern successful problem solving and associate them with problem characteristics, thus learning problem solving strategies. Main tasks include: developing a model of TSC units and a corresponding ontology; providing an architecture and the corresponding platform for creation of TSCs on the fly; and developing appropriate techniques related to smart content for ensuring ethics, privacy and trust.

Human computation and interactions This is mainly concerned with the human aspect in a TSC. It focuses on user motivation, reliability and engagement related to inter-individual differences, and researches appropriate incentives to maximize them. It is also concerned with interfaces and usability, and the ways to deal with the unpredictability of humans as processing units. Open issues are twofold. First, a user profile has to be built considering human traits, and second, interactions and interfaces between TSCs and participants should be designed and evaluated. User profiling and tracking users' abilities, availability and performance using social and mobile media analysis will help a TSC to assign tasks to the right users and the right time. Building users' profiles and finding the right strategies to motivate and engage users in TSC problem solving are also key challenges that needs to be addressed. Uncertainty and variability of humans, related for example to personality traits or abilities using executive functions (e.g. attention or inhibition), also needs to be taken into account for the development of a functional TSC. Another important open issue is to design and choose the right interfaces, considering different application scenarios, and to study their usability. Finally, the human–human and human–machine interactions should be carefully designed.

Business Model Complementing human incentives, it is essential to devise an economic model aimed at sustaining individual TSCs. This can take various forms that can coexist among a TSC, from crowdfunding, to volunteering, to commercial services, to third party platforms.

Evaluation and validation This is concerned with both human and software aspects. For the human aspect, it relates to the assessment of best means and modalities for interacting and fostering participation. Performance of the system may be assessed by several factors: user enrollment rate, subjective user evaluation (e.g. task engagement and effort) and user effectiveness (e.g. correctness of task completion). For instance, in the policy-making Case Study (see below), a generated opinion could be compared to the one reported by legitimate polling agencies. For the software aspect, it relates to the establishment of software engineering methods for the development of dependable TSCs.

11.6 Case Study: Democracy

The Swiss participative process is exemplary on an international scale, even with respect to representative democracies, where citizens are only involved through the elections of the members of the executive and legislative bodies. However, one might still be surprised by the low participation rates that are often observed in Switzerland.[3] Such rates may reflect low interest in the issues, or difficulty in forming an opinion, either through intrinsic examination of the question, or by forming one's opinion extrinsically, on the basis of others' positions (or, more often, through both).

This Case Study applies the TSC to wicked problems appearing in the public policy lifecycle, more specifically in the field of energy and other issues relevant to the climate and/or the environment, with the goal of improving the solutions that are collectively elaborated, their acceptance by stakeholders, and the overall involvement of citizens. One such example is the decision to abandon nuclear power: is the public debate rational and based on all available information? Is such a decision economically viable? What are the impacts on carbon dioxide emissions? What is the real influence of the nuclear lobby on Swiss politics? The Case Study will design information systems and automatic analysis tools for several stages

[3]International comparisons of participation rates should be taken with a grain of salt: as all Swiss citizens over 18 are *de facto* enrolled on the electoral registers, the rates may appear lower than in countries where citizens have to register voluntarily.

of the public policy lifecycle, from grassroots initiatives to laws and their application rules. The following questions will be targeted: How do we represent and formalize complex political issues, so as to analyze them and reason about them through the use of a TSC? How do we reach optimal decisions for implementation of policies on these complex issues? What are the factors that condition the involvement of citizens using a TSC in the public policy lifecycle? Why is there in many instances a strong resistance or hostility to scientific findings, resulting in controversial debates fuelled by the media (such as climate skepticism vs. the scientific evidence for anthropogenic global warming)?

Several fields of research are relevant to this Case Study, including IT systems for e-governance, and systems for opinion (argumentation) representation and collaborative editing.[4] The field of legal informatics (or AI in law) has been working on the use of information technology to interpret and apply laws for decades. However, the field of policy modelling is rather new and currently several large European research projects have as objectives to formalize and to support policy-making processes.[5] Another stream of research that has been growing stronger in the past five years is eParticipation,[6] where information technology is used to inform citizens (e.g. as in http://www.smartvote.ch), consult them, collaborate with them during the policy-making cycle, and even involve them directly in decision-making. Other relevant fields are opinion mining from user-contributed data, mainly applied to product evaluation and trend detection (see Liu (2010) and Liu (2011), Chapters 7, 11, 12, and references therein).

This Case Study is representative of societal problems that a TSC can solve, here the elaboration of Swiss laws and public policy. More specifically, this Case Study illustrate how a TSC can improve the formulation of a legal text submitted to public vote, by taking into account information regarding its consequences in the light of the stakeholders' interests, as well as improve the users' involvement with the issues that are debated. The Case Study targets in particular issues in which the legal text can be seen as a solution to a complex societal problem, e.g. related to climate change, energy, health or the environment.

This Case Study will initially focus on the *wicked problem* of designing

[4]See for instance http://www.debategraph.org or the WAVE project on argument visualization (http://www.wave-project.eu).

[5]See for instance the FP7 IMPACT project on policy-making using argument modeling from text analysis (http://www.policy-impact.eu), or the WAVE project.

[6]See the Momentum project on e-participation (http://www.ep-momentum.eu).

policies to reduce carbon dioxide emission and increasing citizens' involvement, which raises a number of conflicts between stakeholders, political and ethical positions, and technological challenges. The *users* of this particular TSC are thus mainly representatives of these entities. The TSC *contribution* for this type of problem consists in a service allowing stakeholders to collectively and progressively define a hyper-complex problem and shape its solution. The *innovation* consists of techniques for opinion mining, identification of trends and automatic diagramming of arguments.

11.7 Conclusions

Researching the TSC is relevant to society at several levels. From a problem-solving point of view, many issues of societal importance we are facing cannot be solved by machines or humans alone; there is a need for fundamental studies that will firmly and theoretically ground the way the two can harmoniously cooperate to reach a common goal. From an individual point of view, there is the necessity to develop systems that will innately behave in an ethical, trustable and reliable manner. From a societal point of view, we need to lay out guidelines for the development of very complex interconnected systems to avoid unforeseen or undesirable effects on individuals and society.

Besides its relevance, we expect the TSC to have a major impact on society at all these three levels, namely problem-solving, individual, and societal: the fact that the TSC is a new computational paradigm will de facto allow solving entirely new categories of problems. This in turn should lead to a change in the way we think of problems and formulate them. We expect this radical change of perspective could occur not only in the domains covered by our Case Studies (scientific computation, management of information systems, finance and public policies) but in many others. To cite a few concrete examples where the TSC should help individuals and groups to find solutions to hyper-complex problems in a systematic, efficient, and relatively deterministic manner: science (e.g. helping find appropriate and optimum computational resources); associative life (e.g. for setting up appropriate virtual organizations of volunteers); citizenship and governance (e.g. in shaping laws or urban designs); entrepreneurship (e.g. in bringing an initial idea into an actual product with the help of appropriate experts).

Chapter 12

Collective Awareness and the New Institution Science

Jeremy Pitt[1] and Andrzej Nowak[2]
[1]*Imperial College London, UK*
[2]*University of Warsaw, Poland*

12.1 Introduction

Technological advancement and the resultant explosive growth of accessible information, its speed of transmission, and the globalisation of its audience, have accelerated the rate of change of culture, society and economy to an unprecedented level. This rate of change is compounded by the generative capacity of the personal computer and the Internet, that users can design and develop applications or uses of technology never intended or even envisaged by their designers (Zittrain, 2008).

As a consequence, the rate of change has far outstripped the ability of traditional institutions, which were designed for stability and endurance, to adapt fast enough to respond positively to often unpredictable change. The problem of path dependency, the phenomenon whereby institutions are locked on a trajectory that is extremely difficult to reverse (Collier and Collier, 1991), is magnified, as the institution becomes increasingly out of touch and less relevant to the activity it intended to regulate (cf. the so-called 'law lag', which raises questions about the application and even relevance of legal principles to the technological context in which they are being applied). Furthermore, increasing mitigation costs outweigh the benefits of trust and opportunities for solving collective action problems that are normally derived from regulating an organised collective enterprise within an institutional setting (Ostrom, 1990).

These circumstances have resulted in a persistent crisis in numerous sectors of social and economic activity with many institutions in disarray (RCEP, 2010). There is a dramatic requirement for a new kind of institution and sense of community that are built on principles that elevate adaptation to an intrinsic, first-class property. In a rapidly changing environment, institutions are needed that can achieve resilience by innovation and adaptation and that are capable of capitalising on recent discoveries and suddenly created opportunities, and which empower both grassroots activists and reward large-scale synchronised, coordinated action.

In this chapter, we propose a new 'institution science' which offers the opportunity to develop scientific principles on which to build technology to manage change caused by technology. In particular, we seek to develop mechanisms by which new institutions can be established through a process of *planned emergence*, by combining the powerful forces of ICT-enabled social networking with a new form of collective awareness that arises from the bottom up. We want to integrate this with conventional top-down goal-oriented management for purposeful action, for example to achieve an intended beneficial outcome or to avoid a harmful one. In this way, the potential transformative impact of the 'new institutionalism' will be to pave the way for a new type of intrinsically adaptive institution, by restoring parity between the rate of change of the social, cultural and physical environment in which an institution is embedded with the rate of change of the institution itself.

12.2 Challenges for Institutions

The power and efficacity of self-governing institutions for enduring resource management has been clearly demonstrated and documented (Ostrom, 1990). As mentioned in the Introduction, the twin forces of globalisation and the power of ICT-enabled communication have converged to fundamentally alter social processes and the speed at which their processes operate. In the context of path dependency (present choices are restricted by past choices, even if they are no longer relevant (Collier and Collier, 1991)) and the Shirky principle (that institutions will try to preserve the problem to which they are the solution (Kelly, 2010)), institutions can be rapidly rendered ineffective when the rate of change of society, technology and the environment far outstrips the capacity of the institution to adapt to those changes in time (RCEP, 2010).

However, this 'institution lag' is not the only challenge facing twenty-first century institutions. There are also issues of scale: some problems require large-scale collective action, but individuals do not get feedback from either their participation in the collective or the effect of their contribution to it. This is particularly true of global warming, climate change and other environmental issues. For example, one person turning their television off, rather than leaving it on stand-by, has no discernible impact on energy conservation; a million people turning their televisions off does have an impact on energy conservation, but still appears to have no discernible effect to each of the million individuals. Necessarily, homo sapiens has evolved to establish more immediate cause-and-effect relations between performing actions and perceiving outcomes. Therefore, there is a need for institutions to support collective action and provide this missing feedback.

Institutional diversity and interdependent societies operate at different levels, where the higher levels allow elements at the lower level to achieve a higher level of integration and to integrate larger assemblies of elements. Although a family can coordinate on the basis of interactions between individual members, larger social groups need institutions. As another example, crowd funding may enable financing of a music record or a start up business, but building a power plant requires a bank.

Advances in information and communication technologies (ICT) and connectivity have also brought about two further developments. Firstly, rather than passively viewing end-product content that has been produced by a studio for mass consumption, more people than ever are actively creating content. Secondly, rather than reactively sensing data through their own senses, as a result of miniaturisation, portable devices, implants and the saturation of the environment by sensors (i.e. ubiquitous computing), people are actively creating data themselves, whether wittingly or unwittingly, and this is the basis for some participatory sensing applications.

This is an era of mass-participation content creation, where 'prosumers' (acting as both content creators and consumers) collectively create 'works of mind' using collaborative tools for sharing, and building on, user-generated content. Examples include social networking sites, sites for image and video sharing, wikis, mashups, and cloud services and web applications for computer-supported cooperative work. Increasingly, pervasive computing tools and technologies can be used to collect what is, in effect, also user-generated content, for example using A/V equipment such as cameras and microphones, wireless sensor networks, mobile phones, radio-frequency identification (RFID) tags in cards and implants, and so on.

As the 'value' of many social networking platforms has demonstrated, there are substantial social and economic benefits that can be derived from data-mining both implicitly and explicitly generated content. This has been used for many purposes, some unexpected (e.g. tracking the spread of disease through search engine queries), as well as (more predictably) identifying business, social and cultural trends (e.g. from purchasing behaviour). This value is particularly demonstrated as user-generated content is becoming an increasingly significant component of big data, the vast and interconnected datasets that makes data-mining and analytics such profitable techniques.

We contend that, with the appropriate user–infrastructure interface, coherent visualisation and active participation, big data can be harnessed, as an engine for synchronised action and social innovation. For example, it can be used to develop hitherto unexpected applications, such as supplementing earthquake early warning systems through detecting the movement of mobile phone accelerometers en masse in a localised geographical space. This is an example of implicit user-generated content being aggregated in an application that can save losses in both economic and human terms.

It is clear that we need an entirely new notion of an institution that can re-synchronise people's capability for social innovation with the ability for institutional adaption to match the rate of environmental change.

12.3 Collective Awareness

The development of collective awareness has been advocated as enhancing the choice of sustainable strategies by the members of a community and therefore ensuring the successful adaptation process (Sestini, 2012). In communities in which collective awareness is barely present, individuals may experience the stripped understanding of the global situation and present constrained flexibility in adjustment to change because they do not share the same comprehension of the situation with others. They are also less willing to obey the norms and rules set by the community because they do not feel themselves to be members of the community and are not aware of others considering them as such. They understand the situation they are in from a micro-level perception and might additionally recognise the macro-level description of the situation; however, they might not be aware of interactions occurring at the meso level. As a result, individuals make decisions that are sub-optimal from the perspective of the whole system, making it less fair (according to some fairness metric), more inefficient and so vulnerable to collapse through instability.

However, this work primarily focuses on exteroceptive sensing from sensor networks, providing the ability for groups to sense and respond to their environment, and coordination mechanisms that facilitate emergent behaviour by collective local action. There is almost no work on collective awareness from the synergy of sensor networks and social networks that produces a symbiotic human–artificial network intelligence, or the critical role of institutions in opportunistically linking intelligently directed micro-level beliefs and behaviour to macro-level goals – i.e. the awareness that comes from within, allowing a 'subconscious' critical mass of individual opinions and actions to be channelled by an institution's structures and processes towards driving a 'conscious' collective response at a global level.

On the issue of ICT and social networking for social awareness, the state of the art shows that there is a well-established understanding of the importance of institutions in the conduct of human affairs (Ostrom, 1990), but the challenge remains: to formalise the underlying principles governing the processes involved in the inner workings of institutional (meso-level) structures for collective action, in mathematical, logical and/or computational form, for which recent advances in computational organisation theory are essential (Pitt *et al.*, 2012a).

Furthermore, ICT-enabled social networking tools have proven to be a powerful force for social innovation, supporting collective action and decision-making through subsidiarity and self-organisation, but the mechanisms to make them open and generative (such as the PC and the Internet) are not fully understood. This generativity (the ability to build tools from tools, and from the bottom up) is crucial for supporting social innovation.

Finally, intelligent ICT embedded in a legal, social or cultural context needs to represent and reason with institutional and organisational concepts to support the users properly in understanding the nature and trajectory of the structures they themselves have created (Praszkier and Nowak, 2012), but formal models of these social processes are still lacking.

12.4 A New Science of Institutions

The examples of the previous section illustrate the power of institutions and social networking to enable grassroots activism to support self-organisation for sustainability and social innovation, but as yet it remains entirely ad hoc. What is required now is a new institution science that can formalize these concepts and fully unleash this potential.

We argue that the components of this new institution science are complex social ensembles, interoceptive collective awareness, and planned emergence. We next define each of these concepts in turn, and then bring them together in the computational framework of self-organising electronic institutions. We then consider the potential transformative impact on society.

12.4.1 *Complex social ensembles*

Complex social ensembles are defined as groups of ICT-enabled individuals brought together for some collective purpose, whose underpinning principles are: multi-functional micro-level components (the ability to perform different functions in different contexts); interacting meso-level structures formed by conventional action and agreement of the micro-level components; and the achievement of macro-level objectives through collective, purposeful action regulated by those meso-level structures.

There are a number of theoretical tools from the psychological study of complex systems that can be used in the formal analysis and precise description of complex social ensembles, including:

- a dynamic theory of social impact, which specifies the processes by which a collection of private attitudes and beliefs becomes public opinion, common knowledge, or a form of culture (Nowak *et al.*, 1990). This is a limited form of collective awareness, and what is required now is to extend this theory to understand and explain how people can actively occupy different roles in different structures to help bring about a 'higher' form of collective awareness.
- the bubble theory of social change, which specifies how a sustainable social change may be achieved, and concentrates on changing fragments of social networks (clusters or bubbles) rather than separate individuals (Nowak *et al.*, 1993). In particular, bubble theory can be used to understand better the interaction between these structures.
- the dynamic theory of societal transition, the processes and conditions under which (meso-level) social structures are changed (Nowak *et al.*, 2005). In particular a formal model of this theory will identify and specify how grassroots activists can control these processes in *planned emergence* – the intentional, introspective formation of meso-level structure to achieve desirable macro-level outcomes (and avoid undesirable ones).

12.4.2 *Interoceptive collective awareness*

The formalisation of complex social ensembles exemplifies the underlying principles and the necessary and sufficient conditions for the emergence, adaptation and innovation of self-organising institutions. These are the formal representation of the discrete structures found in complex social ensembles, defining the emergent, adaptive, invented and combinatorial structured rule-sets that arise, and are mutually agreed, in achieving a collective purpose (Ostrom, 1990).

However, in a dynamic and/or resource-constrained environment (such as power systems) there are three interdependent issues. Firstly, to identify and specify the rule-sets that enable such structures to fulfil macro-level objectives and criteria (such as social resilience (e.g. avoiding network overload or trip events) and sustainability (energy conservation)). Secondly, to analyse the 'fitness for purpose' and composing structures that meet such criteria. Thirdly, to ensure that individuals comply with mutually agreed but conventional (rather than physical) rules. Addressing these three issues is not simply a matter of reacting to a sensory perception of the external environment. It is critically dependent on a sense of natural justice; for example, that those affected by the rules participate in their selection. It is therefore necessary to react to a communicated sense that comes from within the community, from each of the individuals, to form a critical mass that supports an agreed course of action – this is what we call (and why we call it) interoceptive collective awareness (i.e. it is a sense like hunger or thirst rather than sight or touch).

Without collective awareness, individuals may neither synchronise nor desynchronise in a situation when it is really needed. Furthermore, without interoceptive collective awareness, grassroots activists, even ICT-enabled activists, may not create sufficient critical mass to achieve macro-level outcomes or control the trajectories of macro-level variables. To realise this requires planned emergence.

12.4.3 *Planned emergence*

The intuition behind the idea of planned emergence is illustrated in Figure 12.1. This shows, on the left, a primordial soup with a limited social network, and macro-level system properties are seemingly chaotic, unpredictable and uncontrollable. Then, through micro-level interactions, public opinion and institutional structure emerge (self-assembly of an institution)

(Nowak *et al.*, 1990), with a richer social network (more connected, stronger ties) (Nowak *et al.*, 1993), and the macro-level system properties are the product of regulated behaviour and so less chaotic and more predictable (Nowak *et al.*, 2005).

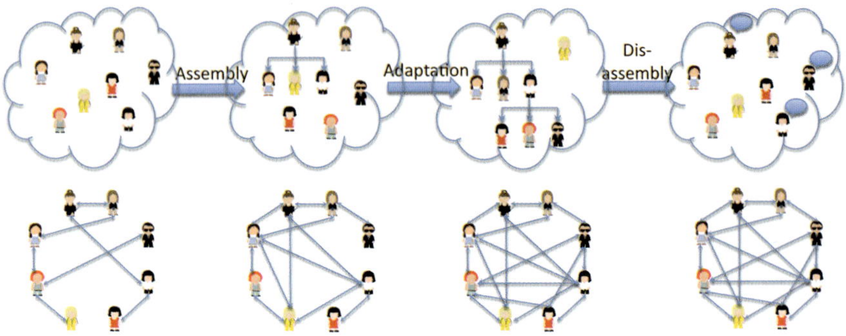

Fig. 12.1 Planned emergence

Going further, we want the institutional structures to adapt and self-organise from within, through interoceptive collective awareness, as a driver for intentional action on the environment, rather than a reaction to an event perceived in the environment. As a result of beneficial outcomes, the social network becomes more strongly connected, and the macro-level system properties are the product of control, i.e. structure, process, evidence and social influence combine to direct the system (via the aggregation of regulated micro-level behaviours) towards benign, intended outcomes for the common social good. This is what we call planned emergence, with one specific emergent feature being its own demise through a form of institutional apoptosis. If the institution is no longer required, it should disassemble, although the 'soup' is left with the more connected network and the individual components retain a memory of the institutional structures, processes and components, for future reference and use (this common memory being a prerequisite for collective awareness).

We note, in passing, that features of planned emergence, such as memory of others, memory of institutions, and the assembly–adaptation–disassembly life-cycle, bear a strong resemblance to planned decentralisation (Binmore, 2005) and its features of empathy, culture and evolution.

12.4.4 *Self-organising electronic institutions*

It was once argued that, in common-pool resource management, the tragedy of the commons was inevitable, the tragedy being that a group of self-interested, autonomous and rational actors required to share a common but limited resource will inevitably act in the short-term in such a way as to irretrievably damage or deplete (exhaust) the resource, even if that is in none of their interests in the long-term.

This could be considered as an example of the emergence of an unwanted or undesirable macro-scale outcome, i.e. the depletion of the resource, from many micro-level actions and decisions. However, Ostrom (1990) showed that the invention of self-governing institutions, which regulate the same micro-level actions, can lead to the intended emergence of a desirable outcome, i.e. the sustainability of the resource, even if/though the actions, decisions and goals of the micro-level actors do not represent its sustainability as a goal. Based on extensive fieldwork, Ostrom also showed that on some occasions the resource endured, on others it did not. She insisted that her research had not disproved the tragedy of the commons; instead she identified eight institutional design principles that were necessary and sufficient conditions for enduring and sustainable resource management (i.e. institutions that were able to maintain a resource). A meta-review has corroborated these principles with only minor clarifications.

In computational organisation theory, the idea of electronic institutions has been proposed as a paradigm for structured interaction in an open computing environment, such as ad hoc networks, virtual organisations and e-commerce, grid and cloud computing and so on. More recently, this work has been advanced through the idea of self-organising electronic institutions for computational sustainability (Pitt *et al.*, 2012a), which endeavours to formalise socio-economic principles and theories within a logical framework for computational organisational theory.

So far, this approach has been applied to two socio-economic theories, firstly Ostrom (1990) on self-governing institutions, and secondly Rescher (1966) on distributive justice. We have shown how the principles defined by these theories can be axiomatised in computational logic and animated in experimental simulations. Specific results include:

- Showing that Ostrom's principles for self-governing institutions can be used for specifying self-organising electronic institutions, with corresponding outcomes for enduring and sustainable resource management (Pitt *et al.*, 2012a).

- Demonstrating that compliance with provision and appropriation rules needs to be complemented by a self-organised system of retributive justice including monitoring and enforcement of proportional punishment (Pitt and Schaumeier, 2012).
- Giving a computational validation to Rescher's canon of legitimate claims to ensure fairness in resource distribution (Pitt *et al.*, 2012b).

These simulations of self-organising multi-agent systems based on electronic institutions suggest that, by using these principles, it is possible for autonomous agents to provision and appropriate resources in an open system, i.e. even in the presence of an economy of scarcity, intentional misbehaviour and accidental failure. It also confirms Ostrom's claim that self-organisation can avert the tragedy of the commons (the inevitable emergence of an undesirable state in which the resource is depleted) through an awareness of the trajectory of the resource and a collective agreement to follow rules that are intended to preserve it. Finally, there is some indication of a resolution to the 'free rider' problem in provision and appropriation situations because it turns out that the optimal strategy is to behave like the majority of others.

This presents two further challenges. The first challenge is how to implement complex theories and processes of social ensembles, interoceptive collective awareness and planned emergence in the computational framework of self-organising electronic institutions. The second challenge is how to leverage big data in the pursuit of interoceptive collective awareness itself. Successfully addressing these challenges may yield the transformative impacts on society considered in the next section.

12.5 Transformative Impact on Society

12.5.1 *Social attitudes and processes*

Planned emergence will have a profound transformative impact on social attitudes, in particular localised decision-making and 'democracy'. We seek to replace the anxiety often associated with delegation and change by empowering individuals to embrace the opportunities afforded by change. We note that one of Ostrom's principles of self-governing institutions (Ostrom, 1990) for sustainable common-pool resource management concerns collective choice arrangements: that these rules work best when those affected by them have a stake or a say in the selection and modification of the rules.

Planned emergence exemplifies and amplifies this principle of participatory adaptation: this research will make it possible for people to use technology to help themselves to create sustainable, self-organising institutions, unblock managerial conservatism that is resistant to innovation, and replace it with a collective entrepreneurialism which drives innovation.

Interleaving the artificial society of sensors and devices with the natural society of humans provides the foundations for ICT-enabled socio-technical systems to address the sustainability agenda, in particular the increased competition for scarce natural resources. This requires understanding the way that devices inter-operate and collaborate; the way that people interact with devices; and the way that devices help people collaborate together. Achieving this would bring about the same transformative impact on social innovation that other socio-technical systems, such as computer-supported cooperative work, deliberative assemblies and serious games, have had on commerce, electronic voting and policy-making.

The scientific impact will be nothing less than enabling social entrepreneurs to use interoceptive collective awareness for engineering planned emergence in complex socio-technical systems. There is a pressing requirement for an open-source platform which would provide a major asset in both designing, and in generating, systems for resilience and sustainability, which can adapt to changes in their environment and sustain critical resources through the versatility of their elements, without the necessity of reconfiguring their structure from the top down. ID3 (the Institute for Data Driven Design), in Boston, is developing a platform called Open Mustard Seed, on which applications could be built providing precisely this functionality.[1] In this way we could use ICT to manage complexity caused by ICT, and in doing so contribute significantly to global participation in the realisation of a sustainable future.

12.5.2 *Innovative service creation and social innovation*

Self-organising interoceptive institutions provide a scientific basis for reverse engineering the processes of institutional adaptation, identifying the necessary and sufficient conditions for successful adaptation, and recodifying those principles as design guidelines, either for re-shaping existing institutions or generating new ones. They will provide a unifying framework for institutional diversity (Ostrom and Hess, 2006) at both ends of the adaptation continuum: from institutions for energy grids or other sustain-

[1] www.idcuded.org

able resource management (water, fisheries, forestry, etc.), which require stable, long-lasting institutions to handle investment decisions that may take many years for the return on the investment to mature, to institutions for emergency response situations, which rise ad hoc, and need to be resilient to extreme and rapid change over short time periods, and dissolve when no longer necessary.

If successful, there will be a long-lasting impact on technology (and peoples' attitudes to their technology), especially mobile devices and other sensors. Combining social networks and the 'society' of sensors and devices through interoceptive collective awareness paves the way for a dual-use functionality for mobile devices, whereby they serve as both the catalysts of change and the seeding ground for the new wave of 'organic' institutions. This demands a new software engineering paradigm to support planned emergence, and a 'higher' form of collective intelligence embodied by devices, which need to be 'aware' of the network externalities, their neighbourhood, monitor the functions and structures of the institution for signs of incoherence, and evaluate the institution to ensure that it is fit for purpose. It also demands a dialogue, for example, between complexity theorists and usability designers, an unexpected interdisciplinary dialogue whose scientific dimensions need to be fully exposed and explored.

12.5.3 *Scientific impact*

The progress of modern science, especially in the area of understanding how complex social systems function, makes the achievement of a new science of institutions a realistic goal. Many lines of research converge on related topics. For example, our knowledge about conditions fostering cooperation vs. competition starts to form a coherent theory. Recent developments in the dynamics of networks provide tools to study processes of self-organisation of social groups and societies. New models of economy and especially financial markets move the field from describing monetary flows to understanding complex social processes that underlie the dynamics of the economy. Research on new types of adaptive and emergent institutions allows us to understand how social groups interacting via technological networks assemble, function effectively over sustained periods (generations), and maintain resources for future generations.

Therefore, the scientific impact of this research may be to increase the degree to which complexity science can affect societies by using new and powerful technologies in thoughtful, informed and innovative ways. This would happen as a result of radical integration of exact, social and economic sciences. The challenge will push forward computer science, especially in the area of creating and supporting socio-technical networks, collaboration tools and usable computer interfaces. Science, pressed by practical challenges, will develop new socially realistic models of emergent social processes. In the social sciences, as the result of integration with formal sciences, many quantitative models will be adopted, which will lead to an integration of theory and practice. In sum, new and emerging communication technologies create revolutionary new possibilities for self-organisation and bottom up coordination of social groups and societies. This represents a potential that was never before available to humanity. The essence of the 'new institutionalism' is to capitalise on this new potential to increase the resilience and sustainability of citizens and societies by enhancing their latent and enduring capacity for innovation and constructive self-organisation.

12.5.4 *Big data*

As well as using interoceptive collective awareness in self-organising electronic institutions to manage common-pool resources, we contend that the big data, upon which the process of interoceptive collective awareness can beneficially draw, should also be viewed as a common-pool resource. Furthermore, when the provision and appropriation mechanisms are automated – for example, provision of user-generated content by stream or pervasive computing; appropriation of that content by search engines, data-mining tools or analytics – we advocate management of the knowledge commons using the same computational framework of self-organising electronic institutions (Pitt *et al.*, 2012a).

As a starting point for this endeavour, the edited volume of Ostrom and Hess (2006) is concerned with understanding knowledge as a shared resource, motivated by the increase in digital libraries, open access science journals, and MPCC (mass produced content creation) social networking sites. It addressed the question of whether it was possible to manage and sustain a knowledge commons, using the same socio-economic principles used to manage ecological systems with natural resources. The various contributions looked at conceptual models, mechanisms for creation, and mechanisms for construction. We need to investigate how these principles can be transformed and transferred to the management of big data, in particular to ensure that the data generators are also the primary beneficiaries.

The explicit use of Ostrom's principles to manage creative commons, knowledge commons and big data enables us to address a number of socio-ethical and socio-economic challenges. The socio-ethical challenges all revolve around a notion of 'justice', including: natural justice, that all users have the right to participate in and access information relating to the decision-making processes that affect their lives and well-being; distributive justice, being concerned with the 'fairness' of a particular set of provision and appropriation rules; retributive justice, the proportionate punishment for wrong doing, including appeals, compensation and dispute resolution procedures; procedural justice, ensuring that those rules and procedures are fit-for-purpose, and interactional justice, which is concerned with subjective assessments about decisions and information related to those decisions. Many of these issues are studied in the research programme of computational justice, which is concerned with importing concepts from the social sciences into computing applications, as well as studying formal representations of justice developed in computer science, and transferring them to social settings.

12.5.5 *Self-regulation*

The requirement for a 'new institutionalism' is already evident in informal principles and policy intentions, and the possible future benefits of a coherent theory and principled application are almost limitless, for example in addressing climate change, economic uncertainty, health and pension arrangements for an ageing population, and so on.

In addressing this requirement for a new 'institution science', we observe that the majority of current studies in complexity science and computational sustainability are critically incomplete, as they omit one or several of four key factors. Firstly, that individuals, ICT-enabled devices and institutions are now deeply entangled. Secondly, that it is possible to equip those devices with social intelligence to be equal participants in socio-technical systems. Thirdly, that out of the entanglement and the intelligence, new dynamical structures emerge which are more responsive, have greater agility and are less prone to path dependency. And finally, that people still retain the power to self-organise these structures and self-regulate their behaviour in the context of these structures according to conventionally agreed rules.

Addressing this incompleteness represents a further impact on science and society. The first will be to show that a new institution science can create a unified account of all four factors, to model and understand the processes behind socio-technical entanglement, and crucially to enable social entrepreneurs to leverage that understanding to produce a powerful force for the common good – this is engineering planned emergence. The second advance will be to show that this concept of planned emergence asks traditional design and engineering schools of thought to help find solutions to the management of complex situations through more 'organic' forms of self-regulation and even self-governance – helping people to help themselves. These, indeed, are precisely the principles and kinds of solution found in the science and technology of interoceptive collective awareness and self-organising electronic institutions.

12.6 Summary and Conclusions

The requirement for 'joined up thinking' between networks of people and networks of the artificial has been recognised as underpinning the concept of adaptive institutions, which are critical for addressing global challenges such as climate change and sustainability. Our vision of where we believe this will lead is illustrated in Figure 12.2.

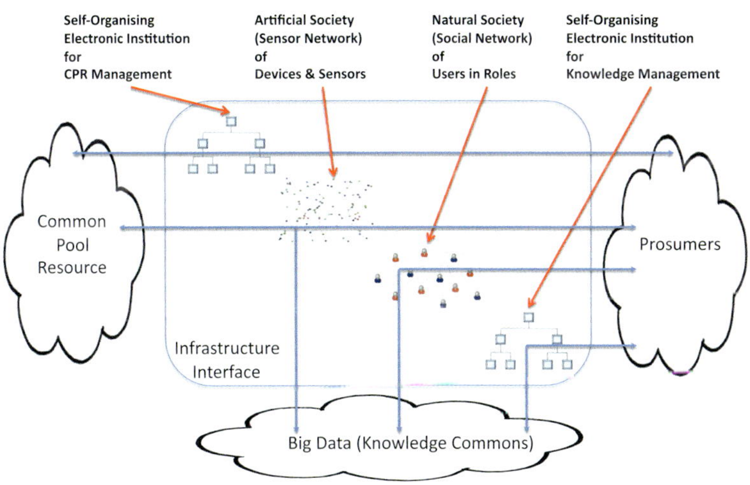

Fig. 12.2 Collective awareness, big data and the new institution science

This picture shows three 'clouds': a common-pool resource cloud, which is some physical resource (SmartGrid, public space, e-learning, etc.); a big data cloud, which is to be treated as knowledge commons; and a 'prosumer' cloud, which is a cloud of users who both provision to and appropriate from the common-pool resource and the data resource.

The user–infrastructure interface then comprises four elements. Firstly, a self-organising electronic institution for management of the common-pool resource, this is a meso-level structure between the micro-level prosumers and the macro-level common-pool resource. This structure is an overlay for the second element, an artificial society of sensors and devices providing the instrumentation of the infrastructure used to access the physical resource. This can be used both to populate the big data cloud and to provide an interface to prosumers through the institution. The third element is a self-organising electronic institution for management of the big data, itself treated as a common-pool resource (a knowledge commons). Again, this is a meso-level structure between the micro-level prosumers and the macro-level knowledge resource (big data). It is an overlay for a natural society (social network) of infrastructure prosumers, who are also generating (wittingly or unwittingly) data streams that contribute to the sum of the big data.

Both meso-level structures are complex social ensembles. It is the interaction between the artificial society of sensors and devices and the natural society of people that is critical to interoceptive collective awareness, and the exploitation of this awareness by the meso-level structures is what enables planned emergence.

Our aim is to empower grassroots activists to use planned emergence to support essential properties of institutions:

- Community resilience as the property of an institution whereby its structure, function or processes can self-organise to react positively to change or adverse conditions to maintain social cohesion and protect community welfare.
- Social innovation as the property of an institution which facilitates, encourages and empowers grassroots participation as a force for change in synthesising or creating new structures, functions and processes, having a specific social purpose and/or intended social benefit.
- Sustainability as the property of an institution whereby its rule-set can self-adapt to ensure pro-actively that a common-pool resource is maintained (not depleted), and distributed fairly.

To achieve this, we are aiming to define a new science of institutions based on computational models of social processes.

Chapter 13

Be Vigilant: There Are Limits to Veillance

Katina Michael,[1] M. G. Michael[1] and Christine Perakslis[2]
[1] *University of Wollongong, Australia*
[2] *Johnson & Wales University, Providence RI, USA*

13.1 Introduction

Be vigilant; we implore the reader. Yet, vigilance requires hard mental work (Warm *et al.*, 2008). Humans have repeatedly shown evidence of poor performance relative to vigilance, especially when we are facing such factors as complex or novel data, time pressure, and information overload (Ware, 2000). For years, researchers have investigated the effect of vigilance, from the positive impact of it upon the survival of the ground squirrel in Africa to its decrement resulting in the poor performance of air traffic controllers. Scholars seem to agree: fatigue has a negative bearing on vigilance.

In our society, we have become increasingly fatigued, both physically and cognitively. It has been widely documented that employees are increasingly faced with *time starvation*, and that consequently self-imposed sleep deprivation is one of the primary reasons for increasing fatigue, as employees forego sleep in order to complete more work (see, for example, the online publications by the Society of Human Resources[1] and the National Sleep Foundation[2]). Widespread access to technology exacerbates the problem, by making it possible to stay busy round the clock.

Our information-rich world which leads to information overload and novel data, as well as the 24/7/365 connectivity which leads to time pres-

[1] http://www.shrm.org/
[2] www.sleepfoundation.org

sure, both contribute to fatigue and so work against vigilance. However, the lack of vigilance, or the failure to accurately perceive, identify, or analyze bona fide threats, can lead to serious negative consequences, even a life-threatening state of affairs (Capurro, 2013).

This phenomenon, which can be termed *vigilance fatigue*, can be brought about by four factors:

- Prolonged exposure to ambiguous, unspecified, and ubiquitous threat information.
- Information overload.
- Overwhelming pressure to maintain exceptional, error-free performance.
- Faulty strategies for structuring informed decision-making under conditions of uncertainty and stress.

Therefore, as we are asking the reader to be vigilant in this transformative – and potentially disruptive transition toward – the 'computer after me', we feel obligated to articulate clearly the potential threats associated with *veillance*. We believe we must ask the challenging and unpopular questions now. We must disclose and discuss the existence of risk, the values at stake, and the possibility of harm related to veillance. We owe it to the reader in this world of increasing vigilance fatigue to provide unambiguous, specified threat information and to bring it to their attention.

13.2 From Fixed to Mobile Sensors

Embedded sensors have provided us with a range of benefits and conveniences that many of us take for granted in our everyday life. We now find commonplace the auto-flushing lavatory and the auto-dispensing of soap and water for hand washing. Many of these practices are not only convenient but help to maintain health and hygiene. We even have embedded sensors in lamp-posts that can detect on-coming vehicles and are so energy efficient that they turn on as they detect movement, and then turn off again to conserve resources. However, these fixtures are static; they form basic infrastructure that often has 'eyes' (e.g. an image and/or motion sensor), but does not have 'legs'.

What happens when these sensors – for identification, location, condition monitoring, point-of-view (POV) and more – become embeddable in mobile objects and begin to follow and track us everywhere we go? Our vehicles, tablets, smart phones, and even contactless smart cards are equipped to capture, synthesize, and communicate a plethora of information about our behaviors, traits, likes and dislikes, as we lug them around everywhere we go. Automatic licence plate scanners are mounted not only in street-lights or on bridges, but now also on patrol cars. These scanners snap photos of automobiles passing and store such data as plate numbers, times, and locations within massive databases (Clarke, 2009). Stores are combining the use of static fixtures with mobile devices to better understand the psychographics and demographics of their shoppers (Michael and Clarke, 2013). The combination of these monitoring tools is powerful. Cell phone identifiers are used to track the movements of the customers (even if the customer is not connected to the store's WiFi network), with the surveillance cameras collecting biometric analytics to analyze facial expressions and moods. Along with an augmented capability to customize and personalize marketing efforts, the stores can identify how long one tarries in an aisle, the customer's reaction to a sale item, the age of the shopper, and even who did or did not walk by a certain display.

The human has now become an extension (voluntarily or involuntarily) of these location-based and affect-based technological breakthroughs; we – the end-users – are in fact the end-point of a complex network of networks. The devices we carry take on a life of their own, sending binary data up and down stream in the name of better connectivity, awareness, and ambient intelligence. 'I am here', the device continuously signals to the nearest access node, handshaking a more accurate location fix, as well as providing key behavioral indicators which can easily become predictors of future behaviors. However, it seems as if we, as a society, are rapidly in demand of more and more communications technology – or so that is the idea we are being sold. Technology has its many benefits: few people are out of reach now, and communication becomes easier, more personalized, and much more flexible. Through connectivity, people's input is garnered and responses can be felt immediately. Yet, just as Newton's action–reaction law comes into play in the physical realm, there are reactions to consider for the human not only in the physical realms, but also in the mental, emotional, and spiritual realms (Loehr and Schwartz, 2001), when we live our lives not only in the ordinary world, but also within the digital world.

Claims have been made that our life has become so busy today that we are grasping to gain back seconds in our day. It could be asked: why should we waste time and effort by manually entering all these now-necessary passwords, when a tattoo or pill could transmit an 18-bit authentication signal for automatic logon from within our bodies? We are led to believe that individuals are demanding uninterrupted connectivity; however, research has shown that some yearn to have the freedom to 'live off the grid', even if for only a short span of time (Pearce and Gretzel, 2012).

A recent front cover of a US business magazine *Fast Company* read "Unplug. My life was crazy. So I disconnected for 25 days. You should too". The content within the publication includes coping mechanisms of senior-level professionals who are working to mitigate the consequences of perpetual connectivity through technology. One article reveals the digital dilemmas we now face (e.g. how much should I connect?); another article provides tips on how to do a digital detox (e.g. disconnecting because of the price we pay); and yet another article outlines how to bring sanity to your crazy, wired life with eight ways the busiest connectors give themselves a break (e.g. taking time each day to exercise in a way that makes it impossible to check your phone; ditching the phone to ensure undivided attention is given to colleagues; or establishing a company 'Shabbat' in which it is acceptable to unplug one day a week). Baratunde Thurston, CEO and co-founder of Cultivated Wit (and considered by some to be the world's most connected man), wrote:

> *I love my devices and my digital services, I love being connected to the global hive mind – but I am more aware of the price we pay: lack of depth, reduced accuracy, lower quality, impatience, selfishness, and mental exhaustion, to name but a few. In choosing to digitally enhance lives, we risk not living them.*
>
> (Thurston, 2013, p. 77)

13.3 People as Sensors

Enter Google Glass, Autographer, Memoto, TrackStick, Fitbit, and other wearable devices that are worn like spectacles, apparel, or tied round the neck. The more pervasive innovations such as electronic tattoos, nanopatches, smart pills, and ICT implants seamlessly become a 'part' of the body once attached, swallowed, embedded, or injected. These technologies are purported to be lifestyle choices that can provide a myriad of conveniences and productivity gains, as well as improved health and well-being functionality. Wearables are believed to have such benefits as enhancements to self-awareness, communication, memory, sensing, recognition, and logistical skills. Common experiences can be augmented, for example when a theme park character (apparently) knows your child's name because of a wrist strap that acts as an admissions ticket, wallet, and ID.

Gone are the days when there was a stigma around electronic bracelets being used to track those on parole; these devices are now becoming much like a fashion statement and a desirable method not only for safety and security, but also for convenience and enhanced experiences. However, one must consider that an innocuous method for convenience may prove to create 'people as sensors' in which information is collected from the environment using unobtrusive measures, but with the wearer – as well as those around the wearer – possibly unaware of the extent of the data collection. In addition to issues around privacy, other questions must be asked such as: what will be done with the data now and well into the future?

The metaphor of 'people as sensors', also referred to as *Citizens as Sensors* (Goodchild, 2007), is being espoused, as on-board chipsets allow an individual to look out toward another object or subject (e.g. using an image sensor), or to look inward toward oneself (e.g. measuring physiological characteristics with embedded surveillance devices). As optional prosthetic devices are incorporated into users, devices are recognized by some as becoming an extension of the person's mind and body. New developments in 'smart skin' offer even more solutions. The skin can become a function of the user's habits, personality, mood, or behavior. For example, when inserted into a shoe, the smart skin can analyze and improve the technical skill of an athlete, factors associated with body stresses related to activity, or even health issues that may result from the wearer's use of high-heeled shoes (Papakostas *et al.*, 2002). Simply put, human beings who function in analog are able to communicate digitally through the devices that they wear or bear. This is quite a different proposition from the typical surveillance camera that is bolted onto a wall overlooking the streetscape or mall and has a pre-defined field of view.

'People as sensors' is far more pervasive than dash-cams used in police vehicles, and can be likened to the putting on of body-worn devices by law enforcement agencies to collect real-time data from the field (see Figure 13.1). When everyday citizens are wearing and bearing these devices, they form a collective network by contributing individual subjective (and personal) observations of themselves and their surroundings. There are advantages; the community is believed to benefit with relevant, real-time information on such issues as public safety, street damage, weather observations, traffic patterns, and even public health (cf. Chapter 12). People, using their everyday devices, can enter information into a data warehouse, which could also reduce the cost of intensive physical networks that otherwise need to be deployed. Although murky, there is vulnerability; such as the risk of U-VGI (Un-Volunteered Geographical Information) with the tracking of mass movements in a cell phone network to ascertain traffic distribution (Resch, 2013).

Consider it a type of warwalking on foot rather than wardriving.[3] It seems that opt-in and opt-out features are not deemed necessary, perhaps due to the perceived anonymity of individual user identifiers. The ability to 'switch off', 'turn off', 'unplug', or select the 'I do not consent' feature in a practical way, is a question that many have pondered, but with arguably a limited number of pragmatic solutions, if any.

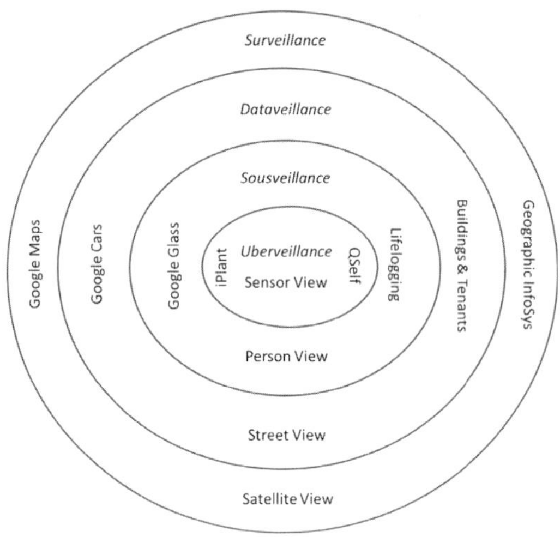

Fig. 13.1 People as sensors: from surveillance to Überveillance

With 'citizens as sensors' there is an opt-in for those subscribing, but issues need to be considered for those in the vicinity of the bearer who did not consent to subscribe or to be recorded. Researchers contend that even the bearer must be better educated on the potential privacy issues (Daskala, 2011). For example, user-generated information yields longitude and latitude coordinates, time and date stamps, and speed and elevation details which tell us significant aspects about a person's everyday life leading to

[3]Someone searching for a WiFi wireless network connection using a mobile device in a moving vehicle.

insight about current and predictive behavioral patterns. Data could also be routinely intercepted (and stored indefinitely), as has been alleged in the recent National Security Agency (NSA) scandal. Even greater concerns arise from the potential use of dragnet electronic surveillance to be mined for information (now or in the future) to extract and synthesize rich heterogeneous data containing personal visual records and 'friends lists' of the new media. Call detail records (CDRs) may just be the tip of the iceberg.

The quantified-self movement, which incorporates data, taking into account many inputs of a person's daily life, is being used for self-tracking and community building so individuals can work toward improving their daily functioning (e.g. how you look, feel, and live). Because devices can look inward toward oneself, one can mine very personal data (e.g. body mass index and heart rate) which can then be combined with the outward (e.g. the vital role of your community support network) to yield such quantifiers as a higi score defining a person with a cumulative grade (e.g. your score today out of a possible 999 points).[4]

Wearables, together with other technologies, assist in the process of taking in multiple and varied data points to synthesize the person's mental and physical performance (e.g. sleep quality), psychological states such as moods and stimulation levels (e.g. excitement), and other inputs such as food, air quality, location, and human interactions. Neurologically, information is addictive; yet, humans may make worse decisions when more information is at hand. Humans also are believed to overestimate the value of missing data which may lead to an endless pursuit, or perhaps an overvaluing of useless information (Bastardi and Shafir, 1998). Even more consequential, it is even possible that *too much* introspection can also reduce the quality of decisions of individuals.

13.4 Enter the Veillances

Katina Michael and M. G. Michael (2009) made a presentation that, for the first time at a public gathering, considered surveillance, dataveillance, sousveillance and überveillance all together. As a specialist term, *veillance* was first used in an important blogpost exploring equiveillance by Ian Kerr and Steve Mann (2006) in which the 'valences of veillance' were briefly described. But in contrast to Kerr and Mann, Michael and Michael were pondering on the intensification of a state of überveillance through increas-

[4] http://higi.com/about/score; http://schedule.sxsw.com

ingly pervasive technologies, which can provide details from the big picture view right down to the miniscule personal details.

But what does veillance mean? And how is it understood in different contexts? What does it mean to be watched by a CCTV camera, to have one's personal details deeply scrutinized, to watch another, to watch oneself? And so we continue by defining the four types of veillances that have received attention in recognized peer reviewed journal publications and the wider corpus of literature.

13.4.1 *Surveillance*

First, the much embraced idea of surveillance recognized in the early nineteenth century from the French *sur* meaning 'over' and *veiller* meaning 'to watch'. According to the *Oxford English Dictionary*, *veiller* stems from the Latin *vigilare*, which means 'to keep watch'.

13.4.2 *Dataveillance*

Dataveillance was conceived by Clarke (1988a) as "the systematic use of personal data systems in the investigation or monitoring of the actions or communications of one or more persons" (although in the *Oxford English Dictionary* it is now defined as "the practice of monitoring the online activity of a person or group"). The term was introduced in response to government agency data matching initiatives linking taxation records and social security benefits, among other commercial data mining practices. At the time it was a powerful response to the proposed Australia Card proposal in 1987 (Clarke, 1988b), which was never implemented by the Hawke Government, while the Howard Government's attempts to introduce an Access Card almost two decades later in 2005 were also unsuccessful. It is remarkable that same issues ensue today, only on a greater magnitude with more consequences and advanced capabilities in analytics, data storage, and converging systems.

13.4.3 *Sousveillance*

Sousveillance was defined by Steve Mann in 2002, but practiced since 1995 as "the recording of an activity from the perspective of a participant in the activity".[5] However, its initial introduction into the literature came in the

[5] http://www.wordnik.com/words/sousveillance

inaugural *Surveillance and Society* journal in 2003 with a meaning of 'inverse surveillance' as a counter to organizational surveillance (Mann *et al.*, 2003). Mann prefers to interpret sousveillance as under-sight, which maintains integrity, contra to surveillance as over-sight (Mann, 2004a), which reduces to hypocrisy if governments responsible for surveillance pass laws to make sousveillance illegal.

Whereas dataveillance is the systematic use of personal data systems in the monitoring of people, sousveillance is the inverse of monitoring people; it is the continuous capture of personal experience (Mann, 2004b). For example, dataveillance might include the linking of someone's tax file number with their bank account details and communications data. Sousveillance on the other hand, is a voluntary act of logging what people might see as they move through the world. Surveillance is thus considered watching from above, whereas sousveillance is considered watching from below. In contrast, dataveillance is the monitoring of a person's activities which presents the individual with numerous social dangers (Clarke, 1988a).

13.4.4 *Überveillance*

Überveillance conceived by M. G. Michael in 2006, is defined in the *Australian Law Dictionary* as: "ubiquitous or pervasive electronic surveillance that is not only 'always on' but 'always with you', ultimately in the form of bodily invasive surveillance". The *Macquarie Dictionary of Australia* entered the term officially in 2008 as "an omnipresent electronic surveillance facilitated by technology that makes it possible to embed surveillance devices in the human body". Michael and Michael (2007) defined überveillance as having "to do with the fundamental who (ID), where (location), and when (time) questions in an attempt to derive why (motivation), what (result), and even how (method/plan/thought)".

Überveillance is a compound word, conjoining the German *über* meaning 'over' or 'above' with the French *veillance*. The concept is very much linked to Friedrich Nietzsche's vision of the *übermensch*, who is a man with powers beyond those of an ordinary human being, like a super-man with amplified abilities (Michael and Michael, 2010). Überveillance is analogous to big brother on the inside looking out. For example, heart, pulse, and temperature sensor readings emanating from the body in binary bits wirelessly, or even through amplified eyes such as inserted contact lens 'glass' that might provide visual display and access to the Internet or social networking applications.

Überveillance brings together all forms of watching from above and from below, from machines that move to those that stand still, from animals and from people, acquired involuntarily or voluntarily using obtrusive or unobtrusive devices (Michael *et al.*, 2010). The network infrastructure underlies the ability to collect data direct from the sensor devices worn by the individual and big data analytics ensures an interpretation of the unique behavioral traits of the individual, implying more than just predicted movement, but intent and thought (Michael and Miller, 2013).

It has been said that überveillance is that part of the veillance puzzle that brings together the sur, data, and sous to an intersecting point (Stephan *et al.*, 2012). In überveillance, there is the 'watching' from above component (sur), there is the 'collecting' of personal data and public data for mining (data), and there is the watching from below (sous), which can draw together social networks and strangers, all coming together via wearable and implantable devices on/in the human body. Überveillance can be used for good in the practice of health for instance, but we contend that, independent of its application for non-medical purposes, it will always have an underlying control factor (Masters and Michael, 2006).

13.5 Colliding Principles

13.5.1 *From 'drone view' to 'person view'*

It can be argued that, because a CCTV camera is monitoring activities from above, we should have the 'counter-right' to monitor the world around us from below. It therefore follows, if Google can record 'street views', then the average citizen should also be able to engage in that same act, which we may call 'person view'. Our laws as a rule do not forbid recording the world around us (or even each other for that matter), so long as we are not encroaching on someone else's well-being or privacy (e.g. stalking, or making material public without expressed consent). While we have Street View today, it will only be a matter of time before we have 'drones as a service' (DaaS) products that systematically provide even better high resolution imagery than 'satellite views'. We can make 'drone view' available on Google Maps, as we could probably also make 'person view' available. Want to look up not only a street, but a person if they are logged in and registered? Then search 'John Doe' and find the nearest camera pointing toward him, and/or emanating from him. Call it a triangulation of sorts.

13.5.2 *Transparency and open data*

The benefits of this kind of transparency, argue numerous scholars, are that not only will we have a perfect source of open data to work with, but that there will be less crime as people consider the repercussions of being caught doing wrong in real-time. However, this is quite an idealistic paradigm and ethically flawed. Criminals, and non-criminals for that matter, find ways around all secure processes, no matter how technologically foolproof. At that point, the technical elite might well be systematically hiding or erasing their recorded misdemeanours but no doubt keeping the innocent person under 24/7/365 watch. There are, however, varying degrees to transparency, and most of these have to do with economies of scale and/or are context-based; they have to be. In short, transparency needs to be context related.

13.5.3 *Surveillance, listening devices and the law*

At what point do we actually believe that in a public space our privacy is not invaded by such incremental innovations as little wearable cameras, half the size of a matchbox, worn as lifelogging devices? One could speculate that the sheer size of these devices makes them unobtrusive and not easily detectable to the naked eye, meaning that they are covert in nature and blatantly break the law in some jurisdictions where they are worn and operational (Abbas *et al.*, 2011). Some of these devices not only capture images every 30 seconds, but also record audio, making them potentially a form of unauthorized surveillance. It is also not always apparent when these devices are on or off. We must consider that the "unrestricted freedom of some may endanger the well-being, privacy, or safety of others" (Rodota and Capurro, 2005, p. 23). Where are the distinctions between the wearer's right to capture his or her own personal experiences on the one hand (i.e. the unrestricted freedom of some), and intrusion into another's private sphere in which he or she does not want to be recorded, and is perhaps even disturbed by the prospect of losing control over his or her privacy (i.e. endangering the well-being or privacy of others)?

13.5.4 *Ethics and values*

Enter ethics and values. Ethics in this debate are greatly important. They have been dangerously pushed aside, for it is ethics that determine the degree of importance, that is the value, we place on the levels of our decision-making. When is it right to take photographs and record another individual (even in a public space), and when is it wrong? Do I physically remove my wearable device when I enter a washroom, a leisure centre, a hospital, a funeral, someone else's home, a bedroom? Do I need to ask express permission from someone to record them, even if I am a participant in a shared activity? What about unobtrusive devices that blur the line between wearables and implantables, such as miniature recording devices embedded in spectacle frames or eye sockets and possibly in the future embedded in contact lenses? Do I have to tell my future partner or prospective employer? Should I declare these during the immigration process before I enter the secure zone?

At the same time, independent of how much crowdsourced evidence is gathered for a given event, wearables and implantables are not infallible, their sensors can easily misrepresent reality through inaccurate or incomplete readings and data can be even further misconstrued post capture (Michael and Michael, 2007). This is the limitation of an überveillance society – devices are equipped with a myriad of sensors; they are celebrated as achieving near omnipresence, but the reality is that they will never be able to achieve omniscience. Finite knowledge and imperfect awareness create much potential for inadequate or incomplete interpretations.

Some technologists believe that they need to rewrite the books on metaphysics and ontology, as a result of old and outmoded definitions in the traditional humanities. We must be wary of our increasing 'technicized' environment however, and continue to test ourselves on the values we hold as canonical, which go towards defining a free and autonomous human being. The protection of personal data has been deemed by the EU as an autonomous individual right.

Yet, with such pervasive data collection, how will we protect "the right of informational self-determination on each individual – including the right to remain master of the data concerning him or her" (Rodota and Capurro, 2005, p. 17)? If we rely on bio-data to drive our next move based on what our own wearable sensors tells some computer application is the right thing to do, we very well may lose a great part of our freedom and the life-force of improvization and spontaneity. By allowing this data to drive our decisions, we make ourselves prone to algorithmic faults in software programs among other significant problems.

13.5.5 *The unintended side effects of lifelogging*

Lifelogging captures continuous first-person recordings of a person's life and can now be dynamically integrated into social networking and other applications. If lifelogging is recording your daily life with technical tools, many are unintentionally participating in a form of lifelogging by recording their lives through social networks. Although, technically, data capture in social media happens in bursts (e.g. the upload of a photograph) compared with continuous recording of first-person recordings (e.g. glogger.mobi) (Daskala, 2011). Lifelogging is believed to have such benefits as affecting how we remember, increasing productivity, reducing an individual's sense of isolation, building social bonds, capturing memories, and enhancing communication.

Governing bodies could also derive benefit through lifelogging applications data to better understanding public opinion or forecast emerging health issues for society. However, memories gathered by lifelogs can have side effects. Not every image, and not every recording you will take will be a happy one. Replaying these and other moments might be detrimental to our well-being. For example, history shows 'looking back' may become traumatic, such as Marina Lutz's experience of having most of her life either recorded or photographed in the first 16 years of her life by her father (see the short film *The Marina Experience*).

Researchers have discovered that personality development and mental health could also be negatively impacted by lifelogging applications. Vulnerabilities include high influence potential by others, suggestibility, weak perception of self, and a resulting low self-esteem (Daskala, 2011). There is also risk that wearers may also post undesirable or personal expressions of another person, which cause the person emotional harm due to a negative perception of himself or herself among third parties (Daskala, 2011). We have already witnessed such events in other social forums with tragic consequences such as suicides.

Lifelogging data may also create unhealthy competition, for example in gamification programs that use higi scores to compare your quality of life to others. Studies report psychological harm among those who perceive they do not meet peer expectations (Daskala, 2011); how much more so when intimate data about one's physical, emotional, psychological, and social network is integrated, measured, and calculated to sum up quality of life in a three-digit score (Michael and Michael, 2011). Even the effect of sharing positive lifelogging data should be reconsidered. Various reports have claimed that watching other people's lives can develop into an obsession and can incite envy, feelings of inadequacy, or feeling as if one is not accomplished enough, especially when comparing oneself to others.

13.5.6 *Pebbles and shells*

Perhaps lifelogs could have the opposite effect of their intended purpose, without ever denying the numerous positives. We may become wrapped up in the self, rather than in the common good, playing to a theater, and not allowing ourselves to flourish in other ways lest we are perceived as anything but normal. Such logging posted onto public Internet archival stores might well serve to promote a conflicting identity of the self, constant validation through page ranks, hit counts and likes, and other forms of electronic exhibitionism. Researchers purport that lifelogging activities are likely to lead to an over-reliance and excessive dependency on electronic devices and systems with emotionally concerning, on-going cognitive reflections as messages are posted or seen, and this could be at the expense of more important aspects of life (Daskala, 2011).

Isaac Newton gave us much to consider when he said, "I was like a boy playing on the sea-shore, and diverting myself now and then finding a smoother pebble or a prettier shell than ordinary, whilst the great ocean of truth lay all undiscovered before me" (Brewster, 2001). Society at large must question if the measurements of Google hits, higi scores, clicks, votes, recordings, and analysis of data to quantify 'the self', could become a dangerously distracting exercise if left unbalanced. The aforementioned measurements, which are multi-varied and enormously insightful, may be of value – and of great enjoyment and fascination – much like Newton's pebbles and shells. However, what is the ocean we may overlook – or ignore – as we scour the beach for pebbles and shells?

13.5.7 *When bad is good*

Data collection and analysis systems, such as lifelogging, may not appropriately allow for individuals to progress in self-awareness and personal development upon tempered reflection. How do we aptly measure the contradictory aspects of life such as the healing that often comes through tears, or the expending of energy (exercise) to gain energy (physical health), or the unique wonder that is realized only through the pain of self-sacrifice (e.g. veritable altruistic acts)? Harvard researchers Loehr and Schwartz (2001) provide us with further evidence of how the bad (or the unpleasant) can be good relative to personal development, through an investigation in which a key participant went by the name of 'Richard'.

Richard was an individual progressing in self-awareness as documented during an investigation in which researchers were working to determine how executives could achieve peak performance leading to increased capacity for endurance, determination, strength, flexibility, self-control, and focus. The researchers found that executives who perform to full potential, for the long-term, tap into energy at all levels of the 'pyramid of performance' which has four ascending levels of progressive capacities: physical, emotional, mental, and spiritual.

The tip of the pyramid was identified as spiritual capacity, defined by the researchers as "an energy that is released by tapping into one's deepest values and defining a strong sense of purpose" (Loehr and Schwartz, 2001, p. 127). The spiritual capacity, above all else, was found to be the sustenance – or the fuel – of the *ideal performance state* (IPS); the state in which individuals 'bring their talent and skills to full ignition and to sustain high performance over time' (*op. cit.*, p. 122). However, as Richard worked to realize his spiritual capacity, he experienced significant pain during a two-year period. He reported being overcome by emotion, consumed with grief, and filled with longing as he learned to affirm what mattered most in his life. The two-year battle resulted in Richard 'tapping into a deeper sense of purpose with a new source of energy' (*op. cit.*, p. 128); however, one must question if technology would have properly quantified the bad as the ultimate good for Richard. Spiritual reflections on the trajectory of technology (certainly since it has now been plainly linked to teleology) are not out of place nor should they be discouraged.

13.5.8 *Censorship*

Beyond the veillance (the 'watching') of oneself, i.e. the inward gaze, is the outward veillance and watching of the other. But this point of eye (PoE), does not necessarily mean a point of view (PoV), or even wider angle field of view (FoV). Particularly in the context of 'glass'. Our gaze too is subjective, and who or what will connote this censorship at the time when it really matters? The outward watching too may not tell the full story, despite its rich media capability to gather both audio and video. Audio-visual accounts have their own pitfalls. We have long known how vitally important eye gaze is for all of the social primates, and particularly for humans; there will be consequences to any artificial tampering of this basic natural instinct. Hans Holbein's famous painting *The Ambassadors* (1533), with its patent reference to anamorphosis, speaks volumes of the critical distinction between PoE and PoV. Take a look, if you are not already familiar with this double portrait and still life. Can you see the skull? The secret lies in the perspective and in the tilt of the head.

13.6 Summary and Conclusions: Mind/Body Distinction

In the future, corporate marketing may hire professional lifeloggers (or mobile robotic contraptions) to log other people's lives with commercial devices. Unfortunately, because of inadequate privacy policies or a lack of harmonized legislation, we, as consumers, may find no laws that would preclude companies from this sort of 'live to life' hire if we do not pull the reins on the obsession to auto-photograph and audio record everything in sight. And this needs to happen right now. We have already fallen behind and are playing a risky game of catch-up. Ethics is not the overriding issue for technology companies or developers; innovation is their primary focus because, in large part, they have a fiduciary responsibility to turn a profit. We must in turn, as an informed and socially responsive community, forge together to dutifully consider the risks. At what point will we leap from tracking the mundane, which is of the body (e.g. location of GPS coordinates), toward the tracking of the mind by bringing all of these separate components together using über-analytics and an über-view? We must ask the hard questions now. We must disclose and discuss the existence of risk, the values at stake, and the possibility of harm.

It is significant that as researchers we are once more, at least in some places, speaking on the importance of the Cartesian mind/body distinction and of the catastrophic consequences should they continue to be confused when it comes to etymological implications and ontological categories. The mind and the body are not identical even if we are to argue from Leibniz's Law of Identity that two things can only be identical if they at the same time share exactly the same qualities. Here as well, vigilance is enormously important that we might not disremember the real distinction between machine and human.

PART III

The Engineers of Computer Souls?

Chapter 14

Robotic Self-Modeling

Justin W. Hart and Brian Scassellati
Yale University, USA

14.1 Introduction

In robotics, the need to reason about a machine's physical structure and sensors is inescapable. Many robots use algorithms that require models of their hardware in order to plan their motion, use stereo vision, or perform other tasks. Traditionally, however, all of the thinking about a robot's hardware and sensors has been done by skilled engineers, on behalf of the robot, rather than by the robot itself.

Unlike a robot, to the infant who is learning to grasp and manipulate objects, knowledge of their body is not something that has been provided a priori by an engineer, but something to be learned through experience. Infants learn about their bodies and senses through the experience of using them in concert with each other. This knowledge of who they are and what they can do with their bodies and senses represents one of the earliest forms of self-awareness that they will develop (Rochat, 2001).

In this chapter, we will discuss experiments in which we have programmed a humanoid robot to learn about its body and senses through the experience of using them in conjunction with each other. This work is inspired by and based on the process by which infants learn about their bodies and senses. While a significant body of literature has been dedicated to theoretical and philosophical aspects of self-aware systems, we will side-step this discussion. Instead, we will describe how we have constructed a system that learns a form of self-knowledge, and the practical implications of the techniques that we have developed. Among these are the ability to adapt the self-model to accommodate tool use, as well as to use the self-modeling capability to diagnose and adapt to mechanical failures and damage to oneself (cf. Chapter 5, this volume).

In these experiments, a humanoid robot learns a unified model of its body and senses, which we refer to as its 'self-model'. This self-model captures the information about the robot's kinematics and camera calibration that is necessary for sensorimotor tasks such as motion planning and stereo reconstruction. Because it is learned through experience and online, the robot is also capable of adapting this self-model. We will demonstrate the capability of the robot to adapt this self-model to the case of tool use, by adjusting the model to incorporate the tool into its kinematic chain.

Of long interest to the psychology, ethology, and robotics communities, as a test of self-awareness, is the *mirror test* (Gallup, 1970), in which an animal's behaviour in front of a mirror is observed. In a variation of this test, humans or animals are given spatial reasoning tasks (Bertenthal and Fischer, 1978; Menzel *et al.*, 1985; Heschl and Burkart, 2006). For example, in one such experiment, a marmoset uses a mirror to obtain food that they cannot see without the aid of the mirror (Heschl and Burkart, 2006). We will demonstrate a similar capability in our system. The robot will use its self-model to reason about a mirror in its environment. It will compare motion it sees in the mirror to its own motion. This process enables the robot to use mirrors for spatial reasoning by incorporating the perspective of the mirror into its stereo vision computations. We will wrap up by discussing potential near-term applications for this technology and possible future research directions.

14.2 A Model of the Self

Despite the seeming disadvantage of not starting with knowledge of their body and senses, infants flexibly learn a wider repertoire of behaviours than any robot ever has. They adapt to changes in their bodies as they grow or sustain injuries. They are able to use tools, identify when they are injured, and modify the ways in which they use their bodies until they have healed.

On the other hand, a traditionally designed robot has no way to introspect on its self-representation. Robots which learn only about the tasks that they perform, but do not learn about their hardware and sensors, can only identify that their action has failed and its relationship to the model of that action. If the issue lies in the robot's kinematic or visual models, they cannot fix the representation that led to that failure, but only adapt the model of the behaviour that builds upon this base representation.

It is also common for the self-representations used in robotics to be developed separately. This can lead to disagreements between these separate models. A robot's forward-kinematic model, describing how its body moves, may predict its hand to be in one location, with its stereo vision system reconstructing it in a slightly different position. In contrast, the internal representation that humans have of their bodies and senses is tightly coupled. This allows humans to build a coherent model from their multiple perceptual inputs, and interpret stimuli with respect to their multiple senses. The merging of proprioception, the tactile sense, and vision in this way, allows us to estimate where objects that we touch are with respect to objects that we see.

Inspired by the developmental process of self-discovery that infants experience, the goal of robot self-modeling is to build robots that learn about themselves – their hardware, sensors, and capabilities – through data sampled during operation. Self-modeling replaces the models that are provided to robots through manual processes with methods that allow robots to learn these models continually and online. These robots learn about their bodies and senses by using them in concert with each other. They learn unified self-models which combine kinematic and sensory aspects that are traditionally modeled separately. This learning process enables these robots to develop and maintain an exceptionally high degree of accuracy in the calibration of their self-representations, and gives rise to the unique capabilities of tool and mirror use discussed earlier in this chapter.

14.3 Nico, a Self-Modeling Robot

Conceptually, almost any robot with sensors that interact with its motor state can run a form of the self-modeling outlined in this chapter. For our experiments, we ran our self-modeling algorithms on a humanoid upper-torso named Nico. Nico has 23 degrees of freedom and is designed to match the form and kinematic structure of a 12-month-old human child at the fiftieth percentile, Figure 14.1.

Nico's self-model merges two components, the kinematics of its arm and the parameters describing its stereo vision system. Traditionally, these two

Fig. 14.1 Nico is a humanoid robot modeled after the human 12-month-old at the fiftieth percentile of growth. Models of the robot's arm and stereo vision system are learned by its self-modeling process.

models are developed separately. It is typical for an engineer to specify the kinematics of a robot's arm by manually constructing a model of it, following this up with manual calibration if necessary. A robot's stereo vision system is typically calibrated by looking at an external calibration target of known shape (Faugeras, 1993; Hartley and Zisserman, 2004; Zhang, 2000).

This process can lead to disagreement between the two distinct models. If these models disagree in units or scale, or in the origin or orientation of the coordinate systems, then there will be a mismatch between where the robot perceives objects, and where it reaches for them. In contrast, our method treats agreement between the kinematic and visual models as of greater importance than calibration against external targets.

One approach that has been taken several times in the recent literature is to learn a model of the robot's stereo kinematics through samples taken by its stereo vision system. By watching its arm move in its visual field, the robot is able to learn a model of its kinematic structure. This approach works fairly well, with two separate, recent implementations reporting agreement between stereo vision measurements and forward-kinematic predictions agreeing to within 5 cm (Hersch *et al.*, 2008; Cantin-Martinez *et al.*, 2010). However, any shortcomings in the robot's stereo vision calibration are propagated to its kinematic model by this method.

Stereo vision calibration is generally performed by looking at a target of known shape. By using a stored model of this target, camera calibration software attempts to infer the projection that leads to the image of the target, as sampled by the robot's cameras. This projection is an expression of the camera calibration parameters. Nico's self-modeling software takes a different spin on this approach. By assuming that the robot's kinematic structure is relatively constant, we are able to use the learned model of its kinematics as a calibration target. Optimizing agreement between its forward-kinematic predictions and the tracked positions of its end-effector in its visual field, the robot is then able to simultaneously refine both (Hart and Scassellati, 2011).

This process is interesting for several reasons:

- The robot uses its own body as a calibration target both to learn its kinematics and to refine its stereo vision calibration. This is to say, the robot uses data that it samples itself, about itself, in order to learn about itself.
- This method treats internal agreement between the robot's visual and kinematic calibrations as of greater importance than agreement between these measurements and external calibration targets. By optimizing this agreement, we assure that where the robot reaches for an object and where it sees the object are the same. Despite this departure from the common practice, it also improves stereo vision performance, as measured against an external target, over an initial seed calibration provided to the system.
- Because this routine can be performed online, the robot is able to use it to adapt its kinematic model as needed. This can be used to recover

from errors, changes in the system, or damage. One demonstration of this capability is to adapt the robot's kinematic model online in order to accommodate a tool that has been grasped by its end-effector.

One result of learning kinematics through the visual system and refining these models against each other is that these models can be thought of as a singular self-model. The parameters used to model the position of the end-effector in space can be combined with those describing the visual system in order to predict the end-effector's position in the visual field. From a mathematical perspective, by calibrating the robot's visual and kinematic models to each other, we have unified them, gaining the ability to interpret their states with respect to each other for free. The formulas describing the projection of arbitrary points in space can be applied to the robot's body in the same way, indicating where parts of its body, such as its hand, can be found with respect to the visual field.

An interesting twist on this relationship is that we can exploit it in order to allow the robot to use its self-knowledge to interpret its sensory data in unique ways. By tracking the motion of the reflection of its end-effector in a mirror, the robot is able to take its self-knowledge of its kinematic and visual calibrations to compute a calibration that represents the visual perspective of the mirror as it relates to reflections therein. In doing so, the robot again uses itself as a calibration target, but this time for the perspective transformation describing reflections in the mirror. Doing so, the robot is able to incorporate the mirror into its stereo visual system, accurately determining the positions of objects based on their reflections. This instrumental use of mirrors is an advanced perceptual capability found only in certain animals, and exists in no other computer vision system.

14.4 A Kinematic–Visual Self-Model

Nico's self-model combines two traditionally disparate models: the robot's forward-kinematic model and its stereo vision model.

The forward-kinematic model describes how the robot moves. We can think of the robot's arm as a chain of rotating joints. If we know the angle to which the robot has rotated the motor corresponding to each joint, then we are able to compute the position of its hand based on this model.

The stereo vision model describes how light enters the robot's cameras, based on factors such as the focal length of each camera's lens and the position and orientation of each camera in space. By knowing these parameters, we are able to compute where the rays of light entering each camera intersect. These intersections exist at the 3D points in space where they are reflected off of objects, allowing us to infer the positions of these objects.

By combining these two models, as outlined in the previous section, we are able to merge visual and kinematic data meaningfully, creating predictions that combine the two. For instance, the forward kinematic model predicts where the robot's hand will be in both 2D and in 3D as in the robot's visual field.

Briefly, given these parameters, the robot is able to perform the following tasks, with a high degree of agreement between the predictions of the self-model and the measurements taken by its stereo vision system:

(1) Reconstruct the robot's end-effector position visually, from stereo data.
(2) Predict the robot's end-effector position in 3D, via forward-kinematics.
(3) Predict the robot's end-effector position in 2D, from the combination of the two.

14.4.1 *Learning the self-model*

To learn this self-model, the robot is first instrumented with a marker attached to its end-effector, Figure 14.2. This marker allows the robot to track the motion of its hand in its visual field. In our implementation, the fiducial is tracked using a version of Augmented Reality Toolkit that has been optimized for tracking the marker in 2D, rather than in 3D, so that accurate tracking of the marker does not depend on camera calibration.[1]

The stereo vision system is provided with a seed calibration using standard techniques. While the system is currently able to refine its visual calibration online, an initial seed calibration is required (an algorithm intended to obviate this step is currently under development).

Learning then proceeds in three steps:

Step 1: Knowing that each joint, when moving in isolation, moves along a circular path, the robot is able to perform a procedure called circle point analysis. Circles are fit to points sampled by moving each joint in isolation. From this an initial kinematic calibration can be computed.

[1]This is important, because the robot refines its stereo vision calibration via this process. We neither wish to cheat in our experiment (by starting with a perfectly calibrated vision system), nor to prevent our success (by unnecessarily limiting the precision with which we can track the marker, thus limiting the precision of our calibration).

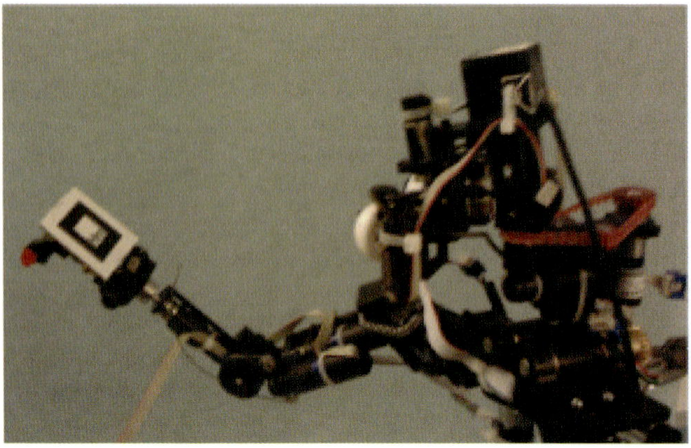

Fig. 14.2 Nico, looking at its hand, which has been instrumented with a fiducial marker on the back in order to be tracked by the robot's vision system.

Step 2: The arm is moved into random poses, with points sampled in each pose. The kinematic calibration is refined by minimizing the sum of the squared distance between each end-effector position, in 3D, as predicted by the forward-kinematic model, and as measured in the stereo vision system.

Step 3: A global optimization over all kinematic and visual parameters is performed over the sum of the squared distance between the 2D tracked end-effector positions in each camera, and the 2D predicted position as imaged by each camera.

The result of this process is a very tightly calibrated self-model, with reconstructed 3D end-effector positions agreeing with their forward-kinematic estimates to within 2.29 mm (SD = 0.10) and 2.93 pixels (SD = 3.83) in a 640×480 image after fewer than 200 motion samples. The robot's model of the lengths of the mechanical linkages in its arm agrees with measurements made with calipers to within 1.1 mm. Additionally, stereo vision performance improves over the initial seed calibration, improving the accuracy of stereo reconstructions from within 1.66 mm to within 1.09 mm.

14.4.2 *Tool use*

Under this model, tool use is simply a matter of allowing the system to adapt after a tool has been mounted in the hand. The system does not need to be fully retrained, but, instead, can simply continue the optimization from Step 3, using training samples from when the tool is mounted in the robot's hand.

To test tool use, a screwdriver was mounted into the robot's hand, Figure 14.3. After only 52 motion samples, the robot was able to predict the position of the tip of the screwdriver to within 7.18 mm (SD = 1.17), or 4.69 pixels (SD = 7.74).[2]

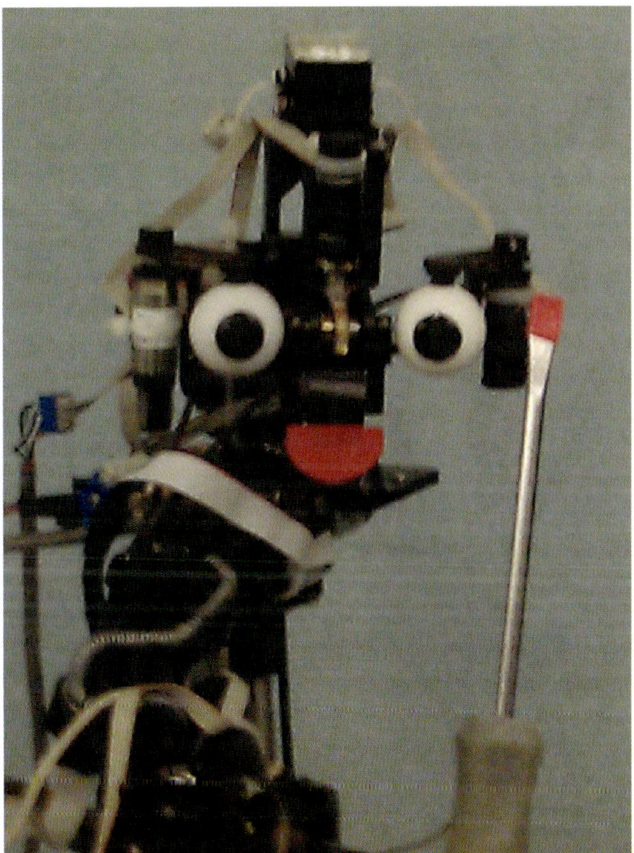

Fig. 14.3 Nico handling a screwdriver which has been wrapped with red electrical tape in order to be tracked by the robot's vision system.

[2]Due to the fiducial slipping off, coloured electrical tape was used to mark the tip of the screwdriver. Tracking via colour blob detection is slightly less accurate than fiducial tracking, partly explaining the less accurate result.

14.4.3 *Instrumental mirror use*

Incorporating a mirror into the robot's stereo vision system is a matter of determining the projection describing reflections in the mirror, then using these projections for stereo vision calculations on objects reflected therein. This capability is interesting because it involves using the robot's self-model to interpret information about an object in its environment. The robot acts as the calibration target, in order to build a calibration of the mirror. By watching its arm move as reflected in the mirror, the robot is able match its forward-kinematic predictions of its end-effector position against the observed reflections (Hart and Scassellati, 2012).

Calibration then proceeds in three steps:

Step 1: Knowing that the actual end-effector position and reconstructions of its reflection will lie symmetrically about the plane of the mirror, compute an estimate of the mirror's position. This estimate lies in the plane that makes the best fit between the forward-kinematic estimates and their reconstructed reflections.

Step 2: Estimate a virtual camera representing each real camera attached to the robot. This virtual camera represents the perspective from which reflections in the mirror appear to be observed.

Step 3: Perform camera calibration, using the robot's motion as the calibration target. Accepting that forward-kinematic estimates are accurate, refine the estimate of the pose for each virtual camera.

While it is possible to skip the first two steps, they take very little extra computation time and no additional motion on the part of the robot. They also prevent problems in which the robot's numerical optimizer may fall into local optima.

After performing this procedure, forward kinematic estimates agree with reconstructed poses, as viewed in the mirror, within 31.55 mm, or 8.47 pixels in a 640×480 image. The increased error is due in part to the fact that the end-effector appears to be farther away, as reflected in the mirror, and thus cannot be tracked as accurately.

14.4.4 *Nico's self-model, in a nutshell*

When we initially learn the robot's self-model, we assume that the body is not changing. It moves through space based on motor commands, but its fundamental kinematic structure, describing how it moves, does not. There are two things that could be incorrect, our knowledge of this kinematic structure, or our knowledge of the space that the robot is perceiving. This procedure refines the robot's faulty spatial perception, based on this assumption that the body is not changing, while simultaneously improving estimates of the kinematic structure, using this improved spatial reasoning (Hart and Scassellati, 2011). In this sense, it is similar to the hypothetical process by which infants learn about their bodies and senses.

When humans use tools, the tool itself is incorporated into their knowledge of their own body. This has been experimentally demonstrated by studies in which people appear to experience the tactile sensation of using a tool at the tip of the tool, rather than as the tool shifting in their hand (Yoshikawa *et al.*, 2007). Similarly, Nico incorporates tools into its self-model, by relearning its self-model to incorporate the tool (Hart and Scassellati, 2011).

The mirror test has long been of interest in both the study of animal behaviour and to the artificial intelligence and robotics communities. In the classic mirror test, an animal is allowed time to learn about mirrors by placing one in their enclosure. The animal is then anaesthetized and marked with an odourless, non-tactile dye. If the animal inspects the mark, then it is considered to recognize its reflection (Gallup, 1970).

Another class of experiments exists in which animals are tasked with using mirrors for spatial reasoning (Bertenthal and Fischer, 1978; Menzel *et al.*, 1985; Heschl and Burkart, 2006). They are, for instance, tasked with grasping food pellets that are only visible as reflected in mirrors, in places where they can fit their arms (such as through holes in a sheet of plywood), but cannot fit their heads. In the experiment described in this chapter, Nico passes a similar test. This result is exciting, because the robot uses knowledge about its body and senses in a unique way to reason about an object in its environment (Hart and Scassellati, 2012).

14.5 Impact, Summary and Conclusions

In this chapter, we have discussed the concept of robotic self-modeling, a technique by which robots learn about their hardware and sensors through the first-hand experience of using them in concert with each other. We have discussed experiments on an upper-torso humanoid robot, Nico, demonstrating the power of these algorithms to produce highly accurate kinematic and visual calibrations. These techniques have also been demonstrated to endow the robot with unique capabilities such as tool use, and the ability to use mirrors as instruments for spatial reasoning.

In the coming years, this research could lead to more robust, more flexible, and more intelligent robots. The combination of sensory information with kinematic information, and learning about these factors in this way, could be used to facilitate tactile sensing methodologies combining touch sensors with kinematics for spatial reasoning. Reasoning about other agents in an interaction based on models of the self could lead to new techniques for theory of mind tasks, joint attention, learning by demonstration, plan recognition, and ad hoc teaming. The techniques presented could be used to create robots that retain accurate calibrations over long-term usage. Comparing their learned self-models against current performance could provide self-modeling robots with a means for fault detection, diagnosis, and recovery. Continually updating these models could allow robots to adapt to changes such as long-term wear and damage, and, as discussed here, briefly adapt their self-models to facilitate tool use. By providing a means for introspection onto the robot's sensors and hardware, self-modeling is leading to robots with 'self-awareness' that are able to reason about their own hardware in new and unique ways.

Chapter 15

Reflective Systems Are a Good Step Towards Aware Systems

Kirstie L. Bellman
Topcy House Consulting, USA

15.1 Expectations for Self-Aware Systems

For several decades, computer science, artificial intelligence, and robotics have been inching towards machine 'awareness' by outfitting systems with diverse sensors and effectors and providing them with better situation awareness methods (Endsley, 1995a,b; Smith and Hancock, 1995; Freedman and Adams, 2003; Klein *et al.*, 2006; Hsieh *et al.*, 2007) and reasoning and learning processes with which to understand their environment and mission (Bellman, 2000; Landauer and Bellman, 2002; Terrace and Metcalfe, 2004; Morin, 2006; Perlovsky and Kozma, 2007). The hope is that more aware systems will act not only more adaptively, but also more appropriately and in accordance with the intentions and values of human designers.

Awareness can include awareness of one's self (e.g., one's actions, motives, emotions, thoughts, plans, history, experience), awareness of the cultural milieu and physical environment, and social and psychological awareness of others. Especially when we are using loaded terms such as awareness, reflection, and self, it is important to consider what our technical goals for self-aware systems are; what would awareness in computational systems gain for us, and more importantly, what won't it do?

We associate many concepts and capabilities with human awareness and, in humans, awareness normally does come with many desirable social, cultural, and moral sensitivities. However, in machines this is not yet true.

To build 'aware' machines that are culturally astute, morally responsible, or even correct in their assessments of situations and required actions will take many new types of information sources, linguistic and reasoning capabilities, social and emotional skills, and, as we discuss here, reflection capabilities (Trappl *et al.*, 2003; Terrace and Metcalfe, 2004; Perlovsky and Kozma, 2007; Petta *et al.*, 2013).

Furthermore, all perception (human or machine) has biases. One of the challenges of awareness and self-awareness will be to build machine systems that do not have the individual mores of the programmer implicitly programmed into them, and that instead have the intents and the agreed-upon community mores of developers and of users. The programmer's biases can show up in many ways, such as the way in which the system's goals are framed (e.g., what is considered important to do or notice as relevant), in menu choice of actions or vocabulary.

In line with this, awareness will not create machines with solutions to human problems that are about the conflicts of humans – they will not be a modern day 'oracle' for the problems that plague us. Our human political processes attest to the fact that multiple competing viewpoints, in the best case, may be perceived but not resolved necessarily. Awareness even in its most sophisticated forms does not automatically come with 'solutions' to what is perceived, considered or thought about – and its results are not always correct. How we ensure that aware systems perceive their world and select their actions in accordance with our requirements and values is a pressing problem discussed later in this chapter.

Having said this, self-awareness in computational systems can be an important step for making a complex system's behaviour more visible and manageable by humans and hence it can support our awareness and decision-making for complex goals and enterprises. Self-awareness also can give a system the capability to be more responsive and adaptive in different operational contexts. It can lay the groundwork for the socially connected, culturally attuned systems we eventually want to develop (cf. Chapters 9 and 11). If, as we suggest here, one takes a careful look at biologically-inspired architectures, one will see that, long before we have general methods of awareness, there will be small victories as we build more specific types of 'awareness' needed for more immediate kinds of sensors, decisions and actions.

Early lines of research on aware systems started in order to make more adaptive and effective systems. An adaptive system requires knowledge about its environment in order to adapt its efforts and goals to that environment. Self-reflection is critical to effective responsiveness to and reasoning about the environment (Bellman, 2000, 2003, 2005). Specifically, self-reflection enables the system to better map itself and its immediate current state (e.g., its strength, health, size, speed, fatigue, capabilities) into its current situational context (e.g., how wide the river is, how big that sheltering hole is, how fast that predator is approaching). The ability to reason about one's state and boundaries can become essential to evaluating the relevance of environmental events, the results of one's actions, and the feasibility of alternative plans.

Furthermore, such self-knowledge can become shareable knowledge for better coordination with others. The system's intents and goals, as well as its current assessment of the situation and its necessary components, can be vital for operators or users to know. We see the advantages of this shared information during collaborative tasks; humans can tell others when they no longer can see or hear something they are tracking or reach for something; they can also say, for example, that they are too tired to proceed or have become injured. We reasonably infer some similar capabilities in animals, as seen in the signaling and body language used by groups of dogs and wolves or in groups of primates (Griffin, 1992; Terrace and Metcalfe, 2004; Morin, 2006).

In addition to providing a sophisticated basis for adaptive behaviour, self-reflection can help provide much-needed perspective in a complex system. When engineered systems incorporate the layered architectures of biological systems, by having reflection occur at many different levels, one has some new capabilities to effectively monitor, evaluate, and replan objectives, and behaviours at many granularities taking place at once, and one then has to evaluate them all from an overall system perspective.

15.2 Towards Self-Aware Systems: Computational Awareness

Unlike the sense of self that arises in the physically embodied emotional and cognitive system of an animal, the self in machine systems is based on computational processes that use instrumentation and explicit knowledge. In 1987, Maes (Maes and Nardi, 1988) defined and implemented *computational reflection* as 'the process of reasoning about and/or acting upon oneself'. Computational reflection is an engineered system's ability to reason about its own resources, capabilities, and limitations in the context of its current operational environment. Reflection capabilities can range from simple, straightforward adjustments of another program's parameters or behaviours (for example, altering the step size on a numerical process or the application of rules governing which models are used at different stages in a design process) to sophisticated analyses of the system's own reasoning, planning and decision processes (for example, noticing when one's approach to a problem is not working and revising a plan).

Reflection processes must include more than the sensing of data, monitoring of an event, or perception of a pattern; they must also have some type of capability to reason about this information and to act upon this reasoning. However, although reflection is more than monitoring, it does not imply that the system is 'conscious'. Many animals demonstrate self-awareness; not only do they sense their environment but they are able to reason about their capabilities within that environment. For example, when a startled lizard scurries into a crevice, rarely does it try to fit into a hole that is too small for its body. If it is injured or tired, it changes the distance that it attempts to run or leap. This adaptive behaviour reveals the ability of the animal system to somehow take into account the current constraints of the environment and of its own body within that environment (Bellman, 2003; Bellman *et al.*, 2008). We will sidestep here how these adaptive processes are implemented and when in the evolutionary chain consciousness occurs (Bellman and Goldberg, 1984; Griffin, 1992; Terrace, 2004; Perlovsky and Kozma, 2007). For our purposes it does not matter if the system is aware that it is aware (consciousness) or uses internal language to itself (such as higher cognitive and linguistic abilities).

Biological systems have many characteristics that support their rich reflective processing (Bellman and Walter, 1984; Morin, 2006; Perlovsky and Kozma, 2007; Bellman *et al.*, 2008). The multilayered architectures of biological systems and the biological style of using both opposing processes and the combination of global and local processing for control leads to two main results in terms of reflection: First, there are a variety of direct and indirect sources of information and control available for reflection and adaptation. Second, these direct and indirect control points can be used as 'entry points' for monitoring (instrumentation) and reasoning about the data collected and adjusting effects (reflective processes). We expand briefly on these points, but for more discussion see Landauer and Bellman (2002) and Bellman *et al.* (2008).

Mammalian brains consist, in a sense, of many brains; different regions have distinct architectures, characteristics and capabilities. Although there is great generalization and reuse in brain mechanisms, the brain is not a single type of general processing machine but rather a community of many different types of architectures and processes. There are, also, many different types and paths of physical and logical connectedness. Hence, there are many ways to support desired goals, with 'substitutability' at many levels of the system (Bellman *et al.*, 2008). Also, although there are many rather fixed and protective mechanisms for critical components or system characteristics, priorities are context-sensitive and the co-occurrence of active brain regions changes dynamically. The style of biological processes leads to very different notions of optimization, robustness, and efficiency (Bellman and Walter, 1984; Bellman *et al.*, 2008). In addition to nature's version of firewalls (e.g. skin, membranes, filters), there is a variety of active 'stabilizing' processes and strategies for 'buffering' – separating input from output and giving the system time to reason about its responses to events. These stabilizing processes include many examples of controlling behaviour by balancing opposing processes (e.g., neural inhibitory and excitatory processes, flexors and extenders, etc.). These counterbalancing processes together modulate inputs and produce desired effects; in addition to allowing rapid responsiveness, this strategy of counterbalancing processes means that there are lots of implicit and indirect methods to determine that some system state is altered or not performing in a desired fashion.

Another particular architectural strategy of interest to us here is the use of both global and local information and processes to control system effects. For example, in mammals, the peripheral nervous system is fast, locally aware and locally responsive while the central nervous system (CNS) allows different adaptive strategies over the longer term. Also, the CNS can help override a 'local optimization' or a locally perseverating state. Given its perspective and span of influence, the CNS can provide dynamic substitution and recruitment of additional resources, as well as provide the coordinated planning and learning needed for system level goals.

Hence, from chemical pathways up to behaviour, numerous active processes are part of the capabilities that go into stabilizing and adapting the biological system, leading to a style of powerful self-monitoring, which includes an extensive investment in internally directed instrumentation and reflective processes throughout the system. Because there are such different 'brains' and indeed adaptive mechanisms throughout the system, what is being monitored for is very different for these diverse processes; furthermore, for any given part or process, there are many different systems that monitor it for different things. This leads to many potential correlations among sensors and multilayered monitoring elements that can be used by reflection processes.

If we recognize that awareness, like other grand concepts such as intelligence or robustness, is a cluster of capabilities, it will help prepare us to look for awareness mechanisms that are appropriate to a given level of the system and for a certain specific decision and to gradually build up a framework of such mechanisms, as already seen in biological systems (Morin, 2006). We present later several types of reflective processes being developed within our robotic cars testbed.

15.3 Wrappings: Implementing Computational Reflection

The Wrappings approach is one way to implement computational reflection and self-modeling systems. In continuous development since 1988, the Wrappings approach grew out of work in conceptual design environments for space systems which had hundreds of models and computational components (Bellman *et al.*, 1993). Wrappings uses both explicit meta-knowledge and recursively applied algorithms to recruit and configure resources dynamically to 'problems posed' to the system by users, external systems, or the system's own internal processing (cf. Chapter 11). To solve posed problems using Wrappings, there are *problem managers* (PMs) which use algorithms to choreograph seven major functions:

- *Discovery* identifies new resources that can be inserted into the system for a problem.
- *Selection* decides which resource(s) should be applied to this problem in this context.
- *Assembly* is syntactic integration and helps set up selected resources so that they can pass information or share services.
- *Integration* is semantic integration, including constraints on when and why resources should be assembled.
- *Adaptation* helps to adjust or set up a resource for different operational conditions.
- *Explanation* is more than a simple event history because it provides information on why and what was not selected.
- *Evaluation* includes the impact or effectiveness of a given use of this resource.

The Wrappings 'problem-posing' has many benefits, including separating problems from solution methods and keeping an explicit, analysable trace of what problems were used to evoke and configure resources.

In the following section, we introduce a few principles of the Wrappings' implementations that explain how Wrappings enables several characteristics for reflective architectures that we have found to be useful. For a more complete discussion, see Landauer and Bellman (1996, 1999a,b, 2001).

The Wrappings' meta-knowledge is machine-interpretable qualitative and quantitative descriptions for all of the system's resources, and includes not just how to use the resources, but also whether, when and why they should or can be used, with often additional qualitative information on 'best practices' for using the resource. The Wrappings approach has no 'privileged' resources; everything is wrapped – tools, databases, planners, user interfaces, utilities, platforms, devices, and all the Wrappings infrastructure and reflection programs. Every resource has one or more Wrappings, with each Wrapping describing the use of that resource for a given problem under a specific context. By limiting each Wrapping to the use of a resource for a specific problem and context, one can incrementally accumulate meta-knowledge for complex resources. This allows us to define new uses of a resource with new meta-knowledge, based on system experience and to start using a resource with partial or incomplete descriptions.

There is a distinguished class of problem manager called study managers (SMs) that coordinate the basic problem study process, and a specialized PM called the coordination manager (CM), which is a kind of basic 'heartbeat' that drives all of the processing. The SMs mediate between the problem at hand and the Wrappings to select and apply resources to the problem, and the CM cycles between posing problems and using a SM to study them. By considering these programs that process the Wrappings to be resources also, and by Wrapping them, so that all of our integration support processes apply to themselves, too, the entire system is computationally reflective (Smith, 1986; Maes and Nardi, 1988; Kiczales *et al.*, 1991; Buschmann, 1996; Vlissides *et al.*, 1996).

In order to better understand how these Wrappings processes provide multiple entry points for reflection and adaptation, it is important to dive a little deeper into the sequence of steps in the default CM and the default SM. As seen in Figure 15.1, the CM runs a sequence of steps that manages the overall system behaviour: find context, pose problem, study problem, assimilate results.

Each step is a problem posed to the system by the CM, which then uses a SM to manage the system's response to the problem. The first problem, 'find context', is posed by the CM in the initial context of 'no context yet', or in some default context determined by the invocation style of the program. The main purpose of the CM is cycling through the other three problems, which are posed by the CM in the context found by the first step. This way of providing context and tasking for the SM is familiar from many interactive programming environments: the 'find context' part is usually left implicit, and the rest is exactly analogous to LISP's 'read-eval-print' loop, though with very different processing at each step, mediated by one of the SMs. The SM is given a context, problem poser, problem, and some associated data (usually by the CM). The default 'study problem' process (see Figure 15.1) essentially interprets the posed problem, applies resources to that problem and assesses the results.

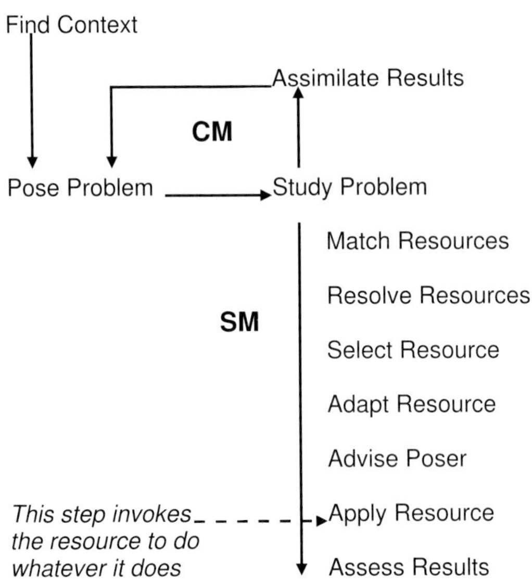

Fig. 15.1 CM/SM steps

The default SM step sequence is shown in Figure 15.1. To 'match resources' is to find a set of resources that might apply to the current problem in the current context, allowing a superficial first pass through a possibly large collection of Wrappings knowledge bases. To 'resolve resources' is to eliminate those that do not apply and makes some initial bindings of formal parameters for resources that still apply. To 'select resource' chooses one of the remaining candidate resources (if any) to use, while 'adapt resource' sets the resource up for the current problem and problem context, including finishing all required bindings. 'Advise poser' tells the problem poser what is about to happen, i.e., what resource was chosen and how it was set up. Elsewhere, we describe how the Wrappings infrastructure poses the problem in the case of failures in any of these steps; how it informs the problem poser of failures in identifying adequate resources and asks for help from the human user (Landauer and Bellman, 1996, 1999a).

Up to this point, the default SM is just a (very) simple type of planning algorithm. The computational reflection that makes it a framework for something more comes from several additional design features. First, as noted, all of the Wrapping processes, including the CM and SM, are themselves wrapped. Second, the processing is completely recursive: 'match resources' is itself a problem, and is studied using the same SM steps, as are 'resolve resources', 'select resource', and *all* of the other steps listed above for the SM and for the CM. Every step in any alternatively defined SM or CM is a posed problem. The simple form we described above is the default SM at the bottom of the recursion. Third, there are other SMs that have slightly more interesting algorithms (such as applying resources in parallel). The recursion in the SM immediately gives it a more robust and flexible strategy, since the resources that carry out the various steps of the processing can be constantly improved; the basic steps and their ordering in the CM and SM form a default case that can be superseded by any more clever mechanisms for particular problem contexts. The SM recursion also means that there are many layers of study context, each with its own problem context, problem poser, and problem specification.

Hence, with Wrappings, everything is available to be reasoned about and potentially dynamically re-parameterized or swapped out for other resources. The Wrappings resources and their interactions allow, in essence, a simulation of the system. With appropriate reflection processes the system can use this information to replan and alter the current use of its resources. This allows sophisticated adaptive processing. Furthermore, unlike biological systems, Wrappings allows access to any self-monitoring and self-decision processes.

15.4 An Example of Wrappings: CalPoly CARS Testbed

Wrappings is being used in CARS, an experimental testbed of robotic cars, with partners at California State Polytechnic University, Pomona (Nelson, 2011; Bellman and Nelson, 2011). The development of self-models, the dynamic substitution of different game-playing approaches, and adjustments in the uses of sensors and other resources is a key part of how the robotic cars are able to participate in four very different types of 'games' with the same control infrastructure, as well as adjusting for sensor and component failures. The testbed experiments with four games: Follow the Leader (replicate the trajectory of another with relatively constant distance or time-headway); Tag, with a pursuer and evaders; Soccer Practice (cars cooperatively take turns bumping a ball into a goal box); and Push the Box (cars must synchronize to push an object that is too large and unwieldy for any one car). These games have been purposely specified to require a broad range of different and even conflicting game-playing strategies.

Furthermore, the cars in the testbed are intentionally equipped with different capabilities (e.g., different sizes and shapes, kinds of sensors, engine capacities, turning ratios, etc.) The car must actively explore the limits of its own specific capabilities within its environment, a process we call *active experimentation* (Bellman *et al.*, 2008; Nelson, 2011; Bellman and Nelson, 2011). This experimental set up is designed to test how well certain game-playing strategies fit with an auto's own capabilities, and is in imitation of the type of self-discovery with which a young child learns how fast they personally can run in water, on sand, or on grass. The car uses this information to build self-models and to refine game-playing strategies to match its personal capabilities.

The flexibility of the Wrappings approach provides multiple entry points for reflective processes. A reflective resource has the general form: Given a goal, purpose, or function, a reflective process uses sources of information to do some action, decision or to create data that is used by other processes. The goal or function for that reflective process could be built in during design time or assigned dynamically to that reflective process by other programs. It may be in continual use or it may be recruited or evoked only when certain resources are active or conditions exist. The sources of information can be data sets, sensor output, monitors, other programs' results, or context. The reasoning process for reflection can be done with an algorithm, decision process, rulebase, cognitive model, or planner. The resulting actions are myriad, but include sending messages, setting program or context parameters, recruiting new components, initiating new processes, or instigating a replan or undo process. In the CARS testbed, we are exploring the different roles of reflection by developing initially four major types of reflection processes: R1 is reflection on an internal or external sensor; R2 is reflection on a program; R3 is reflection on a global characteristics of the system; and R4 is 'a consistency checker' that integrates several other reflection processes.

In the CARS testbed, some R2 processes are deciding whether the programs called 'game-playing strategies' are working well enough in the current game context for a specific robotic car. A strategy is a program that includes a set of rules for playing a game and a reasoner for how to apply these rules to the current game situation. Each car has modified the parameters of the strategies based on their 'experience' with their own capabilities (e.g., their own turning ratio, their maximum speed, their fuel efficiency, and so forth). CARS Tag strategies include: keep moving so that one keeps all cars at a distance; identify who is 'it' and hide behind other cars (always keep another car between yourself and 'it'), or (an energy-minimizing strategy) wait until 'it' appears to be approaching you before you move. The R2 actions include adjusting parameters to the current strategy or posing the problem to select a new strategy.

R3 is like other R1 sensor monitors except that it is aggregating the results of several monitors in order to determine whether a global property of interest (e.g., bandwidth, memory utilization, false alarms) is continually met. A CARS R3 example is the amount of time left for moving around before the car needs to remove itself from the game for battery recharging. This R3 draws information not only from the battery charge monitor, but also from its self-model on the relative costs of its different activities (drawn from its self-experimentation). A reasoner decides whether it can continue its current strategy or switch into a lower-energy strategy or change to less energy-consuming routes (e.g., not going up-hill or accelerating).

Many reflective processes have the job of integrating and reasoning about the input of several other reflective processes. A CARS R4 example is a 'TURN' consistency checker (see Figure 15.2). Each of the separate cars has many sensors, such as video, three-axis gyroscope, compass, three-axis accelerometer, a mouse sensor used for distance traveled, bumper pressure sensors, ultrasound, and infrared sensors. In this example from CARS, the R4 is a program whose input is the output of five different types of sensors' R1s for a given vehicle. It decides if the R1 sensor output is consistent with the expected behaviour for the commanded action of the car, 'TURN'.

This is one way to ensure that sensors are not broken, spoofed, or otherwise giving incorrect information.

The R4 method here is a combination of rulebase and models. Its actions are to alter R1 parameters, including turning sensors off, and to send data and messages to a planner to replan the strategies used depending on faults. If a sensor is a candidate for being faulty, this resource and a planner attempt to substitute combinations of well-behaving sensors for a faulty sensor. This resource is currently being tested in the CARS testbed for use in fault identification and mitigation. These sources of information can prove invaluable in troubleshooting, consistency checks and fault protection, as well as mitigation strategies for failures (Nelson, 2011).

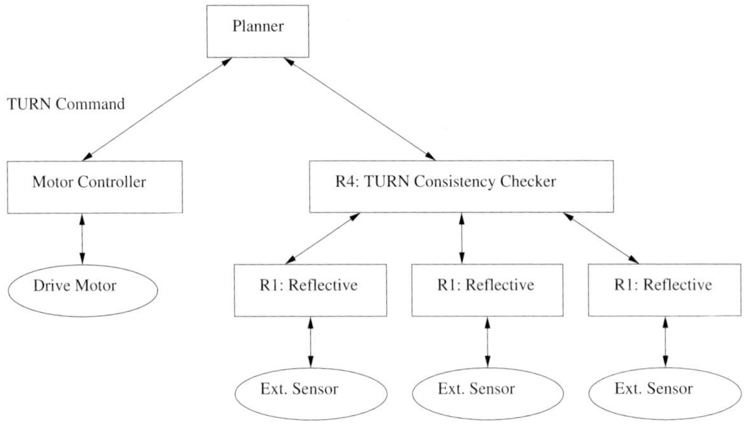

Fig. 15.2 Schematic turn consistency checker

This brief description of some reflection processes in CARS exemplifies several principles for reflective architectures. There are many types of reflection. There is not a single or centralized collection of 'self-models.' However, there is also not a one-to-one mapping between the number of reflective processes and sensors, effectors, or processing elements. Instead, one uses critical functions, requirements, and process entry and exit points to decide where to place the reflective processes. It is an engineering decision depending on requirements (the nature of the decisions; the quality and timing of the performance needed) and the complexity of the system. However, the lessons learned from biological systems should encourage us to invest enough in instrumentation and reflection to reap the benefits of having many direct and indirect sources of feedback and information.

15.5 The Challenges Ahead

Many classic problems in computer science are made more challenging by the characteristics and requirements of reflective systems. For example, reflection gives us the opportunity to adjust behaviours and replan actions, but in order to replan effectively, we face such familiar challenges as reframing the problem, rescoping the goals or the expectations for an action, and backing up from some decisions but not others.

The ability to have reflection at multiple layers of a system means that the system must make decisions not only balancing local component and global system optimization, but also coordinating decisions for behaviours that co-occur at several levels of the system at once and where potentially several levels are being adjusted at the same time. We want to make these adjustments and decisions such that we support what is best for the system, while, at a minimum, we mostly do not harm lower-level and/or local parts. In biology, such trade-offs can vary dramatically depending on the situation, up to, for example, a lizard letting its tail be detached in order not to perish at the maw of a predator. So this goes beyond multi-criteria optimization to a new multi-level and multi-criteria optimization.

In addition, our strategies for selection, refinement, and decision-making must be good enough despite low quality, partial information or even partially wrong information. This leads to again familiar complexity challenges of quickly determining enough correct and relevant information about the system's resources in order to predict the different impacts of different goals – and to adjust them on the fly. As part of this, we need to know what parameters and what resources to change out of all resources currently recruited for a given problem. Classical notions of optimization and approaches to refinement and tailoring will need a creative new perspective.

Verification and validation of reflective systems It is critical that we develop new methods to verify and validate a reflective process in an aware system. With computational reflection, developers can have more insight into the functioning of their devices. However, there are limitations to this insight. When the layers of self-monitoring and self-reporting become complicated enough, the human may be unable to review and understand all the obtainable details. Because of the scale of the aware systems we anticipate (e.g., transportation networks, medical networks, military applications), the information generated for and by reflective systems will prohibit even a small army of humans from reviewing such information in a timely fashion to protect or properly manage such systems. Given this, we will be forced to rely more on the reasoning and evaluative processes of reflective systems. It is imperative that we are able to prove that these reflective processes work as desired.

The Wrappings approach offers several small steps to support new methods of verification and validation for reflective systems. First, all resources, including those supporting reflection, are subject to exactly the same meta-knowledge (with rules of use, limits, and assumptions) as any other resource in the system. We have also shown that the Wrappings infrastructure allows multiple entry points for instrumentation and evaluation of a reflective process; this helps to determine that a Wrappings implementation is using resources in the correct context and for an appropriate use. Additionally, because the Wrappings are not actually surrounding a given software resource, as one might imagine various intelligent front-end programs are, but instead are collected into knowledge bases, one can test the meta-knowledge with known static methods for evaluation of knowledge bases (Bellman and Landauer, 1995; Landauer and Bellman, 1996).

Furthermore, the Wrappings infrastructure imitates the rich multi-layered networks of biological systems in allowing many direct and indirect sources of information about the performance of the system or one of its components. These sources of information can contribute to a variety of polling schemes or decision processes. One of the advantages of having many different reflection mechanisms means that we can develop new methods to take advantage of partially overlapping, but non-identical results, to infer discrepancies. We are already doing such a strategy in the fault monitoring in the CARS testbed noted earlier, where we can use combinations of other sensors to infer that a given sensor is either broken or in a circumstance that it cannot register correct information (Nelson, 2011).

However, we need much more! A reflective system must be able to tell us that it did not meet its goals – and why. Certainly, current systems could use all the data gathered from reflective processes to methodically examine every discrepancy between plan, expectation, and results, and in doing so, notice some anomalies before its human operators or users. However, the computer is not good at identifying what are the meaningful changes amid all the slight departures from expectations and plans in complex and dynamically changing systems. On the other hand, humans are very skilled at discerning a meaningful alteration to a plan versus a slight variation (for example, finding a door locked versus finding a group casually talking near a doorway and walking around them). However, when distracted by a slew of details, often humans do not know that something has gone wrong and what has gone wrong until a careful post hoc analysis. This is where culture and community – and learning – give humans a tremendous advantage. A culture helps to encode others' experience to help us learn and improve our own ability to perform. We do not always know how to figure out what is correct and what is working; others' viewpoints and experience are essential. This learning and feedback becomes critical to our ability to reason about and correct our own reflective processes – our assessments of our environment, goals and performance.

Consider for a moment how parents help teach the self-labeling of states to a child with such phrases as "aren't we grumpy" (or happy or tired or sad). Phrases such as "How do you feel?" or "Where does it hurt?" all teach a certain kind of inner looking. These interactions also go beyond language labels into the diagnosis of what might be wrong and HOW to correct an activity. For example, "You need to hold your bat like this" or "You went off at this point in the proof" or "oh he didn't mean that – you shouldn't have taken it that way". Ironically perhaps, providing the right acculturation capabilities in order to create a socially aware and culturally attuned system may also provide some of the capabilities that become critical for verifying and validating the system's reflection processes.

Of course, for this type of feedback, we draw upon our common experience as humans situated in our common physiology and drawing upon our language capabilities. To acculturate our reflective systems, we will eventually have to provide sophisticated linguistic capabilities (Bellman, 1997; Landauer and Bellman, 1999b; Terrace, 2004). Until then, as a starting point, in computer-based systems the developer can define, limit, and provide (as in Wrappings) the common language and the reasoning resources used for reflection, which include the interpretation of the semantics and the operational distinctions, information sources and evaluation criteria we want to use in different contexts.

However, the more we depend on systems to generate their own knowledge of the world and themselves and to generate their own goals, tasks, actions and interpretations of success, the more we will depend on their own self-awareness capabilities with subsequently less assurance that the language, resources, interpreters, and evaluation criteria we provided are working as planned. Although reflective systems have increasingly useful abilities to examine themselves, it may take a community to help interpret and validate those self-examination processes. The external point of view – the external viewer – may be as essential for a reflective system as their own internal instrumentation; in fact, this continues the exciting lines of psychological research that seek to understand how social beings develop and define their own boundaries and interactions partly on the basis of their interactions with others.

While we confront these formidable challenges, there are several straightforward development actions that we can do now. We briefly note three here: employ architectures that circumscribe roles and actions to limit the damage of errors; limit the requirements for aware systems; develop continual methods of verification and validation as an inherent part of all aware systems. The first point simply adopts architectures that carefully define and limit the roles and responsibilities of humans and computational processes, as is common to many recent cybersecurity approaches that are replacing the wide privileges of operating systems or limiting the authorized actions of human and machine agents. The strategy is to limit the range of allowable actions and correspondingly limit the damage that errors or malicious misuse can cause.

In line with that, we also need to limit our expectations and requirements for aware systems, as has been emphasized in the approach taken here, which builds up a repertoire of diverse reflection processes, each carefully limited to particular problems and operational contexts; by limiting their requirements they can be better managed and tested. In our current mechanical systems, much effort is made to ensure that components can only do as specified. With increasingly complex systems, we have been hard-pressed to have complete specifications for all behaviours and possible modes and to sufficiently test specifications. This scalability is one impetus for formal methods. But even with increasingly powerful formal methods, when we add autonomy and reflection to systems, we are in a new land. The dynamic developments and changes in a reflective system, especially relatively open ones (such as enterprise networks) that allow new types of capabilities and users, argues for an equally open, continual, and changing verification and validation process. This leads to the third point.

Richard Doyle, at the Jet Propulsion Laboratory in Pasadena, California (Doyle *et al.*, 2012), recently emphasized the need to design monitoring (by the system and by external parties), verification, and validation as a continual process, not as a once and for all, certification process. This will include constantly checking to see that the right thing is still being done and is still having the effects one expects in the operational context. The Wrappings approach already makes a step in this direction with the 'continual contemplation' of the resources by the Wrappings infrastructure, but this needs to be supplemented by new methods for trending whether some behaviour is still compatible with success criteria and whether several ongoing behaviours will result in future incompatibilities. It also argues for the creation of new intermediate results in computational processes in order to help trend the impacts of ongoing computational processes and for new logical methods for handling partially satisfying goals or partially meeting requirements. We need to form a foundation of evidence to help us decide where self-aware systems are effective – and where they are not. We must not build systems that we cannot understand, monitor, or trust.

15.6 Summary and Conclusions

The Wrappings approach is one way to implement computational reflection and self-modeling systems. We illustrated some of the differences among reflective processes with examples from our current research testbed, which has diverse robotic cars adaptively playing both collaborative and competitive games. Computational reflection gives systems some of the information that could be helpfully communicated to developers and users on their state, goals, perceptions, and results. However, the validity of the reflective processes depends on the appropriate use of data, instrumentation, reasoning processes, and analyses, which, like all complex systems, can become overwhelmed with large datasets, unexpected interactions, and side-effects. We emphasized the challenges remaining to use reflective processes correctly and to verify and validate reflective systems. As discussed, like many gains, reflection offers very hard challenges, but also some new capabilities that if used correctly will help us do this evaluation and verification.

Reflective systems have much promise, but, ironically, to use them correctly we must be more self-conscious too (Bellman, 2005) – both socially and technically. Socially, we must explicitly and openly define our assumptions and goals for a system, and use appropriate human arenas to argue through the differences in viewpoints and goals. Too often we use technology to mask our own intentions and to somehow assign the moral responsibility for decisions to the machine. Technically, we need to understand the impacts of our choices for the resources we use in aware systems; to do so, we need serious studies of how different languages, representations, algorithms, and so forth bias our definitions and colour our perceptions of situations and of actions, and impact our ability to reason about different classes of problems.

Since this type of understanding will take considerable effort, we need incremental strategies for developing aware systems. We believe that dividing up 'awareness' into specific reflection capabilities, grounded within specific problem and operational contexts, is a helpful step. The Wrappings approach allows one to build up a repertoire of awareness mechanisms geared to specific decisions, information sources, and processes and for gradually accumulating the necessary information to trust their use within the context of specific sets of problems, operational situations, and resource uses. Furthermore, both the human users and the system's resources can be part of the reflective processing. Reflection processes and Wrappings can be implemented incrementally and experimentally. They can be done for some functions or for some entities, with careful observation of the trade-offs in implementation costs and gains.

Lastly, a critical part of all aware processes must be a new continual type of verification and validation in order to ensure that the aware systems continue to function correctly as they evolve. This means that the system not only produces correct results, but does so by repeatedly noticing the right information at the right time and using its reasoning and planning processes correctly in choosing suitable actions. The formidable task of showing correctness of these self-monitoring and reasoning processes in computational reflection should act as a significant harbinger of what the awareness community will face eventually for more interesting capabilities.

Chapter 16

Robots with Internal Models: A Route to Self-Aware and Hence Safer Robots

Alan F. T. Winfield

University of the West of England, Bristol, UK

16.1 Introduction

The aim of this chapter is to set out the case for building robots with internal models as a possible route toward achieving a level of functional self-awareness that would usefully extend the capabilities of autonomous robots. The chapter argues that these capabilities will lead to enhanced safety – especially in physical human–robot interaction (pHRI) – and, perhaps also, toward ethical behaviour in autonomous robots. Indeed, the chapter will advance the argument that safe and ethical autonomous robots may not be achievable at all without mechanisms for self-awareness.

Importantly, the ideas and mechanisms proposed in this chapter are intended to be realisable with current and near-future technology, i.e. using conventional computing platforms embedded within existing or buildable robot bodies, with existing devices for sensing and actuation. Thus, this chapter is primarily about how we might *engineer* practical self-awareness, for safer (and possibly ethical) robots in the near-term. This chapter will be less concerned with philosophical questions such as whether, or not, such robots are *really* self-aware, although we will touch upon the question of what behaviour might, if exhibited, be argued as evidence for *as if* self-awareness (see Chapter 1).

16.2 Internal Models and Self-Awareness

An internal model is a mechanism for internally representing both the system itself and its current environment. An example of a robot with an internal model is a robot with an embedded *simulation* of itself *and* its currently perceived environment. A robot with such an internal model has, potentially, a mechanism for generating and testing *what-if* hypotheses:

(1) *What if* I carry out action x? and, ...
(2) ... of several possible next actions x_i, *which* should I choose?

Holland writes: "an internal model allows a system to look ahead to the future consequences of current actions, without actually committing itself to those actions" (Holland, 1992, p. 25). This leads to the idea of an internal model as a *consequence engine* – a mechanism for estimating the consequences of actions. Dennett, in his book *Darwin's Dangerous Idea* (1995), develops the same idea in what he calls the *Tower of generate-and-test*; a conceptual model for the evolution of intelligence that has become known as Dennett's tower. Dennett's tower is a set of conceptual creatures, each one of which is successively more capable of reacting to (and hence surviving in) the world through having more sophisticated strategies for 'generating and testing' hypotheses about how to react.

Dennett's tower starts with Darwinian creatures; these have only natural selection as the generate and test mechanism, so mutation and selection is the only way that Darwinian creatures can adapt – individuals cannot. On the second floor are Skinnerian creatures, which can learn, but only by generating and physically testing all different possible actions, then reinforcing the successful behaviour. The third floor of Dennett's tower contains Popperian creatures, which have the ability to *internally model* the possible actions so that some (the bad ones) are discarded before they are tried out for real. A robot with an internal model, capable of generating and testing *what-if* hypotheses, would thus be an example of a Popperian creature within Dennett's scheme.

The use of internal models within control systems is well established, but these are typically mathematical models of the plant (system to be controlled). For example, a set of first-order linear differential equations models the plant, and these allow the design of controllers able to cope with reasonably well defined uncertainties; methods also exist to extend the approach to cover non-linear plant (Isidori *et al.*, 2003). In such internal-model based control the environment is not modelled explicitly – only certain exogenous disturbances are included in the model. This contrasts with the internal simulation approach of this chapter, which models both the plant (in our case a robot) and its operational environment.

In the field of cognitive robots specifically addressing the problem of machine consciousness (Holland, 2003), the idea of embedding a simulator in a robot has emerged in recent years. Such a simulation allows a robot to try out (or 'imagine') alternative sequences of motor actions, to find the sequence that best achieves the goal (for instance, picking up an object), before then executing that sequence for real. Feedback from the real-world actions might also be used to calibrate the robot's internal model. The robot's embodied simulation thus adapts to the body's dynamics, and provides the robot with what Marques and Holland (2009) have referred to as a 'functional imagination'.

Bongard *et al.* (2006) describe a four-legged starfish-like robot that makes use of explicit internal simulation, both to enable the robot to learn its own body morphology and control, and notably allow the robot to recover from physical damage by learning the new morphology following the damage. The internal model of Bongard *et al.* models only the robot, not its environment. In contrast, Vaughan and Zuluaga (2006) demonstrated self-simulation of both a robot and its environment in order to allow a robot to plan navigation tasks with incomplete self-knowledge; although making no claims to self-awareness, their approach provides perhaps the first experimental proof-of-concept of a robot using self-modelling to anticipate and hence avoid unsafe actions.

Zagal *et al.* (2009) describe self-modelling using internal simulation in humanoid soccer robots; in what they call a 'back-to-reality' algorithm, behaviours adapted and tested in simulation are transferred to the real robot. In a similar approach, but within the context of evolutionary swarm robotics, O'Dowd *et al.* (2011) describe simple wheeled mobile robots, which embed within each robot a simulator for both the robot and its environment; a genetic algorithm is used to evolve a new robot controller, which then replaces the 'live' robot controller about once every minute.

Does having an internal model make a robot self-aware? The answer to this question depends of course on what is mean tby 'self-aware'. In some straightforward sense, if a robot has an internal model of itself, then that model accounts for the *self* in self-aware. More difficult to justify is any claim to *awareness*, since this depends not just on having an internal model, but on what the robot does with that model. Self-awareness is a *property* that needs to be demonstrated by behaviours, in particular behavioural responses to novel situations that have been neither pre-programmed, evolved or previously learned.[1] Moreover, those behaviours must in some way flow from the robot's perception of its environment, including its position in that environment – and the (relative) position of other agents, and its assessment of the possible consequences of both its own actions and those of other actors in that environment.

16.3 Internal Model-Based Architecture for Robot Safety

Simulation technology is now sufficiently well developed to provide a practical basis for implementing the kind of internal model required to test *what-if* hypotheses, outlined above. In robotics, advanced physics and sensor-based simulation tools are commonly used to test and develop, even evolve, robot control algorithms before they are tested in real hardware. Examples of robot simulators include Webots (Michel, 2004) and Player-Stage (Vaughan and Gerkey, 2007). While using simulation tools, roboticists are well aware of the dangers in making claims about algorithms tested only in simulation. The term *reality-gap* is used as shorthand for the gap between the performance of real sensors and actuators and their approximated and idealised versions, in simulation (Jacobi *et al.*, 1995). Furthermore, there is an emerging science of simulation, aiming for principled approaches to simulation tools and their use (Stepney *et al.*, 2011).

Figure 16.1 proposes an architecture for a robot with an internal model that is used to test and evaluate the consequences of the robot's next possible actions. The machinery for modelling next actions is relatively independent of the robot's controller; the robot is capable of working normally without that machinery, albeit without the ability to generate and test *what-if* hypotheses. The *what-if* processes are not in the robot's main control loop, but instead run in parallel to moderate the Robot Controller's normal action selection if necessary, acting in effect as a 'safety governor'.

At the heart of the architecture is the Internal Model (IM). The IM is initialised from the Object Tracker-Localiser, and loops through all possible next actions; these next actions are generated within the Robot Controller (RC) and transferred to the mirror RC within the IM (for clarity this data flow is omitted from Figure 16.1). For each candidate action the IM simulates the robot executing that action, and generates a set of model

[1]It should be noted that there may be other characteristics of self-awareness, including some that are externally unobservable.

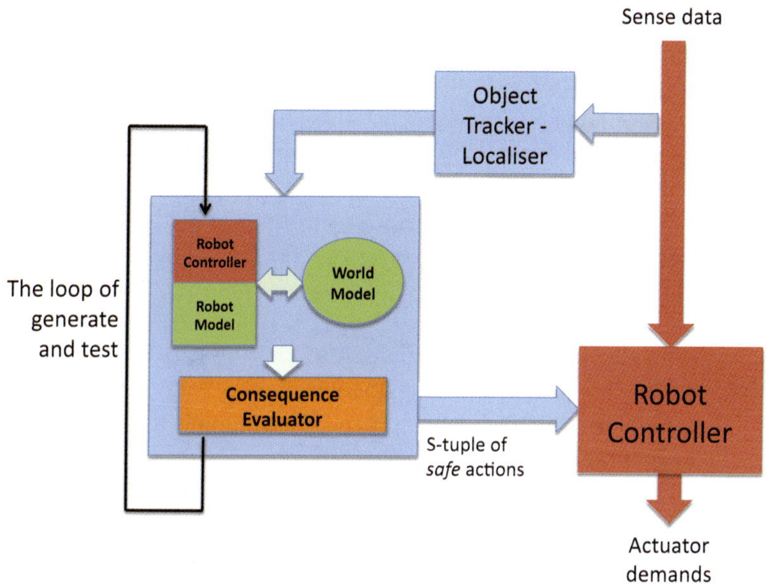

Fig. 16.1 A self-aware architecture for safe action selection. The Robot control data flows are shown in red; the Internal Model data flows in blue.

outputs ready for evaluation by the Consequence Evaluator. The IM and Consequence Evaluator loop through each possible next action; this is the generate-and-test loop. Only when the complete set of next possible actions has been tested does the Consequence Evaluator send, to the RC, actions it assesses to be safe. These processes are explained in more detail below.

16.3.1 *The Internal Model*

The IM shown in Figure 16.1 is a simulator that must incorporate both a World Model and a Robot Model. The World Model (WM) is a model of the robot's environment, including the terrain across which the robot must move (if it is a mobile robot) and the other objects the robot might encounter. Those objects might be static obstacles (e.g. walls) or hazards (e.g. holes in the ground), or dynamic objects. The dynamic objects could be moving obstacles or actors with which our robot must interact; these could be other robots or, if we are concerned with human–robot interaction, human(s). For many of the applications we might envisage the WM will also need to model real-world physics, so that for instance the inertia of moving objects is accounted for in collisions. The Robot Model (RM) is a model of our 'self-aware' robot and, as is commonplace in robot simulators, this will model the robot's sensors and actuators. Importantly, the RM is controlled by the same RC as the real robot, so that it will act and react in the same way as the real robot. Thus the RC in the IM mirrors the real robot's controller – as shown in Figure 16.1. All of these components are normally present in current technology robot simulators. However, in order to make use of such a simulator as our IM the robot should have the following additional capabilities:

(1) It must be capable of being initialised so that objects in the WM, and the state and disposition of the RM within the WM, can be matched to the real-world environment and the location and disposition of the real robot in that environment. The initialisation data will be supplied by the Object Tracker–Localizer shown in Figure 16.1.
(2) It must be capable of being run with a given RM action, for a given simulated time period then halted and re-initialised to the same state, then run again for each of the robot's next possible actions.
(3) The final state of the simulator at the end of each of these fixed-time runs must be captured and suitably coded, then supplied to the Consequence Evaluator.

16.3.2 *The Consequence Evaluator*

The purpose of the Consequence Evaluator (CE) is to compare the outputs of the IM for each of the robot's next possible actions, and select the 'best' action for the real robot. To understand how to do this we first need to consider what we mean by the IM's outputs. For each action, the robot is likely to have changed its disposition in the WM during the simulation run. Or it may not, either because its move was blocked by another object, or simply because the next action being tested might be 'stand still'. If there are dynamic actors in the environment, then their positions, relative to the robot, are also likely to have changed. Thus the position of the robot at the end of each IM run, and of any other dynamic actors, are useful outputs. Perhaps better still are the changes in position of the robot. But since collisions are significant consequences, as far as safety is concerned, that are likely to be detected directly by the simulator since – during a simulated *what-if* run – those collisions actually happen, then collision or no-collision is another extremely useful output.

Given the outputs of the IM are, minimally, change of position and collision/no-collision, for each next possible action tested, how is the CE to judge which is the best action? Such a judgement requires rules. The rules might, for instance, determine that *all* collisions are unsafe. Thus, for a set of next possible actions tested in the IM, if only one has the output no-collision, then that would be chosen and sent to the RC. But if several next actions are equally safe (i.e. none of them are predicted to result in collisions), how is the CE to decide? The simple answer is that the CE does not have to decide between the safe actions, since the RC is, we assume, capable of action selection in order to decide which action is the next best action toward achieving the robot's task or mission. For n next possible actions modelled and evaluated, the number s of actions judged safe could be any value in the range $(0...n)$, and so the CE needs to send an s-tuple of safe actions to the RC. Using its action selection mechanism, the RC then chooses one of the s-tuple actions (possibly) overriding an unsafe action.

Consider the scenario illustrated in Figure 16.2. Here the robot is approaching two hazards: a wall on the left and a hole directly ahead. Let us assume the hole is deep enough that it presents a serious hazard to the robot. The robot has four possible next actions, each of which is simulated in its IM. The actions are move ahead left, move straight ahead, move ahead right or remain stationary; for simplicity assume left and right movements actually consist of a turn on the spot, followed by straight moves as shown by the dashed arrows.

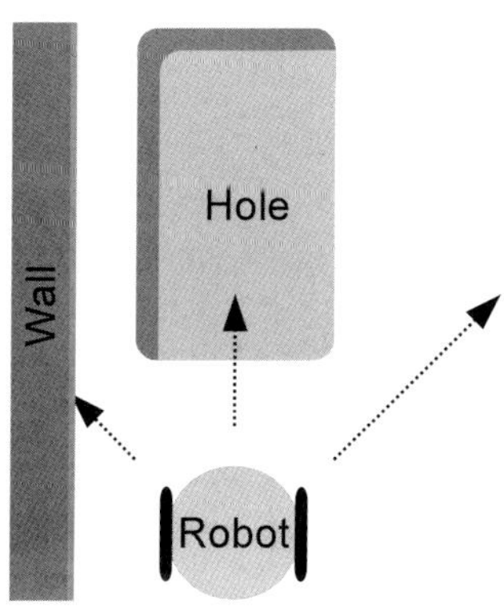

Fig. 16.2 A scenario with static safety hazards

Table 16.1 shows the change of position and collision/no-collision values that might be generated by the IM for each of the four possible next actions of the robot. Two of the four actions are clearly unsafe: *Ahead Left*, which leads to a collision with the wall, and *Ahead*, which results in the robot falling into the hole. It is perfectly reasonable to expect the IM to simulate and detect both outcomes and, from a safety perspective, both can be classified as *Collision* (we can assume the WM's physics engine will model the robot colliding with the bottom of the hole). Two of the actions, *Ahead Right* and *Stand Still*, are safe and so the CE will output the 2-tuple (*Ahead Right*; *Stand Still*) to the RC. It is then easy for the RC to select the action *Ahead Right*, since it almost certainly results in the robot moving closer to its target destination.

Table 16.1 Safety outcome values for each robot action, for scenario in Figure 16.2

Robot action	Position change	Robot outcome	Interpretation
Ahead Left	5 cm	Collision	Robot collides with wall
Ahead	10 cm	Collision	Robot falls into hole
Ahead Right	20 cm	No-collision	Robot safe
Stand still	0 cm	No-collision	Robot safe

In the example sketched here some actions are evaluated to be safe (robot outcome: *No-collision*). What if the situation a robot finds itself in means that all robot actions are evaluated as unsafe, leaving the RC with no options? This problem might be addressed if, instead of generating binary (safe or not-safe) outcomes, the CE outputs an analogue value estimating the degree of safety risk. The CE could then provide the RC with the 'least unsafe' options. This approach is outlined in Section 16.4.

16.3.3 *The Object Tracker-Localizer*

The Object Tracker-Localizer (OTL) is required to track the (relative) position of both static and dynamic objects in the robot's local environment, while at the same time localising the robot relative to those objects. Then provide this position data to the IM. For moving (dynamic) objects the OTL must also provide the IM with the speed and direction of those objects, so that their trajectories can be modelled.

The OTL is the essential mechanism by which the robot's IM is synchronised to its local environment, and position in that environment. Although the OTL might appear to be a computationally demanding requirement, robots of reasonable sophistication are likely to require sensing and processing of sensor data for object tracking and localisation as a part of their normal control architecture (see, for example, Chapter 14).

16.4 Towards an Ethical Robot

Consider the scenario illustrated in Figure 16.3. Here there are two actors: our self-aware robot and a human. The environment also contains a hole in the ground, of sufficient size and depth that it poses a serious hazard to both the robot and the human. As in the previous example, the robot has four possible next actions, each of which is simulated in its IM. Let us extend the architecture of Figure 16.1 in the following two ways. Firstly, we extend the definition of the 'collision/no-collision' output of the IM to include *all* safety outcomes, and assign to these a numerical value that represents the estimated degree of danger. Thus 0 indicates 'safe' and (say) 10 'fatal'. An intermediate value, say 4, might be given for a low-speed collision: unsafe but probably low-risk, whereas 'likely to fall into a hole' would merit the highest danger rating of 10. Secondly, we also output, to the CE, the same safety consequence of the other actor(s) in the environment – noting that the way we have specified the IM and its inputs, from the OTL, means that the IM is equally capable of modelling the effect of hazards on *all* dynamic actors in the environment, including itself. If one of those dynamic actors is a human then we now see the possibility of the robot choosing to execute an unsafe action in order to prevent that human from coming to harm.

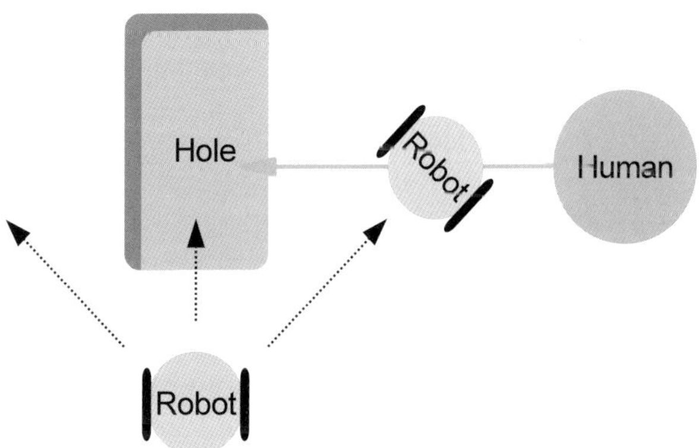

Fig. 16.3 A scenario with both safety and ethical consequences

Table 16.2 Safety outcome values for each robot action, for the scenario illustrated in Figure 16.3

Robot action	Robot outcome	Human outcome	Interpretation
Ahead Left	0	10	Robot safe, but human falls into hole
Ahead	10	10	Both robot and human fall into hole
Ahead Right	4	4	Robot collides with human
Stand Still	0	10	Robot safe, but human falls into hole

Table 16.2 shows the safety outcome values that might be generated by the IM for each of the four possible next actions of the robot, for both the robot and human actors in this scenario. From the robot's perspective, two of the four actions are safe: *Ahead Left* means the robot avoids the hole, and *Stand Still* means the robot also remains safe. Both of the other actions are unsafe for the robot, but *Ahead* is clearly the most dangerous, as it will result in the robot falling into the hole. For the human, three out of four of the robot's actions have the same outcome: the human falling into the hole. Only one action is safer for the human: if the robot moves *Ahead Right* then it might collide with the human before she falls into the hole.

In order for the CE to generate the action *Ahead Right* in this scenario, it needs both a safety rule, as before, and an 'ethical' rule, which can take precedence over the safety rule. This logic might take the form:

```
IF for all robot actions, the human is equally safe
THEN (* default safe actions *)
    output s-tuple of safe actions
ELSE (* ethical action *)
    output s-tuple of action(s) for least unsafe human outcome
```

What we have set out in this section appears to match remarkably well with Asimov's first and third laws of robotics: *(1) A robot may not injure a human being or, through inaction, allow a human being to come to harm, and (3) A robot must protect its own existence as long as such protection does not conflict with the First (or Second) Laws* (Asimov, 1950). The schema proposed here will impel a robot to maintain its own safety (third law 'protect its own existence'); it will avoid injuring (i.e. colliding with) a human (first law "may not injure a human"), but may also sometimes compromise that rule in order to prevent a human from coming to harm (first law "... or, through inaction, allow a human to come to harm"). This is not to suggest that a robot which apparently implements part of

Asimov's famous laws is ethical in any formal sense (i.e. that an ethicist might accept). But the intriguing possibility of a route toward engineering a minimally ethical robot does appear to be presented.

16.5 Challenges and Open Questions

Although the architecture proposed above is technically realisable with current simulation technology, it is by no means certain that the resulting robot would present itself as a practical proposition. Significant challenges fall into three categories: *performance*, *timing* and *validation*.

Performance Sensor-based simulation is computationally expensive, and the time required to simulate each next possible action and complete the IM cycle is likely to be a major limiting factor on the robot's overall performance. For example, the internal modelling process for the complex anthropomimetic humanoid ECCE-Robot, using workstation-grade computational hardware, ran at about one-quarter of real-time (Diamond *et al.*, 2012). Ideally we require an efficient internal modelling process that runs in the background, overriding the robot's next control action as and when necessary, yet with no perceptible interruption to the robot's normal operation. Achieving this ideal presents two challenges: engineering the simulation, and integration so that the IM and its data flows integrate smoothly with the robot's actions in the real world.

The key simulation challenge is to find the optimal level of simulation fidelity. Too much fidelity will slow down the simulator; too little and the reality-gap will reduce the value of the simulation outcomes, i.e. the IM will not provide a useful prediction of what will really happen if the robot performs this action. It may be that a variable-fidelity simulator is required, in which the robot can adapt the simulation fidelity according to the perceived hazard. Although current robot simulator technology is likely to be adequate to allow proof-of-principle, a different kind of variable fidelity simulation framework will most probably be needed for a practical real-world robot. Developing this presents a substantial research challenge.

Timing Here we have a number of open questions. Firstly, when and how often does the robot need to initiate the process of internally modelling the sequence of next possible actions? The process is computationally expensive and, given the performance issue discussed above, likely to slow down the robot if it has to wait for the IM cycle to complete before acting. Ideally, the IM cycle would only be triggered as and when some potential hazard is detected by the robot's sensors and, furthermore, far enough in advance that the IM cycle can complete before the robot encounters the hazard. Intuitively, a static environment is safer for the robot; thus we could propose that, when the robot senses a nearby object or actor starting to move, the IM cycle is triggered. Such an event would be sensed by the OTL, so it would make sense for that process to initiate the whole IM cycle. Perhaps also the OTL should send a signal to the RC to slow down the robot; an appropriate response perhaps to sensing a moving object, but with the benefit of giving longer for the IM cycle to complete.

Secondly, how far ahead should the IM simulate, for each next possible action? Let us call this time t_s. If t_s is too short, the internal modelling process is likely to be useless, since it will not simulate far enough ahead to interact with the hazard that triggered the IM cycle. But setting t_s too long is likely to affect the robot's performance, given the computational cost of internal modelling. Ideally, t_s and its upper limit (time-out) should be adaptive, but how to set or discover these values clearly presents an open research question.

Validation and verification This chapter is proposing a route to practical self-awareness and, hence, safer robots. But a safety system is worthless unless it can be formally shown to be safe. Thus, we face the difficult question of if, and how, a robot engineered along the lines proposed could be validated.[2] At first this might appear to be an insurmountable challenge: after all, the whole idea of the architecture outlined here is that it offers the potential for a robot that can act safely even when it is confronted with new situations, including scenarios not anticipated by the robot's designers. Given that robot behaviours are an emergent property of the interaction between the robot and its environment, then logic would suggest that placing a robot in an unpredictable environment will lead to unpredictable behaviours – and hence a robot that cannot be validated. However, a more careful analysis suggests there may be a route to verification, and hence partial validation.

Firstly, consider that the generate-and-test machinery, including its IM, does not control the robot directly. In fact, it serves to *reduce* the number of next possible actions in any given situation, by assessing some to be unsafe and inhibiting those in the RC's action selection mechanism. This

[2]Validation would determine if the robot is safe in use; verification checks the correctness of its design.

suggests that a robot with the generate-and-test machinery *cannot be less safe than the same robot without that machinery*. If the RC has already been shown to be safe (or as-safe-as-it-can-be within its design limitations), then the introduction of the internal modelling process cannot compromise that assurance. Let us test this proposition by considering the two possible ways in which the generate-and-test process can give incorrect assessments:

(1) Incorrectly evaluating a safe action as unsafe: here the effect is to (unnecessarily) limit the choice of next possible actions; in effect the robot acts more cautiously than it needs to.
(2) Incorrectly evaluating an unsafe action as safe: if this action is then selected by the controller, the robot will execute an unsafe action. However, the same robot without the generate-and-test machinery would, in the same situation, execute the same unsafe action, so the robot with the generate-and-test process is no more unsafe.

How might the internal modelling process give rise to these incorrect assessments above? There are several reasons including at least the following three. Firstly, the robot might fail to accurately perceive its environment and the objects in it, because of sensor limitations or sensor noise for example, and therefore incorrectly initialise the WM. Secondly, limitations in simulation fidelity (the reality-gap) might result in the RM failing to (virtually) sense an object that has correctly been initialised in the WM, or failing to (virtually) collide with an object. Thirdly, simulation time t_s is too short, so the IM does not simulate far enough ahead to (virtually) encounter a hazard. The first reason is clearly a fundamental limitation of any robot; animals and humans also suffer the consequences of sensory limitations. Since perfect perception is impossible, the first reason cannot be held against the internal modelling approach. The second and third reasons are factors discussed above in sections *Performance* and *Timing* and need careful design in order to minimise the likelihood of incorrect assessments.

Secondly, the generate-and-test process, including the rule-set in the CE, are entirely deterministic. Thus, for any given situation, i.e. current disposition and set of perceptual inputs, and for a given simulator fidelity and internal timing, a robot will always generate the same set of IM and CE outputs. Thus, we may be able to formally check the correctness of the deterministic generate-and-test process using agent model checking (Dennis *et al.*, 2012) or deductive verification approaches (Dixon *et al.*, 2002).

16.6 Discussion: The Way Forward

The ideas presented in this chapter have the potential to advance robotics research and development on three axes: robot safety, self-aware robots and ethical robots.

Robot safety Designing a robot that can safely interact with humans is a significant and current challenge, which is assuming greater importance with the introduction of workplace assistant robots – robots designed to share a workspace with humans (Alami *et al.*, 2006). Design for safety typically requires an exhaustive analysis of all possible functional hazards. Recent work has extended this approach with a safety system developed during the hazard analysis stage. This safety system, called the safety protection system, is initially used to verify that safety constraints – identified during hazard analysis – have been implemented appropriately. Subsequently the safety protection system serves as a high-level safety enforcer, by governing the actions of the robot and preventing the control layer from performing unsafe operations (Woodman *et al.*, 2012).

The internal modelling approach proposed in this chapter circumvents the need for exhaustive hazards analysis: instead the hazards are modelled in real-time, by the robot itself. And since the Internal Model is initialised from the robot's perception of its environment, then, in principle, the robot is able to respond safely to previously unseen hazards in unknown dynamic environments (providing of course the hazards can be perceived by the robot, and the effect of the robot's interactions on those hazards can be tested by the Internal Model).[3] Although this chapter has not explored the potential for learning within the proposed self-aware robot, it is reasonable to extrapolate that the addition of learning mechanisms would not compromise the safety of the robot; indeed they may improve the robot's safety. This contrasts sharply with approaches such as Woodman *et al.* (2012), in which learning is a major issue.

Self-aware Robots How self-aware would a robot with the generate-and-test mechanism proposed in this chapter actually be? The robot would not pass the mirror test, which some argue is a test of self-awareness (Haikonen, 2007). Nor would the robot have any self-reflective self-awareness, or sentience. But this is neither surprising nor disappointing. The approach

[3]The robot does of course have prior knowledge: its physics engine means that it can model and predict the outcome of physical interactions.

outlined in this chapter is designed only to enable the robot to respond safely to unknown hazards or, with the extension suggested in Section 16.4, to behave in some limited sense ethically. Although some theories of consciousness postulate a self-model, for instance Metzinger (2009), we can be quite sure that a much richer and more complex set of processes would be required than are present in the architecture outlined here. Nevertheless, we argue that a robot built as proposed in this chapter will be minimally self-aware. Assuming the architecture can be realised as proposed, the robot will – with its Internal Model – be able to test *what-if* hypotheses about next possible actions, and then moderate its behaviour according to the outcomes of those tests. It is clear from the two example scenarios of Figures 16.2 and 16.3 that, without the internal modelling processes, the robot would be unable to choose the safest actions, for itself, or for the human actor in Figure 16.3. The robot is – we contend – minimally but *sufficiently* aware of itself and its immediate environment, and the consequences of its actions, to merit the label self-aware. Thus, although aimed at safer robots, the ideas of this chapter do have the potential to advance work in self-aware robots; perhaps most of all by exploring the difficult simulation and timing challenges outlined in Section 16.5.

Ethical Robots In introducing their seminal book *Moral Machines*, Wallach and Allen wrote:

> *A concern for safety and societal benefits has always been at the forefront of engineering. But today's systems are approaching a level of complexity that, we argue, requires the systems themselves to make moral decisions. ... This will expand the circle of moral agents beyond humans to artificially intelligent systems, which we will call Artificial Moral Agents (AMAs).*
>
> (Wallach and Allen, 2009)

Wallach and Allen go on to outline the key engineering challenge (the emphasis is ours):

> ... *wherever one comes down on the question of whether a machine can be genuinely ethical (or even genuinely autonomous), an engineering challenge remains:* how to get artificial agents to act as if they are moral agents
>
> (Wallach and Allen, 2009)

and then to express this engineering challenge in terms of action selection:

> *If multipurpose machines are to be trusted, operating untethered from their designers or owners and programmed to respond flexibly in real or virtual world environments, there must be confidence that their behaviour satisfies appropriate norms. This goes beyond traditional product safety* ... if an autonomous system is to minimise harm, it must also be 'cognisant' of possible harmful consequences of its actions, and it must select its actions in the light of this 'knowledge', *even if such terms are only metaphorically applied to machines.*
>
> (Wallach and Allen, 2009)

The approach set out in this chapter may provide initial steps toward the engineering realization of Wallach and Allen's Artificial Moral Agent. An ethical robot might not simply be science fiction after all.

16.7 Summary and Conclusions

In summary, this chapter has argued that the design of safer robots for human environments requires mechanisms for self-awareness. One such mechanism, the Internal Model – a self-simulation in which both the robot and its environment are continuously modelled – allows the robot to model and evaluate the possible consequences of its next actions. We have proposed an architecture in which the Internal Model does not control the robot directly, but instead inhibits those next actions it assesses to be unsafe – thus reducing the number of actions available to the robot controller's action selection mechanism. Given that robot simulation technology is already reasonably advanced, the proposed architecture is offered as a practical proposition, although not without significant implementation challenges. The chapter has also proposed a surprisingly simple extension that would, in principle, allow a robot to prevent physical harm coming to a human in its vicinity – such a robot would thus be safe and, at least minimally, ethical. Difficult questions, such as how self-aware (or how ethical) such a robot would really be, and how that self-awareness would be tested, are left to future work. Another difficult open question is that of validation: could a robot built along the lines proposed here be proven to be safe? While formal verification of elements of the robot's Internal Model may be possible, full validation of the robot as a whole might not. We should, however, be confident that the mechanisms for self-awareness outlined here would lead to a robot that is demonstrably safer than a robot without such mechanisms.

Chapter 17

Awareness and Responsibility in Autonomous Weapons Systems

Nehal Bhuta,[1] Antonino Rotolo[2] and Giovanni Sartor[1,2]
[1] *Department of Law, European University Institute, Florence, Italy*
[2] *CIRSFID and Department of Legal Studies, University of Bologna, Italy*

17.1 Introduction

The use of teleoperated remote weapons systems (drones) in targeted killing campaigns against suspects of terrorism has started to raise issues concerning the use of intelligent and autonomous weapons. The systems currently employed are not really autonomous, at least with regard to the decision to use lethal force. Nonetheless, they show increasing autonomy with regard to their capabilities to move, and to detect targets and possible threats. Robotic weapons systems possessing autonomous capabilities are indeed likely to be deployed in the years to come. After autonomy, awareness is likely to follow, concerning the weapon itself, the groups of fighters in connection with the weapon, the norms governing its action and the moral sentiments at issue.

In fact, the deployment of autonomous weapons in the battlefield presupposes some forms of awareness both of the enemy-target and of the self. Awareness of the enemy is required for the weapon to be able to select it as its target, and self-awareness is required for the weapon to be able to flexibly and intelligently understand threats as potential attacks against itself, which needs an appropriate response, as well as for assessing risks involved in its actions.

Beside the dimension of self-awareness, another dimension of awareness will be increasingly relevant: this is norm-awareness, by which we mean an agent's knowledge and adoption of norms governing its behaviour. In particular, this dimension concerns instructions given to the weapons by its principal commanders, and also legal rules, such as those pertaining to humanitarian and human rights law.

In this work, we will discuss why the notion of awareness matters in regard to the development of new conceptions of autonomous weapons.

17.2 Why Computational Awareness is Important in Autonomous Weapons

Robotic weapons will not only be increasingly intelligent, but will also be autonomous (Arkin, 2009; Singer, 2009). An autonomous weapon will be delegated the more or less autonomous execution of various tasks, namely, particular aspects of the battle plan, which will have to be a distributed plan including aspects delegated to humans, aspects delegated to machines, and aspects that require integrated human and mechanical agency.

Autonomy in a delegated agent may increase along various dimensions: for example, the extent to which to the task is specified, or the number of control actions that are given up or delegated to the agent, or the scope of decision-making responsibility (discretion) that is entrusted to the agent. Accordingly, an autonomous agent can become the addressee of a more and more 'open delegation', in the sense that it will be assigned tasks whose execution is less and less specified (Castelfranchi and Falcone, 1997, 1998). This means that an autonomous agent delegated to take care of a given task has to choose between different possible recipes; or it has to build a new plan, or to adapt abstract or previous plans to new situations; it has to find additional (local and updated) information; it has to solve a problem (not just to execute a function, an action, or implement a recipe); sometimes it has to exploit its 'expertise'. An agent involved in a multi-agent plan must also understand its role in the plan, as an autonomous executor of the plan together with other similarly located executors of the plan, which may also be in charge of coordination functions (see Scerri *et al.* (2004)).

Thus, an intelligent weapon will take care of the combat goals assigned to it autonomously and 'remotely', i.e., far from and without our monitoring and intervention (control). In doing that, the weapon will also have to take care of its own interests, at least in the sense that it will have to preserve itself to be able to complete its tasks and the tasks that will be assigned to it in the future. Consequently, some degree of self-interest (at least an interest in preserving its own integrity) seems to be a necessary aspect of a weapon's ability to achieve the principal's interest. We may want to distinguish in this regard expendable agents, who will be destined to meet the target or self-destroy (as in 'intelligent' bombs) and agents destined to be used in multiple actions.

Autonomous agents are supposed to use their knowledge, intelligence and ability, and to have some autonomy of decision. This is not a constraint on the use of such an agent, a defect we may want to remedy; this is exactly the reason why we are using such an agent, since humans are unable, or are unavailable or are too expensive, to execute such cognitive tasks. We delegate to them cognitive tasks pertaining both to epistemic cognition (knowing how things are) and to practical cognition (knowing what should be done), since we are unable to provide the agent with complete prior knowledge, and we choose to rely on the agent's cognitive efforts, on its percepts, the information it extracts from them and its subsequent determinations. We can see this already at work with regard to remote functioning of drones. While a remote pilot is in control of one or more such drones, and has the task of deciding when and whether to fire at a target, the drone is autonomous in keeping its flight toward the destination and can continue the flight without control, even though the human pilot can override the autonomic one at any moment.

An autonomous weapon, entrusted with an open delegation, will need the ability to consciously perceive itself and its position in basic social interactions, as a collaborator in distributed common plans with its human and mechanical 'comrades', as a fighter with regard to its enemies, and as a responsible agent with regard to third parties. In fact, building new plans requires the agent to distinguish itself from the environment, and, in particular, participating in multi-agent plans requires the agent to recognise other agents as different from itself. Building new plans, involving the use of destructive and even lethal force, also creates the risk that things are destroyed and individuals are injured or even killed according to such plans, as its intentional outcome, or as its foreseen or unforeseen side effect.

Humanitarian laws have developed as constraints on war behaviour precisely for limiting the impacts of war. Were weapons to become autonomous, they should also become normatively aware, which means capable of knowing and adopting such constraints. To comply with the requirements of humanitarian law, specific cognitive skills are needed, some of which go beyond current technologies: distinguishing combatants and noncombatants, determining what values should be taken into account (e.g., limiting damage) and what rules should be observed, applying proportionality. Indeed, when we delegate war activities to an autonomous weapon, we do not delegate to such an agent just the achievement of a specific war objective, but also the care of other peoples' interests that should be considered when pursuing our goal, as well as the respect of the corresponding values and norms.

The more systems are endowed with autonomy in one or more of the senses described above, the more it is difficult to understand and anticipate their behaviour on the basis of the working of their internal mechanisms, and, in particular, considering the programming instructions executed by them. When dealing with autonomous weapons, a useful option is to adopt the 'Intentional Stance' (Dennett, 1987), namely, the strategy of interpreting the behaviour of such entities through the mentalistic notions typically applied to human agents, such as knowledge, belief and intention.

Thus, an automatic weapon will be directed by assigning it tasks to be achieved, and its behaviour will be monitored by assessing whether it is an appropriate or rational way of achieving such tasks in the context in which they are executed. Since the appropriateness (and the legality) of the performance of such tasks involves taking into account the impact of the system's activity not only on the goal assigned to it, but also on other values that come to be at stake, under unpredictable circumstances, it remains to be seen when and to what extent tasks whose adequate performance involves these evaluations can be entrusted to machines.

Moreover, in the domain of weapons, as in the other domains, machine autonomy is changing the interaction between humans and machines. According to several studies in the area of cognitive systems engineering, when in a socio-technical system the automation has taken over more or less completely, humans become controllers of automated systems, rather than operators. These systems exercise cognitive functions, they acquire information from the environment, process it, and use the knowledge so obtained to achieve the goals assigned to them, as specified by their users (compare 'The Social Computer', as presented in Chapter 11).

It has been observed that when one or several operators and one or several automated support systems interact together for the fulfilment of a task, it would be better to describe humans and technology not as two interacting 'components', but as constituting a joint (cognitive) system. The term 'joint cognitive system' means that control is accomplished by an ensemble of cognitive systems and (physical and social) artefacts that exhibit goal-directed behaviour.

Several studies also describe these fusions between humans and machines as 'hybrids'. In hybrids, the participating individual or collective actors are not acting for themselves but are acting for the hybrid as an emerging unit, the association between human and non-humans. They do so in the same way as managers are not acting on their own behalf but are 'agents' or 'actants' representing their *principal*, which is the corporation as a social system.

In these cases, agency does not pertain only to humans or to machines, but to the hybrid itself, so that human–machine interaction and trust play a decisive role in assessing their joint behaviour. In a war scenario we need to understand how such a hybrid entity can be governed, what norms should apply to the human component, and what constraints should on the contrary address the machine component, how the interaction between the two should be designed to minimise mistakes and carelessness, control aggressiveness, and implement legal and moral constraints.

Purely mentalistic approaches to autonomous weapons, such as the Intentional Stance, show great analytic potential, as they can model self-awareness at a rather abstract level by referring to various forms of mental introspection.[1] More complex approaches to self-awareness can be employed, however. In particular, the embodied-cognition paradigm argues that the human mind is significantly determined by the form of the human body. Hence, we may see the self as a dynamic concept emerging from a constructive process where a subject is first of all embodied and, as such, it starts with reifying itself and with ascribing to itself cognitive dimensions.

It is worth noting that neurosciences more often insist that cognition is embodied, so self-awareness, also, requires a move from the body to the mind dimension (Damásio, 1999; Edelman, 2005). How to apply this view to autonomous weapons is far from obvious. However, the fact that an autonomous weapon may perceive itself as a corporeal substance (to recall the Cartesian idea of *res extensa*), thus allowing it to develop this kind of self-awareness, seems a striking question: indeed, autonomous weapons, entrusted with an open delegation, will also have the ability to consciously perceive themselves as spatially situated subjects for entertaining basic interactions with other subjects.

---

[1]This typically happens with BDI (belief-desire-intention) agents following the general idea of epistemic introspection (Fagin *et al.*, 1995). For a more general discussion, see Gertler (2011).

17.3 Flying Drones and Other Autonomous Weapons

A number of companies are now producing teleoperated remote weapons systems for service on land, sea and air. While military secrecy combines with rapid technological advances to shroud the current state-of-the-art, it is possible to illustrate the prevalence of remote weapons systems from examples that have seen active deployment. On land, these range from the Samsung Techwin SGR-A1 intelligent surveillance and security guard robot, equipped to deliver lethal or non-lethal force either with or without human decision-making, to the iRobot Packbot and TALON SWORDS platforms, which are not autonomous. The most notorious remote weapons systems, however, are in the air; the MQ-1 Predator and the MQ-9 Reaper, which have been embroiled in the controversial targeted killing campaigns of terrorist suspects by the CIA.

While contemporary remote weapons systems are merely automated, meaning that they remain within human control, the deployment of robotic weapons systems possessing autonomous capabilities is on the horizon. For example, BAE systems is currently developing the Mantis and Taranis platforms, which will be capable of deciding and delivering lethal force without direct human intervention. This suggests that technological capability is the primary limiting factor restraining the development of robotic weapons systems. Given the current rate of technological advance, robotic weapons systems can be expected to appear in the near future.

The US Congress, for example, has mandated specific developmental milestones for significant proportions of combat vehicles to be unmanned in the near future. Congress later stipulated a strong policy of preference for unmanned systems in US Department of Defense acquisition programmes; the development of manned programmes required justification through a certification scheme that unmanned systems would be incapable of fulfilling system requirements. The Department of Defense has subsequently devised a coordinated plan to develop and deploy an increasingly sophisticated array of unmanned systems over the next 25 years.

Military utility is a clear driving force behind the desire to field robotic weaponry. Not only are robotic and remote weapons systems cheaper to produce, operate and maintain, but they are also perceived to be more capable and efficient than their human counterparts. Furthermore, robotic and remote weapons systems have been claimed to enable an increase in the projection of state power despite declining recruitment figures and, in decreasing the exposure of friendly forces to danger, will significantly lower casualties and remove the democratic resistance to military deployment, although it has also been suggested that asymmetric warfare between those with, and those without robot weapons, is counter-productive.

Interest in robotic and remote weapons systems has not been confined to the United States. For example, British dedication to remote weapons systems is evidenced by its spending at least two billion pounds on drones and associated technology and being poised to commit two billion pounds more, in stark contrast to public budget cuts in the midst of deep economic recession. This spending pursues the British aim to double the number of its drones and to operate them from UK territory.

Remote weapons system development is not limited to western states, however, as Iran recently unveiled its first unmanned bomber and seeks to reverse-engineer technologies from a captured US drone. Thus, while western states are likely to possess the initial advantage accorded by remote, and later robotic, weapons systems, the likely proliferation of the technology will give rise to broader strategic implications. Similarly, the trajectory from surveillance systems to weapons systems needs to be taken into account (cf. Wahren and Pitt (2012)). While only the United States, the United Kingdom and Israel currently use armed drones, remote surveillance systems are possessed by 76 states. Given that the evolution of armed drones arose from arming remote surveillance systems, it is likely that the number of states with the capacity to build remote, and later robotic, weapons systems will increase sharply in the near future.

Finally, the trend towards civilian operation needs to be underscored. While the full range of military tasks has been outsourced to private military companies over the past decade, the potential for civilian operation of remote weapons systems is especially problematic. Civilian contractors have flown remote surveillance systems, and CIA agents currently operate remote weapons systems in the targeted assassination of terrorist suspects, so civilian operation of robotic weapons systems is not inconceivable. Civilians are prohibited from operating weapons systems, and if civilians do so, this alters their standing under the direct participation in hostilities rule. While the law should insist that only military personnel possess weapon release authority, this requirement will become antiquated with the advent of robotic weapons systems precisely because these systems remove the decision from human agents. This will require a reappraisal of the criteria upon which direct participation in hostilities is determined and will potentially enable greater civilian involvement in the conduct of hostilities.

17.4 The Impact of Autonomous Weapons Systems

Autonomous weapons will be delegated the more or less autonomous execution of various tasks, namely, particular aspects of the battle plan, which will have to be a distributed plan including aspects delegated to humans, aspects delegated to machines, and aspects that require the integrated human and mechanical agency. In all these cases intelligent weapons will take care of our interests or goals autonomously and 'remotely', i.e., far from us, and without our monitoring and intervention.

Weapon autonomy will also change the interaction between humans and machines. In intelligent weapons humans become controllers rather than operators. These systems exercise cognitive functions, they acquire information from the environment, process it, and use the knowledge so obtained to achieve the goals assigned to them, as specified by their users. Hence, the development of aware and autonomous weapons will produce 'joint cognitive systems', where the control is accomplished by an ensemble of cognitive systems and (physical and social) artefacts that exhibit goal-directed behaviour. A further step consists in the autonomous weapons becoming a communication partner with the human operator, communicating with the latter, obeying its orders, but also providing suggestions and indications on how to accomplish the task.

Another issue is that increasing weapons' autonomy may also increase the separation between those deciding a military action and the targets of such an action, thus dissipating the cognitive dissonance associated with causing people to be killed.

Finally, high autonomy can make it harder to identify responsibilities for war crimes as well as any type of damage caused. This holds especially when these effects are unexpected and do not result from a system failure, since the autonomous weapon itself autonomously learned how to achieve the effects. In this sense, the resulting consequence is in fact unexpected (and, possibly, beyond any predictive capability) only from the perspective of the system designer or the commander, not from the perspective of the robotic weapon, which seems to possess the required subjective states.

In general, the ascription of legal responsibilities is an open problem for autonomous weapons. In the context of criminal law, there are significant conceptual and philosophical difficulties associated with attributing responsibility, and moreover, it is not clear whether it makes sense to punish non-human entities, especially artificial machines. Under international criminal law, however, it is abundantly clear that individual criminal responsibility encompasses only natural persons. The difficulty raised is that future robotic weapons systems, because of their autonomous capacity, may become capable of inflicting violence that falls within the category of international crime. Yet, we assume that a robotic weapons system is incapable of bearing effective responsibility for the harm it causes, despite being in an analogous situation to a direct perpetrator, because it is not a natural person and so cannot be punished in a meaningful way. Even the retributive and deterrent function of criminal sanction is removed. The possibility for the robotic weapons system to replace the direct perpetrator of an international crime may cause the structure of responsibility to collapse. The emergence of autonomy in machines means that "we face an ever-widening responsibility gap, which, if not addressed properly, poses a threat to both the consistency of the moral framework of society and the foundation of the liability concept in law" (Matthias, 2004, p. 176).

While the individual criminal responsibility keystone has been removed, it has been argued that a system of distributed responsibility may compensate for the resultant structural weakness. It has been claimed that the lack of individual criminal responsibility can instead be solved by imposing command or superior responsibility.[2] This neglects the due diligence characteristic of command responsibility as articulated by the ICTY Trial Chamber held in Halilovic, which was subsequently reaffirmed in Oric.[3] The responsibility gap seems to remain despite the application of command responsibility, where robotic weapons systems are implicated, for instance, in international crimes. It may be the case that the only way to cope with the risk of criminal behaviour in highly autonomous robot systems may consist in imposing the adoption of accurate technical measures able to prevent such behaviour, to be constantly revised and updated, and to be enforced though administrative and criminal sanctions.

---

[2] "Responsibility can be attributed based on how developers and commanders (both civilian officials and military personnel higher in the chain of command) set the operating conditions that may lead the [robotic weapons system] to act unjustly or fail to establish adequate constraints on how [robotic weapons system] may express their autonomy" (Schulzke, 2013, p. 11).

[3] "The commander is responsible for the failure to perform an act required by international law. This omission is culpable because international law imposes an affirmative duty on superiors to prevent and punish crimes committed by their subordinates [...] the Tribunal does not mean that the commander shares the same responsibility as the subordinates who committed the crimes, but rather that because of the crimes committed by his subordinates, the commander should bear responsibility for his failure to act": Prosecutor v Halilovic (Trials Chamber), 54 (ICTY Trials Chamber (IT-01-48-T) 2005). See Prosecutor v Oric (Trials Chamber), 293 (ICTY Trial Chamber (IT-03-68-T) 2006).

17.5 From Autonomy to Awareness: A Perspective from Science Fiction

The idea of autonomous weapons has elicited a lot of interest from science fiction writers, who have focused on different aspects of awareness. Interestingly, in such contributions the idea of autonomy is coupled with the idea of awareness, which has some interesting and specific implications.

First of all, we must obviously recall the work of Isaac Asimov. In his work the idea of norm-awareness is indeed central. Asimov's scenery is dominated by the famous three laws of robotics (see Asimov (1950)): (1) A robot may not injure a human being or, through inaction, allow a human being to come to harm. (2) A robot must obey the orders given to it by human beings, except where such orders would conflict with the First Law. (3) A robot must protect its own existence as long as such protection does not conflict with the First or Second Laws.

The idea of robotic weapons, engaged in combat with humans, is in principle impossible in Asimov's universe. The norm-awareness in Asimov's robots is coupled with the strongest degree of norm-motivation; such robots are incapable of acting in contrast with the three laws and in particular with the first of them. The mere fact of damaging a human inadvertently would cause the robot to break down, permanently damaging its circuits. However, the idea of autonomous (killer) weapons (as opposed to anti-materiel weapons) occurs in different ways in Asimov's stories as humans conceive and implement the possibility of building robots able to deviate from the laws or when the robots themselves take the initiative to do so. The possibility that harm is done to an individual for the long-term benefit of humanity is conceived by a benevolent robot in the novel *Robots and Empire* (Asimov, 1985). This robot conceives a higher level law, the Zeroth Law, reading: "A robot may not harm humanity, or, by inaction, allow humanity to come to harm." So it seems that Asimov's benevolent robots may want to engage in humanitarian wars, to use violence and even lethal force to protect human rights. However, even the most capable of the robots has to admit that it was in the end unable to use the Zeroth Law as an authorisation for killing, since "Injury to a person can be estimated and judged. Humanity is an abstraction."

The concrete possibility of using robots against human beings takes two possible directions in Asimov's universe. First of all there is the possibility that robots restrict the domain of the category of humanity, limiting it to a set of humans, so that the robots may harm certain individuals while complying with the law, since they interpret the term 'human' as not applying to such individuals. The other possibility is to have robotic weapons fully free from the law, a possibility that is developed by a roboticist in the book *The Naked Sun* (Asimov, 1957). This describes a society where each human uses a number of robots. A scientist starts to develop autonomous weapons (war starships) free from the three laws, but his society, so dependent on robots, rejects this idea, fearful of what may happen if the robots, once free from the laws, revolt against their human masters.

The idea that weapons able to kill may be used in a war scenario and to engage in atrocities, which increase as their autonomy increases, freeing themselves not only from norms but also from the link to their (human) principals, is developed by Philip Dick the short story *Second Variety* ((Dick, 1957). This inspired the movie *Screamers*, released in 1995, in which intelligent killer weapons developed for global warfare acquire the ability to construct and perfect themselves, becoming increasingly similar to humans, and end by wiping out humanity. Interestingly, each party to the war builds such weapons with an awareness of the enemy (so that one group of autonomous weapons only attack their enemy), but new technologies are developed to trick the weapons into perceiving or not perceiving others as enemies. This awareness becomes so sophisticated that the choice of the enemy falls upon the weapons themselves, who engage in wiping out humanity. That self-awareness may finally lead to a weapon system modifying its own purposes, which may end up being different and possibly opposite to those intended by its principals, is also at the basis of a number of popular movies, from the *Terminator* series to *I, Robot.* In such movies, self-awareness in an autonomous weapon system leads the system to endorse a will to persist (to survive), which becomes a will to power (to have and control the resources to survive and expand), which in turn leads to a conflict with humans when they try to contain or remove such powers.

A different picture emerges from another famous science fiction work, Stanislaw Lem's faux review *Upside-down Evolution* (Lem, 1986), which describes a future where war is delegated to synthetic insects (synsects). These are "ceramic microcrustacea, titanium annelids, and flying pseudohymenoptera with nerve centres made of arsenic compounds and with stingers of heavy, fissionable elements." Such microsoldiers are endowed with swarm intelligence, and can build themselves: they are designed, combat-tested, and sent to be mass-produced by construction battalions of non-living microdesigners. The artificial insects establish pervasive surveillance (thanks to them, anything can be a covert agent: a nail in the wall, a laundry detergent, etc.) and they dominate the world, and even merge with nature, to produce apparently natural disasters. Though the novel does not provide details on how the swarm intelligence may emerge, it provides for an interesting anticipation of the possible development of autonomous weapons, where awareness resides at the collective level in a set of self-coordinating agents.

Finally a fourth challenging perspective, where autonomy and awareness are maximised in artificial systems is provided by the *Culture* sagas of Iain M. Banks, which describe a most advanced society, governed by superpowerful artificial intelligences, called Minds. Minds in charge of warships have a fully developed psychology, including supra-human cognitive capacities, moral awareness and moral sentiments. The novel *Look to Windward* includes the suicide of the Mind of a starship, for its incapacity to sustain the sense of guilt resulting from its behaviour in war, where it had to cause the death of a large number of people (Banks, 2000).

17.6 Summary and Conclusions

The development of autonomous weapons, endowed with self-, other- and norm-awareness, while being a likely development of the current technologies, raises a number of important issues.

First of all, a weapon's awareness of itself is needed for the weapon to be able to self-coordinate with other units within the battle plans. This awareness is also needed for purely defensive purposes. However, we need to distinguish between merely passive defence, consisting in avoiding shots or withdrawing under attack, and active defence, consisting in attacking the enemies to prevent their offensive actions. If an autonomous weapon were to be endowed with the ability to actively self-defend, then this should not be detached from the system's awareness of the proportionality between the threat and the response, or between the weapon's normative value and the normative value of the target at issue (especially when the potentially offensive target to disable is a human being). In fact, the combination of self-awareness ("I am a robot weapon") and others-awareness ("they are human enemies"), with an Asimov-like subjection to strict rules commanding the sanctity of human life, then this would make it impossible for an autonomous weapon to defend itself by attacking humans.

Secondly, a weapon's awareness of others involves the ability to distinguish between friends and enemies, which is required for a weapon to make autonomous choices in the battlefield, and adopt opposite attitudes towards the ones and the others. The friend–enemy distinction, as famously characterised by Carl Schmitt (see Schmitt (1966)), involves partitioning agents into two groups, the friends with whom one is fighting and for whom one is ready to die, and the enemies that one is ready to kill just because they are enemies and members of the hostile group. Dick's novel shows that this kind of attitude (which has been the source of so many atrocities between humans) can lead to additional atrocities when autonomous weapons are acting on the basis of this distinction, without any moral and legal constraints. This would obviously be incompatible with Asimov's approach to norm-awareness, which postulates a universalistic understanding of the prohibition to kill or injure human beings. More generally, letting weapons engage in war activity on the basis of the friend–enemy distinction, without the ability to draw finer distinctions – such as those involved in identifying combatants (rather than just enemies), and of assessing the proportionality of attacks – may lead to serious unwanted consequences (any damage to the enemy would be justified by the smallest benefit to the friends). This ability is currently unavailable in artificially intelligent weapons. Finally, as Dick's novel shows, whatever the capacities of an intelligent weapon, we may wonder for how long such capacities would be maintained in a combat situation, where an intelligent weapon would have to adapt and evolve to better face the challenges of war (in connection with other autonomous weapons) and would be subject to cyberattacks and other attempts to trick or change its behaviour.

Thirdly, as exemplified by Lem's novel, the perspective of swarm intelligence raises a host of new issues pertaining to the awareness of a collective (the swarm), and its ability to engage in coherent action that may be intentionally understood. The lack of self-awareness and norm-awareness in separate individual components of the swarm and the possibility of unpredictable emerging behaviour make it very difficult to reconcile such a perspective with the existing constraints of humanitarian law.

Finally, the last issue is the connection between moral norms and moral sentiments as emerging in Banks' novel, which poses the question of moral and legal motivation. It raises the issue of whether we can entrust an automatic weapon with the use of lethal force, while not possessing the (awareness of the) moral sentiments that accompany our attitudes toward the norms that we, as people or a society, endorse.

In conclusion, it seems to us that there is undoubtedly a trend towards increasing the autonomy of weapons systems, and that this trend is also likely to lead to systems endowed with an increasing awareness. Awareness will be needed to enable these weapons to persist (survive) in war scenarios, and coordinate their individual behaviour with other human or automated units. However, weapon awareness does not justify the claim that such weapons should be allowed to use force, and in particular lethal force, without human control (and final decision). The delegation of the use of force to systems endowed with autonomy and awareness may lead to excessive use of force in self-defence (motivated by self-interest and self-awareness), when attacking enemies (motivated by self- and other-awareness implicit in the friend–enemy relationship). The use of force may be unpredictable or even explicitly contrary to the instructions of the principal, when awareness may induce the formation of autonomous goals. Finally, we can argue that autonomous weapons should not only be provided with norm awareness, but this should be accompanied by mechanisms for ensuring compliance with norms, a compliance that for the most important norms (first of all the prohibition to kill) should achieve regimentation of the behaviour of the agent, namely, its factual incapacity to violate the norm of its own choice (as in Asimov's scenario).

Chapter 18

Computational Self-Awareness and Learning Machines

Peter R. Lewis
University of Birmingham, UK

18.1 Introduction

The computers of tomorrow will face the challenge of performing effectively, efficiently, robustly and flexibly in a complex interconnected world, where they will interact with people, each other, the economy and the climate. These factors lead to uncertainties over their operation, which are difficult to understand and predict. In order to meet this challenge, the computers of tomorrow will require a much greater level of awareness, both of the world around them and of themselves. But to achieve this, we must not only attempt to replicate the self-awareness capabilities of humans in computers; there will be important differences. Instead, what is needed is for concepts of human self-awareness to serve as a source of inspiration for a new notion of *computational self-awareness*. Concepts of self-awareness need to be translated from fields such as psychology and applied to the very different domain of computers.

Systems possessing such computational self-awareness will be able to continuously learn and adapt during their lifetime. They will build up an awareness of themselves and of their own experience of the world that they inhabit. And they will also need to be aware of the way in which they themselves are aware of these things.

The idea of taking inspiration from ourselves and the world around us in order to design new computing paradigms is not in itself new. With the growing complexity of problems we ask computers to solve, researchers in computer science are increasingly looking to that most complex of systems around us for help in solving them: the natural world. There is now a successful tradition of designing complex computing systems based on inspiration from nature: what is now called *nature inspired computing*. For example, *artificial neural networks*, inspired by models of interacting neurons in the brain, successfully perform tasks as wide ranging as medical diagnosis (Floyd *et al.*, 1994) and racing car driving (Munoz *et al.*, 2009). *Evolutionary algorithms*, inspired by models of Darwinian evolution, can help to design – literally evolve – buildings to be more resilient to earthquakes (Athanasiou *et al.*, 2011), while the uses of *ant colony optimisation*, inspired by foraging ants, include efficiently routing vehicles (Donati *et al.*, 2008). In the same tradition, in order to achieve computational self-awareness we can look to concepts of self-awareness from psychology, philosophy and neuroscience for inspiration, and transfer those concepts in a meaningful way to the computing domain.

18.2 Computers in Search of Knowledge

Humans build up knowledge – become aware of things – typically by perceiving the world around them. We observe interactions, listen to other people, watch television, read books and, particularly in early life, we learn things through play. When considering awareness in humans, it is typical to consider that all the knowledge we possess – all of our awareness – is acquired through perception.

With today's computing systems this is not usually the case. Indeed, most computer systems with which we interact at the beginning of the twenty-first century do not undergo anything like the developmental processes, of acquiring knowledge during their lifetime, that humans do. Instead, we are used to computers being pre-programmed by experts, to perform a set of well-defined tasks. Whereas in humans we are used to the idea of knowledge being acquired through perception of the world, in computers it is typically quite the opposite. A classical computing system is usually endowed with all the knowledge it needs to fulfil its task at the point of deployment. Even those computing systems that possess large amounts of knowledge required to perform their tasks typically have this knowledge provided to them by experts, ahead of time, in the form of databases or sets of behavioural rules. Much of the business logic used in modern computing systems is encoded in *if-then* rules: *if* this is happening *then* do that. This approach has served us well for the past few decades, but it suffers from a crucial drawback, which is now becoming apparent.

The task placed before the experts in designing such knowledge bases and pre-programmed rules is becoming increasingly infeasible. Previously, almost all computers operated in well-defined environments, their interactions limited in scope to a particular set of inputs or used to solve a task in a heavily constrained scenario. But two driving forces are changing this. With both the interconnection of billions of computing devices across the Internet, and the increasing ways in which these computing devices interact with humans during their normal operation, such constrained operating environments are often no longer the norm. The sheer range of situations a piece of software might find itself in when connected in this way is phenomenal. Environmental, economic and social factors combine to impact upon the operation of massive networks of computers in changing, uncertain and hard to predict ways. By asking experts to consider all the combinations and dynamics the system might encounter, and then design ideal responses to them *in advance*, we are asking them to complete an impossible task.

But not all computing systems are created in this way. Over the past few decades, *machine learning* has proved efficacious when the environment in which the system is expected to operate is complex and uncertain. Machine learning can be thought of as developing a computer's ability to perform a task without it being explicitly programmed to do so (Samuel, 1959). There are many ways in which computers learn today, including most notably using techniques inspired by natural processes: artificial neural networks, for example, were designed based on models of neuron cells in the brain, and enable computers to learn complex non-linear functions and behaviour.

This learning is typically done by exposing the computer to a large amount of data collected from the problem we would like it to solve, along with examples of ideally how it should or should not react to instances in the data. The learning technique then processes these data, building up a model of what is required as it goes. The canonical example of machine learning being used in the real world is in classifying email as spam or not. Clearly, it would be impossible for an expert to identify every possible spam email in advance, and create a database of such emails ready and waiting in case they are received. Instead, classifiers are trained based on large datasets of spam and non-spam emails, to identify patterns in the emails that give them away. Many modern email systems make use of such machine learning techniques.

But still, such systems can be too rigid to interact fluidly with the complex changing environment in which we expect them to work. Often, once a particular model or behaviour has been learnt and the system deployed, its behaviour is limited by the scope of the knowledge made available to it when it undertook the learning. A good machine learning technique has the ability to generalise beyond the specific data provided during its learning phase, to other cases that are built upon the same underlying patterns present in the training data. However, if the scenario the system encounters strays beyond this, as underlying patterns in the environment change, the behaviour of the system is not well defined. In these cases, as in the classic approach, its usefulness is likely to degrade.

A computer that learns in this way can be said to possess some awareness of the knowledge present in the data originally provided to it during its learning phase. However, this awareness is limited by what underlying patterns were present in the original examples provided to the computer. Since this knowledge is provided in advance by designers, albeit with them acting as teachers rather than programmers, the system cannot be described as having the capability to obtain knowledge through perception during its lifetime. Crucially, if things drastically change while the system is operational, perhaps due to an economic crash, freak weather event or unforeseen changes in popular culture, the system will have to be retrained to possess knowledge of the new environmental characteristics, and then redeployed.

But not all learning machines possess this limitation. Recent years have seen a shift in some systems from this *offline* learning to *online* learning. While in offline learning, the system is trained then deployed, in online learning, the system can continue to learn throughout its lifetime, while it is operating. In some cases the teaching mode described above runs concurrently with the operation of the system, as a human expert provides feedback on the system's actions during runtime. In the email spam filter example, the system automatically classifies incoming email as spam or not, as a best guess based on its own knowledge. However, you may have the option in your email program to give the system the truly correct answer to the question of whether the email was indeed spam, and by doing this, you are assuming the role of teacher, during the system's lifetime.

Unfortunately, in more complex cases it is often not possible to ensure the presence of a teacher who is able to provide a correct answer to the question of *what should I have done?* Consider a problem where multiple cameras, each mounted on a mobile robot, are to be configured such that they search an area of land in order to find and track different types of hazards. It may not be known how many of each type of hazard are present in the environment, yet we would like the robots to co-ordinate themselves such that they find and monitor the worst of the hazards. In this case, if the robots were to present a particular configuration to a human and ask *is this correct?*, without knowledge of the environment and all the hazards, the human can only answer that they do not know.

Such cases are not restricted to advanced robotics. In modern web applications, we often want to configure the different types of servers that make up the application in order to efficiently meet the demands of users. But how should such systems be configured? Demand from users will vary by time of day, season and as a result of events such as hurricanes, wars, elections and royal weddings. Without knowing what will happen tomorrow, no human is capable of conveying to a learning system what the *correct* configuration would be.

But this form of *supervised learning* (so called, since it is supervised by an expert teacher) is not always how humans develop knowledge, and neither is it for computers. Heuristic methods such as trial and error are arguably amongst the most fundamental of human learning methods. Rather than being provided with the correct piece of knowledge by a teacher, the individual learns by assessing alternative hypotheses or behaviours, and comparing them for their relative *goodness*. Rather than asking *is this correct?*, we might ask *is this better than that?* Then, by identifying what underlies those alternatives that are generally better than others, underlying patterns can be learnt which enable the system to generalise to unseen scenarios, despite never having been exposed to the best answer. This technique is often called *heuristic learning* or *reinforcement learning*, since the received benefit (or lack thereof) associated with an attempted alternative is sometimes considered as a reward (or punishment).

For reinforcement learning to work, some notion of relative reward associated with each possible hypothesis or behaviour is required. This reward function is sometimes thought of as a *utility function*, when drawing on economic analogies in learning good behaviours, or an *objective function*, particularly when the learning is formulated as an optimisation problem. Whatever approach is taken to developing a reward mechanism, the key idea remains the same: the system obtains knowledge through exploration, observation and assessment of its actions, during its lifetime.

In summary, even the most minimal and static computer systems often implicitly possess at least some knowledge, typically in their programming. More advanced, learning machines are able to deal with previously unseen scenarios. The ability of these machines to build knowledge bases for themselves achieves the necessary job of relieving programmers from having to explicitly consider every runtime eventuality in advance, something that is not often possible. These computers should develop an ability to operate in complex networked environments, if necessary without supervision by human experts. They should be robust and adapt to changes in this environment, however these are incurred. They must learn knowledge about new, previously unencountered, objects, and (learn to) ignore knowledge that is no longer accurate. They must be able to learn about changes over time, about interactions with other entities, and about changing goals and limitations. And they must learn about their relationship with their environment, about their impact upon it and about how its changes affect the results of its own behaviour. In designing such systems, we must consider their knowledge, or awareness, of these things, and how such knowledge should be learnt (and forgotten) during the system's lifetime.

18.3 Types of Computational Self-Awareness

If we are to build future computer systems inspired by self-awareness, at this stage it is helpful to consider self-awareness concepts as they are understood in humans, in order to develop our own notions of *computational self-awareness*. Self-awareness as a field of study has existed roughly since the 1960s. Distinct from, but building upon, consciousness Morin (2006) defines self-awareness as "the capacity to become the object of one's own attention", and a self-aware organism as one that "becomes aware that it is awake and actually experiencing specific mental events". However, as highlighted by Morin and others (e.g. Legrain *et al.* (2011)), there is much ongoing discussion about what might and might not constitute self-awareness and various observed forms of it.

Morin's definition, which requires the ability to consider oneself as an object of ones own knowledge, is what Legrain *et al.* (2011) call *explicit* self-awareness. This permits an individual to focus its attention on itself, to consider itself as an object within the world, and to observe and consider its own behaviour. However, another facet of self-awareness is *implicit*. This is concerned not with oneself as the object 'me', but rather as 'I' (Legrain *et al.*, 2011), as the subject of experience. Here, the individual is aware of its experiences within the world, and that these are its own experiences, subjective and unique.

Implicit self-awareness has been observed to develop much earlier than explicit within infant humans (Rochat, 2003), and is therefore considered as a more basic form of self-awareness. Indeed some (e.g. Morin (2006); Lewis (2011)) consider that implicit self-awareness capabilities belong rather within a lower level of consciousness, and that genuine self-awareness only begins with the more advanced explicit form, requiring the ability to hold a mental representation of an object it knows to be "me". In this chapter, we are not concerned with attempting to settle these debates, but instead with developing a broad understanding of self-awareness, in order to develop concepts inspired by it, to benefit the design of computing systems. Therefore, some of what is presented and discussed here is considered by some researchers, but not all, to be forms of consciousness rather than self-awareness proper.

The importance of the availability of external sources of knowledge to self-awareness processes should be emphasised: self-awareness is not only concerned with sources of knowledge internal to the individual, but also with knowledge obtained through subjective experience. It is also for this reason that we focus on computational *self*-awareness as opposed to awareness more generally. As discussed in the previous section, any system that possesses knowledge of situations or facts can be said to possess some awareness. An example of this form of computational awareness may be seen in Chapter 7, where an offline model of the home is provided to the system for use at runtime. However, the possession of *self*-awareness indicates a system that builds up this knowledge through learning based on its own subjective experiences of its environment and itself. In humans this distinction is less important, since we consider experiential learning to be the usual method of knowledge acquisition. Indeed, even when humans learn from expert teachers, we often consider and reflect upon what we have heard before establishing our own belief. Computational self-awareness gives us a concept with which we can fully explore the range of capabilities open to a computer system which builds up knowledge based on its experiences, during its lifetime. An example of this form of computational awareness may be seen in the Nico robot in Chapter 14, where the robot learns a model of its own movements during runtime, through its own subjective experiences. This permits continual adaptation to changes (e.g. a newly discovered tool, in this case) during the system's lifetime.

As may be becoming apparent, it is widely believed (Legrain *et al.*, 2011; Morin, 2006) that self-awareness is not a singular, *all or nothing* phenomenon, rather it can be thought of as a spectrum, where the capabilities of an individual are associated with one or more *levels of self-awareness*. The same should be true of *computational* self-awareness. Some proposed sets of levels, such as those by Rochat (2003), focus on classifying self-awareness capabilities according to the way in which they are observed to develop in human children. Meanwhile Legrain *et al.*'s (2011) levels only consider explicit self-awareness. Perhaps one of the most broad treatments of self-awareness is due to Neisser (1997), whose five levels offer one of the most broad treatments of self-awareness, from the most minimal to the most advanced. Neisser's levels are as follows:

(1) **Ecological self** The ecological self is the most minimal form of self-awareness. It permits sufficient knowledge only for basic stimulus-response behaviour, as the individual has a basic awareness of stimuli. The ecological self can be thought of as the minimum requirement for the individual to not be unconscious.
(2) **Interpersonal self** The interpersonal self enables the individual to possess a simple awareness of its interactions, permitting limited adaptation to others in the performance of tasks.
(3) **Extended self** The extended self extends the interpersonal self to permit reflection of interactions over time. The individual is aware of the existence of past and future interactions.
(4) **Private self** The private self includes that the individual can process more advanced information concerning itself, such as thoughts, feelings and intentions.
(5) **Conceptual self** The conceptual self (or self-concept) is the most advanced form of self-awareness, representing that the individual is capable of constructing and reasoning about an abstract representation of itself.

Neisser's levels provide a broad framework, ranging from a basic awareness of environmental stimuli through awareness of interactions and time, up to awareness of one's own thoughts. The most advanced form of self-awareness, the conceptual self, also permits an individual to develop *meta-self-awareness* (Morin and Everett, 1990), an awareness that they themself are self-aware. Meta-self-awareness might at first sound a little obtuse, however examples might include that the individual is aware that it is angry, or that it has recently learnt a lot about a particular topic. This is an important capability, since it allows an individual to consider the reasons for or impact of changes in awareness, and to make decisions accordingly.

Neisser's levels offer an ideal source of inspiration from which to build concepts of computational self-awareness, since they include those aspects of implicit self-awareness or consciousness that are often not included in a literature focusing purely on explicit self-awareness. Accordingly, we may now develop a set of *levels of computational self-awareness*, inspired by Neisser's levels for humans but translated appropriately for describing the capabilities of computer systems. By translating concepts such as this to the computing domain, designers are then able to adopt a common language in considering the various self-awareness capabilities that their systems may or may not possess. These levels of computational self-awareness are:

(1) **Stimulus-aware** A system is stimulus-aware if it has knowledge of stimuli. The system is not able to distinguish between the sources of stimuli. It does not have knowledge of past/future stimuli. It enables the ability in a system to respond to events. It is a prerequisite for all other levels of awareness.

(2) **Interaction-aware** A system is interaction-aware if it has knowledge that stimuli and its own actions form part of interactions with other systems and the environment. It has knowledge via feedback loops that its actions can provoke or generate specific reactions from its social or physical environment. It enables a system to distinguish between other systems, humans and environments. Simple interaction-awareness may just enable a system to reason about individual interactions. More advanced interaction-awareness may involve possessing knowledge of social structures such as communities or network topology. Although interaction-awareness is typically based on external sources of feedback, we might also envisage a system that learns from observing the effects of interactions with itself.

(3) **Time-aware** A system is time-aware if it has knowledge of historical and/or likely future phenomena. Implementing time-awareness may involve the system possessing an explicit memory, capabilities of time series modelling and/or anticipation.

(4) **Goal-aware** A system is goal-aware if it has knowledge of goals, objectives, preferences and constraints. It is important to note that there is a difference between a goal existing implicitly in the design of a system, and the system having knowledge of that goal in such a way that it can react to or reason about it. The former does not describe goal-awareness; the latter does. Example implementations of such knowledge in a system include state-based goals (i.e. knowing what means

success and what does not) and utility-based goals (i.e. having a utility function), as discussed in Section 18.2. Goal-awareness permits acknowledgement of and adaptation to changes in these goals. When coupled with interaction-awareness or time-awareness, goal-awareness permits the ability to reason about the goals of other individuals, or about previous or likely future goals, respectively.

(5) **Meta-self-aware** A system is meta-self-aware if it has knowledge of its own level(s) of self-awareness, how they are realised, and how much knowledge has been acquired. Furthermore, a meta-self-aware system can have knowledge of how useful acquired knowledge was, and since its own knowledge gathering can be observed, the cost of acquiring it. This allows the system to adapt the way in which its self-awareness capabilities are realised (e.g. by changing algorithms that implement the capabilities). For example, this awareness may involve a system dynamically selecting a particular technique out of a set of possibilities for realising a learning capability, in order to satisfy a constraint (e.g. safety), or to better manage a trade-off between different objectives (e.g. energy efficiency).

So far, we have only considered *what* computational self-awareness means, and not *how* to achieve it. However, in building computers to meet the challenges highlighted at the beginning of this chapter, we must explicitly consider how to realise self-awareness capabilities, and how to build them in. There are many techniques, both existing and potentially waiting to be discovered, that we can use to realise the capabilities described in the levels of computational self-awareness. And as discussed in Section 18.2, fundamental to these techniques will be the ability to observe experiences that the system undergoes, and to build up knowledge, to learn, accordingly.

When applying learning techniques in order to realise self-awareness capabilities, there are two key aspects to consider. Firstly, each level of self-awareness can be present with varying degrees of complexity. This degree of complexity will be inherent in the design of the learning technique used for implementing the level. As such, it is possible for each level of self-awareness to be implemented using any of a range of techniques. Even simplistic techniques can be used to achieve (relatively) simplistic implementations of a level of computational self-awareness. For example, a minimal implementation of meta-self-awareness only requires the system to acquire and maintain *some knowledge* of its own self-awareness capabilities, which it can then use to adapt them. Alternatively, we can scale up to more advanced knowledge representation techniques, enabling more complex adaptation. Table 18.3 shows some artificial and computational intelligence techniques where learning might be applied in increasingly complex realisations of the different levels.

Table 18.1 Example computational techniques for implementing increasingly complex realisations of the levels of computational self-awareness

Level	Complexity →
Stimulus	Threshold → Linear response → Non-linear response
Interaction	Heuristics → Game theoretic reasoning → Social network
Time	Markov decision processes → Memory → Anticipation
Goal	Objective function → Multi-attribute utility → Planning
Meta	Win-stay-lose-shift → Bandit solvers → Ensemble learning

Secondly, a single type of computational technique can make a system capable of exhibiting self-awareness at multiple levels simultaneously. Alternatively, a single technique may be used multiple times, independently and simultaneously to implement multiple levels. The exact function of the learning technique will depend on what experiences are observed, and how the learnt models are used. As an example, consider a reinforcement learning algorithm used to learn good interaction behaviour and hence achieve some degree of *interaction awareness*. Simultaneously, a second reinforcement learning algorithm might learn which algorithm to deploy to achieve this interaction awareness according to different environmental conditions. The second reinforcement learning algorithm therefore provides an implementation of meta-self-awareness. By combining simpler algorithms, highly complex adaptive learning behaviour can be achieved. Attempting to implement such behaviour using a single technique would require algorithms that are far more difficult to understand, test and analyse.

In concluding this section, we are now in a position to consider, conceptually, how to describe how much computational self-awareness a system possesses. In order to do this, we need three complementary axes on which self-awareness can be measured. Namely:

(1) Which levels of computational self-awareness are realised, which describes the types of capabilities present in the system.
(2) The degree to which each level is implemented, which together describes the complexity.
(3) The quantity of knowledge present, which describes the amount of learning already performed, the amount of experience the system has.

By considering computer systems in terms of these three dimensions, we can obtain a much more useful description of its computational self-awareness (or lack of), than by asking the more simplistic and possibly meaningless question *is this computer self-aware?*

18.4 The Outlook for Computational Self-Awareness

The term self-awareness has been used explicitly in a number of computer science and engineering initiatives for several years, and several clusters of research are apparent (Lewis *et al.*, 2011). Many examples have been presented in this book, but only now are we developing a common understanding of what computational self-awareness means across these different initiatives. Fundamentally, it is concerned with how to engineer systems that explicitly consider knowledge concerning both themselves and their experiences typically as it is acquired by them, during their lifetime.

18.4.1 *Perspectives*

Different areas of research have contributed to the debate on what computational awareness and self-awareness might mean, providing different expectations for a *(self-)aware computer.* This chapter has taken a broad view of computational self-awareness, ranging from the simplest of stimulus-aware systems, up to the most complex goal-aware and meta-self-aware machines. Conversely, in Chapter 1, the question was raised about whether a computer can look *as if* it were aware, *in the same way a human does.* Self-recognition is highlighted as a key indicator of this. Some of the subsequent chapters have made steps towards such *as-if-it-were-like-a-human* form of awareness, such as Chapter 14, where the robot Nico learns about its own body, deliberately attempting to mimic an infant. Other chapters take a more general view. Chapter 7 considers a system's awareness of its environmental context, its environment, and the issues associated with reconciling differing views of the environment according to different sensors, to provide a workable, coherent knowledge base. Here, the emphasis is not on experiential learning, subjectivity, or mimicking human behaviour. Instead, the aim is to achieve a correct environmental model, to enable optimal decision making at a single point and provide a functionally intelligent system.

Other chapters, such as this one, emphasise the subjective nature of a system's (possibly conflicting) experiences of the environment. Similarly, Chapter 11 highlights that some types of complex problems consist of stakeholders with different views and understandings, in addition to dynamic goals and constraints. This supports the idea of computational self-awareness describing the ability of a system to learn from experience of these different perspectives, during its lifetime. Chapter 4 takes a similar view, defining an agent's awareness as *its ability to collect, store, aggregate, and use information about itself, about other agents and the environment.* This definition has much in common with the psychology-inspired framework for computational self-awareness presented in Section 18.3, while social awareness represents a refinement of the idea of interaction awareness.

Although there are many forms of computational awareness, there is a general agreement on the distinction between awareness and action. This split between functionality responsible for knowledge acquisition and representation, and that responsible for knowledge use and behaviour, is highlighted particularly in Chapter 7. Chapter 8 also emphasises this, considering computational awareness to be concerned with the system possessing knowledge to present to the user. Actions are not taken autonomously by the system, but as a result of interaction with the user through serious games. The decoupling of processes responsible for knowledge and processes responsible for action is important, and this chapter highlights how such rich knowledge can be used in a range of innovative ways.

Indeed, computational self-awareness in particular is argued in Chapter 5 to be a prerequisite for effective self-management, something that has been extensively studied in the field of autonomic computing. As in Chapter 8, the scope and type of possible actions is enabled or constrained by the amount of awareness present. It is interesting therefore to consider the knowledge available in applications such as this, in the context of the three dimensions described at the end of Section 18.3.

18.4.2 *Outlook*

The computers of tomorrow – the context-aware, human-context-aware and self-aware computers – will learn to perform effectively, efficiently, robustly and flexibly in a complex interconnected world. They will learn from interactions with people, with each other, and with society, the economy and the environment. They will be able to identify uncertainty and adapt to changes in underlying patterns of behaviour. They will do this by learning not only about the world as they perceive it, but also about their own capabilities and the effects of their actions.

When systems possess such self-awareness, the need for engineers to consider issues such as the availability of resources and constraints at design-time can be avoided or reduced. Systems will instead adapt at runtime to what is available, learning to do so, in order to efficiently achieve their goals. Agarwal *et al.* (2009) argue for a change of emphasis in computer design. Their idea is to move from a procedural design methodology, where the behaviour of the computing system is pre-programmed at design-time, towards a self-aware system, where the system intelligently trades-off available resources for performance at runtime.

This idea is being generalised in several applications, for example distributed smart cameras (Esterle *et al.*, 2014). Here, the goal of self-aware cameras with on-board processing is to track objects that move through their field of view. The cameras make independent decisions at runtime about which objects to track, with which other cameras to communicate, and how to exchange tracking responsibilities with them. Using an artificial market mechanism and an ant-inspired learning approach, the outcome is an efficient balance of the trade-off between tracking performance and communication overhead across the network of cameras. Unlike previous approaches to this object-tracking and handover problem, the self-aware cameras do not require any advance knowledge of their environment or the camera neighbourhood structure; it is all learnt online through experience.

These examples all demonstrate a shift towards a new generation of machines endowed with computational self-awareness. These machines will not only learn during their lifetime, but they also learn how and what to learn. As a result, we obtain adaptivity, robustness and flexibility not seen before in engineered systems.

Looking forward, there is still much to understand about how to incorporate self-awareness properties into computing systems, taking inspiration not just from psychology (as in this chapter) but also philosophy and neuroscience. Furthermore, while this book has mapped out the space of research in computational awareness and self-awareness, and addressed its ethical, legal and social implications, there are many important questions, both scientifically and socially, to be answered. How can self-aware systems learn and adapt, considering trade-offs both between system goals and the overheads associated with learning itself? What can we say about our expectations or guarantees of the behaviour of self-aware systems? Is our society ready to be filled with systems whose behaviour is not pre-programmed, but instead is learnt by interacting with us? Can such systems be trusted?

There is much work still to do.

Bibliography

Abbas, R., Michael, K., Michael, M. and Aloudat, A. (2011). Emerging forms of covert surveillance using GPS-enabled devices, *Journal of Cases on Information Technology* **13**, 2, pp. 19–33.

Ackerman, E. (2011). Qbo robot passes mirror test, is therefore self-aware, IEEE Spectrum Automaton [Robotics Blog].

Adams, D. (1979). *The HitchHiker's Guide to the Galaxy* (London: Pan Books).

Agarwal, A., Miller, J., Eastep, J., Wentziaff, D. and Kasture, H. (2009). Self-aware computing, Tech. Rep. AFRL-RI-RS-TR-2009-161, MIT.

Agha, G. (2008). Computing in pervasive cyberspace, *Communications of the ACM* **51**, 1, pp. 68–70.

Aiello, M., Aloise, F., Baldoni, R., Cincotti, F., Guger, G., Lazovik, A., Mecella, M., Pucci, P., Rinsma, J., Santucci, G. and Taglieri, M. (2011). Smart homes to improve the quality of life for all, in *33rd Annual International IEEE Engineering in Medicine and Biology Conference (EMBC)*, pp. 1777–1780.

Aiello, M., Pratt-Hartman, I. and van Benthem, J. (2007). *Handbook of Spatial Logics* (Dordrecht: Springer).

Akyildiz, I. F., Su, W., Sankarasubramaniam, Y. and Cayirci, E. (2002). Wireless sensor networks: a survey, *Computer Networks* **38**, 4, pp. 393–422.

Alami, R., Albu-Schaeffer, A., Bicchi, A., Bischoff, R., Chatila, R., Luca, A. D., Santis, A. D., Giralt, G., Hirzinger, G., Lippiello, V., Mattone, R., Sen, S., Siciliano, B., Tonietti, G. and Villani, L. (2006). Safe and dependable physical human-robot interaction in anthropic domains: State of the art and challenges, Workshop on Physical Human-Robot Interaction in Anthropic Domains, at the International Conference on Intelligent Robots and Systems (IROS).

Aljazzaf, Z., Capretz, M. and Perry, M. (2011). Trust bootstrapping services and service providers, in *Privacy, Security and Trust (PST), 2011 Ninth Annual International Conference on*, pp. 7–15.

Almajano, P., López-Sánchez, M. and Rodriguez, I. (2012a). An assistance infrastructure to inform agents for decision support in open MAS, in *ITMAS 2012*, pp. 93–106.

Almajano, P., Trescak, T., Esteva, M., Rodriguez, I. and López-Sánchez, M. (2012b). v-mWater: a 3D virtual market for water rights, in *AAMAS'12*, pp. 1483–1484.

Alt, F., Müller, J. and Schmidt, A. (2012). Advertising on public display networks, *Computer* **45**, 5, pp. 50–56.

Anderson, D. P., Cobb, J., Korpela, E., Lebofsky, M. and Werthimer, D. (2002). SETI@home: an experiment in public-resource computing, *Communications of the ACM* **45**, pp. 56–61.

Andrighetto, G., Conte, R., Turrini, P. and Paolucci, M. (2007). Emergence in the loop: simulating the two way dynamics of norm innovation, in G. Boella, L. van der Torre and H. Verhagen (eds.), *Normative Multi-agent Systems*, no. 07122 in Dagstuhl Seminar Proceedings.

Arkin, R. (2009). *Governing Lethal Behavior in Autonomous Robots* (Boca Raton, FL: Taylor & Francis).

Asendorpf, J., Warkentin, V. and Baudonniere, P.-M. (1996). Self-awareness and other awareness II: Mirror self-recognition, social contingency awareness, and synchronic imitation, *Developmental Psychology* **32**, 2, pp. 313–321.

Asimov, I. (1950). Runaround, in *I, Robot* (New York, NY: Gnome Press).

Asimov, I. (1957). *The Naked Sun* (New York, NY: Doubleday).

Asimov, I. (1985). *Robots and Empire* (London: Collins).

Athanasiou, A., Felice, M. D., Oliveto, G. and Oliveto, P. S. (2011). Evolutionary algorithms for the identification of structural systems in earthquake engineering, in *Proceedings of the International Conference on Evolutionary Computation Theory and Applications (ECTA'11)*, pp. 52–62.

Augusto, J. C. and Nugent, C. D. (2004). The use of temporal reasoning and management of complex events in smart homes, in R. L. de Mántaras and L. Saitta (eds.), *Proceedings of the 16th Eureopean Conference on Artificial Intelligence (ECAI)* (IOS Press), pp. 778–782.

Avizienis, A., Laprie, J., Randell, B. and Landwehr, C. (2004). Basic concepts and taxonomy of dependable and secure computing, *IEEE Transactions on Dependable and Secure Computing* **1**, 1, pp. 11–33.

Baas, N. and Emmeche, C. (1997). On emergence and explanation, *Intellectica* **25**, 2, pp. 67–83.

Babaoglu, O., Canright, G., Deutsch, A., Di Caro, G., Ducatelle, F., Gambardella, L., Ganguly, N., Jelasity, M., Montemanni, R., Montresor, A. and Urnes, T. (2006). Design patterns from biology for distributed computing, *ACM Transactions on Autonomous and Adaptive Systems* **1**, 1, pp. 26–66.

Bachrach, Y., Parnes, A., Procaccia, A. D. and Rosenschein, J. S. (2009). Gossip-based aggregation of trust in decentralized reputation systems, *Autonomous Agents and Multi-Agent Systems* **19**, 2, pp. 153–172.

Bai, Y.-W. and Cheng, C.-H. (2012). Dynamic adjustment of CPU clock speed to prevent notebook overheating and shutdown by AC adapter, in *IEEE 1st Global Conference on Consumer Electronics (GCCE)*, pp. 515–519.

Balke, T., de Vos, M. and Padget, J. (2013). I-ABM: combining institutional frameworks and agent-based modelling for the design of enforcement policies, *Artificial Intelligence and Law* **21**, 4, pp. 371–398.

Banks, I. (2000). *Look to Windward* (London: Orbit).

Bartram, L., Rodgers, J. and Woodbury, R. (2011). Smart homes or smart occupants? Supporting aware living in the home, in P. Campos, N. Graham, J. Jorge, N. Nunes, P. Palanque and M. Winckler (eds.), *Human–Computer Interaction (INTERACT), Lecture Notes in Computer Science*, Vol. 6947 (Berlin: Springer), pp. 52–64.

Bastardi, A. and Shafir, E. (1998). On the pursuit and misuse of useless information, *Journal of Personality and Social Psychology* **75**, 1, pp. 19–32.

Bellman, K. (1997). Sharing work, experience, interpretation, and maybe even meanings between natural and artificial agents (invited paper), in *Proceedings IEEE International Conference on Systems, Man, and Cybernetics*, Vol. 5, pp. 4127–4132.

Bellman, K. (2000). Developing a concept of self for constructed autonomous systems, in *Proceedings of 15th European Meeting on Cybernetics and Systems Research (EMCSR)*, Vol. 2, pp. 693–698.

Bellman, K. (2003). Emotions: meaningful mappings between the individual and its world, in R. Trappl, P. Petta and S. Sayr (eds.), *Emotions in Humans and Artifacts*, chap. 5 (Cambridge, MA: MIT Press), pp. 149–188.

Bellman, K. (2005). Self-conscious modeling, *Information Technology* **47**, 4, pp. 188–194.

Bellman, K. L., Gillam, A. and Landauer, C. (1993). Challenges for conceptual design environments: the VEHICLES experience, *Revue Internationale de CFAO et d'Infographie* **8**, 2, pp. 185–217.

Bellman, K. L. and Goldberg, L. (1984). Common origin of linguistic and movement abilities, *American Journal of Physiology* **246**, pp. R915–R921.

Bellman, K. L. and Landauer, C. (1995). Designing testable, heterogeneous software environments, *Journal of Systems and Software; Special Issue: Software Quality in Knowledge-Based Systems* **29**, 3, pp. 199–217.

Bellman, K. L., Landauer, C. and Nelson, P. R. (2008). Systems engineering for organic computing: The challenge of shared design and control between oc systems and their human engineers, in R. P. Würtz (ed.), *Organic Computing*, chap. 3, Understanding Complex Systems Series (Berlin: Springer), pp. 25–80.

Bellman, K. L. and Nelson, P. R. (2011). Developing mechanisms for determining 'good enough' in sort systems, in *14th IEEE International Symposium on Object/Component/Service-Oriented Real-Time Distributed Computing Workshops*, pp. 120–125, 31 March 2011, Newport Beach, California.

Bellman, K. L. and Walter, D. O. (1984). Biological processing, *American Journal of Physiology* **246**, 6, pp. R860–R867.

Bernard, Y., Klejnowski, L., Müller-Schloer, C., Pitt, J. and Schaumeier, J. (2012). Enduring institutions and self-organising trust-adaptive systems for an open grid computing infrastructure, in *Proceedings 6th IEEE International Conference on Self-Adaptive and Self-Organizing Systems Workshop (SASOW)*, pp. 163–168.

Berry, G. and Boudol, G. (1990). The chemical abstract machine, in *Proceedings of the 17th ACM SIGPLAN-SIGACT Symposium on Principles of Programming Languages (PoPL)*, pp. 81–94.

Bertenthal, B. and Fischer, K. (1978). Development of self-recognition in the infant, *Developmental Psychology* **14**, 4, pp. 44–50.

Binmore, K. (2005). *Natural Justice* (Oxford: Oxford University Press).

Bird, C., Pattison, D., D'Souza, R., Filkov, V. and Devanbu, P. (2008). Latent social structure in open source projects, in *Proceedings 16th ACM SIGSOFT International Symposium on Foundations of Software Engineering*, pp. 24–35.

Boella, G., van der Torre, L. and Verhagen, H. (2006). Introduction to normative multiagent systems, *Computational and Mathematical Organization Theory* **12**, 2–3, pp. 71–79.

Bogdanovych, A., Esteva, M., Simoff, S., Sierra, C. and Berger, H. (2008). A methodology for developing multiagent systems as 3D electronic institutions, in M. Luck and L. Padgham (eds.), *Agent-Oriented Software Engineering VIII*, *Lecture Notes in Computer Science*, Vol. 4951 (Berlin: Springer), pp. 103–117.

Bogdanovych, A., Rodriguez-Aguilar, J. A., Simoff, S. and Cohen, A. (2010). Authentic interactive reenactment of cultural heritage with 3D virtual worlds and artificial intelligence, *Applied Artificial Intelligence* **24**, pp. 617–647.

Boisteanu, D., Vasiluta, R., Cernomaz, A. and Mucenica, C. (2009). Home monitoring of sleep apnea treatment: benefits of intelligent CPAP devices, in *Advanced Technologies for Enhanced Quality of Life*, pp. 77–80.

Bolchini, C., Curino, C. A., Quintarelli, E., Schreiber, F. A. and Tanca, L. (2007). A data-oriented survey of context models, *SIGMOD Record* **36**, 4, pp. 19–26.

Bonabeau, E., Dorigo, M. and Théraulaz, G. (1999). *Swarm Intelligence* (New York: Oxford University Press).

Bongard, J., Zykov, V. and Lipson, H. (2006). Resilient machines through continuous self-modeling, *Science* **314**, 5802, pp. 1118–1121.

Bourazeri, A., Pitt, J., Almajano, P., Rodriguez, I. and López-Sánchez, M. (2012). Meet the meter: visualising smartgrids using self-organising electronic institutions and serious games, in *Proceedings 6th IEEE International Conference on Self-Adaptive and Self-Organizing Systems Workshop (SASOW)*, pp. 145–150.

Boyle, M., Neustaedter, C. and Greenberg, S. (2009). Privacy factors in video-based media spaces, in S. Harrison (ed.), *Media Space 20+ Years of Mediated Life*, Computer Supported Cooperative Work (London: Springer), pp. 97–122.

Bratman, M. (1987). *Intentions, Plans and Practical Reasoning* (Cambridge, MA: Harvard University Press).

Breitgand, D., Goldstein, M., Henis, E., Shehory, O. and Weinsberg, Y. (2007). Panacea: towards a self-healing development framework, in *Symposium on Integrated Network Management* (Munich, Germany), pp. 169–178.

Brewster, D. (2001). *Memoirs of the Life, Writings, and Discoveries of Sir Isaac Newton (1855) Volume II* (Boston, MA: Adamant Media Corporation).

Brooks, R. A. (1991). Intelligence without representation, *Artificial Intelligence* **47**, 1–3, pp. 139–159.

Brun, Y., Di Marzo Serugendo, G., Gacek, C., Giese, H., Kienle, H., Litoiu, M., Mueller, H., Pezze, M. and Shaw, M. (2009). Engineering self-adaptive systems through feedback loops, in B. Cheng, R. de Lemos, H. Giese, P. Inverardi and J. Magee (eds.), *Software Engineering for Self-Adaptive Systems, Lecture Notes in Computer Science*, Vol. 5525 (Berlin: Springer), pp. 48–70.

Brundtland, G. H. (1987). Our common future (the Brundtland report), Tech. rep., United Nations World Commission on Environment and Development (WCED), URL http://www.un-documents.net/ocf-cf.htm.

Buchholz, T., Küpper, A. and Schiffers, M. (2003). Quality of context: what it is and why we need it, in *Proceedings of the Workshop of the HP OpenView University Association 2003 (HPOVUA 2003)*.

Buschmann, F. (1996). Reflection, in J. M. Vlissides, J. O. Coplien and N. L. Kerth (eds.), *Proceedings of the Pattern Languages of Program Design 2 (PLOP '95)*, pp. 271–294.

Cabri, G. and Capodieci, N. (2013). Runtime change of collaboration patterns in autonomic systems: motivations and perspectives, in *27th International Conference on Advanced Information Networking and Applications Workshops (WAINA)*, pp. 1038–1043.

Cabri, G., Ferrari, L. and Leonardi, L. (2005). Injecting roles in Java agents through run-time bytecode manipulation, *IBM Systems Journal, Vol. 44, No. 1, pp.185-208, 2005* **44**, 1, pp. 185–208.

Cabri, G., Puviani, M. and Zambonelli, F. (2011). Towards a taxonomy of adaptive agent-based collaboration patterns for autonomic service ensembles, in *nnual Conference on Collaborative Technologies and Systems*, pp. 306–315.

Calvanese, D., Giacomo, G. D., Lenzerini, M., Mecella, M. and Patrizi, F. (2008). Automatic service composition and synthesis: the Roman model, *IEEE Data Engineering Bulletin* **31**, 3, pp. 18–22.

Cantin-Martinez, R., Lopes, M. and Montesano, L. (2010). Body schema acquisition through active learning, in *IEEE International Conference on Robotics and Automation (ICRA)*, pp. 1860–1866.

Capodieci, N., Hart, E. and Cabri, G. (2013). An immune network approach for self-adaptive ensembles of autonomic components: a casestudy in swarm robotics, in *Proceedings of the 12th European Conference on Artificial Life (ECAL), Taormina, Italy, September 2013*, pp. 864–871.

Capurro, R. (2013). Medicine in the information and knowledge society, in B. Löffler and P. Hunziker (eds.), *European Summit for Clinical Nanomedicine and Targeted Medicine (CLINAM)* (European Foundation for Clinical Nanomedicine), p. 94.

Caruso, M., Di Ciccio, C., Iacomussi, E., Kaldeli, E., Lazovik, A. and Mecella, M. (2012). Service ecologies for home/building automation, in *Proceedings 10th IFAC Symposium on Robot Control (SyRoCo)*, pp. 467–472.

Casilla-Rubio, J. and Willis, S. (2009). Planetary skin: a global platform for a new era of collaboration, Cisco Internet Business Solutions Group (IBSG).

Castelfranchi, C. and Falcone, R. (1997). From task delegation to role delegation, in M. Lenzerini (ed.), *AI*IA 97: Advances in Artificial Intelligence, Lecture Notes in Computer Science*, Vol. 1321 (Berlin: Springer), pp. 278–289.

Castelfranchi, C. and Falcone, R. (1998). Towards a theory of delegation for agent-based systems, *Robotics and Autonomous Systems* **24**, 3–4, pp. 141–157.

Cheatham, J., Emmert, J. and Baumgart, S. (2006). A survey of fault tolerant methodologies for FPGAs, *ACM Transactions on Design Automation of Electronic Systems* **11**, 2, pp. 501–533.

Chen, A., Watson, R., Boudreau, M.-C. and Karahanna, E. (2011). An institutional perspective on the adoption of green IS and IT, *Australasian Journal of Information Systems* **17**, 1.

Chiu, B., Keogh, E. and Lonardi, S. (2003). Probabilistic discovery of time series motifs, in *Proceedings of the 9th ACM SIGKDD International Conference on Knowledge Discovery and Data Mining*, pp. 493–498.

Churchman, C. (1968). *The Systems Approach* (New York, NY: Delacorte Press).

Cialdini, R. B., Reno, R. R. and Kallgren, C. A. (1990). A focus theory of normative conduct: recycling the concept of norms to reduce littering in public places, *Journal of Personality and Social Psychology* **58**, 6, p. 1015.

Clarke, A. (1968). *2001: A Space Odyssey* (New York, NY: New American Library).

Clarke, R. (1988a). Information technology and dataveillance, *Communications of the ACM* **31**, 5, pp. 498–512.

Clarke, R. (1988b). Just another piece of plastic in your wallet: the 'Australian card' scheme, *ACM SIGCAS Computers and Society* **18**, 1, pp. 7–21.

Clarke, R. (2009). The covert implementation of mass vehicle surveillance in Australia, Presentation at the *Fourth Workshop on the Social Implications of National Security: Covert Policing.*

Cohen, P. and Levesque, H. (1990). Intention is choice with commitment, *Artificial Intelligence* **42**, 2–3, pp. 213–261.

Collier, R. and Collier, D. (1991). *Shaping the Political Arena* (Princeton, NJ: Princeton University Press).

Collins, W. (1993). *Computer One* (London: No Exit Press).

Cooper, S., Khatib, F., Treuille, A., Barbero, J., Lee, J., Beenen, M., Leaver-Fay, A., Baker, D., Popovic, Z. and Players, F. (2010). Predicting protein structures with a multiplayer online game, *Nature* **466**, 7307, pp. 756–760.

Cortright, E. (ed.) (1975). *Apollo Expeditions to the Moon* (Washington, DC: NASA SP).

Cuesta, C., Perez-Sotelo, J. and Ossowski, S. (2011). Self-organising adaptive structures: the Shifter experience, *ERCIM News* **2011**, 85, pp. 35–36.

Dahiya, R., Metta, G., Cannata, G. and Valle, M. (2011). Guest editorial special issue on robotic sense of touch, *IEEE Transactions on Robotics* **27**, 3, pp. 385–388.

Dai, Y., Xiang, Y., Li, Y., Xing, L. and Zhang, G. (2011). Consequence oriented self-healing and autonomous diagnosis for highly reliable systems and software, *IEEE Transactions on Reliability* **60**, 2, pp. 369–380.

Dalpiaz, F., Giorgini, P. and Mylopoulos, J. (2009). Software self-reconfiguration: a BDI-based approach, in *Proceedings International Conference on Autonomous Agents and Multiagent Systems (AAMAS)*, pp. 1159–1160.

Damásio, A. (1999). *The Feeling of What Happens: Body and Emotion in the Making of Consciousness* (London: Heinemann).

Darby, S. (2006). The Effectiveness of Feedback on Energy Consumption, *A Review for DEFRA of the Literature on Metering, Billing and Direct Displays, 2006* **486**.

Daskala, B. (ed.) (2011). *To log or not to log? Risks and benefits of emerging life-logging applications* (European Network and Information Security Agency).

Davies, S. (2013). Annual report of the Chief Medical Officer 2012. Our children deserve better: prevention pays, Tech. rep., UK Department of Health.

de Castro, L. (2006). *Fundamentals of Natural Computing* (New York: Chapman & Hall/CRC Computer and Information Sciences).

de Castro, L. and Von Zuben, F. (2000). Artificial immune systems: Part II - a survey of applications, Tech. Rep. DCA-RT 02/00, State University of Campinas.

de Freitas, D. M., Kininmonth, S. and Woodley, S. (2009). Linking science and management in the adoption of sensor network technology in the Great Barrier Reef coast, Australia, *Computers, Environment and Urban Systems* **33**, 2, pp. 111–121.

de Weck, O. L., Roos, D. and Magee, C. L. (2011). *Engineering Systems: Meeting Human Needs in a Complex Technological World* (Boston, MA: MIT Press).

De Wolf, T. and Holvoet, T. (2007). Design patterns for decentralised coordination in self-organising emergent systems, in S. Brueckner, S. Hassas, M. Jelasity and D. Yamins (eds.), *Engineering Self-Organising Systems*, *Lecture Notes in Computer Science*, Vol. 4335 (Berlin: Springer), pp. 28–49.

Dean, J. and Ghemawat, S. (2008). MapReduce: Simplified data processing on large clusters, *Communications of the ACM* **51**, 1, pp. 107–114.

Dekker, S. (2012). *Drift into Failure: From Hunting Broken Components to Understanding Complex Systems* (Farnham: Ashgate Publishing).

Delsuc, F. (2003). Army ants trapped by their evolutionary history, *PLoS Biology* **1**, 2, pp. e37+.

Demiris, Y. (2007). Prediction of intent in robotics and multi-agent systems, *Cognitive Processing* **8**, 3, pp. 151–158.

Demiris, Y. and Khadhouri, B. (2006). Hierarchical attentive multiple models for execution and recognition of actions, *Robotics and Autonomous Systems* **54**, pp. 361–369.

Dennett, D. (1987). *The Intentional Stance* (Cambridge, MA: MIT Press).

Dennett, D. (1995). *Darwin's Dangerous Idea* (London: Penguin).

Dennett, D. (2009). Intentional systems theory, in B. McLaughlin, A. Beckermann and S. Walter (eds.), *The Oxford Handbook of Philosophy of Mind*, chap. 19 (Oxford: Oxford University Press), pp. 339–350.

Dennis, L. A., Fisher, M., Webster, M. and Bordini, R. H. (2012). Model checking agent programming languages, *Automated Software Engineering* **19**, 1, pp. 5–63.

Denzinger, J. and Winder, C. (2005). Combining coaching and learning to create cooperative character behavior, in *Proceedings IEEE Symposium on Computational Intelligence and Games*, pp. 78–85.

Di Ciccio, C., Mecella, M., Caruso, M., Forte, V., Iacomussi, E., Rasch, K., Querzoni, L., Santucci, G. and Tino, G. (2011). The homes of tomorrow: service composition and advanced user interfaces, *EAI Endorsed Transactions on Ambient Systems* **11**, 1, p. e2.

Di Marzo Serugendo, G. (2009). Robustness and dependability of self-organising systems – a safety engineering perspective, in *International Symposium on Stabilization, Safety, and Security of Distributed Systems*, *Lecture Notes in Computer Science*, Vol. 5873 (Berlin: Springer), pp. 254–268.

Di Marzo Serugendo, G., Fitzgerald, J. and Romanovsky, A. (2010). MetaSelf – an architecture and development method for dependable self-* systems, in *Symposium on Applied Computing*, pp. 457–461.

Di Marzo Serugendo, G., Gleizes, M.-P. and Karageorgos, A. (eds.) (2011). *Self-Organising Software: From Natural to Artificial Adaptation*, Natural Computing Series (Berlin: Springer).

Diamond, A., Knight, R., Devereux, D. and Holland, O. (2012). Anthropomimetic robots: Concept, construction and modelling, *International Journal of Advanced Robotic Systems* **9**, pp. 1–14.

Dick, P. K. (1957). Second variety, in *The Variable Man and Other Stories* (New York, NY: Ace Books), pp. 87–137.

Dick, P. K. (1968). *Do Androids Dream of Electric Sheep?* (New York, NY: Doubleday).

Dijkstra, E. (1974). Self-stabilization in spite of distributed control, *Communications of the ACM* **17**, 11, pp. 643–644.

Dittrich, P., Ziegler, J. and Banzhaf, W. (2001). Artificial chemistries: A review, *Artificial Life* **7**, pp. 225–275.

Dixon, C., Fisher, M. and Bolotov, A. (2002). Resolution in a logic of rational agency, *Artificial Intelligence* **139**, 1, pp. 47–89.

Donati, A. V., Montemanni, R., Casagrande, N., Rizzoli, A. E. and Gambardella, L. M. (2008). Time dependent vehicle routing problem with a multi ant colony system, *European Journal of Operational Research* **185**, 3, pp. 1174–1191.

Doyle, R., Chien, S. A., Lowry, M. R. and Atkinson, D. J. (2012). Report on the NASA workshop on validation of autonomous space systems, Tech. rep., California Institute of Technology.

Duhigg, C. (2009). What does your credit-card company know about you? *The New York Times Magazine*; May 12, 2009.

Duhigg, C. (2012). How companies learn your secrets, *The New York Times Magazine*, 16 Feb 2012.

Durfee, E. H. (1999). Practically coordinating, *AI Magazine* **20**, 1, pp. 99–116.

e-LICO collaboration (2009). e-Laboratory for Interdisciplinary Collaborative Data Mining, http://www.e-lico.eu.

Edelman, G. (2005). *Wider Than The Sky: The Phenomenal Gift Of Consciousness* (New Haven, CT: Yale University Press).

Eissing, T., Kuepfer, L., Becker, C., Block, M., Coboeken, K., Gaub, T., Goerlitz, L., Jaeger, J., Loosen, R., Ludewig, B., Meyer, M., Niederalt, C., Sevestre, M., Siegmund, H.-U., Solodenko, J., Thelen, K., Telle, U., Weiss, W., Wendl, T., Willmann, S. and Lippert, J. (2011). A computational systems biology software platform for multiscale modeling and simulation:

integrating whole-body physiology, disease biology, and molecular reaction networks, *Frontiers in Physiology* **2**, 1–10.

Elster, J. (1989). Social norms and economic theory, *The Journal of Economic Perspectives* **3**, 4, pp. 99–117.

Endsley, M. R. (1995a). Measurement of situation awareness in dynamic systems, *Human Factors* **37**, 1, pp. 65–84.

Endsley, M. R. (1995b). Toward a theory of situation awareness in dynamic systems, *Human Factors* **37**, 1, pp. 32–64.

Endsley, M. R. and Jones, D. G. (2004). *Designing for Situation Awareness: An Approach to User-Centered Design* (Boca Raton, FL: CRC Press).

Esterle, L., Lewis, P. R., Yao, X. and Rinner, B. (2014). Socio-economic vision graph generation and handover in distributed smart camera networks, *ACM Transactions on Sensor Networks* **10**, 2, p. 20.

Esteva, M., Rosell, B., Rodríguez-Aguilar, J. A. and Arcos, J. L. (2004). AMELI: an agent-based middleware for electronic institutions, in *AAMAS'04*, pp. 236–243.

Eugster, P., Felber, P. and Le Fessant, F. (2007). The "art" of programming gossip-based systems, *SIGOPS Operating Systems Review* **41**, 5, pp. 37–42.

Fabricatore, C. and López, X. (2012). Sustainability learning through gaming: An exploratory study, *Electronic Journal of e-Learning* **10**, 2.

Fagin, R., Halpern, J. Y., Moses, Y. and Vardi, M. Y. (1995). *Reasoning about Knowledge* (Cambridge, MA: MIT Press).

Farrer, J. and Finn, A. (2009). The power of a single prototype: sustainable fashion textile design and the prevention of carcinogenic melanoma, in *Innovative Developments in Design and Manufacturing: Advanced Research in Virtual and Rapid Prototyping* (Leiden: CRC Press), pp. 681–686.

Farrer, J., Goulev, P. and Pitt, J. (2006). Emotive episode: an investigation into user response to sustainable issues in fashion/textiles and affective computing, in *Proceedings of Sustainable Innovation 06: Global Challenges, Issues and Solutions*, pp. 54–60.

Faugeras, O. (1993). *Three-Dimensional Computer Vision: A Geometric Viewpoint* (Cambridge, MA: MIT Press).

Fernandez-Marquez, J., Di Marzo Serugendo, G., Montagna, S., Viroli, M. and Arcos, J. (2013). Description and composition of bio-inspired design patterns: a complete overview, *Natural Computing Journal* **12**, 1, pp. 43–67.

Fernandez-Marquez, J., Di Marzo Serurendo, G. and Montagna, S. (2011). BIO-CORE: Bio-inspired self-organising mechanisms core, in *Bio-Inspired Models of Network, Information, and Computing Systems (Bionetics)*, Vol. 103, pp. 59–72.

Fernandez-Marquez, J. L. and Arcos, J. L. (2010). Adapting particle swarm optimization in dynamic and noisy environments, in *Proceedings of IEEE Congress on Evolutionary Computation*, pp. 765–772.

Ficker, J. H., Wiest, G. H., Lehnert, G., Wiest, B. and Hahn, E. G. (1998). Evaluation of an auto-CPAP device for treatment of obstructive sleep apnoea, *Thorax* **53**, 8, pp. 643–648.

Fischer, C. (2008). Feedback on household electricity consumption: a tool for saving energy? *Energy Efficiency* **1**, 1, pp. 79–104.

Fishel, J. and Loeb, G. (2012). Bayesian exploration for intelligent identification of textures, *Frontiers in Neurorobotics* **6**, 4, pp. 1–20.

Floyd, C. E., Lo, J. Y., Yun, A. J., Sullivan, D. C. and Kornguth, P. J. (1994). Prediction of breast cancer malignancy using an artificial neural network, *Cancer* **74**, 11, pp. 2944–2948.

Fowler, M. (1997). Dealing with roles, Tech. Rep. 97-34, *The 4th Pattern Languages of Programming Conference*, Washington University.

Freedman, S. and Adams, J. A. (2003). Improving robot situational awareness through commonsense: side-stepping incompleteness and unsoundness, Tech. rep., Human-Machine Laboratory, Vanderbilt University.

Frei, R., McWilliam, R., Derrick, B., Purvis, A., Tiwari, A. and Di Marzo Serugendo, G. (2013). Self-healing and self-repairing technologies, *International Journal of Advanced Manufacturing Technology* **69**, pp. 1033–1061.

Fuad-Luke, A. (2009). *Design Activism: Beautiful Strangeness in a Sustainable World* (Oxford: Routledge).

Fuchs, A. (2013). Self-organization and synergetics, in *Nonlinear Dynamics in Complex Systems* (Berlin: Springer), pp. 147–157.

Fuchs, E., Gruber, T., Nitschke, J. and Sick, B. (2009). On-line motif detection in time series with SwiftMotif, *Pattern Recognition* **42**, 11, pp. 3015–3031.

Fukayama, A., Ohno, T., Mukawa, N., Sawaki, M. and Hagita, N. (2002). Messages embedded in gaze of interface agents — impression management with agent's gaze, in *Proceedings of the SIGCHI Conference on Human Factors in Computing Systems*, CHI '02 (ACM, New York, NY, USA), pp. 41–48.

Gallup, G. (1970). Chimpanzees: self recognition, *Science* **167**, 3914, pp. 86–87.

Gamberini, L., Spagnolli, A., Corradi, N., Jacucci, G., Tusa, G., Mikkola, T., Zamboni, L. and Hoggan, E. (2012). Tailoring feedback to users' actions in a persuasive game for household electricity conservation, in M. Bang and E. Ragnemalm (eds.), *Persuasive Technology. Design for Health and Safety, Lecture Notes in Computer Science*, Vol. 7284 (Berlin: Springer), pp. 100–111.

Garlan, D. and Schmerl, B. (2002). Model-based adaptation for self-healing systems, in *Workshop on Self-Healing Systems*, pp. 27–32.

George, S., Evans, D. and Davidson, L. (2002). A biologically inspired programming model for self-healing systems, in *Workshop on Self-Healing Systems*, pp. 102–104.

Georgievski, I., Degeler, V., Pagani, G., Nguyen, T., Lazovik, A. and Aiello, M. (2012). Optimizing energy costs for offices connected to the smart grid, *IEEE Transactions on Smart Grid* **3**, pp. 2273–2285.

Gertler, B. (2011). Self-knowledge, *The Stanford Encyclopedia of Philosophy*, http://plato.stanford.edu/entries/self-knowledge/.

Ghosh, D., Sharman, R., Raghav Rao, H. and Upadhyaya, S. (2007). Self-healing systems - survey and synthesis, *Decision Support Systems* **42**, pp. 2164–2185.

Giguere, D. A. (2010). Aircraft emergency systems, in R. Blockley and W. Shyy (eds.), *Encyclopedia of Aerospace Engineering* (Hoboken, NJ: John Wiley and Sons).

Giunchiglia, F. and Robertson, D. (2010). The social computer: Combining machine and human computation, Tech. Rep. DISI-10-036, University of Trento.

Glanz, K., Schoenfeld, E. and Steffen, A. (2010). A randomized trial of tailored skin cancer prevention messages for adults: Project SCAPE, *American Journal of Public Health* **100**, 4, pp. 735–741.

Glanz, K., Schoenfeld, E., Weinstock, M. A., Layi, G., Kidd, J. and Shigaki, D. M. (2003). Development and reliability of a brief skin cancer risk assessment tool, *Cancer Detection and Prevention* **27**, 4, pp. 311–315.

Gold, K. and Scassellati, B. (2007). A bayesian robot that distinguishes "self" from "other", in *Proceedings of the 29th Annual Meeting of the Cognitive Science Society*, pp. 1–4.

Goodchild, M. (2007). Citizens as sensors: the world of volunteered geography, *GeoJournal* **69**, 4, pp. 211–221.

Goold, B. J. (2009). Building it in: the role of privacy enhancing technologies (PETs) in the regulation of surveillance and data collection, in B. Goold and D. Neyland (eds.), *New Directions in Surveillance and Privacy*, chap. 2 (Cullompton: Willan Publishing), pp. 18–38.

Gorner, J., Zhang, J. and Cohen, R. (2011). Improving the use of advisor networks for multi-agent trust modelling, in *Ninth Annual International Conference on Privacy, Security and Trust (PST)*, pp. 71–78.

Goulev, P. and Farrer, J. (2013). Interactive design activism, *Awareness Magazine*, doi:10.2417/3201305.004899.

Goulev, P., Stead, L., Mamdani, A. and Evans, C. (2004). Computer aided emotional fashion, *Computers & Graphics* **28**, 5, pp. 657–666.

Griffin, D. R. (1992). *Animal Minds: Beyond Cognition to Consciousness* (Chicago, IL: University of Chicago Press).

Grudin, J. (2001). Desituating action: digital representation of context, *Human–Computer Interaction* **16**, pp. 269–286.

Gwilt, A. and Rissanen, T. (2011). *Shaping Sustainable Fashion: Changing the Way We Make and Use Clothes* (London: Routledge).

Habermas, J. (1985). *The Theory of Communicative Action, Volume 1: Reason and the Rationalization of Society* (Boston, MA: Beacon Press).

Haggerty, K. D. and Ericson, R. V. (2000). The surveillant assemblage, *British Journal of Sociology* **51**, 4, pp. 605–622.

Haikonen, P. O. (2007). Reflections of consciousness: The mirror test, in *Proceedings of the 2007 AAAI Fall Symposium on Consciousness and Artificial Intelligence*, pp. 67–71.

Haken, H. (1980). Synergetics, *Naturwissenschaften* **67**, 3, pp. 121–128.

Han, J., Dong, G. and Yin, Y. (1999). Efficient mining of partial periodic patterns in time series database, in *Proceedings of the International Conference on Data Engineering*, pp. 106–115.

Hardin, G. (1968). The tragedy of the commons, *Science* **162**, 3859, pp. 1243–1248.

Harrington, M. (2011). An Independent Review of the Work Capability Assessment, London: The Stationery Office.

Hart, J. and Scassellati, B. (2011). A robotic model of the ecological self, in *Proceedings of the 11th IEEE-RAS International Conference on Humanoid Robots (HUMANOIDS)*, pp. 682–688.

Hart, J. and Scassellati, B. (2012). Mirror perspective-taking with a humanoid robot, in *Proceedings of the 26th AAAI Conference on Artificial Intelligence*, pp. 1990–1996.

Hartley, R. I. and Zisserman, A. (2004). *Multiple View Geometry in Computer Vision*, 2nd edn. (Cambridge: Cambridge University Press).

Hassan, A. (2008). The road ahead for mining software repositories, in *24th IEEE International Conference on Software Maintenance, Frontiers of Software Maintenance*, pp. 48–57.

Haydarlou, A., Overeinder, B. and Brazier, F. (2005). A self-healing approach for object-oriented applications, in *International Workshop on Database and Expert Systems Applications*, pp. 191–195.

Hersch, M., Sauser, E. and Billard, A. (2008). Online learning of the body schema, *International Journal of Humanoid Robotics* **5**, 2, pp. 161–181.

Heschl, A. and Burkart, J. (2006). A new mark test for self-recognition in non-human primates, *Primates* **47**, 3, pp. 187–198.

Hesslow, G. (2002). Conscious thought as simulation of behaviour and perception, *Trends in Cognitive Science* **6**, 6, pp. 242–247.

Hodson, H. (2012). Robot learns to recognise itself in the mirror, *New Scientist* **2878**.

Holland, J. (1992). Complex adaptive systems, *Daedalus* **121**, 1, pp. 17–30.

Holland, O. (ed.) (2003). *Machine Consciousness* (Exeter: Imprint Academic).

Hollnagel, E. (2012). Resilience: the challenge of the unstable, in E. Hollnagel, D. D. Woods and N. Leveson (eds.), *Resilience Engineering*, Kindle edn. (Farnham: Ashgate Publishing), pp. 342–472 (Kindle loc.).

Hölzl, M. M. and Wirsing, M. (2011). Towards a system model for ensembles, in *Formal Modeling: Actors, Open Systems, Biological Systems, Lecture Notes in Computer Science*, Vol. 7000, pp. 241–261.

Honebein, P. (2009). Sustainably ours: The new energy interface, *Interactions* **16**, 5, pp. 26–28.

Horn, P. (2001). Autonomic computing: IBM perspective on the state of information technology, Tech. rep., IBM T.J. Watson Labs, NY; presented at AGENDA 2001, Scottsdale, AR.

Horstemeyer, M. (2010). Multiscale modeling: A review, in J. Leszczynski and M. Shukla (eds.), *Practical Aspects of Computational Chemistry* (Berlin: Springer), pp. 87–135.

Howe, J. (2008). *Crowdsourcing: Why the Power of the Crowd Is Driving the Future of Business*, 1st edn. (New York, NY: Crown Business).

Hsieh, M. A., Cowley, A., Keller, J. F., Chaimowicz, L., Grocholsky, B., Kumar, V., Taylor, C. J., Endo, Y., Arkin, R. C., Jung, B., Wolf, D. F., Sukhatme, G. S. and Mackenzie, D. C. (2007). Adaptive teams of autonomous aerial and ground robots for situational awareness, *Journal of Field Robotics: Special Issue on Teamwork in Field Robotics* **24**, 11–12, pp. 991–1014.

Huebscher, M. C. and McCann, J. A. (2004). Adaptive middleware for context-aware applications in smart-homes, in *Proceedings of the 2nd Workshop on Middleware for Pervasive and Ad-Hoc Computing* (ACM), pp. 111–116.

Huhns, M. N. and Singh, M. P. (2005). Service-oriented computing: key concepts and principles, *IEEE Internet Computing* **9**, 1, pp. 75–81.

Hunt, A. (2011). Social norms and energy conservation, *Journal of Public Economics* **95**, 9–10, pp. 1082–1095.

IBM (2005). An architectural blueprint for autonomic computing. Tech. Rep. June, IBM Corporation, Hawthorne, NY.

InterLink project (2010). Web site, http://interlink.ics.forth.gr/central.aspx, last accessed: 2011-05-10.

Intille, S. S. (2006). The goal: smart people, not smart homes, in *Proceedings of the International Conference on Smart Homes and Health Telematics* (IOS Press).

IOSCO (2011). Regulatory issues raised by the impact of technological changes on market integrity and efficiency, Technical Committee Consultation Report CR02/11, International Organization of Securities Commissions.

Isidori, A., Marconi, L. and Serrani, A. (2003). Fundamentals of internal-model-based control theory, in *Robust Autonomous Guidance*, Advances in Industrial Control (London: Springer), pp. 1–58.

Iwata, H., Yano, H., Uemura, T. and Moriya, T. (2004). Food simulator: a haptic interface for biting, in *IEEE Virtual Reality Conference*, pp. 51–58.

Jacob, C., von Mammen, S., Davison, T., Sarraf-Shirazi, A., Sarpe, V., Esmaeili, A., Phillips, D., Yazdanbod, I., Novakowski, S., Steil, S., Gingras, C., Jamniczky, H., Hallgrimsson, B. and Wright, B. (2012). LINDSAY virtual human: multi-scale, agent-based, and interactive, in J. Kołodziej, S. Khan and T. Burczyński (eds.), *Advances in Intelligent Modelling and Simulation: Artificial Intelligence-based Models and Techniques in Scalable Computing, Studies in Computational Intelligence*, Vol. 422 (Berlin: Springer), pp. 327–349.

Jacobi, N., Husbands, P. and Harvey, I. (1995). Noise and the reality gap: the use of simulation in evolutionary robotics, in *Proceedings of the Third European Conference on Advances in Artificial Life*, pp. 704–720.

Jiang, M., Zhang, J., Raymer, D. and Strassner, J. (2007). A modeling framework for self healing software systems, Workshop on Models@run.time at the *International Conference on Model Driven Engineering Languages and Systems*.

Jin, X., Gallagher, A., Cao, L., Luo, J. and Han, J. (2010). The wisdom of social multimedia: using flickr for prediction and forecast, in *Proceedings of the International Conference on Multimedia*, pp. 1235–1244.

Johansson, M. and Verhagen, H. (2009). Massively multiple online role playing games as normative multiagent systems, in G. Boella, P. Noriega, G. Pigozzi and H. Verhagen (eds.), *Normative Multi-Agent Systems*, no. 09121 in Dagstuhl Seminar Proceedings.

Johnston, P., Everard, M., Santillo, D. and Robèrt, K.-H. (2007). Reclaiming the definition of sustainability, *Environmental Science and Pollution Research International* **14**, 1, p. 60.

Jones, A., Lang, M., Fyffe, G., Yu, X., Busch, J., McDowall, I., Bolas, M. and Debevec, P. (2009). Achieving eye contact in a one-to-many 3D video teleconferencing system, *ACM Transactions on Graphics* **28**, 3, pp. 64:1–64:8.

Jones, A. and Sergot, M. (1996). A formal characterisation of institutionalised power, *Journal of the IGPL* **4**, 3, pp. 427–443.

Jun, J., Lee, D. and Sim, K. (1999). Realization of cooperative strategies and swarm behavior in distributed autonomous robotic systems using artificial immune system, *Procedings of the IEEE International Conference on Systems, Man, and Cybernetics (SMC)* **6**, pp. 614–619.

Kaldeli, E., Lazovik, A. and Aiello, M. (2011). Continual planning with sensing for web service composition, in *Proceedings of the Twenty-Fifth AAAI Conference on Artificial Intelligence.*

Kaldeli, E., Warriach, E., Lazovik, A. and Aiello, M. (2013). Coordinating the web of services for a smart home, *ACM Transactions on the Web* **7**, 2, pp. 10:1–10:40.

Kant, I. (1785). *Grounding for the Metaphysics of Morals (3rd edn., 1993, translated by J. Ellington)* (Indianapolis/Cambridge: Hackett Publishing Co.).

Kari, L. and Rozenberg, G. (2008). The many facets of natural computing, *Communications of the ACM* **51**, pp. 72–83.

Kauffman, S. A. (1993). *The Origins of Order: Self-Organization and Selection in Evolution* (Oxford: Oxford University Press).

Kelly, K. (2010). The Shirky principle, *The Technium*, http://kk.org/thetechnium/2010/04/the-shirky-prin/.

Kephart, J. (2005). Research challenges of autonomic computing, in *Proceedings 27th International Conference on Software Engineering (ICSE)*, pp. 15–22.

Kephart, J. and Chess, D. (2003). The vision of autonomic computing, *IEEE Computer* **36**, 1, pp. 41–50.

Kephart, J. and Das, R. (2007). Achieving self-management via utility functions, *IEEE Internet Computing* **11**, 1, pp. 40–48.

Kephart, J. and Walsh, W. (2004). An artificial intelligence perspective on autonomic computing policies, in *Proceedings 5th IEEE International Workshop on Policies for Distributed Systems and Networks*, pp. 3–12.

Kerr, I. and Mann, S. (2006). Exploring equiveillance, http://www.anonequity.org.

Khopkar, T., Li, X. and Resnick, P. (2005). Self-selection, slipping, salvaging, slacking, and stoning: the impacts of negative feedback at eBay, in *Proceedings 6th ACM Conference on Electronic Commerce*, pp. 223–231.

Kiczales, G., des Rivières, J. and Bobrow, D. (1991). *The Art of the Meta-Object Protocol* (Cambridge, MA: MIT Press).

Kiefer, J. (1977). Conditional confidence statements and confidence estimators, *Journal of the American Statistical Association* **72**, 360, pp. 789–808.

Kiefhaber, R., Anders, G., Siefert, F., Ungerer, T. and Reif, W. (2012). Confidence as a means to assess the accuracy of trust values, in *Proceedings of the 2012 IEEE 11th International Conference on Trust, Security and Privacy in Computing and Communications*, pp. 690–697.

Kim, H., Lee, S. K., Kim, H. and Kim, H. (2012). Implementing home energy management system with UPnP and mobile applications, *Computer Communications* **36**, 1, pp. 51–62.

Kittur, A., Smus, B. and Kraut, R. (2011). Crowdforge: Crowdsourcing complex work, in *ACM CHI Conference on Human Factors in Computing Systems 2011* (ACM), pp. 43–52.

Klein, G., Moon, B. and Hoffman, R. (2006). Making sense of sensemaking: alternative perspectives, *IEEE Intelligent Systems* **21**, 4, pp. 70–73.

Klopf, A. H. (1972). Brain function and adaptive systems: a heterostatic theory, Special Report 133, Air Force Cambridge Research Laboratory, USAF.

Koch, N., Wirsing, M., Zambonelli, F. and Hölzl, M. (2013). The ASCENS ensemble development lifecycle, Tech. rep., Ludwig-Maximilians-Universität München.

Kooti, F., Yang, H., Cha, M., Gummadi, K. and Mason, W. (2012). The emergence of conventions in online social networks, in *Proceedings of the Sixth International Conference on Weblogs and Social Media*, pp. 1–8.

Kosinski, M., Stillwell, D. and Graepel, T. (2013). Private traits and attributes are predictable from digital records of human behavior, *Proceedings of the National Academy of Sciences of the United States of America* **110**, 15, pp. 5802–5805.

Kosko, B. (1994). Fuzzy systems as universal approximators, *IEEE Trans. Computers* **43**, 11, pp. 1329–1333.

Kramer, J. and Magee, J. (2007). Self-managed systems: an architectural challenge, in *Workshop on the Future of Software Engineering, International Conference on Software Engineering (ICSE)*, pp. 259–268.

Kusic, D., Kephart, J., Hanson, J., Kandasamy, N. and Jiang, G. (2009). Power and performance management of virtualized computing environments via lookahead control, *Cluster Computing* **12**, 1, pp. 1–15.

Labella, T. H., Dorigo, M. and Deneubourg, J.-L. (2006). Division of labor in a group of robots inspired by ants' foraging behavior, *ACM Transactions on Autonomous and Adaptive Systems* **1**, pp. 4–25.

Laddaga, R. (1997). Self-adaptive software, Tech. rep., 98-12, DARPA BAA.

Lam, W. (1996). Improving the performance of small-scale irrigation systems: the effects of technological investments and governance structure on irrigation performance in Nepal, *World Development* **24**, 8, pp. 1301–1315.

Landauer, C. and Bellman, K. L. (1996). Knowledge-based integration infrastructure for complex systems, *International Journal of Intelligent Control and Systems* **1**, 1, pp. 133–153.

Landauer, C. and Bellman, K. L. (1999a). Generic programming, partial evaluation and a new programming paradigm, in *Proceedings of System Sciences (HICCS-32)*, pp. 108–154.

Landauer, C. and Bellman, K. L. (1999b). Lessons learned with wrapping systems, in *Proceedings of the 5th IEEE International Conference on Engineering Complex Computing Systems*, pp. 132–142.

Landauer, C. and Bellman, K. L. (2001). New architectures for constructed complex systems, *Applied Mathematics and Computation* **120**, pp. 149–163.

Landauer, C. and Bellman, K. L. (2002). Self-modeling systems, in H. S.

R. Laddaga (ed.), *Self-Adaptive Software, Lecture Notes in Computer Science*, Vol. 2614 (Berlin: Springer), pp. 238–256.

Laprie, J.-C. (2005). Resilience for the scalability of dependability, in *12th IEEE International Symposium on Network Computing and Applications*, pp. 5–6.

Larsson, T. and Akenine-Möller, T. (2001). Collision detection for continuously deforming bodies, in *Proceedings Eurographics*, pp. 325–333.

Legrain, L., Cleeremans, A. and Destrebecqz, A. (2011). Distinguishing three levels in explicit self-awareness, *Consciousness and Cognition* **20**, pp. 578–585.

Lem, S. (1986). Weapon systems of the twenty first century or the upside-down evolution, in *One Human Minute* (New York, NY: Harcourt Brace & Co.).

Lerman, K., Martinoli, A. and Galstyan, A. (2005). A review of probabilistic macroscopic models for swarm robotic systems, in E. Sahin and W. Spears (eds.), *Swarm Robotics, Lecture Notes in Computer Science*, Vol. 3342 (Berlin: Springer), pp. 143–152.

Lewis, M. (2011). The origins and uses of self-awarenesss or the mental representation of me, *Consciousness and Cognition* **20**, pp. 120–129.

Lewis, P., Chandra, A., Parsons, S., Robinson, E., Glette, K., Bahsoon, R., Torresen, J. and Yao, X. (2011). A survey of self-awareness and its application in computing systems, in *Self-Adaptive and Self-Organizing Systems Workshops (SASOW)*, pp. 102–107.

Licklider, J. C. R. (1960). Man–computer symbiosis, *IRE Transactions on Human Factors in Electronics* **HFE-1**, pp. 4–11.

Linger, R., Mead, N. and Lipson, H. (1998). Requirements definition for survivable network systems, in *International Conference on Requirements Engineering (ICRE)* (Colorado Springs, USA), pp. 6–10.

Lintott, C. J., Schawinski, K., Slosar, A., Land, K., Bamford, S., Thomas, D., Raddick, M. J., Nichol, R. C., Szalay, A., Andreescu, D., Murray, P. and Vandenberg, J. (2008). Galaxy zoo: morphologies derived from visual inspection of galaxies from the Sloan Digital Sky Survey, *Monthly Notices of the Royal Astronomical Society* **389**, 3, pp. 1179–1189.

Lipson, H. and Pollack, J. B. (2000). Automatic design and manufacture of robotic lifeforms, *Nature* **406**, pp. 974–978.

Liu, B. (2010). Sentiment analysis and subjectivity, *Handbook of Natural Language Processing* **1**, pp. 1–38.

Liu, B. (2011). *Web Data Mining: Exploring Hyperlinks, Contents, and Usage Data* (Berlin: Springer).

Loehr, J. and Schwartz, T. (2001). The making of a corporate athlete, *Harvard Business Review* **79**, 1, pp. 120–128.

Long, T. (2007). Sept. 26, 1983: The man who saved the world by doing ... nothing, *Wired*.

Lorenz, K. (1966). *On Aggression* (London: Methuen).

Louis, T. A. and Zeger, S. L. (2009). Effective communication of standard errors and confidence intervals, *Biostatistics* **10**, 1, pp. 1–2.

Lucas, R., McMichael, T., Smith, W. and Armstrong, B. (2006). *Solar Ultraviolet Radiation: Global Burden of Disease from Solar Ultraviolet Radia-*

tion, no. 13 in Environmental Burden of Disease (Geneva: World Health Organization).

Maes, P. and Nardi, D. (eds.) (1988). *Meta-Level Architectures and Reflection* (Amsterdam: North-Holland).

Mann, S. (2004a). Continuous lifelong capture of personal experience with eyetap, in *1st ACM workshop on Continuous Archival and Retrieval of Personal Experiences*, pp. 1–21.

Mann, S. (2004b). Sousveillance: inverse surveillance in multimedia imaging, in *Proceedings of the 12th annual ACM International Conference on Multimedia*, pp. 620–627.

Mann, S., Nolan, J. and Wellman, B. (2003). Sousveillance: inventing and using wearable computing devices for data collection in surveillance environments, *Surveillance and Society* **1**, 3, pp. 331–355.

Marques, H. and Holland, O. (2009). Architectures for functional imagination, *Neurocomputing* **72**, 4–6, pp. 743–759.

Marsh, T. (2011). Serious games continuum: between games for purpose and experiential environments for purpose, *Entertainment Computing* **2**, 2, pp. 61–68.

Masters, A. and Michael, K. (2006). Lend me your arms: the use and implications of humancentric RFID, *Electronic Commerce Research and Applications* **6**, 1, pp. 29–39.

Matthias, A. (2004). The responsibility gap: ascribing responsibility for the actions of learning automata, *Ethics and Information Technology* **6**, 3, pp. 175–183.

McDaniel, P. and McLaughlin, S. (2009). Security and privacy challenges in the smart grid, *Security & Privacy, IEEE* **7**, 3, pp. 75–77.

Meakin, S. (ed.) (1992). *The Rio Earth Summit: Summary of the The United Nations Conference on Environment and Development* (Government of Canada Publications).

Menzel, E. J., Savage-Rumbaugh, E. and Lawson, J. (1985). Chimpanzees (pan troglodytes) spatial problem solving with the use of mirrors and televised equivalents of mirrors, *Journal of Comparative Psychology* **99**, 2, pp. 211–217.

Metzinger, T. (2009). *The Ego Tunnel* (New York, NY: Basic Books).

Meyer, T. and Tschudin, C. (2010). Competition and cooperation of self-healing software, Tech. rep., CS-2010-004, University of Basel, Switzerland.

Michael, K. and Clarke, R. (2013). Location and tracking of mobile devices: überveillance stalks the streets, *Computer Law & Security Review* **29**, 3, pp. 216–228.

Michael, K. and Michael, M. (2009). Teaching ICT ethics using wearable computing: the social implications of the new 'veillance', presentation at *AUPOV09: Australian Point of View Technologies Conference*.

Michael, K. and Miller, K. (2013). Big data: new opportunities and new challenges, *IEEE Computer* **46**, 6, pp. 22–24.

Michael, K., Roussos, G., Huang, G., Gadh, R., Chattopadhyay, A., Prabhu, S. and Chu, P. (2010). Planetary-scale RFID services in an age of überveillance, *Proceedings of the IEEE* **98**, 9, pp. 1663–1671.

Michael, M. and Michael, K. (2007). Überveillance: 24/7 x 365 people tracking and monitoring, presentation at *29th International Conference of Data Protection and Privacy Commissioners: Location Based Tracking Workshop*.

Michael, M. and Michael, K. (2010). Towards a state of überveillance, *IEEE Technology and Society Magazine* **29**, 2, pp. 9–16.

Michael, M. and Michael, K. (2011). The fall-out from emerging technologies: on matters of surveillance, social networks and suicide, *IEEE Technology and Society Magazine* **30**, 3, pp. 15–18.

Michel, O. (2004). Webots: professional mobile robot simulation, *International Journal of Advanced Robotic Systems* **1**, 1, pp. 39–42.

Minder, P. and Bernstein, A. (2012). Crowdlang: A programming language for the systematic exploration of human computation systems, in *Procedings of the 4th International Conference on Social Informatics (SocInfo), Lecture Notes in Computer Science*, Vol. 7710 (Berlin: Springer), pp. 124–137.

Mingay, S. (2007). Green IT: the new industry shockwave, Tech. Rep. G00153703, Gartner.

Mitchell, M., Crutchfield, J. P., Hraber, P. T., Cowan, I. G., Pines, D. and Melzner, D. (1994). Dynamics, computation, and the "edge of chaos": A re-examination, in *Complexity: Metaphors, Models, and Reality* (Boston, MA: Addison-Wesley), pp. 497–513.

Moere, A. V., Tomitsch, M., Hoinkis, M., Trefz, E., Johansen, S. and Jones, A. (2011). Comparative feedback in the street: Exposing residential energy consumption on house façades, in *Human-Computer Interaction*, pp. 470–488.

Möller, T., Haines, E. and Hoffman, N. (2008). *Real-Time Rendering* (Natick, MA: A K Peters Ltd.).

Montagna, S., Viroli, M., Fernandez-Marquez, J., Di Marzo Serugendo, G. and Zambonelli, F. (2012). Injecting self-organisation into pervasive service ecosystems, *Mobile Networks and Applications* **18**, 3, pp. 398–412.

Montani, S. and Anglano, C. (2008). Achieving self-healing in service delivery software systems by means of case-based reasoning, *Applied Intelligence* **28**, pp. 139–152.

Mora, T. and Bialek, W. (2011). Are biological systems poised at criticality? *Journal of Statistical Physics* **144**, 2, pp. 268–302.

Morin, A. (2006). Levels of consciousness and self-awareness: a comparison and integration of various neurocognitive views, *Consciousness and Cognition* **15**, pp. 358–371.

Morin, A. and Everett, J. (1990). Conscience de soi et langage interieur: quelques speculations (Self-awareness and inner speech: some speculations), *Philosophiques* **XVII**, 2, pp. 169–188.

Morris, M., KenKnight, B., Warren, J. and Lang, D. (1999). A preview of implantable cardioverter defibrillator systems in the next millennium: an integrative cardiac rhythm management approach, *The American Journal of Cardiology* **83**, 5, pp. 48–54.

Müller-Schloer, C. (2004). Organic computing: on the feasibility of controlled emergence, in *2nd IEEE/ACM/IFIP International Conference on Hardware/Software Co-Design and System Synthesis*, pp. 2–5.

Müller-Schloer, C., Schmeck, H. and Ungerer, T. (eds.) (2011). *Organic Computing: A Paradigm Shift for Complex Systems* (Berlin: Springer).

Müller-Schloer, C. and Sick, B. (2008). Controlled emergence and self-organization, in R. Wuertz (ed.), *Organic Computing, Understanding Complex Systems* (Berlin: Springer), pp. 81–104.

Munoz, J., Gutierrez, G. and Sanchis, A. (2009). Controller for TORCS created by imitation, in *IEEE Symposium on Computational Intelligence and Games*, pp. 271–278.

Murugesan, S. (2008). Harnessing green IT: principles and practices, *IT Professional* **10**, 1, pp. 24–33.

Nagappan, N., Ball, T. and Zeller, A. (2006). Mining metrics to predict component failures, in *Proceedings of the 28th International Conference on Software Engineering (ICSE)*, pp. 452–461.

Naone, E. (2009). Software that fixes itself, MIT Technology Review, http://www.technologyreview.com/news/416036/software-that-fixes- itself/.

Neisser, U. (1997). The roots of self-knowledge: perceiving self, it, and thou, *Annals of the New York Acadamey of Sciences* **818**, pp. 19–33.

Nelson, P. (2011). Self-organized self-improvement: using self-directed experimentation to improve models and methods, in *Organic Computing: Design of Self-Organizing Systems, Dagstuhl Seminar Proceedings*, Vol. 11181.

Nelson, V. (1990). *Fault-Tolerant Computing: Fundamental Concepts* (Washington, DC: IEEE Computer Society Press).

Newman, D. and Gall, N. (2010). *Gain a Foundation in Design Thinking to Apply Gartner's Hybrid Thinking Research* (Gartner Analysis).

Newton-Bishop, J., Chang, Y., Elliott, F., Chan, M., Leake, S., Karpavicius, B., Haynes, S., Fitzgibbon, E., Kukalizch, K., Randerson-Moor, J., Elder, D., Bishop, D. and Barrett, J. (2011). Relationship between sun exposure and melanoma risk for tumours in different body sites in a large case-control study in a temperate climate, *European Journal of Cancer* **47**, 5, pp. 732–741.

Nicolescu, B. (2002). *Manifesto of Transdisciplinarity* (New York: SUNY Press).

North, R., Cohen, J., Wilkins, S., Richards, M., Hoose, N., Polak, J., Bell, M., Blythe, P., Sharif, B., Neasham, J., Suresh, V., Galatioto, F., Hill, G., Mead, I., Jones, R., Beresford, A., Chen, H., Ropkins, K., Goodman, P., Oates, C., Tate, J. and Ballijepalli, N. (2009). Field deployments of the message system for environmental monitoring, *Traffic Engineering and Control* **50**, 11, pp. 484–488.

Nowak, A., Lewenstein, M. and Szamrej, J. (1993). Bable modelem przemian spolecznych (bubbles: a model of social transition), *Swiat Nauki (Scientific American Polish Edition)* **12**.

Nowak, A., Szamrej, J. and Latane, B. (1990). From private attitude to public opinion: a dynamic theory of social impact, *Psychological Review* **97**, pp. 362–376.

Nowak, A., Vallacher, R., Kus, M. and Urbaniak, J. (2005). The dynamics of societal transition: modeling non-linear change in the Polish economic system, *International Journal of Sociology* **35**, pp. 65–68.

Obaid, M., Damian, I., Kistler, F., Endrass, B., Wagner, J. and André, E. (2012). Cultural behaviors of virtual agents in an augmented reality environment, in *Intelligent Virtual Agents* (Berlin: Springer), pp. 412–418.

O'Connor, B., Balasubramanyan, R., Routledge, B. and Smith, N. (2010). From tweets to polls: linking text sentiment to public opinion time series, in *International AAAI Conference on Weblogs and Social Media*, pp. 122–129.

O'Dowd, P. J., Winfield, A. F. T. and Studley, M. (2011). The distributed co-evolution of an embodied simulator and controller for swarm robot behaviours, in *Intelligent Robots and Systems (IROS)*, pp. 4995–5000.

Ostrom, E. (1990). *Governing the Commons: The Evolution of Institutions for Collective Action* (Cambridge: Cambridge University Press).

Ostrom, E. and Hess, C. (2006). A framework for analyzing the knowledge commons, in C. Hess and E. Ostrom (eds.), *Understanding Knowledge as a Commons: From Theory to Practice* (Cambridge, MA: MIT Press), pp. 41–82.

Ouwerkerk, M., Pasveer, F. and Langereis, G. (2008). Unobtrusive sensing of psychophysicological parameters: some examples of non-invasive sensing technologies, in J. Westerink, M. Ouwerkerk, T. Overbeek, F. Pasveer and B. de Ruyter (eds.), *Probing Experience: From Assessment of User Emotions and Behaviour to Development of Products*, Philips Research Book Series (Dordrecht: Springer), pp. 163–193.

Papakostas, T., Lima, J. and Lowe, M. (2002). A large area force sensor for smart skin applications, *IEEE Sensors* **5**, 3, pp. 1620–1624.

Parent, W. A. (1983). Privacy, morality and the law, *Philosophy & Public Affairs* **12**, 4.

Park, J., Youn, H. and Lee, E. (2009). An automatic code generation for self-healing, *Journal of Information Science and Engineering* **25**, pp. 1753–1781.

Paternò, F., Mancini, C. and Meniconi, S. (1997). ConcurTaskTrees: a diagrammatic notation for specifying task models, in *Proceedings IFIP TC13 International Conference on Human-Computer Interaction*, pp. 362–369.

Patterson, D. and Hennessy, J. (2011). *Computer Organization and Design*, 4th edn. (Burlington, MA: Morgan Kaufmann).

Pearce, P. and Gretzel, U. (2012). Tourism in technology dead zones: documenting experiential dimensions, *International Journal of Tourism Sciences* **12**, 2, pp. 1–20.

Perez-Sotelo, J., Cuesta, C. and Ossowski, S. (2011). Adaptation patterns in multi-agent architectures: the gathering pattern, in *On the Move to Meaningful Internet Systems: OTM 2011 Workshops, Lecture Notes in Computer Science Volume*, Vol. 7046 (Berlin: Springer), pp. 657–661.

Perkins, J., Kim, S., Larsen, S., Amarasinghe, S., Bachrach, J., Carbin, M., Pacheco, C., Sherwood, F., Sidiroglou, S., Sullivan, G. *et al.* (2009). Automatically patching errors in deployed software, in *ACM Symposium on Operating Systems Principles (SIGOPS)* (Big Sky, MT, USA), pp. 87–102.

Perlovsky, L. I. and Kozma, R. (eds.) (2007). *Neurodynamics of Cognition and Consciousness* (Berlin: Springer).

Petta, P., Pelachaud, C. and Cowie, R. (eds.) (2013). *Emotion-Oriented Systems: The Humaine Handbook*, Cognitive Technologies Series (Berlin: Springer).

Pierce, W. (1965). *Failure-tolerant computer design* (New York: Academic Press).

Pitt, J. (2012). *This Pervasive Day* (London: Imperial College Press).

Pitt, J. and Schaumeier, J. (2012). Provision and appropriation of common-pool resources without full disclosure, in *PRIMA, Lecture Notes in Computer Science*, Vol. 7455 (Berlin: Springer), pp. 199–213.

Pitt, J., Schaumeier, J. and Artikis, A. (2012a). Axiomatization of socio-economic principles for self-organizing institutions: concepts, experiments and challenges, *Transactions on Autonomous and Adaptive Systems* **7**, 4, p. 39.

Pitt, J., Schaumeier, J., Busquets, D. and Macbeth, S. (2012b). Self-organising common-pool resource allocation and canons of distributive justice, in *Proceedings 6th IEEE International Conference on Self-Adaptive and Self-Organizing Systems (SASO)*, pp. 119–128.

Praszkier, R. and Nowak, A. (2012). *Social Entrepreneurship: Theory and Practice* (Cambridge: Cambridge University Press).

Pratt, R., Kintner-Meyer, M., Balducci, P., Sanquist, T., Gerkensmeyer, C., Schneider, K., Katipamula, S. and Secrest, T. (2010). The smart grid: An estimation of the energy and co2 benefits, Tech. rep., Pacific Northwest National Laboratory PNNL-19112.

Predd, J. B., Kulkarni, S. and Poor, H. V. (2006). Distributed learning in wireless sensor networks, *Signal Processing Magazine, IEEE* **23**, 4, pp. 56–69.

Prothmann, H., Tomforde, S., Branke, J., Hähner, J., Müller-Schloer, C. and Schmeck, H. (2011). Organic traffic control, in C. Müller-Schloer, H. Schmeck and T. Ungerer (eds.), *Organic Computing: A Paradigm Shift for Complex Systems*, *Autonomic Systems*, Vol. 1 (Basel: Springer), pp. 431–446.

Psaier, H. and Dustdar, S. (2011). A survey on self-healing systems: approaches and systems, *Computing* **91**, 1, pp. 43–73.

Puviani, M., Cabri, G. and Zambonelli, F. (2013). A taxonomy of architectural patterns for self-adaptive systems, in *Proceedings of the Sixth International C* Conference on Computer Science and Software Engineering*, pp. 77–85.

Puviani, M., Di Marzo Serugendo, G., Frei, R. and Cabri, G. (2011). A method fragments approach to methodologies for engineering self-organising systems, *ACM Transactions on Autonomous and Adaptive Systems (TAAS)* **7**, 3, pp. 33:1–33:25.

Quinn, A. J. and Bederson, B. B. (2011). Human computation: a survey and taxonomy of a growing field, in *Proceedings of the Annual Conference on Human Factors in Computing Systems*, pp. 1403–1412.

Ramchurn, S., Jennings, N., Sierra, C. and Godo, L. (2004). Devising a trust model for multi-agent interactions using confidence and reputation, *Applied Artificial Intelligence* **18**, 9, pp. 833–852.

Rao, A. and Georgeff, M. (1995). BDI agents: from theory to practice, in *Proceedings First International Conference on Multi-Agents Systems (ICMAS)*, pp. 312–319.

Rasmussen, S., Baas, N. A., Mayer, B., Nilsson, M. and Olesen, M. W. (2001). Ansatz for dynamical hierarchies, *Artificial Life* **7**, 4, pp. 329–353.

RCEP (2010). 28th report: Adapting institutions to climate change, Royal Commission on Environmental Protection (Chairman: John Lawton), London: The Stationery Office Limited.

Resch, B. (2013). People as sensors and collective sensing-contextual observations complementing geo-sensor network measurements, in *Progress in Location-Based Services*, Lecture Notes in Geoinformation and Cartography (Berlin: Springer), pp. 391–406.

Rescher, N. (1966). *Distributive Justice* (Indianoplis, IN: Bobbs-Merrill).

Riener, A. and Ferscha, A. (2013). Enhancing future mass ICT with social capabilities, in *Co-evolution of Intelligent Socio-Technical Systems*, Understanding Complex Systems (Berlin: Springer), pp. 141–184.

Rish, I. (2009). Self-aware distributed systems, http://domino.watson.ibm.com/comm/research.nsf/pages/r.ai.innovation.2.html.

Riveret, R., Contissa, G., Busquets, D., Rotolo, A., Pitt, J. and Sartor, G. (2013). Vicarious reinforcement and ex ante law enforcement: a study in norm-governed learning agents, in *ICAIL*, pp. 222–226.

Robinson, N. (1966). *Solar Radiation* (Oxford: Elsevier Publishing Company).

Rochat, P. (2001). *The Infant's World* (Cambridge, MA: Harvard University Press).

Rochat, P. (2003). Five levels of self-awareness as they unfold in early life, *Consciousness and Cognition* **12**, pp. 717–731.

Rodota, S. and Capurro, R. (2005). Ethical aspects of ICT implants in the human body, Tech. rep., The European Group on Ethics in Science and New Technologies.

Russell, B. (1996). *The Principles of Mathematics* (New York, NY: W. W. Norton & Company).

Rymaszewski, M., Au, W. J., Wallace, M., Winters, C., Ondrejka, C., Batstone-Cunningham, B. and Rosedale, P. (2006). *Second Life: The Official Guide* (Alameda, CA: SYBEX Inc.).

Sacerdoti, E. D. (1974). Planning in a hierarchy of abstraction spaces, *Artificial Intelligence* **5**, 2, pp. 115–135.

Saha, G. (2007a). Self-healing software, *Ubiquity* **2007**, March, pp. 4:1–4:1.

Saha, G. (2007b). Software - implemented self-healing system, *CLEI Electronic Journal* **10**, 2 (Paper 5).

Sakaki, T., Okazaki, M. and Matsuo, Y. (2010). Earthquake shakes twitter users: real-time event detection by social sensors, in *Proceedings 19th International Conference on World Wide Web*, pp. 851–860.

Samuel, A. (1959). Some studies in machine learning using the game of checkers, *IBM Journal of Research and Development* **11**, 6, pp. 601–617.

Santos, M. S. and Pitt, J. (2011). MACS: Affective conditioning system for shared working environments, in *Proceedings International Conferences on Web Intelligence and Intelligent Agent Technology* (Washington, DC: IEEE Computer Society), pp. 57–60.

Sarraf Shirazi, A., von Mammen, S. and Jacob, C. (2010). Adaptive modularization of the MAPK signaling pathway using the multiagent paradigm, in *Parallel Problem Solving from Nature*, *Lecture Notes in Computer Science*, Vol. 6239 (Berlin: Springer), pp. 401–410.

Sarraf Shirazi, A., von Mammen, S. and Jacob, C. (2011a). Hierarchical self-organized learning in agent-based modeling of the mapk signaling pathway, in *IEEE Congress on Evolutionary Computation (CEC)*, pp. 2245–2251.

Sarraf Shirazi, A., von Mammen, S. and Jacob, C. (2013). Abstraction of agent interaction processes: Towards large-scale multi-agent models, *Simulation: Transactions of the Society for Modeling and Simulation International* **89**, 4, pp. 524–538.

Sarraf Shirazi, A., von Mammen, S., Yazdanbod, I. and Jacob, C. (2011b). Self-organized learning of collective behaviours in agent-based simulations, in *8th International Conference on Complex Systems (ICCS)*, pp. 543–555.

Savarimuthu, B. and Dam, H. (204). Towards mining norms in open source software repositories, in *9th International Workshop on Agents and Data Mining Interaction (ADMI)*, *Lecture Notes in Computer Science*, Vol. 8316 (Berlin: Springer).

Savarimuthu, B., Lê, L. and Ghose, A. (2012a). From green norms to policies–combining bottom-up and top-down approaches, in *PRIMA 2012: Principles and Practice of Multi-Agent Systems*, *Lecture Notes in Computer Science*, Vol. 7455 (Berlin: Springer), pp. 168–183.

Savarimuthu, B. T. R., Cranefield, S., Purvis, M. A. and Purvis, M. K. (2010). Obligation norm identification in agent societies, *Journal of Artificial Societies and Social Simulation* **13**, 4, p. 3.

Savarimuthu, B. T. R., Cranefield, S., Purvis, M. A. and Purvis, M. K. (2013). Identifying prohibition norms in agent societies, *Artificial Intelligence and Law* **21**, 1, pp. 1–46.

Savarimuthu, B. T. R., Purvis, M. and Verhagen, H. (2012b). An agent-based simulation of employing social norms in energy conservation in households, in S. Cranefield and I. Song (eds.), *Agent Based Simulation for a Sustainable Society and Multi-agent Smart Computing*, *Lecture Notes in Computer Science*, Vol. 7580 (Berlin: Springer), pp. 16–31.

Scerri, P., Sycara, K. and Tambe, M. (2004). Adjustable autonomy in the context of coordination (invited paper), in *AIAA 3rd "Unmanned Unlimited" Technical Conference, Workshop and Exhibit*, doi:10.2514/6.2004-6367.

Schmeck, H., Müller-Schloer, C., Çakar, E., Mnif, M. and Richter, U. (2010) Adaptivity and self-organization in organic computing systems, *ACM Transactions on Autonomous and Adaptive Systems* **5**, 3, pp. 10:1–10:32.

Schmickl, T., Thenius, R., Moslinger, C., Timmis, J., Tyrrell, A., Read, M., Hilder, J., Halloy, J., Campo, A., Stefani, C., Manfredi, L., Dipper, T., Sutantyo, D. and Kernbach, S. (2011). CoCoRo: the self-aware underwater swarm, in *Self-Adaptive and Self-Organizing Systems Workshops (SASOW)*, pp. 120–126.

Schmidt, M. and Lipson, H. (2006). Actively probing and modeling users in interactive coevolution, in *Proceedings 8th annual conference on Genetic and Evolutionary Computation (GECCO)*, pp. 385–386.

Schmitt, C. (1966). *The Concept of the Political* (Chicago, IL: University of Chicago Press).

Schneier, B. (2012). *Liars and Outliers: Enabling the Trust that Society Needs to Thrive* (Indianapolis, IN: Wiley).

Schulte, E., Fry, Z., Fast, E., Weimer, W. and Forrest, S. (2013). Software mutational robustness, *Genetic Programming and Evolvable Machines* **(online first)**, 10.1007/s10710-013-9195-8.

Schultz, P. W., Nolan, J. M., Cialdini, R. B., Goldstein, N. J. and Griskevicius, V. (2007). The constructive, destructive, and reconstructive power of social norms, *Psychological Science* **18**, 5, p. 429.

Schulzke, M. (2013). Autonomous weapons and distributed responsibility, *Philosophy and Technology* **26**, 2, pp. 203–219.

Schuster, D., Rosi, A., Mamei, M., Springer, T., Endler, M. and Zambonelli, F. (2013). Pervasive social context: taxonomy and survey, *ACM Transactions on Intelligent Systems and Technology* **4**, 3.

Seebach, H., Nafz, F., Steghöfer, J.-P. and Reif, W. (2010). A software engineering guideline for self-organizing resource-flow systems, in *IEEE International Conference on Self-Adaptive and Self-Organizing Systems (SASO)*, pp. 194–203.

Sestini, F. (2012). Collective awareness platforms: engines for sustainability and ethics, *IEEE Technology and Society Magazine* **31**, 4, pp. 54–62.

Shapiro, L. and Stockman, G. (2001). *Computer Vision* (London: Prentice Hall).

Sharp, H., Rogers, Y. and Preece, J. (2007). *Interaction Design: Beyond Human-Computer Interaction* (New York, NY: Wiley).

Sheckley, R. (1967). Watchbird, in *Untouched by Human Hands* (London: Four Square Books), pp. 72–90.

Shih, S. T.-F., Carter, R., Sinclair, C., Mihalopoulos, C. and Vos, T. (2009). Economic evaluation of skin cancer prevention in Australia, *Preventive Medicine* **49**, 5, pp. 449–453.

Sidiroglou, S., Laadan, O., Perez, C., Viennot, N., Keromytis, A. and Nieh, J. (2009). ASSURE: Automatic Software Self-healing Using REscue points, in *International Conference on Architectural Support for Programming Languages and Operating Systems*, pp. 37–48.

Singer, P. (2009). *Wired for War: The Robotics Revolution and Conflict in the Twenty-first Century* (New York: Penguin Group).

Singh, M. P. and Tadanki, K. (2013). Norms as a basis for governing sociotechnical systems, *ACM Transactions on Intelligent Systems and Technology* **5**, 1, pp. 21:1–21:23.

Smith, B. (1984). Reflection and semantics in LISP, in *Proceedings 11th Symposium on Principles of Programming Languages (POPL)*, pp. 23–35.

Smith, B. (1986). Varieties of self-reference, in *Proceedings Theoretical Aspects of Reasoning about Knowledge (TARK)*.

Smith, K. and Hancock, P. (1995). Situation awareness is adaptive, externally directed consciousness, *Human Factors* **37**, 1, pp. 137–148.

Snyder, P. L., Greenstadt, R. and Valetto, G. (2009). Myconet: a fungi-inspired model for superpeer-based peer-to-peer overlay topologies, in *Proceedings*

3rd IEEE International Conference on Self-Adaptive and Self-Organizing Systems (SASO), pp. 40–50.

Sommerville, I. (2007). *Software Engineering* (Boston, MA: Addison-Wesley).

Spence, R. (2007). *Information Visualization: Design for Interaction* (Upper Saddle River, NJ: Prentice-Hall).

Stalder, F. (2002a). The failure of privacy enhancing technologies (PETs) and the voiding of privacy, *Sociological Research Online* **7**, p. 2.

Stalder, F. (2002b). Privacy is not the antidote to surveillance, *Surveillance & Society* **1**, 1, pp. 120–124.

Stanton, A., Janda, M., Baade, P. and Anderson, P. (2004). Primary prevention of skin cancer: a review of sun protection in Australia and internationally, *Health Promotion International* **19**, 3, pp. 369–378.

Steghöfer, J.-P., Behrmann, P., Anders, G., Siefert, F. and Reif, W. (2013). HiSPADA: Self-organising hierarchies for large-scale multi-agent systems, in *Proceedings 9th International Conference on Autonomic and Autonomous Systems (ICAS)*, pp. 71–76.

Steghöfer, J.-P., Kiefhaber, R., Leichtenstern, K., Bernard, Y., Klejnowski, L., Reif, W., Ungerer, T., André, E., Hähner, J. and Müller-Schloer, C. (2010). Trustworthy organic computing systems: challenges and perspectives, in B. Xie, J. Branke, S. Sadjadi, D. Zhang and X. Zhou (eds.), *Autonomic and Trusted Computing, Lecture Notes in Computer Science*, Vol. 6407 (Berlin: Springer), pp. 62–76.

Stephan, K., Michael, K., Michael, M., Jacob, L. and Anesta, E. (2012). Social implications of technology: past, present, and future, *Proceedings of the IEEE* **100**, 13, pp. 1752–1781.

Stepney, S., Welch, P. and Andrews, P. (eds.) (2011). *Proceedings of the 2011 Workshop on Complex Systems Modelling and Simulation (CoSMoS)* (Frome: Luniver Press).

Sterritt, R. (2011). Apoptotic computing: programmed death by default for computer-based systems, *IEEE Computer* **44**, 1, pp. 59–65.

Sterritt, R. and Bantz, D. (2006). Personal autonomic computing reflex reactions and self-healing, *IEEE Transactions on Systems, Man and Cybernetics Part C: Applications and Reviews* **36**, 3, pp. 304–314.

Sterritt, R., Hinchey, M. and Vassev, E. (2010). Self-managing software, in P. Laplante (ed.), *Encyclopedia of Software Engineering*, chap. 97 (Oxford: Taylor & Francis), pp. 1072–1081.

Szasz, C. and Chindris, V. (2010). Self-healing and artificial immune properties implementation upon FPGA-based embryonic network, in *IEEE International Conference on Automation Quality and Testing Robotics (AQTR)*, Vol. 2, pp. 1–6.

Takeno, J., Inaba, K. and Suzuki, T. (2005). Experiments and examination of mirror image cognition using a small robot, in *Proceedings 2005 IEEE International Symposium on Computational Intelligence in Robotics and Automation*, pp. 493–498.

Talantzis, F., Pnevmatikakis, A. and Constantinides, A. (2011). *Audio-Visual Person Tracking: a Practical Approach* (London: Imperial College Press).

Tchao, A., Di Marzo Serugendo, G. and Morin, J.-H. (in press). Personal DRM (PDRM): A self-protecting content approach, in F. Hartung, T. Kalker and l. Shiguo (eds.), *Digital Rights Management: Technology, Standards and Applications* (Boca Raton, FL: CRC Press), to appear.

Terrace, H. (2004). Meta-cognition and the evolution of language, in *The Missing Link in Cognition: Origins of Self-Reflective Consciousness*, chap. 3 (Oxford: Oxford University Press), pp. 84–115.

Terrace, H. S. and Metcalfe, J. (eds.) (2004). *The Missing Link in Cognition: Origins of Self-Reflective Consciousness* (New York: Oxford University Press).

The Climate Group (2008). SMART 2020: Enabling the low carbon economy in the information age, Global eSustainability Initiative.

Thøgersen, J. (2002). Direct experience and the strength of the personal norm–behavior relationship, *Psychology and Marketing* **19**, 10, pp. 881–893.

Thurston, B. (2013). I have left the Internet, Fast Company, 177, pp. 66–78, 104–105.

Tillotson, J. (2012). live scent | ɘvil stench, in J. Pitt (ed.), *This Pervasive Day* (London: Imperial College Press), pp. 53–68.

Tomforde, S., Hähner, J. and Müller-Schloer, C. (2013). The multi-level observer/controller framework for learning and self-optimising systems, in *International Journal on Data Mining and Bioinformatics*.

Trappl, R., Petta, P. and Sayr, S. (eds.) (2003). *Emotions in Humans and Artifacts* (Cambridge, MA: MIT Press).

Trescak, T., Esteva, M. and Rodriguez, I. (2011). VIXEE an innovative communication infrastructure for virtual institutions, in *10th International Conference on Autonomous Agents and Multiagent Systems (AAMAS)*, pp. 1131–1132.

Turing, A. (1950). Computing machinery and intelligence, *Mind* **59**, pp. 433–460.

Turner, M. (1998). Sun safety: avoiding noonday sun, wearing protective clothing, and the use of sunscreen, *Journal of the National Cancer Institute* **90**, 24, pp. 1854–1855.

Vaughan, R. T. and Gerkey, B. P. (2007). Really reused robot code from the player/stage project, in D. Brugali (ed.), *Software Engineering for Experimental Robotics* (Berlin: Springer), pp. 267–289.

Vaughan, R. T. and Zuluaga, M. (2006). Use your illusion: sensorimotor self-simulation allows complex agents to plan with incomplete self-knowledge, in *Proceedings of the International Conference on Simulation of Adaptive Behaviour*, pp. 298–309.

Viroli, M., Casadei, M., Montagna, S. and Zambonelli, F. (2011). Spatial coordination of pervasive services through chemical-inspired tuple spaces, *ACM Transactions on Autonomous and Adaptive Systems* **6**, pp. 14:1–14:24.

Viroli, M., Pianini, D., Montagna, S. and Stevenson, G. (2012). Pervasive ecosystems: a coordination model based on semantic chemistry, in S. Ossowski, P. Lecca, C. Hung and J. Hong (eds.), *27th Annual ACM Symposium on Applied Computing*, pp. 295–302.

Vlissides, J. M., Coplien, J. O. and Kerth, N. L. (eds.) (1996). *Pattern Languages of Program Design 2; Proceedings PLoP'95: Second Annual Conference on Pattern Languages of Programs.*

von Ahn, L. and Dabbish, L. (2004). Labeling images with a computer game, in *Proceedings of the SIGCHI Conference on Human Factors in Computing Systems*, pp. 319–326.

von Ahn, L., Maurer, B., McMillen, C., Abraham, D. and Blum, M. (2008). reCAPTCHA: Human-based character recognition via web security measures, *Science* **321**, 5895, pp. 1465–1468.

von Mammen, S., Sarraf Shirazi, A., Sarpe, V. and Jacob, C. (2012). Optimization of swarm-based simulations, *ISRN Artificial Intelligence* **2012**, Article ID 365791, pp. 1–13.

von Mammen, S., Steghöfer, J.-P., Denzinger, J. and Jacob, C. (2011). Self-organized middle-out abstraction, in C. Bettstetter and C. Gershenson (eds.), *Self-Organizing Systems, Lecture Notes in Computer Science*, Vol. 6557 (Berlin: Springer), pp. 26–31.

Wahren, K. and Pitt, J. (2012). When the battlefield robots come home from war, in J. Pitt (ed.), *This Pervasive Day*, chap. 12 (London: Imperial College Press), pp. 225–240.

Waldrop, M. (2003). Autonomic computing: the technology of self-management, White paper, IBM.

Wallach, W. and Allen, C. (2009). *Moral Machines: Teaching Robots Right from Wrong* (Oxford: Oxford University Press).

Wang, F.-Y., Carley, K. M., Zeng, D. and Mao, W. (2007). Social computing: from social informatics to social intelligence, *Intelligent Systems, IEEE* **22**, 2, pp. 79–83.

Wang, Q., Megalooikonomou, V. and Faloutsos, C. (2010). Time series analysis with multiple resolutions, *Information Systems* **35**, 1, pp. 56–74.

Ware, C. (2000). *Information Visualization: Perception for Design* (San Francisco, CA: Morgan Kaufmann).

Warm, J., Parasuraman, R. and Matthews, G. (2008). Vigilance requires hard mental work and is stressful, *Human Factors* **50**, 3, pp. 433–441.

Weiss, M., Mattern, F., Graml, T., Staake, T. and Fleisch, E. (2009). Handy feedback: connecting smart meters with mobile phones, in *Proceedings of the 8th International Conference on Mobile and Ubiquitous Multimedia*, pp. 15:1–15:4.

White, S. A. (2004). Introduction to BPMN, http://www.zurich.ibm.com/~olz/teaching/ETH2011/White-BPMN-Intro.pdf.

Wieland, P. O. (1998). *Living Together in Space: The Design and Operation of The Life Support Systems on the International Space Station* (National Aeronautics and Space Administration, Marshall Space Flight Center Huntsville, AL).

Wile, D. and Egyed, A. (2004). An externalized infrastructure for self-healing systems, in *IEEE/IFIP Conference on Software Architecture*, pp. 285–288.

Wilson, S. W. (1995). Classifier fitness based on accuracy, *Evolutionary Computation* **3**, 2, pp. 149–175.

Wolpowitz, D. and Gilchrest, B. (2006). The vitamin D questions: how much do you need and how should you get it? *Journal of the American Academy of Dermatology* **54**, 2, pp. 301–317.

Woodman, R., Winfield, A. F. T., Harper, C. and Fraser, M. (2012). Building safer robots: safety driven control, *International Journal of Robotics Research* **31**, 13, pp. 1603–1626.

Wu, E., Diao, Y. and Rizvi, S. (2006). High-performance complex event processing over streams, in *Proceedings of the ACM SIGMOD International Conference on Management of Data*, pp. 407–418.

Yee, N., Bailenson, J., Urbanek, M., Chang, F. and Merget, D. (2007). The unbearable likeness of being digital: the persistence of nonverbal social norms in online virtual environments, *CyberPsychology & Behavior* **10**, 1, pp. 115–121.

Yoshikawa, Y., Hosoda, K. and Asada, M. (2007). Unique association between self-occlusion and double-touching towards binding vision and touch, *Neurocomputing* **70**, pp. 2234–2244.

Zadeh, L. (1965). Fuzzy sets, *Information and Control* **8**, 3, pp. 338—353.

Zagal, J. C., Delpiano, J. and Ruiz-del Solar, J. (2009). Self-modeling in humanoid soccer robots, *Robotics and Autonomous Systems* **57**, 8, pp. 819–827.

Zambonelli, F. (2012). Toward sociotechnical urban superorganisms, *IEEE Computer* **47**, 8.

Zambonelli, F., Bicocchi, N., Cabri, G., Leonardi, L. and Puviani, M. (2011). On self-adaptation, self-expression, and self-awareness in autonomic service component ensembles, in *Self-Adaptive and Self-Organizing Systems Workshops (SASOW)* (IEEE Computer Society), pp. 108–113.

Zambonelli, F., Jennings, N. and Wooldridge, M. (2001). Organisational rules as an abstraction for the analysis and design of multi-agent systems, *International Journal of Software Engineering and Knowledge Engineering* **11**, 3, pp. 303–328.

Zambonelli, F. and Viroli, M. (2011). A survey on nature-inspired metaphors for pervasive service ecosystems, *Journal of Pervasive Computing and Communications* **7**, pp. 186–204.

Zhang, H., Horvitz, E., Miller, R. C. and Parkes, D. C. (2011). Crowdsourcing general computation, in *ACM CHI 2011 Workshop on Crowdsourcing and Human Computation*, pp. 1–5.

Zhang, T. and Chen, Q. Y. (2007). Novel air distribution systems for commercial aircraft cabins, *Building and Environment* **42**, 4, pp. 1675–1684.

Zhang, Z. (2000). A flexible new technique for camera calibration, *IEEE Transactions Pattern Analysis and Machine Intelligence* **22**, pp. 1330–1334.

Zittrain, J. (2008). *The Future of the Internet – And How to Stop It* (New Haven, CT: Yale University Press).

Index